American College of Physicians

MKSAP® 15

Medical Knowledge Self-Assessment Program®

Neurology

Neurology

Contributors

David W. Dodick, MD, Book Editor[2]
Professor of Neurology
Neurology Residency Program Director
Mayo Clinic Arizona
Phoenix, Arizona

Jack Ende, MD, MACP, Associate Editor[1]
Professor of Medicine
University of Pennsylvania
Chief, Department of Medicine
Penn Presbyterian Medical Center
Philadelphia, Pennsylvania

Richard J. Caselli, MD[1]
Professor and Chair
Department of Neurology
Mayo Clinic Arizona
Scottsdale, Arizona

Bart M. Demaerschalk, MD, MSc, FRCP(C)[2]
Director, Cerebrovascular Diseases Center
Associate Professor of Neurology
Division of Cerebrovascular Diseases
Division of Critical Care Neurology
Department of Neurology
Mayo Clinic Arizona
Phoenix, Arizona

Brent P. Goodman, MD[1]
Assistant Professor of Neurology
Department of Neurology
Mayo Clinic Arizona
Scottsdale, Arizona

Katherine H. Noe, MD, PhD[1]
Assistant Professor of Neurology
Department of Neurology
Mayo Clinic Arizona
Phoenix, Arizona

Dean M. Wingerchuk, MD, MSc, FRCP(C)[2]
Professor of Neurology
Multiple Sclerosis Clinic
Division of Demyelinating Diseases
Mayo Clinic Arizona
Scottsdale, Arizona

Editor-in-Chief

Patrick C. Alguire, MD, FACP[1]
Director, Education and Career Development
American College of Physicians
Philadelphia, Pennsylvania

Neurology Reviewers

Dawn E. DeWitt, MD, MSc, FACP, FRACP[2]
Richard A. Fatica, MD[1]
Thomas E. Finucane, MD, FACP[1]
Faith T. Fitzgerald, MD, MACP[1]
Jeffrey L. Jackson, MD, MPH, FACP[1]
Kevin A. Kahn, MD[2]
Bashar Katirji, MD, FACP[1]
Steven L. Lewis, MD[1]
Mark E. Pasanen, MD, FACP[1]
Steven F. Reichert, MD, FACP[1]

Neurology ACP Editorial Staff

Ellen McDonald, PhD, Senior Staff Editor
Sean McKinney, Director, Self-Assessment Programs
Margaret Wells, Managing Editor
Charles Rossi, Senior Associate of Clinical Content Development
Shannon O'Sullivan, Editorial Coordinator

ACP Principal Staff

Steven E. Weinberger, MD, FACP[2]
Deputy Executive Vice President
Senior Vice President, Medical Education and Publishing

D. Theresa Kanya, MBA[1]
Vice President, Medical Education and Publishing

Sean McKinney[1]
Director, Self-Assessment Programs

Margaret Wells[1]
Managing Editor

Charles Rossi[1]
Senior Associate of Clinical Content Development

Becky Krumm[1]
Senior Staff Editor

Ellen McDonald, PhD[1]
Senior Staff Editor

Amanda Neiley[1]
Staff Editor

Katie Idell[1]
Production Administrator/Editor

Valerie Dangovetsky[1]
Program Administrator

John Murray[1]
Editorial Coordinator

Shannon O'Sullivan[1]
Editorial Coordinator

Developed by the American College of Physicians

---

1. Has no relationships with any entity producing, marketing, re-selling, or distributing health care goods or services consumed by, or used on, patients.

2. Has disclosed relationships with entities producing, marketing, re-selling, or distributing health care goods or services consumed by, or used on, patients. See below.

Conflicts of Interest

The following contributors and ACP staff members have disclosed relationships with commercial companies:

Bart M. Demaerschalk, MD, MSc, FRCP(C)
Research Grants/Contracts
Abbott (CHOICE, ACT I), Vernalis UK, Neurobiological Technologies, AGA, St. Jude Medical
Honoraria
Genentech, Hoffman Roche
Consultantship
Genentech
Other
Neurobiological Technologies, Neuralieve

Dawn DeWitt, MD, MSc, FACP, FRACP
Consultantship
Sanofi-Aventis

David W. Dodick, MD
Research Grants/Contracts
Abbott (CHOICE, ACT I), Allergan, AstraZeneca, Advanced Bionics, Advanced Neurostimulation Systems, Medtronic, Alexza
Honoraria
Merck, GlaxoSmithKline, Neuralieve, Solvay, Ortho-McNeil, Coherex, MAP, Eli Lilly, Endo, Minster
Consultantship
Merck, GlaxoSmithKline, Neuralieve, Eli Lilly, St. Jude Medical, Ortho-McNeil, Solvay, Coherex, MAP, Endo, Minster

Kevin A. Kahn, MD
Employment
UNC Hospitals, Dept. of Neurology
Research Grants/Contracts
UCB Pharmaceuticals
Honoraria
Pfizer, Ortho-McNeil
Speakers Bureau
Pfizer, Ortho-McNeil

Steven E. Weinberger, MD, FACP
Stock Options/Holdings
Abbott, GlaxoSmithKline

Dean M. Wingerchuk, MD, MSc, FRCP(C)
Research Grants/Contracts
Genentech, Genzyme
Consultantship
Genentech

Acknowledgments

The American College of Physicians (ACP) gratefully acknowledges the special contributions to the development and production of the 15th edition of the Medical Knowledge Self-Assessment Program® (MKSAP 15) of Scott Thomas Hurd (Senior Systems Analyst/Developer), Ricki Jo Kauffman (Manager, Systems Development), Michael Ripca (Technical Administrator/Graphics Designer), and Lisa Torrieri (Graphic Designer). The Digital version (CD-ROM and Online components) was developed within the ACP's Interactive Product Development Department by Steven Spadt (Director), Christopher Forrest (Senior Software Developer), Ryan Hinkel (Senior Software Developer), John McKnight (Software Developer), Sean O'Donnell (Senior Software Developer), and Brian Sweigard (Senior Software Developer). Computer scoring and reporting are being performed by ACT, Inc., Iowa City, Iowa. The College also wishes to acknowledge that many other persons, too numerous to mention, have contributed to the production of this program. Without their dedicated efforts, this program would not have been possible.

Continuing Medical Education

The American College of Physicians is accredited by the Accreditation Council for Continuing Medical Education (ACCME) to provide continuing medical education for physicians.

The American College of Physicians designates this educational activity for a maximum of 166 *AMA PRA Category 1 Credits*™. Physicians should only claim credit commensurate with the extent of their participation in the activity.

AMA PRA Category 1 Credit™ is available from July 31, 2009, to July 31, 2012.

Learning Objectives

The learning objectives of MKSAP 15 are to:

- Close gaps between actual care in your practice and preferred standards of care, based on best evidence
- Diagnose disease states that are less common and sometimes overlooked and confusing
- Improve management of comorbidities that can complicate patient care
- Determine when to refer patients for surgery or care by subspecialists
- Pass the ABIM certification examination
- Pass the ABIM maintenance of certification examination

Target Audience

- General internists and primary care physicians
- Subspecialists who need to remain up-to-date in internal medicine
- Residents preparing for the certifying examination in internal medicine
- Physicians preparing for maintenance of certification in internal medicine (recertification)

How to Submit for CME Credits

To earn CME credits, complete a MKSAP 15 answer sheet. Use the enclosed, self-addressed envelope to mail your completed answer sheet(s) to the MKSAP Processing Center for scoring. Remember to provide your MKSAP 15 order and ACP ID numbers in the appropriate spaces on the answer sheet. The order and ACP ID numbers are printed on your mailing label. If you have not received these numbers with your MKSAP 15 purchase, you will need to acquire them to earn CME credits. E-mail ACP's customer service center at custserv@acponline.org. In the subject line, write "MKSAP 15 order/ACP ID numbers." In the body of the e-mail, make sure you include your e-mail address as well as your full name, address, city, state, ZIP code, country, and telephone number. Also identify where you have made your MKSAP 15 purchase. You will receive your MKSAP 15 order and ACP ID numbers by e-mail within 72 business hours.

Disclosure Policy

It is the policy of the American College of Physicians (ACP) to ensure balance, independence, objectivity, and scientific rigor in all its educational activities. To this end, and consistent with the policies of the ACP and the Accreditation Council for Continuing Medical Education (ACCME), contributors to all ACP continuing medical education activities are required to disclose all relevant financial relationships with any entity producing, marketing, re-selling, or distributing health care goods or services consumed by, or used on, patients. Contributors are required to use generic names in the discussion of therapeutic options and are required to identify any unapproved, off-label, or investigative use of commercial products or devices. Where a trade name is used, all available trade names for the same product type are also included. If trade-name products manufactured by companies with whom contributors have relationships are discussed, contributors are asked to provide evidence-based citations in support of the discussion. The information is reviewed by the committee responsible for producing this text. If necessary, adjustments to topics or contributors' roles in content development are made to balance the discussion. Further, all readers of this text are asked to evaluate the content for evidence of commercial bias so that future decisions about content and contributors can be made in light of this information.

Resolution of Conflicts

To resolve all conflicts of interest and influences of vested interests, the ACP precluded members of the content-creation committee from deciding on any content issues that involved generic or trade-name products associated with proprietary entities with which these committee members had relationships. In addition, content was based on best evidence and updated clinical care guidelines, when such evidence and guidelines were available. Contributors' disclosure information can be found with the list of contributors' names and those of ACP principal staff listed in the beginning of this book.

Educational Disclaimer

The editors and publisher of MKSAP 15 recognize that the development of new material offers many opportunities for error. Despite our best efforts, some errors may persist in print. Drug dosage schedules are, we believe, accurate and in accordance with current standards. Readers are advised, however, to ensure that the recommended dosages in MKSAP 15 concur with the information provided in the product information material. This is especially important in cases of new, infrequently used, or highly toxic drugs. Application of the information in MKSAP 15 remains the professional responsibility of the practitioner.

The primary purpose of MKSAP 15 is educational. Information presented, as well as publications, technologies, products, and/or services discussed, is intended to inform subscribers about the knowledge, techniques, and experiences of the contributors. A diversity of professional opinion exists, and the views of the contributors are their own and not those of the ACP. Inclusion of any material in the program does not constitute endorsement or recommendation by the ACP. The ACP does not warrant the safety, reliability, accuracy, completeness, or usefulness of and disclaims any and all liability for damages and claims that may result from the use of information, publications, technologies, products, and/or services discussed in this program.

Publisher's Information

Unauthorized Use of This Book Is Against the Law

MKSAP 15 ISBN: 978-1-934465-25-7
Neurology ISBN: 978-1-934465-31-8

Printed in the United States of America.

For order information in the U.S. or Canada call 800-523-1546, extension 2600. All other countries call 215-351-2600. Fax inquiries to 215-351-2799 or e-mail to custserv@acponline.org.

Errata and Norm Tables

Errata for MKSAP 15 will be posted at http://mksap.acponline.org/errata as new information becomes known to the editors.

MKSAP 15 Performance Interpretation Guidelines with Norm Tables, available December 31, 2010, will reflect the knowledge of physicians who have completed the self-assessment tests before the program was published. These physicians took the tests without being able to refer to the syllabus, answers, and critiques. For your convenience, the tables are available in a printable PDF file at http://mksap.acponline.org/normtables.

Table of Contents

Neurology

Neurologic Examination Pearls

Introduction

Although advanced imaging techniques have revolutionized neurologic diagnosis, the clinical examination continues to provide information of value. Included here are several recent and time-tested methods, some evidence based and others experiential, that should be helpful as part of the initial assessment of neurologic problems. For more information on the approach to neurologic symptoms, go to http://www.aan.com/go/education/curricula/internal/toc.

Dementia and Delirium

Two rapid and simple tests that stand out in the evaluation of dementia are the clock-drawing test and the Folstein Mini–Mental State Examination (MMSE). The clock-drawing test involves having the patient draw a clock face on a pre-drawn circle. No further elaboration or instruction is provided, and the test is not timed. A response is normal if the numbers are inserted in the proper order and positioned near the rim of the circle. Missing one number or inappropriate spacing between numbers is scored as normal, provided that the other elements are present; the hands of the clock do not need to be included. In the absence of a parietal lesion or delirium, drawing an abnormal clock is modestly sensitive (48%-75%) but very specific (93%-94%) for the diagnosis of dementia. The MMSE consists of 11 tasks to be completed by the patient. An MMSE score range of 21 to 25 corresponds to mild dementia, 11 to 20 to moderate dementia, and 0 to 10 to severe dementia. A score of 23 points or fewer (maximum score, 30 points) has a sensitivity of 69% to 100% and a specificity of 78% to 99% for diagnosing Alzheimer dementia.

Delirium is an acute state of confusion that may manifest as a reduced level of consciousness, cognitive abnormalities, perceptual disturbances, or emotional disturbances. The Confusion Assessment Method diagnostic algorithm (**Table 1**) is a useful tool in diagnosing delirium; no laboratory tests, imaging studies, or other tests provide greater accuracy (sensitivity, 94%-100%; specificity, 90%-95%). In hospitalized patients, the brief quantitative Benton Orientation Questionnaire efficiently detects and monitors cognitive impairment (dementia, delirium, or both). Points are deducted for each wrong answer: year, −10 per year; month, −5 per month; date, −1 per day; day of week, −1 per day; and time, −1 per half hour.

TABLE 1 The Confusion Assessment Method Diagnostic Algorithm[a]
Feature 1. Acute Onset and Fluctuating Course
This feature is usually obtained from a family member or nurse and is shown by a positive response to the following questions: Is there evidence of an acute change in mental status from the patient's baseline? Did the (abnormal) behavior fluctuate during the day (that is, tend to come and go or increase and decrease in severity)?
Feature 2. Inattention
This feature is shown by a positive response to the following question: Did the patient have difficulty focusing attention, for example, being easily distractible or having difficulty keeping track of what was being said?
Feature 3. Disorganized Thinking
This feature is shown by a positive response to the following question: Was the patient's thinking disorganized or incoherent, such as rambling or irrelevant conversation, unclear or illogical flow of ideas, or unpredictable switching from subject to subject?
Feature 4. Altered Level of Consciousness
This feature is shown by any answer other than "alert" to the following question: Overall, how would you rate this patient's level of consciousness: alert (normal), vigilant (hyperalert), lethargic (drowsy, easily aroused), stuporous (difficult to arouse), or comatose (unarousable)?

[a]The diagnosis of delirium by the confusion assessment method requires the presence of features 1 and 2 and either 3 or 4.

Adapted with permission from Inouye SK, van Dyck CH, Alessi CA, Balkin S, Siegal AP, Horwitiz RI. Clarifying confusion: the confusion assessment method. A new method for detection of delirium. Ann Intern Med. 1990;113(12):947. [PMID: 2240918]

Visual Defects

Visual fields are traditionally tested with either "static" or "kinetic" techniques. For both types, the patient sits approximately 100 cm (39 in) away from the clinician and fixes his/her vision on a static point, usually the examiner's eye. In the static technique, the clinician holds an object at a fixed point in the peripheral field of vision, whereas in the kinetic technique, an object is moved from the extreme peripheral field toward the point of fixation. Except for the detection of a homonymous hemianopia (sensitivity, 80%), both techniques are insensitive for most visual defects.

KEY POINT

- Except for the detection of a homonymous hemianopia, static and kinetic visual field testing techniques are insensitive for most visual defects.

Motor System

Hemiparesis

For lesions involving the motor cortex, the most common method to detect subtle loss of muscle strength is the pronator drift test. In this test, the patient holds the arms outstretched directly in front of the body, with eyes closed; if a cerebral lesion is present, the contralateral arm will drift downward and pronate. Another method is the forearm rolling test, in which the patient is asked to bend the elbows to align the forearms parallel to each other and then to rotate the arms rapidly around each other; in a patient with subtle hemiparesis, the arm contralateral to a hemispheric lesion is held stationary, and the opposite arm rapidly circles it. A final method is to ask the patient to rapidly and simultaneously tap the index fingers against a hard surface; finger tapping is slower contralateral to the hemispheric lesion.

A common clinical problem is underestimating muscle strength in large, powerful muscle groups, such as the hip. To overcome this error, persons age 50 years or older without bone or hip disease should be asked to rise from a chair (without using the arms) 10 times in 25 seconds; failing this test suggests proximal muscle weakness.

KEY POINT

- The forearm rolling test and finger tapping test are sensitive for the detection of subtle hemiparesis.

Muscle Stretch Reflexes

During testing of muscle stretch reflexes, abnormal findings, such as an absent ankle reflex, are frequent in normal persons. Four simple rules can help in the interpretation of apparently abnormal results. (1) An absent reflex is abnormal if accompanied by other lower motoneuron findings (weakness, atrophy, and fasciculations). Hyperreflexia is abnormal if (2) it is accompanied by other upper motoneuron findings (weakness, spasticity, and an extensor plantar response), (3) the response is asymmetric (lower motoneuron if diminished, upper motoneuron if hyperactive), or (4) the response is hyperactive compared with reflexes from a higher spinal level (spinal cord disease).

Ataxia

Although usually discovered by testing the gait, ataxia may require tandem walking for detection in patients with subtle findings. Other commonly used tests for ataxia include the

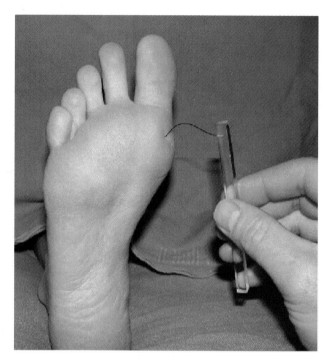

FIGURE 1.
Semmes-Weinstein monofilament test.
In the Semmes–Weinstein monofilament test, patients who cannot reliably detect application of the monofilament to designated sites on the plantar surface of their feet are considered to have lost protective sensation.

Reprinted with permission from Internal Medicine Essentials for Clerkship Students. Philadelphia, PA: American College of Physicians; 2007:Plate 1.

finger-to-nose, heel-to-shin, and rapid alternating movement tests. In the finger-to-nose and heel-to-shin tests, abnormal findings include misjudging the target (too short, too far), jerky movements, and an intention tremor as the finger or heel approaches the nose or shin. The inability to perform rapid alternating movements has the advantage of being quantifiable. Most people can tap two objects 30.5 cm (12 in) apart with their index finger 32 times in 15 seconds, but patients with ataxia cannot (sensitivity, 90%; specificity, 90%).

KEY POINT

- The inability to tap two objects 30.5 cm (12 in) apart with the index finger 32 times in 15 seconds is both highly sensitive and specific for ataxia.

Sensory System

The screening sensory examination is likely to have limited utility in patients with no neurologic symptoms. Most experts believe that testing for touch on the four extremities is probably adequate for such patients, but no data support this practice. In patients at risk for diabetic polyneuropathy, testing for sensation with cotton or pinprick does not detect important abnormalities; alternatively, the Semmes-Weinstein monofilament test is simple, quick, and modestly predictive of future diabetic ulcerations. During the test, the patient is supine with eyes closed and responds when he/she feels the monofilament touching the bottom of the foot. The number of suggested testing sites for each foot has varied from two to ten, but testing the plantar surface of the first and fifth metatarsal heads is probably sufficiently sensitive and specific. The monofilament is held perpendicular to the test site, with enough pressure applied to bow it to a C shape for one second (**Figure 1**). Testing should be randomly repeated twice at each site, as should "sham" applications in which the monofilament is not applied. Protective sensation is considered present if the patient correctly identifies two or more of the three applications, one of which was a sham. The test is abnormal if the patient correctly identifies only one or none of the three applications and is approximately 67% sensitive in predicting future foot ulceration during the subsequent 3 to 4 years.

KEY POINT

- An abnormal monofilament examination is approximately 67% sensitive in predicting future foot ulceration during the subsequent 3 to 4 years.

Bibliography

Goldstein LB, Matchar DB. The rational clinical examination. Clinical assessment of stroke. JAMA. 1994;271(14):1114-1120. [PMID: 8151856]

Stroke

Stroke Classification, Epidemiology, Pathophysiology, and Clinical Evaluation

Stroke results from either ischemic or hemorrhagic causes. Ischemic stroke is classified into categories according to the presumed mechanism of the ischemic brain injury and the pathophysiologic type of the lesion (**Figure 2**). The categories have been defined as large-artery atherosclerotic infarction (extracranial, intracranial, or via artery-to-artery embolism [versus thrombotic occlusion in situ]), embolism from a cardiac source (**Table 2**), small-vessel disease (lacunar stroke), other determined causes (such as dissection, hypercoagulable states, and paradoxical embolism through a patent foramen ovale), and infarcts of undetermined cause (cryptogenic).

Hemorrhagic stroke is classified into categories according to the intracranial location and pathophysiologic type and cause. By compartments, the hemorrhage can occur directly into the brain parenchyma (intracerebral hemorrhage), subarachnoid space, or ventricular system (intraventricular hemorrhage). Intracerebral hemorrhage can be further classified into primary (unrelated to an underlying congenital or acquired brain lesion or abnormality) and secondary (directly related to a congenital or an acquired brain lesion or abnormality) types. Causes of the primary type include hypertension, cerebral amyloid angiopathy, anticoagulant use, thrombolytic use, antiplatelet use, drug use, and other bleeding diathesis; causes of the secondary type include vascular malformations, aneurysms, neoplasms, hemorrhagic transformation of a cerebral infarction, cerebral venous sinus thrombosis, Moyamoya disease, hemorrhagic contusion, and systemic or primary central nervous system vasculitis.

Stroke is the most common life-threatening neurologic disease and is the third leading cause of death in the United States (after diseases of the heart and cancer), accounting for 1 of every 16 deaths; it is the leading cause of long-term disability in adults. Each year, approximately 700,000 people experience a new or recurrent stroke, of which 87% are ischemic; intracerebral and subarachnoid hemorrhagic strokes account for the remainder. The length of time to recover from a stroke depends on its severity. Approximately 50% to 70% of stroke survivors regain functional independence, but 15% to 30% are permanently disabled, and 20% require institutional care by 3 months after onset.

History and clinical findings provide the basis for evaluating patients suspected of having a stroke (**Figure 3**). The presence of acute facial paresis, arm drift, or abnormal speech increases the likelihood of stroke, whereas the absence of all three decreases the odds. Other symptoms associated with stroke include visual loss, diplopia, numbness, weakness, and nonorthostatic dizziness. On the basis of the symptoms and examination findings, the vascular distribution (anterior or posterior circulation) of a stroke can be determined (**Table 3**). Although neuroimaging is required to accurately distinguish ischemic from hemorrhagic stroke, compelling clues that suggest hemorrhagic stroke include headache, nausea, vomiting, hypertension, and progressive worsening of focal neurologic deficits and level of consciousness.

KEY POINTS

- The presence of acute facial paresis, arm drift, or abnormal speech increases the likelihood of stroke, whereas the absence of all three decreases the likelihood.
- Neuroimaging must be performed to distinguish ischemic from hemorrhagic stroke.

Transient Ischemic Attack

Transient ischemic attack (TIA) has traditionally been defined as a focal neurologic deficit that resolves within 24 hours. However, the now widespread and early use of MRI has revealed cerebral infarction in many patients who fit that definition of TIA. Therefore, the proposed revised definition of TIA is a brief episode of neurologic dysfunction attributable to a focal disturbance of brain or retinal ischemia, with clinical

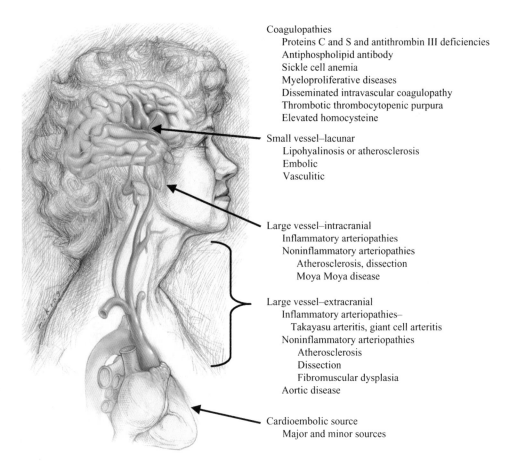

Coagulopathies
    Proteins C and S and antithrombin III deficiencies
    Antiphospholipid antibody
    Sickle cell anemia
    Myeloproliferative diseases
    Disseminated intravascular coagulopathy
    Thrombotic thrombocytopenic purpura
    Elevated homocysteine

Small vessel–lacunar
    Lipohyalinosis or atherosclerosis
    Embolic
    Vasculitic

Large vessel–intracranial
    Inflammatory arteriopathies
    Noninflammatory arteriopathies
        Atherosclerosis, dissection
        Moya Moya disease

Large vessel–extracranial
    Inflammatory arteriopathies–
        Takayasu arteritis, giant cell arteritis
    Noninflammatory arteriopathies
        Atherosclerosis
        Dissection
        Fibromuscular dysplasia
    Aortic disease

Cardioembolic source
    Major and minor sources

FIGURE 2.
Ischemic stroke categories.
Differential diagnosis of sources of ischemic stroke.

symptoms typically lasting less than 1 hour and without imaging evidence of infarction. (See **Table 4** for TIA mimics.)

Up to 20% of patients who have a TIA will have an acute stroke within 90 days, and approximately 50% of these strokes occur within the first 2 days. The ABCD^2 score predicts the risk of stroke at 2, 7, and 90 days after a TIA and is based on Age (1 point if ≥60 years), Blood pressure (1 point if ≥140 mm Hg systolic or 90 mm Hg diastolic), Clinical presentation (2 points for the presence of unilateral weakness or 1 point for speech impairment without weakness), the Duration of symptoms (2 points for ≥60 min and 1 point for 10-59 min), and the presence of Diabetes mellitus (1 point) (**Table 5**).

Emergency department evaluation and hospitalization is recommended for patients who have experienced their first TIA within the past 48 hours to facilitate the early use of thrombolytic therapy if symptoms recur and to expedite diagnostic testing and initiation of secondary prevention treatments. Hospitalization is also recommended for those with multiple or frequently recurring TIAs, a duration of symptoms greater than 60 minutes (probable infarction), symptomatic internal carotid artery stenosis, a known cardioembolic source (such as atrial fibrillation), a known hypercoagulable state, or a moderate or high ABCD^2 score. Patients with a greater than 48-hour history of TIA who have none of these criteria may be evaluated as an outpatient within 7 days.

If a patient was first seen in the emergency department and results of preliminary imaging studies were negative for significant stenosis, then a period of up to 7 days until outpatient evaluation may be appropriate.

Diagnostic testing should include at a minimum electrocardiography, a complete blood count, measurement of serum electrolyte and fasting plasma glucose levels, renal

TABLE 2 Potential Sources of Cardioembolism

High-Risk Sources

Mechanical prosthetic cardiac valve

Mitral stenosis with atrial fibrillation

Atrial fibrillation (other than lone atrial fibrillation)

Left atrial/atrial appendage thrombus

Sick sinus syndrome

Recent myocardial infarction (<4 weeks)

Left ventricular thrombus

Dilated cardiomyopathy

Akinetic left ventricular segment

Atrial myxoma

Infectious endocarditis

Medium- and Low-Risk Sources

Mitral valve prolapse

Mitral annulus calcification

Mitral stenosis without atrial fibrillation

Left atrial turbulence ("smoke")

Atrial septal aneurysm

Patent foramen ovale and atrial septal defect

Atrial flutter

Lone atrial fibrillation

Bioprosthetic cardiac valve

Nonbacterial thrombotic endocarditis

Heart failure

Hypokinetic left ventricular segment

Myocardial infarction (>4 weeks, <6 months)

function testing, a lipid profile, head CT and CT angiography (or brain MRI and magnetic resonance angiography [MRA]), Doppler ultrasonography of the neck, and transthoracic echocardiography. A conventional angiogram may be necessary when the noninvasive assessment is inconclusive. Transesophageal echocardiography with testing for right-to-left shunting across the atrial septum is recommended for patients younger than 45 years when preliminary investigations do not disclose a cause of the TIA. Transesophageal echocardiography is also useful to confirm a presumed proximal source of embolism and evaluate the cardiac valves for vegetation, the proximal aortic arch for atherosclerotic disease, and the left atrium and left atrial appendage for a thrombus or mass lesion.

KEY POINTS

- Transient ischemic attack should be approached with urgency because up to 20% of affected patients will have an acute stroke within 90 days and approximately 50% of these strokes will occur within the first 2 days.
- The ABCD^2 score, which is based on Age, Blood pressure, the Clinical presence of unilateral weakness or speech impairment, the Duration of symptoms, and the presence of Diabetes, predicts the risk of stroke at 2, 7, and 90 days after a transient ischemic attack.
- Emergency department assessment and hospitalization are recommended for patients who have had a first or frequently recurring transient ischemic attack within the past 48 hours.

Acute Stroke

Emergency Evaluation of Acute Stroke

The initial evaluation of patients with a suspected stroke is similar to that of other critically ill patients: stabilization of the airway, breathing, and circulation followed by a secondary assessment of neurologic deficits and comorbidities. The goals should be to identify patients with possible stroke, especially those eligible for acute interventions, to differentiate stroke from stroke mimics (see Table 4), and to identify potential causes of stroke in order to implement early secondary prevention.

The most important piece of historical information in suspected acute stroke is the time of symptom onset. The definition of time of stroke onset is the time a patient reports or was witnessed to have acute onset of stroke symptoms, or the last time the patient was known to be at his or her previous symptom-free state. For patients unable to provide this information or who awaken with stroke symptoms, the time of onset is defined as the time when the patient was last awake and free of symptoms. Additional historical items of interest include circumstances around the development of neurologic symptoms, risk factors for vascular disease, pre-existing cardiovascular and cerebrovascular disease, and history of drug abuse, migraine, seizure, infection, trauma, or pregnancy. Historical data related to eligibility for therapeutic interventions in an acute ischemic stroke are also important. (Characteristics of patients who are candidates for intravenous thrombolytic therapy are discussed later.)

The general physical examination should include vital signs, including temperature and weight, and pulse oximetry reading. Examination of the head and neck can reveal signs of trauma or features of seizure activity (tongue lacerations),

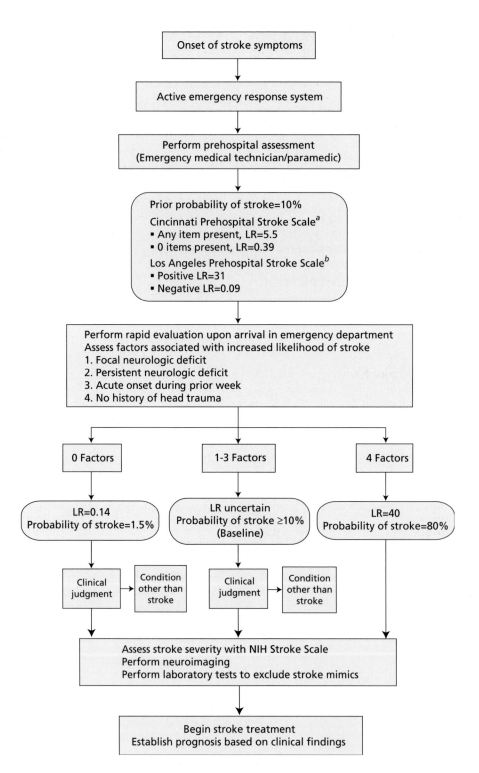

FIGURE 3.

Making a stroke diagnosis.

Algorithm showing the diagnostic steps for a patient with a suspected acute stroke.

LR = likelihood ratio; NIH = National Institutes of Health.

[a]Facial droop, arm drift, and abnormal speech.

[b]History (age >45 years, no history of seizures, symptoms <24 hours, not wheelchair bound), plasma glucose level 60 to 400 mg/dL (3.3 to 22 mmol/L), and examination showing unilateral facial weakness, grip weakness, and arm weakness.

Adapted with permission from Goldstein LB, Simel DL. Is this patient having a stroke? JAMA. 2005;293(19):2392. [PMID: 15900010] Copyright 2005 American Medical Association. All rights reserved.

TABLE 3 Anterior Versus Posterior Circulation: Symptoms and Signs of Cerebral Ischemia

Anterior Circulation	Posterior Circulation
Motor dysfunction of contralateral extremities or face (or both)	Motor dysfunction of ipsilateral face and/or contralateral extremities
Clumsiness	Clumsiness
Weakness	Weakness
Paralysis	Paralysis
Loss of vision in ipsilateral eye	Loss of vision in one or both homonymous visual fields
Homonymous hemianopia	Sensory deficit of ipsilateral face and/or contralateral extremities
Aphasia (dominant hemisphere)	
Dysarthria	Numbness or loss of sensation
	Paresthesias
Sensory deficit of contralateral extremities or face (or both)	Typical but nondiagnostic in isolation
Numbness or loss of sensation	Ataxia (gait or extremities)
Paresthesias	Vertigo
	Diplopia
	Dysphagia
	Dysarthria

carotid disease (by palpation and auscultation for bruit), chronic heart failure (jugular venous distention), giant cell arteritis (temporal artery tenderness), and retinal arteriolar emboli. The cardiac examination should focus on identifying concurrent myocardial ischemia, valvular disease, irregular rhythm, and aortic dissection. Skin and extremity examination may provide clues regarding peripheral artery disease, liver disease, coagulopathies, platelet disorders, bacterial endocarditis, and any injection drug abuse.

The neurologic examination is enhanced by the use of a reliable formal stroke score, such as the National Institute of Health Stroke Scale (**Table 6**). Scores can quantify the degree of neurologic deficit (on the aforementioned scale, <5 is mild, 10-15 is moderate, and >20 is severe), facilitate communication between providers, gauge changes over time, identify possible location of cerebral arterial occlusion, provide early prognosis, and identify patients eligible for particular acute therapies.

Because time is critical, a limited number of diagnostic tests should be performed routinely in patients with suspected acute stroke to differentiate ischemic stroke from hemorrhagic stroke, exclude important alternative diagnoses, assess for serious comorbidities, identify systemic conditions that can mimic or cause stroke or can influence therapeutic options, and search for acute medical or neurologic complications of the stroke (**Table 7**). The goal is for laboratory

TABLE 4 Mimics of Transient Ischemic Attack and Stroke

Transient Ischemic Attack	Stroke
Benign paroxysmal positional vertigo	Brain tumor
Metabolic derangement (such as multiple sclerosis)	Cardiac disease (such as arrhythmia)
Migraine equivalent (variant)	Conversion disorder
Myasthenia gravis	Dementia (with subacute worsening cognitive impairment)
Periodic paralysis	Demyelinating disease
Seizure	Drug overdose
Subdural hemorrhage	Head trauma
Syncope	HSV encephalitis
Thoracic outlet syndrome	Hypertensive encephalopathy
Transient global amnesia	Myasthenia gravis
	Metabolic derangement
	Seizure with postictal hemiparesis
	Syncope
	Systemic infection (such as UTI) unmasking prior stroke-related deficit(s)

HSV = herpes simplex virus; UTI = urinary tract infection.

TABLE 5 Prediction from ABCD² Score of Stroke at 2 Days, 7 Days, and 90 Days After a Transient Ischemic Attack

ABCD² Score Risk Classification	Stroke Risk at 2 Days (%)	Stroke Risk at 7 Days (%)	Stroke Risk at 90 Days (%)
Low risk (score <4 points)	1.0	1.2	3.1
Moderate risk (score 4-5 points)	4.1	5.9	9.8
High risk (score >5 points)	8.1	11.7	17.8

ABCD² score = score based on Age, Blood pressure, Clinical presentation, Duration of symptoms, and presence of Diabetes.

TABLE 6 National Institutes of Health Stroke Scale[a]

1. LOC	5. Visual Fields	12. Sensation (Pin)
0 alert 1 drowsy 2 stuporous 3 coma	0 no visual loss 1 partial hemianopia 2 complete hemianopia 3 bilateral hemianopia	0 normal 1 partial loss 2 severe loss
2. LOC Questions (Ask Month and Age)	**6. Facial Palsy**	**13. Best Language**
0 both correct 1 one correct 2 incorrect	0 normal 1 minor 2 partial 3 complete	0 no aphasia 1 mild–moderate aphasia 2 severe aphasia 3 mute
3. LOC Commands (Close Eyes, Make Fist)	**7–10. Motor (Left/Right Arm and Leg)[b]**	**14. Dysarthria**
0 both correct 1 one correct 2 incorrect	0 no drift 1 drift, doesn't hit bed 2 drifts down to bed 3 no effort against gravity 4 no movement 5 amputation/joint fusion	0 none 1 mild–moderate 2 near to unintelligible or worse 3 intubated/barrier
4. Best Gaze	**11. Limb Ataxia**	**15. Extinction and Inattention**
0 normal 1 partial gaze palsy 2 forced deviation	0 absent 1 present in one limb 2 present in two limbs	0 no neglect 1 partial neglect 2 complete neglect

LOC = level of consciousness.

[a]Scoring: <5, mild neurologic deficit; 10-15, moderate neurologic deficit; >20, severe neurologic deficit.

[b]Motor assessment: While patient is supine, examiner tests each limb separately; limb is held by examiner at a 45-degree angle to the patient and released. Drift is defined as any change in position after the initial release. Limb ataxia assessment should include finger-to-nose and heel-to-toe testing.

Information also available at www.ninds.nih.gov/doctors/NIH_Stroke_Scale_Booklet.pdf. Training is available at no cost at asatrainingcampus.net.

results to be available for review within 45 minutes of arrival of the patient at the emergency department.

KEY POINTS

- The use of a stroke rating scale during the emergency evaluation, preferably the National Institutes of Health Stroke Scale, is recommended to quantify the degree of neurologic deficit and to facilitate communication between health care providers.

- For patients with suspected stroke who are eligible for thrombolysis, the goal is to have imaging completed and interpreted within 45 minutes of arrival in the emergency department.

Brain and Vascular Imaging

A noncontrast CT scan of the brain is the first imaging study to obtain for patients with acute stroke. This scan accurately identifies most cases of intracranial hemorrhage and helps discriminate many nonvascular causes of neurologic symptoms (such as a brain neoplasm). A CT scan can also be used to identify subtle and early signs of infarction (such as loss of gray-white differentiation, sulcal effacement, subtle radiolucency) or arterial occlusion (such as a hyperdense artery sign) (**Figure 4**). The presence of early radiologic evidence of a large infarction is correlated with a higher risk of hemorrhagic transformation after treatment with thrombolytic agents and is associated with poorer outcomes. For potential thrombolysis candidates, the goal is to have a CT scan completed within 25 minutes and interpreted within 45 minutes of arrival at the emergency department.

The multimodal CT approach includes noncontrast CT first, followed by perfusion CT and CT angiography; obtaining these studies should never delay the emergency treatment of a stroke. Results of perfusion CT provide maps of cerebral

TABLE 7 Immediate Diagnostic Studies for Evaluation of a Patient with Suspected Acute Stroke

Patient	Diagnostic Study
All patients	Noncontrast brain CT or brain MRI Plasma glucose measurement Serum electrolyte measurement/kidney function tests Electrocardiography Measurement of markers of cardiac ischemia Complete blood count, including platelet count[a] Prothrombin time/INR measurements[a] Activated partial thromboplastin time measurement[a] Oxygen saturation determination
Selected patients	Liver chemistry studies Toxicology screen Blood alcohol level Pregnancy test Arterial blood gas measurements (if hypoxia is suspected) Chest radiography (if lung disease is suspected) Lumbar puncture (if subarachnoid hemorrhage is suspected and CT scan is negative for blood) Electroencephalography (if seizures are suspected)

[a]Although it is desirable to know the results of these tests before giving recombinant tissue plasminogen activator, thrombolytic therapy should not be delayed while awaiting the results unless (1) there is clinical suspicion of a bleeding abnormality or thrombocytopenia, (2) the patient has received heparin or warfarin, or (3) use of anticoagulation is not known.

Adapted from Christensen H, Fogh Christensen A, Boysen G. Abnormalities on ECG and telemetry predict stroke outcome at 3 months. J Neurol Sci. 2005;234(1-2):99-103. [PMID: 15935384] Copyright 2005 with permission from Elsevier.

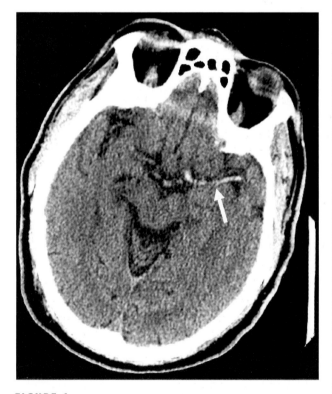

FIGURE 4.
Unenhanced CT scan in acute ischemic stroke.
Unenhanced CT scan of the brain showing early ischemic changes and hyperdense artery (*arrow*) signs.

blood flow and blood volume. Hypoattenuation on a cerebral blood volume map is believed to represent the ischemic core. CT angiograms provide a means of rapidly and noninvasively evaluating the cerebral vasculature in order to provide information about vessel occlusion or stenosis. These techniques have the advantage of rapid data acquisition and can be performed with conventional CT equipment. Disadvantages include the use of iodine contrast and additional radiation exposure. The role of perfusion CT scans (**Figure 5**) in making acute treatment decisions in stroke, however, has not yet been definitively established.

The multimodal MRI approach for acute stroke evaluation includes diffusion-weighted imaging, perfusion-weighted imaging, MRA, and gradient-echo sequences. Standard MRI sequences (T1- and T2-weighting and proton density) are relatively insensitive to early ischemic changes. Diffusion-weighted images have a high sensitivity (88% to 100%) and specificity (95% to 100%) for detecting ischemic lesions, even within minutes of symptom onset; perfusion-weighted images provide relative measures of cerebral hemodynamic status. The ischemic penumbra (brain tissue that is ischemic but not yet infarcted and, therefore, capable of being rescued if successfully reperfused) is roughly approximated on an MRI as the region of perfusion change minus the region of diffusion abnormality (diffusion-perfusion mismatch) (**Figure 6**).

MRI has several advantages over CT in cases of suspected stroke. MRIs are better for distinguishing acute small cortical and subcortical infarcts and brainstem and cerebellar infarctions. The scans are also superior in distinguishing acute from chronic infarctions and identifying silent satellite ischemic lesions that provide information about stroke mechanism (cardioembolism, vasculitis). Limitations include cost, limited availability, longer imaging times, sensitivity to motion, and patient contraindications (such as pacemakers, metal implants, and claustrophobia).

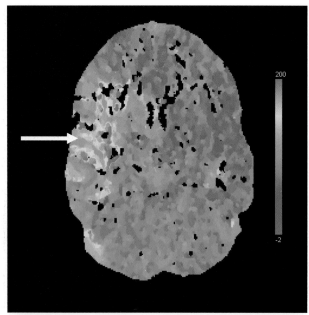

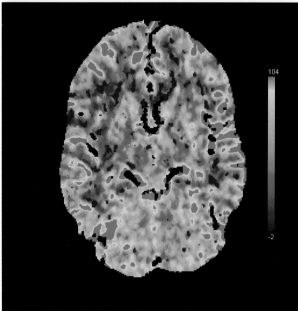

FIGURE 5.
Perfusion CT scans of patients with ischemic stroke.
Top, diminished blood flow is evident in the right middle cerebral artery territory (*arrow*), which indicates the parenchymal zone at risk of infarction if there is no tissue reperfusion. *Bottom*, a minimal blood volume defect is evident in the right middle cerebral artery territory, which indicates that only a small zone of parenchyma is already irreversibly damaged (infarction). The volume of salvageable tissue (or tissue at risk) is the difference between the blood volume defect and the blood flow defect. In this patient, the difference is large, which indicates the presence of a very large potentially salvageable ischemic penumbral zone.

In addition to the aforementioned imaging modalities, transcranial Doppler ultrasonography, carotid duplex ultrasonography, and catheter angiography can be used to detect intracranial and extracranial vessel abnormalities.

Ischemic Stroke

Treatment of Ischemic Stroke

Airway support and ventilatory assistance are recommended for the treatment of patients with acute stroke who have a decreased level of consciousness. Patients with stroke who develop hypoxia should receive supplemental oxygen. Sources of fever should be determined and treated, and antipyretic medications, such as acetaminophen, should be administered to lower temperature in febrile patients with stroke; there is some evidence of an association between elevated temperatures and poor stroke outcome. However, there is no evidence supporting the use of induced hypothermia for the treatment of patients with ischemic stroke. Cardiac monitoring for at least the first 24 hours should be implemented to screen for atrial fibrillation and other potentially serious cardiac arrhythmias that would necessitate emergency cardiac interventions.

The management of arterial hypertension in patients with acute ischemic stroke is controversial. The difficulty involves the compromise between precipitously lowering blood pressure (and thus further compromising blood flow to the tissue undergoing injury) and the risks of hypertension-induced hemorrhagic transformation and worsening cerebral edema. For an uncomplicated ischemic stroke in patients without concurrent acute coronary artery disease or heart failure, antihypertensive medications should be withheld, even in those currently taking antihypertensive medications, unless the systolic blood pressure is greater than 220 mm Hg or the diastolic blood pressure is greater than 120 mm Hg, especially because many patients have spontaneous declines in blood pressure during the first 24 hours after stroke onset. Beyond these levels, a reasonable goal would be to lower systolic blood pressure by approximately 15% during the first 24 hours after stroke onset. If the patient is eligible for thrombolysis, blood pressure must be lowered and stabilized below 185 mm Hg systolic and 110 mm Hg diastolic before thrombolytic therapy is started. Blood pressure may continue to require treatment to maintain the blood pressure below 180 mm Hg systolic and 105 mm Hg diastolic for at least the first 24 hours after thrombolysis treatment. Preferred antihypertensive agents include intravenous labetalol and intravenous nicardipine infusion. Patients with sustained hypertension above recommended levels, despite early antihypertensive therapy, should not be treated with intravenous thrombolysis. These same recommendations

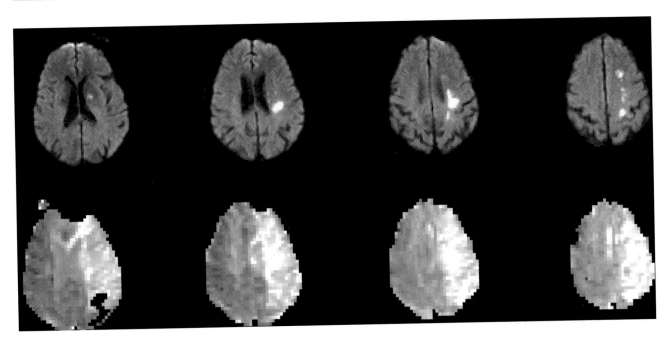

FIGURE 6.
MRIs showing diffusion-perfusion mismatch.
Perfusion-weighted MRIs (*top*) and diffusion-weighted MRIs (*bottom*) illustrate a diffusion-perfusion mismatch.

apply to patients undergoing other acute interventions, including intra-arterial thrombolysis.

Because persistent hyperglycemia during the first 24 hours after stroke is associated with poor outcomes, patients with acute ischemic stroke and plasma glucose levels greater than 140 mg/dL (7.8 mmol/L) should be given insulin; glucose levels should be monitored to avoid hypoglycemia. Normal saline (0.9%) should be used for intravenous fluid hydration rather than dextrose-containing fluids in order not to exacerbate hyperglycemia.

Intravenous Thrombolysis

Intravenous recombinant tissue plasminogen activator (rtPA) therapy for acute ischemic stroke was approved by the U.S. Food and Drug Administration (FDA) in 1996 with specific inclusion and exclusion criteria. Patients with stroke who can be treated with intravenous rtPA have to meet the following criteria:

- Diagnosis of ischemic stroke causing a measurable neurologic deficit (Caution should be used in treatment if major deficits are present.)

- Neurologic signs that do not clear spontaneously

- Stroke symptoms not suggestive of subarachnoid hemorrhage

- Symptom onset less than 3 hours before beginning treatment

- No history of previous intracranial hemorrhage; no head trauma, prior stroke, or myocardial infarction in the previous 3 months; no gastrointestinal or urinary tract hemorrhage in the previous 21 days; no major surgery in the previous 14 days; and no arterial puncture at a non-compressible site in the previous 7 days

- Blood pressure lowered and stabilized (systolic <185 mm Hg, diastolic <110 mm Hg)

- No evidence of active bleeding or acute trauma (such as a fracture) on examination

- No oral anticoagulation or, if on an anticoagulant, an INR of 1.7 or less; activated partial thromboplastin time in the normal range if heparin given in the past 48 hours

- Platelet count of 100,000/µL (100×10^9/L) or greater and plasma glucose level of 50 mg/dL (2.8 mmol/L) or greater

- No seizure with postictal residual neurologic deficits

- No multilobar infarction (a hypodensity > one third of the cerebral hemisphere) on CT scan

- Potential risks and benefits of treatment understood (by patient and family).

The approved dose is 0.9 mg/kg intravenously, with a maximum of 90 mg (10% administered as an intravenous bolus over 1 minute and the remaining 90% in an intravenous infusion over 60 minutes) within 3 hours of onset of stroke symptoms. Favorable outcomes were achieved in 31% to 50% of treated patients compared with 20% to 38% of those given placebo when evaluated at 3 months and again at 1 year. The major risk of treatment was symptomatic intracranial hemorrhage, which occurred in 6.4% of rtPA-treated patients versus 0.6% of those given placebo.

The average estimated number needed to treat (NNT) for one more patient to have a better outcome (by ≥ one grade on the modified Rankin scale [a commonly used scale for measuring the degree of disability or dependence in the daily activities of someone who has had a stroke]) is 3.1 (95% CI, 2.6-3.6); the average estimated number needed to harm (NNH) for one more patient to have a worsened outcome by any degree (≥ one grade on the modified Rankin scale) attributable to rtPA-related symptomatic intracranial hemorrhage is between 29.7 and 40.1. When this information is applied to balancing benefits and adverse effects in clinical practice, intravenous rtPA is 10 times more likely to help than to harm eligible patients with acute ischemic stroke (likelihood of helping versus harming = NNH/NNT). Although written consent is not necessary before administration of rtPA, a full discussion with the patient and family of the potential risks and benefits of treatment is recommended.

Intra-arterial Thrombolysis

Intra-arterial thrombolysis is an option for treatment of selected patients who have had a major stroke within the past 6 hours due to occlusion of a major intracranial artery and who are not candidates for or who have failed to respond to intravenous rtPA. This treatment requires the patient to be at an experienced stroke center with immediate access to cerebral angiography and qualified interventionalists.

Anticoagulation

Urgent anticoagulation—even in instances of presumed cardioembolism (as with atrial fibrillation)—with the goals of preventing early recurrent stroke, halting neurologic worsening, and improving outcomes is not recommended for treatment of patients with acute ischemic stroke because of an increased risk of serious intracranial hemorrhagic complications. For a more detailed discussion, see MKSAP 15 Cardiovascular Medicine.

Antiplatelet Agents

Aspirin is the only antiplatelet agent that has been evaluated for the treatment of acute ischemic stroke. Aspirin, 325 mg, administered within 24 to 48 hours of stroke onset is effective in reducing death and disability. For patients who have received thrombolysis, all antiplatelet medications must be held for 24 hours.

Endovascular Surgical Interventions

Mechanical devices have been used to extract thrombi from occluded intracranial arteries. Although the FDA has approved the use of such devices for reopening intracranial arteries, their clinical utility and appropriate use in the context of available intravenous and intra-arterial thrombolysis have not been firmly established.

Hospital Stroke Unit Admission and Care

The use of comprehensive specialized stroke care (stroke units) and standardized order sets incorporating rehabilitation can substantially reduce morbidity and mortality and so are recommended.

Less severely affected patients should be mobilized to prevent deep venous thrombosis. Subcutaneous administration of anticoagulants (5000 units of unfractionated heparin, subcutaneously, twice daily) is recommended for treatment of immobilized patients to prevent deep venous thrombosis. The use of intermittent external compression devices is recommended for treatment of patients who cannot receive anticoagulation.

Assessment of swallowing is recommended before patients who have experienced strokes start to eat or drink. Patients with dysphagic stroke should be offered enteral tube feedings via a nasogastric tube within the first 24 to 48 hours of admission; nasogastric feeding should be the chosen route within the first 2 or 3 weeks unless there is a strong reason to select a gastric tube (such as intolerance to nasogastric feeding).

If possible, the placement of an indwelling bladder catheter should be avoided because of the associated risk of urinary tract infections.

Treatment of Acute Complications

Patients with major infarctions affecting the cerebral hemisphere or cerebellum are at high risk of brain edema and increased intracranial pressure. Lessening the risk of edema and close monitoring for signs of neurologic worsening, particularly during the first 3 to 5 days after stroke, are recommended. Because many hospitals may not have neurocritical care and neurosurgical expertise, transfer of patients at risk of malignant brain edema to an institution that has such expertise should be considered.

Prophylactic administration of anticonvulsants to patients with stroke who have not had seizures is not recommended.

Patients with acute hydrocephalus secondary to an ischemic stroke, most commonly one that affected the cerebellum, can be treated with placement of a ventricular drain. Decompressive surgical evacuation of the space-occupying cerebellar infarction (generally, >3 cm diameter) can also be used to treat acute hydrocephalus after a stroke and is a potentially lifesaving measure; clinical recovery can be very good, but the impact on morbidity is unknown. Although the efficacy of aggressive medical measures, including osmotic therapy (such as mannitol), intubation, and hyperventilation, is unproved for the treatment of deteriorating patients with malignant brain edema after a large cerebral infarction, the implementation of such measures is recommended when definitive decompressive surgery is being considered. Both the age of the patient and the site of the infarction (dominant versus nondominant hemisphere) may affect decisions about surgery. Although surgery may be recommended for treatment of seriously affected patients, the physician should advise the patient's family about the potential outcomes, including survival with severe disability. Corticosteroids are not recommended as treatment of cerebral edema and increased intracranial pressure complicating acute ischemic stroke.

KEY POINTS

- For patients with acute ischemic stroke (but without cardiac comorbidities) who are not eligible for recombinant tissue plasminogen activator therapy, antihypertensive medications should be withheld unless the systolic blood pressure is greater than 220 mm Hg or the diastolic blood pressure is greater than 120 mm Hg.

- For patients eligible for thrombolysis, blood pressure must be lowered and stabilized below 185 mm Hg systolic and 110 mm Hg diastolic before thrombolytic therapy is started; blood pressure should be maintained below 180 mm Hg (systolic) and 105 mm Hg (diastolic) for at least the first 24 hours after thrombolysis treatment.

- Because persistent hyperglycemia (plasma glucose levels greater than 140 mg/dL [7.8 mmol/L]) during the first 24 hours after stroke onset is associated with poor outcomes, it should be treated in patients with acute ischemic stroke.

- Intravenous recombinant tissue plasminogen activator is recommended for selected patients with ischemic stroke who are treated within 3 hours of symptom onset.

- Patients with major infarctions affecting the cerebral hemisphere or cerebellum are at high risk for the complications of brain edema and increased intracranial pressure; lessening the risk of edema and close monitoring of the patient for signs of neurologic worsening during the first 3 to 5 days after stroke are necessary.

Secondary Prevention of Ischemic Stroke and Transient Ischemic Attack

Treatable Risk Factors

Hypertension

Antihypertensive treatment is recommended for prevention of both recurrent stroke and other vascular events in persons with hypertension who have had an ischemic stroke or TIA and are beyond the hyperacute period. Benefit has been associated with an average reduction of approximately 10 mm Hg for systolic blood pressure and 5 mm Hg for diastolic blood pressure; desirable blood pressure levels have been defined as less than 140 mm Hg systolic and less than 90 mm Hg diastolic in most patients and less than 130 mm Hg systolic and less than 80 diastolic in patients with diabetes mellitus or those with multiple vascular risk factors (per the seventh report of the Joint National Committee on Prevention, Detection, Evaluation, and Treatment of High Blood Pressure).

Lifestyle modifications have been associated with blood pressure reductions and should be included as part of any comprehensive antihypertensive therapy. Although the optimal drug regimen remains uncertain, available data support the use of diuretics and the combination of diuretics and angiotensin-converting enzyme inhibitors to prevent recurrent stroke.

See also MKSAP 15 Cardiovascular Medicine.

Diabetes Mellitus

The goal of glycemic control in patients with diabetes mellitus who have had ischemic stroke or TIA should be to keep glycemic levels as low as is feasible without undue risk for adverse events or an unacceptable burden on patients. A hemoglobin A_{1c} value of less than 7% is a reasonable goal for many, but not all, patients.

More rigorous control of blood pressure (and lipid levels) should be considered in patients with diabetes. Most patients will require more than one agent. Angiotensin-converting enzyme inhibitors and angiotensin II receptor blockers are more effective in reducing the progression of renal disease and are recommended as first-choice medications for patients with diabetes and chronic renal disease.

For more information on diabetes and stroke, see MKSAP 15 Endocrinology and Metabolism.

Lipids

Patients with ischemic stroke or TIA who also have elevated cholesterol levels, comorbid coronary artery disease, or evidence of an atherosclerotic origin of the stroke should be treated according to the National Cholesterol Education Program Adult Treatment Panel III Guidelines, which include lifestyle modification, dietary guidelines, and medication recommendations. Statins are recommended. According to these guidelines, the optimal target goal for cholesterol lowering for those with coronary artery disease or symptomatic atherosclerotic disease is a serum LDL cholesterol level of less than 100 mg/dL (2.6 mmol/L), and for very high-risk persons with multiple risk factors, a reasonable goal is a serum LDL cholesterol level of less than 70 mg/dL (1.8 mmol/L).

Patients with ischemic stroke or TIA of presumed atherosclerotic origin who have no pre-existing indications for statins (that is, they have normal cholesterol levels, no comorbid coronary artery disease, and no evidence of atherosclerosis) are reasonable candidates for treatment with a statin to reduce the risk of vascular events, although the level of supporting evidence is low. Gemfibrozil or niacin may also be considered in patients with ischemic stroke or TIA who have low HDL cholesterol levels.

Modifiable behavioral risk factors that should be addressed include cigarette smoking, excessive alcohol consumption, obesity, and lack of physical activity.

See also MKSAP 15 Endocrinology and Metabolism.

Extracranial Large Artery Atherosclerotic Carotid Disease

For patients with a recent TIA or ischemic stroke (within the past 6 months) who have ipsilateral severe (70%-99%) internal carotid artery stenosis and a life expectancy of greater than 5 years, carotid endarterectomy by a surgeon whose perioperative morbidity and mortality rate is less than 6% is recommended. For patients with a recent TIA or ischemic stroke and ipsilateral moderate (50%-69%) carotid artery stenosis, carotid endarterectomy is also usually recommended, depending on patient-specific factors (such as age, sex, comorbidities, and severity of initial symptoms). When the degree of stenosis is less than 50%, there is no indication for surgery. When carotid endarterectomy is indicated, surgery should occur as soon as possible: within 2 weeks of a small or moderate-sized stroke or TIA and within 6 weeks of a large stroke.

Among patients with symptomatic severe (>70%) internal carotid artery stenosis, carotid endarterectomy is still considered the gold standard of surgical therapies; whether angioplasty or stenting in routine cases is comparable or superior to endarterectomy is still being evaluated in randomized clinical trials. For patients in whom the stenosis is difficult to access surgically, who have medical conditions that greatly increase the risk of surgery, or who have other conditions (such as radiation-induced stenosis or restenosis after endarterectomy), carotid angioplasty and stenting are preferable alternatives to endarterectomy.

In patients with asymptomatic internal carotid artery stenosis of greater than 60%, carotid endarterectomy should be contemplated only if they are medically stable, have severe stenosis, are not too old (<80 years), are expected to have a life expectancy of at least 5 years, and can be operated on at centers with surgeons who have a low perioperative complication rate in asymptomatic patients (<3%).

Extracranial Large Artery Atherosclerotic Vertebrobasilar Disease

Endovascular treatment of patients with symptomatic extracranial large artery atherosclerotic vertebrobasilar disease may be considered when patients continue to experience symptoms directly attributable to posterior circulation ischemia, despite maximal medical therapy with antiplatelet agents, statins, and treatment of other vascular risk factors.

Intracranial Large Artery Atherosclerosis

For patients with hemodynamically significant intracranial stenosis who have symptoms despite medical therapy, the usefulness of endovascular therapy with angioplasty and/or stent placement is uncertain; therefore, this treatment is still considered investigational.

Antithrombotic Therapy for Noncardioembolic Stroke or Transient Ischemic Attack

For patients with either TIA or noncardioembolic ischemic stroke associated with atherosclerosis, small vessel disease, or cryptogenic causes, antiplatelet agents rather than oral anticoagulation are recommended to reduce the risk of recurrent stroke and other cardiovascular events. Aspirin (50-325 mg/d), the combination of aspirin (50 mg) and extended-release dipyridamole (200 mg) twice daily, and clopidogrel (75 mg/d) monotherapy are all acceptable options for initial therapy.

The combination of aspirin and extended-release dipyridamole is more effective than aspirin alone, and clopidogrel may be modestly more effective than aspirin alone on the basis of direct comparison trials. The selection of an antiplatelet agent should be individualized according to patient risk factor profiles, tolerance, and other clinical characteristics. The addition of aspirin to clopidogrel increases the risk of hemorrhage and is not routinely recommended for patients with ischemic stroke or TIA. For patients allergic to aspirin, clopidogrel is a reasonable choice. For patients who have had an ischemic stroke despite taking aspirin, there is no evidence that increasing the dose of aspirin provides additional benefits. Although alternative antiplatelet agents are often considered for noncardioembolic stroke in patients already receiving aspirin, no single agent or combination has been studied in patients who have had an ischemic stroke or TIA while on aspirin therapy.

Treatments for Stroke of Other or Unusual Causes

Arterial Dissections

For patients with ischemic stroke or TIA and extracranial arterial dissection, use of warfarin for 3 to 6 months is preferred (or use of antiplatelet agents when anticoagulation is contraindicated). Beyond 6 months, long-term antiplatelet therapy is reasonable for most of these patients. Anticoagulation beyond 6 months may be considered for patients with recurrent ischemic events. If an acute extracranial arterial dissection is discovered in a patient with headache or neck pain who has no ischemic symptoms, antiplatelet therapy rather than anticoagulation is advised. For patients who have definite recurrent ischemic events despite adequate antithrombotic therapy, endovascular therapy (stenting)—or in rare cases surgery—may be considered.

Cardiac and Hematologic Causes

For a discussion of medical treatments for patients whose strokes or TIAs were caused by a cardioembolism or by paradoxical embolization caused by a patent foramen ovale, see MKSAP 15 Cardiovascular Medicine. For a discussion of treatment of strokes or TIAs caused by hypercoagulable states or hyperhomocysteinemia, see MKSAP 15 Hematology and Oncology.

Stroke in Women

For pregnant women with high-risk thromboembolic conditions (such as known coagulopathy or mechanical heart valves) who have a stroke or TIA, the following options may be considered: (1) adjusted-dose unfractionated heparin throughout pregnancy, such as a subcutaneous dose every 12 hours, with monitoring of activated partial thromboplastin time; (2) adjusted-dose low-molecular-weight heparin, with factor Xa monitoring throughout pregnancy; or (3) unfractionated heparin or low-molecular-weight heparin until gestational week 13, followed by warfarin until the middle of the third trimester when unfractionated heparin or low-molecular-weight heparin is reinstituted until delivery. Pregnant women with lower-risk conditions, such as bioprosthetic heart valves, may be considered for treatment with unfractionated heparin or low-molecular-weight heparin in the first trimester, followed by low-dose aspirin for the remainder of the pregnancy.

For women with a history of ischemic stroke or TIA, neither postmenopausal hormone therapy with estrogen nor premenopausal oral contraceptive therapy is recommended.

KEY POINTS

- For cholesterol lowering in patients with coronary artery disease or symptomatic atherosclerotic disease, statins are recommended, with an optimal target goal of a serum LDL cholesterol level of less than 100 mg/dL (2.6 mmol/L); for very high-risk persons with multiple risk factors, a reasonable goal is less than 70 mg/ dL (1.8 mmol/L).

- Among patients with symptomatic severe (>70%) internal carotid artery stenosis, carotid endarterectomy is still considered the gold standard surgical therapy; in patients in whom the stenosis is difficult to access surgically, who have medical conditions that greatly increase the risk of surgery, or who have other conditions (such as radiation-induced stenosis or restenosis after endarterectomy), carotid angioplasty and stenting are preferable alternatives to endarterectomy.

- Carotid endarterectomy for patients with asymptomatic internal carotid artery stenosis should only be contemplated for those who are medically stable, have severe stenosis, are not too old (age <80 years), are expected to have a life expectancy of at least 5 years, and can be operated on at centers with surgeons who have a low (<3%) perioperative complication rate in asymptomatic patients.

Hemorrhagic Stroke

Intracerebral Hemorrhage

Age greater than 65 years is a risk factor for intracerebral hemorrhage and may provide a cue to physicians for screening and managing modifiable risk factors. Hypertension remains the single most important modifiable risk factor; rigorous treatment of hypertension can prevent intracerebral hemorrhage. Smoking, heavy alcohol use, cocaine use, antithrombotic medication use, and (possibly) a low HDL-cholesterol level are other reported risk factors.

The classic presentation of intracerebral hemorrhage includes the onset of a sudden focal neurologic deficit that progresses over minutes or hours. Other common clinical features include headache, nausea, and vomiting.

CT scans and MRIs are equally reliable in identifying the presence, size, location, and progression of a hematoma. Deep hemorrhages (in the basal ganglia, thalamus, pons, and cerebellum) in hypertensive patients are most often due to the hypertension, whereas lobar hemorrhages in nonhypertensive elderly patients are most often due to cerebral amyloid angiopathy.

The monitoring and management of patients with an acute intracerebral hemorrhage should take place in the intensive care unit because of the acuity of the condition, frequent elevations in intracerebral pressure and blood pressure, risk of rapid deterioration over the ensuing 72 hours, frequent need for intubation and assisted ventilation, and multiple complicating medical issues.

Antiepileptic drug therapy should be reserved for those patients who experience a clinical seizure. The treatment of elevated intracranial pressure should begin with simple measures, such as elevation of the head of the bed, analgesia, and sedation. More aggressive therapies, including use of osmotic diuretics (mannitol and hypertonic saline solution), drainage of cerebrospinal fluid via a ventricular catheter, neuromuscular blockade, and hyperventilation, generally require concomitant monitoring of intracranial pressure and blood pressure, with a goal to maintain a cerebral perfusion pressure above 70 mm. As with ischemic stroke, persistent hyperglycemia (plasma glucose levels >140 mg/dL [7.8 mmol/L]) during the first 24 hours after hemorrhagic stroke is associated with poor outcomes and so should be treated.

In heparin-associated intracerebral hemorrhage, protamine sulfate is used to reverse the coagulopathy. Patients with warfarin-associated intracerebral hemorrhage should be treated with intravenous vitamin K to reverse the effects of the warfarin and with fresh frozen plasma to replace clotting factors. The treatment of patients with intracerebral hemorrhage related to thrombolytic therapy includes urgent empirical therapies to replace clotting factors (cryoprecipitate, 2 bags/10 kg). Emergent surgical evacuation of the hematoma is indicated for patients with a cerebellar hemorrhage greater than 3 cm who are deteriorating neurologically or who have brain stem compression and/or hydrocephalus from ventricular obstruction.

- Deep hemorrhages (in the basal ganglia, thalamus, pons, and cerebellum) in hypertensive patients are often due to the hypertension, whereas lobar hemorrhages in nonhypertensive elderly patients are often due to cerebral amyloid angiopathy.

Aneurysmal Subarachnoid Hemorrhage

Pathophysiology, Risk Factors, and Diagnosis

One in every 20 strokes is caused by a subarachnoid hemorrhage from an intracranial aneurysm. Saccular aneurysms arise at sites of arterial branching, usually at the base of the brain, either on the circle of Willis itself or at a nearby branching point (**Figure 7**). Most intracranial aneurysms will never rupture. The rupture risk increases with the size of the aneurysm.

Modifiable risk factors for subarachnoid hemorrhage include hypertension, smoking, and excessive alcohol intake. Genetic factors obviously play important roles in familial subarachnoid hemorrhage. Intracranial aneurysms have been reported in up to 10% of adults with autosomal dominant polycystic kidney disease.

Sudden headache is the most characteristic symptom of subarachnoid hemorrhage. This headache is generally diffuse and often described as the most severe headache a patient has ever experienced. A sentinel headache (a thunderclap headache in the days or weeks preceding a subarachnoid hemorrhage) occurs in 10% to 40% of patients with subarachnoid hemorrhage; two thirds of these patients have a depressed level of consciousness at presentation. Neck stiffness is a common symptom. Funduscopy is essential to evaluate for subhyaloid hemorrhage, which is found in 15% of these patients (**Figure 8**). Focal neurologic deficits occur from aneurysms that compress a cranial nerve, bleed into brain parenchyma, or cause focal ischemia due to vasospasm. Systemic features may include hypertension, hypoxemia, and electrocardiographic changes. Patients with a subarachnoid hemorrhage may receive a preliminary misdiagnosis (such as migraine headache); this has occurred in 12% to 51% of patients. Without timely detection and definitive management, rerupture occurs in 15% of patients within the first 24 hours and in 40% within the first month.

Obtaining a CT scan is the appropriate first step if a subarachnoid hemorrhage is suspected (**Figure 9**). The ability to detect a subarachnoid hemorrhage on CT is dependent on its volume, the time interval since symptom onset, and the experience of the radiologist. On the first day, extravasated blood will be seen in greater than 95% of patients, but in the following days, this proportion drops off precipitously. In an important minority of patients (~5%) with sudden headache and normal findings on a head CT scan, the cerebrospinal fluid will contain an abnormally elevated erythrocyte count or xanthochromia within 12 hours; angiography subsequently confirms a ruptured aneurysm. Therefore, a lumbar puncture is necessary in any patient with sudden severe headache and normal findings on a head CT scan.

Angiographic studies not only identify the presence of one or more aneurysm, but also allow study of the anatomic configuration of the aneurysm in relation to adjoining arteries, which allows selection of treatment. The sensitivities and specificities of both CT and MRA for detecting an aneurysm, with conventional angiography as the gold standard, are approximately 95% and 100%, but diminish for very small aneurysms (<3 mm). In patients with an acute subarachnoid hemorrhage, CT or MRA should generally be conducted first, followed by the more invasive conventional angiography.

Neurologic Complications

The three main neurologic complications for a patient with a subarachnoid hemorrhage are rebleeding, delayed brain ischemia from vasospasm, and hydrocephalus. In the first few hours after a subarachnoid hemorrhage, up to 15% of patients have a sudden deterioration related to recurrent bleeding. To prevent rebleeding, the aneurysm must be secured by coiling or clipping. During the past decade, endovascular occlusion of aneurysms by detachable coils (**Figure 10**) has emerged as a valuable treatment alternative to surgical clipping in properly selected patients. Nimodipine has been shown to reduce the risk of secondary ischemia after aneurysmal subarachnoid hemorrhages. The typical presentation of acute hydrocephalus is initial alertness followed by a gradual reduction in consciousness over the next few hours.

Unruptured Intracranial Aneurysms

Decisions regarding management of unruptured intracranial aneurysms should be based on the careful comparison of the short- and long-term risks of aneurysmal rupture compared with the risk of intervention. The principal factors that influence the risk of aneurysmal rupture include site, size, morphology, presence of multiple lobes, aneurysm aspect ratio (ratio of length of the aneurysm to neck size), and the presence of a thrombus. The key patient factors include age, medical history, history of prior subarachnoid hemorrhage, positive family history, and the patient's perspective and inclination about observation versus intervention. Natural history data from prospective cohort studies allow valid site- and size-specific rupture rates to be calculated, which can be very useful in routine clinical practice. For patients without prior subarachnoid hemorrhage, the lowest-risk aneurysms (annual rupture risk of approximately 0.05%) were those in the anterior circulation and were less than 7 mm in diameter; for other aneurysm size categories, the annual rupture rates are 0.5% (7-12 mm), 2.9% (13-24 mm), and 8% (>24 mm). For posterior circulation aneurysms, the annual rupture rates

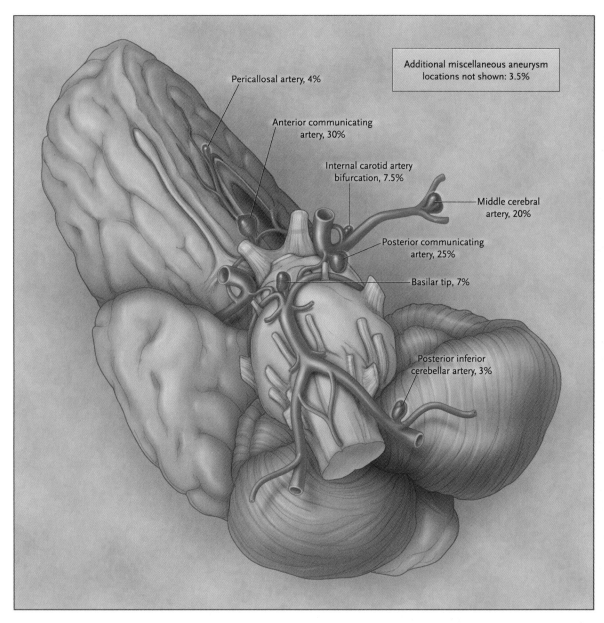

Additional miscellaneous aneurysm locations not shown: 3.5%

Pericallosal artery, 4%

Anterior communicating artery, 30%

Internal carotid artery bifurcation, 7.5%

Middle cerebral artery, 20%

Posterior communicating artery, 25%

Basilar tip, 7%

Posterior inferior cerebellar artery, 3%

FIGURE 7.
The intracranial vasculature showing the most frequent locations of intracranial aneurysms.
Percentages indicate the incidence of intracranial aneurysms.

by aneurysm size are 0.5% (<7 mm), 2.9% (7-12 mm), 3.7% (13-24 mm), and 10% (>24 mm).

KEY POINTS

- A lumbar puncture is necessary for any patient with a sudden severe headache and normal findings on a head CT scan.

- The three main neurologic complications for patients with subarachnoid hemorrhages are rebleeding, delayed brain ischemia from vasospasm, and hydrocephalus.

Recovery After Stroke

Intensive Rehabilitation Programs

Forty percent of patients who have a stroke are left with moderate functional impairment, and 15% to 30% have severe disability. Interventions stressing effective, early, intensive rehabilitation can enhance the recovery process and minimize functional disability. Substantial evidence from meta-analyses and randomized clinical trials indicates that patients do better with a well-organized multidisciplinary approach to postacute

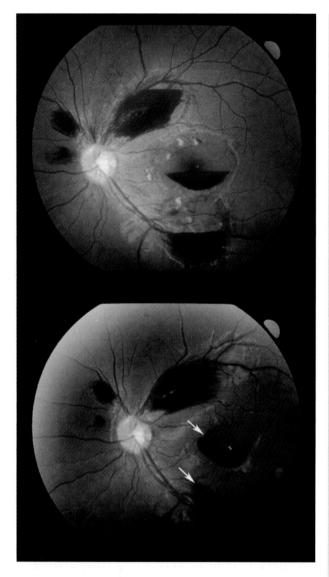

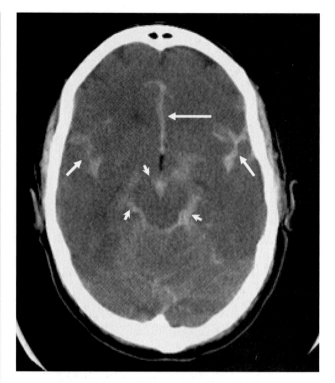

FIGURE 9.
Unenhanced CT scan showing a subarachnoid hemorrhage.
This image shows hyperdensity (blood) in the sylvian fissure (*short arrows*), the interhemispheric fissure (*long arrow*), and the cistern surrounding the brainstem (*arrowheads*).

Studies support early mobilization of patients to prevent complications. Progressive activity should be provided as soon as medically tolerated. Outcomes are anticipated to be better with greater intensity of rehabilitative services.

FIGURE 8.
Funduscopic examination of the left eye showing intraocular hemorrhages.
Intraretinal hemorrhages, white-centered hemorrhages, and a boat-shaped subhyaloid hemorrhage covering the inferior left macula (*top*) are visible with the patient sitting upright. As the patient leans forward (*bottom*), the subhyaloid hemorrhage becomes circular in shape (*arrows*).

Reprinted with permission from Campillo-Artero C. International Committee of Medical Journal Editors' definition of a clinical attack. Annals of Internal Medicine. 2005;143(11):847. [PMID: 16330804]

stroke care. Stroke rehabilitation begins during the acute phase of hospitalization, as soon as the diagnosis is established and life-threatening complications are controlled. The highest priorities of early stroke rehabilitation are to prevent recurrence of stroke, manage comorbidities, prevent complications (such as deep venous thrombosis, bowel and bladder dysfunction, dysphagia and aspiration, spasticity, pain, and depression), minimize impairments, and maximize function.

Bibliography

Adams HP Jr, del Zoppo G, Alberts MJ, et al. Guidelines for the early management of adults with ischemic stroke: a guideline from the American Heart Association/American Stroke Association Stroke Council, Clinical Cardiology Council, Cardiovascular Radiology and Intervention Council, and the Atherosclerotic Peripheral Vascular Disease and Quality of Care Outcomes in Research Interdisciplinary Working Groups [errata in Stroke. 2007;38(6):e38 and Stroke. 2007;38(9):e96]. Stroke. 2007; 38(5):1655-1711. [PMID:17431204]

Duncan PW, Zorowitz R, Bates B, et al. Management of adult stroke rehabilitation care: a clinical practice guideline. Stroke. 2005;36(9):e100-143. [PMID: 16120836]

Goldstein LB, Adams R, Alberts MJ, et al. Primary prevention of ischemic stroke: a guideline from the American Heart Association/American Stroke Association Stroke Council: cosponsored by the Atherosclerotic Peripheral Vascular Disease Interdisciplinary Working Group; Cardiovascular Nursing Council; Clinical Cardiology Council; Nutrition, Physical Activity, and Metabolism Council; Quality of Care and Outcomes Research Interdisciplinary Working Group: the American Academy of Neurology affirms the value of this guideline [erratum in Stroke. 2007;38(1);207]. Stroke. 2006;37(6):1583-1633. [PMID: 16675728]

Goldstein LB, Simel DL. Is this patient having a stroke? JAMA. 2005;293(19):2391-2402. [PMID: 15900010]

FIGURE 10.
Detachable coils used for occlusion of aneurysms.
Three detachable coils used by endovascular surgical neuroradiologists to pack an intracranial aneurysm and prevent rupture and subarachnoid hemorrhage.

Johnston SC, Nguyen-Huynh MN, Schwartz ME, et al. National Stroke Association guidelines for the management of transient ischemic attacks. Ann Neurol. 2006;60(3):301-313. [PMID: 16912978]

Johnston SC, Rothwell PM, Nguyen-Huynh MN, et al. Validation and refinement of scores to predict very early stroke risk after transient ischaemic attack. Lancet. 2007;369(9558):283-292. [PMID: 17258668]

Khaja AM, Grotta JC. Established treatments for acute ischaemic stroke. Lancet. 2007;369(9558):319-330. [PMID: 17258672]

Sacco RL, Adams R, Albers G, et al. Guidelines for prevention of stroke in patients with ischemic stroke or transient ischemic attack: a statement for healthcare professionals from the American Heart Association/American Stroke Association Council on Stroke: cosponsored by the Council on Cardiovascular Radiology and Intervention and the American Academy of Neurology. Stroke. 2006; 37(2):577-617. [PMID: 16432246]

Schwamm LH, Pancioli A, Acker JE III, et al. Recommendations for the establishment of stroke systems of care: recommendations from the American Stroke Association's Task Force on the Development of Stroke Systems. Stroke. 2005;36(3):690-703. [PMID: 15689577]

van der Worp HB, van Gijn J. Acute ischemic stroke. N Engl J Med. 2007;357(6):572-579. [PMID: 17687132]

Dementia

Overview of Dementia

Dementia is a clinical syndrome in which multiple cognitive domains—including memory, language, spatial skills, judgment, and problem solving—are impaired to a disabling degree. Some dementing illnesses can also affect noncognitive neurologic functions (such as gait). Diseases that cause dementia often produce characteristic patterns of cognitive (and sometimes noncognitive) impairment that can aid diagnosis.

Reversible and Nonreversible Causes of Dementia

Cognitive impairment in an elderly person has many potential causes (**Table 8**). The single most important diagnostic goal is to determine whether the cause is reversible or not. Time course, medical context, symptoms, and signs all must be considered. Historical clues suggesting a reversible process include abrupt or rapid onset, fluctuating severity, altered level of consciousness, hypersomnolence, and hallucinations. (None of these clues is absolute, however; for example, Creutzfeldt-Jakob disease is rapidly progressive yet uniformly fatal, and fluctuating severity and visual hallucinations typify dementia with Lewy bodies, an irreversible degenerative disease.) Other clues on mental status testing that suggest a reversible process include inattention, disorientation, and somnolence in the absence of frank amnesia. On physical examination, clues include ataxia, hyperreflexia, tremulousness, and other findings that are often seen in elderly patients but are not part of the typical picture of Alzheimer dementia.

General Diagnostic Considerations

When dementia is suspected, a CT scan or an MRI of the brain should be obtained to identify any structural lesions or other potentially reversible causes. An MRI is generally preferred because of its greater sensitivity for cerebrovascular disease and other disorders. Such brain imaging is important in all patients undergoing initial diagnostic evaluation but need not be repeated routinely in the absence of unexpected changes in disease course. A complete blood count, thyroid

TABLE 8 Common Causes of Cognitive Decline

Pathophysiologic Category of Dementia	Acute/Subacute	Chronic
Vascular	Stroke	Vascular disease
Infectious	Viral encephalitis	Fungal meningitis
Toxic	Acute drug effect (as from amitriptyline)	Chronic drug effect (as from lithium)
Metabolic	Hepatic encephalopathy	Hypothyroidism
Inflammatory	Cerebral vasculitis	Nonvasculitic autoimmune meningoencephalitis
Nutritional	Wernicke-Korsakoff syndrome (thiamine deficiency)	Vitamin B_{12} deficiency
Degenerative	Delirium superimposed on dementia (as with a urinary tract infection)	Alzheimer dementia and related disorders
Epileptic	Seizure; postictal state	Psychomotor status epilepticus
Traumatic	Acute head injury	Sequelae of brain trauma
Psychiatric	Acute psychosis (as in schizophrenia)	Chronic psychosis (as in bipolar affective disorder)
Neoplastic	Primary brain tumor; obstructive hydrocephalus	Meningeal carcinomatosis; communicating hydrocephalus

function tests, a basic metabolic panel, and a serum measurement of vitamin B_{12} level should also be performed. Serologic testing for syphilis should be considered in the appropriate medical setting but is no longer routinely recommended.

An electroencephalogram (EEG) can help identify nonconvulsive status epilepticus, especially in patients with a fluctuating level of consciousness, unusual repetitive movements, or a history of epilepsy. Severe dysrhythmic slowing on an EEG can be a nonspecific indicator of chronic meningitis and thus might prompt more invasive testing (such as a lumbar puncture). In addition, diagnostically characteristic EEG patterns, such as triphasic waves, may be seen in patients with hepatic or uremic encephalopathy.

Lumbar puncture and subsequent cerebrospinal fluid (CSF) examination, although not routinely recommended for all patients with dementia, should be considered in those with fluctuating levels of consciousness, in those at risk for carcinomatous meningitis, in those seemingly too young to be developing a degenerative brain disease, in those at high risk for central nervous system infections, and in those with rapidly progressive disease in whom infection, inflammation, or a neoplasm may have caused chronic meningitis.

Cerebral angiography should be considered only in highly select patients with a high index of suspicion for cerebral vasculitis. Likewise, meningeal and brain biopsy should be considered only in patients in whom inflammatory, infectious, or malignant central nervous system disease is strongly suspected. Usually, there is concurrent evidence of such a disorder based on a severely dysrhythmic EEG, abnormal CSF findings, and often a suggestive medical history of cancer, immune compromise, or autoimmunity. In a patient with suspected cerebral vasculitis or autoimmune encephalopathy, an empiric therapeutic trial of corticosteroids can be considered instead of biopsy, but clear endpoints of success and failure should be established, and the procedure should optimally be performed under neurologic supervision.

Normal Pressure Hydrocephalus

The triad of gait apraxia, dementia (especially with a subcortical pattern), and urinary incontinence is suggestive of normal pressure hydrocephalus (NPH), in particular when these findings are accompanied by enlarged ventricles. NPH is a potentially reversible disorder, but the characteristic triad is nonspecific. Not all patients with dementia who also have gait apraxia and urinary incontinence have NPH, as these symptoms occur eventually in many patients with dementia. Nevertheless, NPH should remain a major diagnostic consideration in patients with this triad of symptoms because it can sometimes be reversed. NPH usually presents as a predominantly shuffling gait disorder (gait apraxia) that is unresponsive to antiparkinsonian medications and may precede or occur in the absence of other symptoms. Although head CT scans and MRIs of the brain in patients with NPH typically show ventriculomegaly that is disproportionate to the degree of cortical atrophy, even the use of a standard ratio of ventricular to brain diameter is unreliable, and NPH can be present even with modest degrees of ventricular enlargement.

There is no universally accepted approach for diagnosing NPH, and the diagnosis is often not made until after some form of treatment is administered. For example, gait improvement after cerebrospinal fluid drainage (best performed with neurologic or neurosurgical consultation) may indicate NPH, as may symptom improvement after surgical placement of a ventriculoperitoneal shunt; the latter procedure, however, has a variable response rate, and most studies report a much higher rate of improvement in the gait disorder than the dementia.

- Clues to potentially reversible dementia include abrupt or rapid onset, fluctuating severity, hypersomnolence, inattention, tremulousness, gait unsteadiness, and hallucinations.

- The initial evaluation of patients with dementia should include CT of the head or MRI of the brain, thyroid and vitamin B_{12} assays, complete blood counts, and a basic metabolic panel.

- The triad of gait apraxia, dementia, and urinary incontinence, especially when accompanied by enlarged ventricles, is suggestive of normal pressure hydrocephalus.

TABLE 9 Diagnostic Classification Scheme for Mild Cognitive Impairment

General
  Symptomatic cognitive complaint
  Normal activities of daily living
  Normal general cognitive function
  Objective cognitive impairment
  Does not meet DSM criteria for dementia
Single domain (symptomatic and objective impairment in one of these categories)
  Memory
  Language
  Visuospatial
  Executive
Multiple domain (symptomatic and objective impairment in two or more of the single domain categories)
Cause
  Degenerative
  Vascular
  Other

DSM = *Diagnostic and Statistical Manual of Mental Disorders.*

Classification of Dementia

Distinctions between cortical and subcortical dementia are evident during the mild to moderate stages of illness but become less clear in later stages. These distinctions help identify the correct diagnosis and predict the types of therapeutic interventions that may become needed. Some diseases that cause subcortical patterns of dementia lead to earlier gait, balance, and swallowing difficulties than occur with most causes of cortical dementia. The defining clinical signs of cortical dementia are aphasia (impaired language), apraxia (impaired movement programming), and agnosia (impaired recognition)—the three "A"s. Subcortical signs primarily include extrapyramidal syndromes and slowing of thought and movement (psychomotor slowing). Cortical signs characterize Alzheimer dementia and the frontotemporal lobar degeneration syndromes of primary nonfluent aphasia, semantic dementia, and frontotemporal dementia (with and without motoneuron disease). Subcortical dementias are primarily found in progressive supranuclear palsy, Parkinson disease with dementia, Huntington disease, and the small-vessel form of vascular dementia. Mixed patterns of dementia characterize cortical basal ganglionic degeneration and dementia with Lewy bodies.

Mild Cognitive Impairment

Early in the course of Alzheimer dementia, patients may not be functionally impaired. The diagnostic term "mild cognitive impairment" (MCI) was originally introduced to describe their condition (abnormal cognitive decline that is not severe enough to produce disability) and define a syndrome of progressive memory impairment. More recently, this diagnosis has evolved by consensus into an entire classification scheme for early, nondisabling cognitive disorders (**Table 9**). The Clinical Dementia Rating (CDR) scale has been used to assess functional impairment and to stage disease in research studies. Although too time consuming for use in most clinical settings, the CDR scale provides a useful conceptual framework that includes the functional categories of memory, orientation, judgment and problem solving, community affairs, home and hobbies, and personal care. Typically, a score of 0 indicates normal cognition, 0.5 MCI, 1.0 mild dementia, 2.0 moderate dementia, and 3.0 severe dementia.

Longitudinal studies of patients with MCI associated with memory loss have shown a conversion rate to dementia of roughly 10% to 15% per year, although conversion rates vary considerably among studies, in part because of different operational definitions of MCI. After 5 years, approximately half of all patients with MCI will meet the criteria for dementia, particularly Alzheimer dementia; after 10 years, most will have Alzheimer dementia (or another dementia syndrome). At autopsy, approximately 80% of patients originally diagnosed with MCI have Alzheimer dementia; other diagnoses that have been confirmed include vascular dementia, frontotemporal dementia, and various less common diseases, with a small percentage of patients showing only the effects of normal aging. In most patients, therefore, MCI associated with memory impairment can be regarded as an early clinical stage of Alzheimer dementia.

- Mild cognitive impairment denotes abnormal cognitive decline that is not severe enough to produce disability.

- Mild cognitive impairment associated with memory loss is often an early stage of Alzheimer dementia, with an annual conversion rate of approximately 10% to 15% per year.

Alzheimer Dementia

Clinical Description and Diagnosis of Alzheimer Dementia

The onset of Alzheimer dementia is insidious and its progression gradual. Alzheimer dementia is characterized by prominent memory loss, anomia, constructional apraxia, anosognosia (impaired recognition of illness), and variable degrees of personality change that cause some patients to become mistrustful and aggressive or frankly delusional and belligerent. Visual variant Alzheimer dementia, or posterior cortical atrophy, is a syndrome in which patients with a similar pathologic process develop progressive visual impairment related to atypically early and severe degenerative involvement of posterior visual cortices that may ultimately result in functional cortical blindness. Other focal variants of Alzheimer dementia are less common but can cause aphasic, apraxic, and frontotemporal patterns of dementia.

Criteria for dementia of the Alzheimer type from the *Diagnostic and Statistical Manual of Mental Disorders*, fourth edition, highlight that memory and other cognitive domains are impaired (aphasia, apraxia, and agnosia) to a functionally disabling degree and that another cause is unlikely. Additionally, the National Institute of Neurological and Communicative Disorders and Stroke–Alzheimer's Disease and Related Disorders Association (NINCDS-ADRDA) use the following categorization criteria:

- Possible Alzheimer dementia—Patient's course is marked by atypical features or coincident, potentially confounding comorbidities.

- Probable Alzheimer dementia—There are multiple domains of functionally disabling impairment, including memory loss.

- Definite Alzheimer dementia—Brain tissue on autopsy confirms the diagnosis in a patient with clinically probable Alzheimer dementia.

There are no widely used biomarkers for Alzheimer dementia, so the goal of the clinical evaluation remains the exclusion of nondegenerative causes. All patients with suspected Alzheimer dementia should undergo the tests mentioned previously for patients with dementia (imaging studies, blood tests) in addition to other tests specific to the patient's medical history. Imaging findings of generalized or medial temporal atrophy are common but nonspecific for Alzheimer dementia. Other diagnostic tests not routinely performed and considered optional at this time include assessment for the apolipoprotein E (APOE) genotype (the e4 allele implies greater likelihood of Alzheimer dementia in a patient with cognitive impairment); fluorodeoxyglucose positron emission tomographic scanning (reduced cerebral glucose metabolism in posterior cingulate, parietal, and temporal cortices is characteristic of Alzheimer dementia); and CSF analysis for amyloid beta (Aβ) amino acids 41-42 (lower levels imply Alzheimer dementia) and phospho-tau (higher levels imply Alzheimer dementia).

Pathology of Alzheimer Dementia

The two hallmark neuropathologic lesions that define Alzheimer dementia are the neuritic amyloid plaque and the neurofibrillary tangle, both of which are generally found in increasing numbers with increasing disease severity (**Figure 11**). In general, neurofibrillary tangle formation is seen first in medial temporal structures and gradually spreads into neocortical regions, with disease progression sparing primary sensorimotor regions until very late in the disease course. Amyloid pathology correlates less well with cognitive loss than does neurofibrillary tangle density, and both correlate less well than does the associated loss of synapses. An unresolved issue with both sets of diagnostic criteria is the significance of plaques and tangles in elderly persons without dementia, since current practice restricts the diagnosis of Alzheimer dementia to those diagnosed with dementia during their lifetimes; this may result in underestimating the number of persons with the disease who die during a preclinical stage.

Risk Factors, Incidence, and Prevalence of Alzheimer Dementia

The most common cause of dementia, Alzheimer dementia accounts for more than half of all cases and increases in frequency with advancing age. Epidemiologic age-specific estimates of incidence and prevalence vary by region and study because of differences in diagnostic criteria and population demographics. There is an exponential increase in both incidence and prevalence with advancing age, at least through the ninth decade. The prevalence of severe dementia from all causes in patients older than 60 years is estimated at 5% and in those older than 85 years between 20% and 50%. The lifetime risk of developing Alzheimer dementia is estimated to be between 12% and 17%.

Besides age, APOE status is the second most important risk factor for Alzheimer dementia. In both familial late-onset Alzheimer dementia and sporadic cases, presence of the APOE e4 allele increases risk, whereas presence of the e2 allele decreases risk. The lifetime risk of Alzheimer dementia in persons without a family history increases from 9% in those without an APOE e4 allele to 29% in those with one copy of the allele. APOE e4 homozygotes make up roughly 2% of the population, and approximately 80% to 90% of them are estimated to develop Alzheimer dementia in their lifetimes. APOE genetic testing is available but not generally recommended for asymptomatic individuals because of the current absence of effective disease-modifying therapy. In limited populations, other genetic factors play a determining role, such as in patients with Down syndrome (trisomy 21) and in autosomal dominant early-onset familial Alzheimer dementia kindreds.

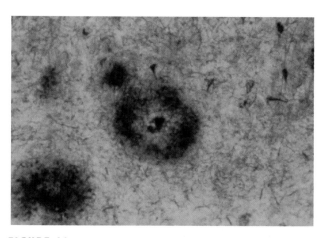
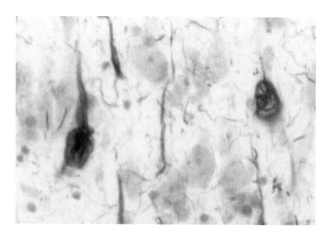

FIGURE 11.
Photomicrograph of the neuropathologic findings of Alzheimer dementia.
Left, neuritic amyloid plaques (Campbell-Switzer stain). *Right*, neurofibrillary tangles (Gallyas stain).

Reprinted with permission from Caselli RJ, Beach TG, Yaari R, Reiman EM. Alzheimer's disease a century later. J Clin Psychiatry. 2006;67(11):1789. [PMID: 17196061] Copyright 2006 Physicians Postgraduate Press. (Photomicrographs courtesy of Dr. Thomas Beach.)

Progression of Alzheimer Dementia

Alzheimer dementia is a gradually progressive disease whose earliest clinical stage is MCI. The mean time from the diagnosis of probable Alzheimer dementia until death is approximately 6 years. Multiple staging schemes of dementia severity between MCI (CDR score = 0.5) and death can be most simply summarized as mild (CDR score = 1.0), moderate (CDR score = 2.0), and severe (CDR score = 3.0).

Mild dementia implies that cognitive loss has progressed to a point of disability in some normal daily activities, such as misplacing items in inappropriate places (putting ice cream in the pantry), becoming lost in familiar places, having difficulty with simple financial transactions (being unable to make change), and experiencing mild deterioration in personal care. Most tasks are completed correctly most of the time, and patients may deny they have a problem (anosognosia).

Moderate-stage Alzheimer dementia is characterized by more severe impairment of cognitive skills, such as language (naming, spelling), and of the ability to perform basic daily activities, such as running a home (preparing meals, managing household finances). Delusional thinking is also characteristic, with stealing and infidelity as two prevalent themes. Patients at this stage cannot generally make a successful pretense of normalcy and require supervision, even if they continue to deny that anything is wrong.

Patients with severe dementia require assistance with all basic activities of daily living, including dressing, bathing, personal hygiene, and eating. Urinary and bowel incontinence develops during this stage. Affected patients are more frankly aphasic (fluent aphasia), agnosic (failure to recognize familiar people and places), and apraxic (inability to write or dress) in addition to having memory loss.

Treatment of Alzheimer Dementia

Alzheimer dementia is best treated with the primary therapeutic modality of caregiving, with the physician largely providing assistance to the caregiver. In this context, pharmacotherapy and lifestyle adjustments can be used.

Pharmacotherapy

There are six major categories of pharmacotherapy to consider in any patient with Alzheimer dementia.

Prevention

There are as yet no proven pharmacologic or other primary prevention therapies for Alzheimer dementia. Some treatments claimed to be effective include use of various drugs, dietary measures, and exercise. However, none has been definitively assessed or is widely accepted as yet.

Intellectual Decline

Two classes of drugs have been approved by the U.S. Food and Drug Administration (FDA) for use to enhance memory and related intellectual skills in patients with Alzheimer dementia: acetylcholinesterase inhibitors and the *N*-methyl-D-aspartate receptor antagonist memantine. Donepezil, galantamine, and rivastigmine are three acetylcholinesterase inhibitors currently approved for the treatment of mild to moderate Alzheimer dementia. As a class, these agents modestly improve cognition, performance of activities of daily living, and functioning as assessed by global measures. For the most part, treatment goals focus on delaying the worsening of these features, although a minority of patients can actually show temporary partial improvement. Memantine is approved as treatment for the moderate to late stages of Alzheimer dementia. After a full therapeutic trial of a medication from one class, there is some evidence to suggest that modest additional benefit may be obtained by adding a medication from the other class.

Dementia with Lewy bodies and vascular dementia usually have concomitant neuropathologic evidence of Alzheimer dementia, and some patients with frontotemporal dementia have a clinical variant of Alzheimer dementia rather than true frontotemporal lobar degeneration. All this suggests (with limited clinical trial support) that using these medications for atypical forms of dementia may also be warranted, although such use is not FDA approved at this time.

Behavioral Decline

Behavioral management of Alzheimer dementia involves the off-label use of medications, and so extra caution is warranted in this setting. The three categories of behavioral problems commonly encountered in patients with Alzheimer dementia and other dementias that are amenable to pharmacologic management are psychosis, depression, and anxiety.

Psychosis includes the symptoms of agitation (particularly sundowning), paranoid delusions, and hallucinations (typically, but not exclusively, visual and more common in patients with dementia with Lewy bodies than Alzheimer dementia). No agents have received FDA approval for the treatment of dementia-related psychosis, but atypical antipsychotic agents, such as quetiapine, are widely used in patients with parkinsonism, for example, because they are less likely to cause or exacerbate extrapyramidal syndromes than are older agents. Two recent studies showed no efficacy of such agents in patients with dementia when used in either a community-based setting or a subspecialty practice. Because the dosages used in both studies were considered by many subspecialists too low to be conclusive, the use of these agents continues. The FDA requires a black box warning label on the use of atypical antipsychotic agents in the treatment of dementia because of the roughly 1.6-fold increased risk of mortality they pose (www.fda.gov/cder/drug/advisory/antipsychotics.htm). Older typical antipsychotic drugs, such as haloperidol, pose an even higher risk of parkinsonism, tardive dyskinesia, and death in patients with Alzheimer dementia. All antipsychotic agents should be avoided in patients with prolonged QT intervals because of the risk of torsades de pointes and ventricular tachycardia.

Drugs with anticholinergic properties, such as tricyclic antidepressants, should be avoided in the treatment of depression in patients with Alzheimer dementia because of the risk of exacerbating confusion. Selective serotonin reuptake inhibitors (SSRIs) are preferred and can sometimes also help ease agitation. However, SSRIs may occasionally precipitate rapid eye movement (REM) sleep behavior disorder (body or limb movements during REM sleep) in patients with an underlying Lewy body–related disorder. Another option is trazadone, although randomized controlled trials of this drug are lacking.

Buspirone or an SSRI may be tried initially to treat anxiety in patients with Alzheimer dementia. If not effective, a low-dose atypical antipsychotic medication (as described earlier) might be considered.

Sleep Disorders

For simple insomnia in patients with Alzheimer dementia, an educational program teaching them and their caregivers the rudiments of sleep hygiene and directing them to set the specific goals of improved nighttime sleep, reduced daytime sleep, and increased daily physical activity may be effective; if this fails, a short-acting sedative-hypnotic, such as zolpidem or zaleplon, may be given either at bedtime or when the patient awakens during the night. Antihistamines, which are generally affordable and accessible, may have adverse effects on cognition and so are not recommended as treatment of simple insomnia in patients with Alzheimer dementia.

Patients with REM sleep behavior disorder exhibit dream-enactment behavior (acting out of dreams during REM sleep); electromyographic recordings in such patients who also have Parkinson disease and related disorders, such as dementia with Lewy bodies, have shown a lack of the muscle atonia typical of sleep because of involvement of cholinergic brainstem nuclei. Low-dose clonazepam can be helpful, but patients should be monitored carefully for benzodiazepine-related exacerbation of cognitive impairment or ataxia. There are anecdotal reports of melatonin efficacy in some patients.

Obstructive sleep apnea (OSA) is not a cause of dementia but can cause mild cognitive problems that may be mistaken for early-stage Alzheimer dementia. OSA is more commonly found in persons with APOE e4, a genetic risk factor of Alzheimer dementia. In patients with OSA and mild cognitive difficulties, treating underlying OSA may improve the cognitive syndrome. If OSA is strongly suspected, a formal sleep study and a trial of continuous positive airway pressure should be attempted.

Although nocturia is not a primary sleep disorder, it is a common reason that some patients with Alzheimer dementia are awake at night and tired during the day.

Other Commonly Associated Disorders

Urinary incontinence is frequently found in patients with Alzheimer dementia and other types of dementia. Two of the most common causes are a flaccid distended bladder, which causes overflow incontinence, and a spastic bladder. Checking the residual amount of urine postvoiding (by ultrasonography in most patients) can distinguish between these two causes. A flaccid distended bladder may require intermittent catheterization. A spastic bladder can usually be managed with peripherally acting anticholinergic agents, such as oxybutynin and tolterodine. These drugs risk exacerbating a patient's confusion but, if started at a low dose and titrated gradually, can often be used safely and effectively. For patients with visual-variant Alzheimer dementia who have cortical visual syndromes, physical and occupational therapy and safety interventions should be considered.

Abrupt Decline

Abrupt cognitive, behavioral, and neurologic deterioration in a patient with Alzheimer dementia and other types of dementia can result from urinary tract infection, pneumonia, medication errors, and various other causes that should prompt a timely and thorough evaluation. Over the protracted course of Alzheimer dementia, many patients may experience an acute delirium, with exacerbated, confused, and slurred speech; somnolence; agitation; tremulousness; unsteadiness; falls; and worsened incontinence. Often, the delirium is due to a superimposed illness (most commonly, a urinary tract infection or pneumonia), a medication error, an injury, or some other cause that must be sought and managed. Postoperative delirium is highly predictable and often easily managed. In a study of elderly patients with hip fracture who did not have dementia, preoperative treatment with low-dose haloperidol reduced the duration and severity of postoperative delirium; the absolute incidence of delirium was also lower, but this difference did not reach statistical significance. Anecdotal reports suggest similar efficacy in patients with dementia, but as yet no controlled trials of haloperidol have been performed in this population.

Lifestyle Changes

The home environment should remain familiar and uncluttered, with ample lighting—especially at night—to prevent falls and injuries. Other home modifications that can be made include installing locks on cabinets, cupboards, and ovens and removing heat- or flame-controlling knobs on stovetops. Families should be instructed to keep poisonous or harmful substances and sharp objects out of reach. Caregivers should be encouraged to register patients with Alzheimer dementia who have a tendency to wander in the Alzheimer's Association's Safe Return Program (www.alz.org/we_can_help_medicalert_safereturn.asp), a national identification program. In the mild stages of Alzheimer dementia, medication taking should be supervised, as should finances. In later stages, caregivers should manage these two activities completely.

Advanced directives can enable a trusted caregiver to become the legal guardian of a patient with Alzheimer dementia. In the absence of current patient competency, living wills, power of attorney, and legal guardianship can provide for the care of a patient and the protection and management of his or her estate.

Memory loss, impaired attention, inability to multitask, and other cognitive disturbances typical of Alzheimer dementia all impair driving skills, as proved in actual road tests and in driving-simulation tests. Patients with Alzheimer dementia who continue to drive, when compared with similarly aged persons without Alzheimer dementia, have two to eight times

the number of collisions. According to a practice parameter of the Quality Standards Subcommittee of the American Academy of Neurology, patients with MCI and a CDR score of 0.5 should be cautioned about driving. Although there is typically no absolute restriction on driving in the absence of an overt driving impairment (reported either by the patient or a reliable observer), physicians should be aware of the reporting requirements in their state. (For instance, California requires physicians to report the diagnosis of Alzheimer dementia to state epidemiologists, who then report the diagnosis to the Department of Motor Vehicles.) The American Academy of Neurology advises that patients with MCI be reassessed every 6 months until their diagnosis converts to Alzheimer dementia, which usually implies that their CDR score has increased to 1.0 (mild dementia) or worse, at which point cessation of driving is advised.

Given that gun ownership is prevalent in the United States and that guns are deliberately kept in an unloaded state in only 17% of households with guns, keeping weapons in secured storage sites and unloading any weapons should be considered when a member of the household has Alzheimer dementia.

Patients with dementia often require behavioral supervision and extensive assistance with activities of daily living, medication use, and essentially every aspect of daily life. Consequently, many are placed in assisted living and skilled nursing facilities. Predictors of placement outside the home include increasing severity of dementia, increased burden of need, and reduced availability of caregivers. Some studies have suggested that treatment with acetylcholinesterase inhibitors may delay nursing home placement by 1 to 2 years, but this suggestion remains controversial.

Future Goals of Treatment for Alzheimer Dementia

Given the pre-eminence of Aβ toxicity in current models of Alzheimer dementia pathogenesis, a growing portfolio of antiamyloid drugs to treat Alzheimer dementia has emerged. For example, because aggregation of Aβ is thought to enhance neurotoxic properties, two Aβ aggregation blockers are currently in clinical trials. Additionally, Aβ immunization has been shown to markedly reduce Alzheimer dementia pathology in animal models. An active immunization trial in humans was ended early, however, because of several cases of T-cell–mediated autoimmune meningoencephalitis. New immunization strategies have since been developed to reduce the T-cell response. In addition, because β-secretase and γ-secretase are thought to generate Aβ, another strategy involves inhibiting β- and γ-secretases (and stimulating α-secretase).

- The two risk factors that account for the greatest number of Alzheimer dementia cases are advanced age and the apolipoprotein E genotype with an e4 allele.

- The acetylcholinesterase inhibitor drugs donepezil, rivastigmine, and galantamine are first-line therapeutic agents for mild to moderate Alzheimer dementia, whereas memantine is a first-line agent for moderate to advanced Alzheimer dementia.

- The use of antipsychotic drugs for the treatment of agitation and psychotic behavior in patients with Alzheimer dementia (and other types of dementia) carries an increased risk of mortality and morbidity and is considered off-label use.

- Abrupt cognitive, behavioral, and neurologic deterioration in a patient with Alzheimer dementia and other types of dementia can result from urinary tract infection, pneumonia, medication errors, and various other causes and thus should prompt a timely and thorough evaluation.

- The American Academy of Neurology advises that patients with mild cognitive impairment and a clinical dementia rating (CDR) of 0.5 should be cautioned about driving and patients with mild Alzheimer dementia (CDR score of 1.0) should cease driving.

Non-Alzheimer Dementias

Vascular Dementia

There are two major types of vascular dementia, the currently preferred term for what was previously known as "multi-infarct dementia." The first type results from infarctions (or hemorrhages) in the territory of the large arteries that produce clinically evident strokes, with a consequent accrual of deficits; these deficits include classic cortical signs such as aphasia and sensorimotor impairment. There is a stepwise process of defined events.

The second type of vascular dementia results from small-vessel cerebrovascular disease caused by arteriolosclerosis or amyloid angiopathy. This form is more common and also more diagnostically subtle in that it typically lacks major defined events. Patients may have psychomotor slowing, a poor learning curve, and relative preservation of naming and other language skills, which reflects a subcortical pathology. Typically, there is no hemiparesis or hemianopia, but patients may have mild features of parkinsonism (without the resting tremor).

Notably, there is a significant association between atherosclerosis of major intracranial arteries and Alzheimer dementia. In fact, small-vessel cerebrovascular disease often presents a mixed pathologic picture of both vascular dementia and Alzheimer dementia, whether the underlying vasculopathy is atherosclerotic or amyloid based. The degree of cognitive impairment, however, correlates better with the degree of neurofibrillary than cerebrovascular pathology at autopsy.

Risk Factors, Incidence, and Prevalence

Cognitive decline has been linked to both cardiovascular disease and atherosclerotic risk factors, including diabetes mellitus, hypercholesterolemia, and high blood pressure; physical activity, such as walking, reduces the risk. Various genetic and nongenetic factors known to increase the risk of vascular disease—including APOE and angiotensin-converting enzyme 1 genotypes, total cholesterol level, lipoprotein A, diabetes mellitus, atrial fibrillation, hypertension, serum APOE levels, and atherosclerosis—have been evaluated as risk factors for vascular dementia and Alzheimer dementia. Improved diabetic control has been associated with a lessening of the risk of Alzheimer dementia, and stroke prevention by any means is associated with reduced cognitive morbidity. The effect of statin use on the prevention or course modification of Alzheimer dementia is still unclear.

The incidence of vascular dementia ranges from 2.6% to 5.2%, and its prevalence from 11.3% to 20.1%, depending on the criteria used. In one longitudinal population-based study, among patients with MCI who progressed to dementia, 60% progressed to Alzheimer dementia and 33% to vascular dementia. Notably, the incidence rate of Alzheimer dementia is higher among individuals with prevalent cardiovascular disease (34.4 per 1000 person-years) than among those without such disease (22.2 per 1000 person-years), which underscores the correlation between vascular dementia and Alzheimer dementia.

Management

Management considerations for vascular dementia are the same as for Alzheimer dementia, except that treatment of causes of cerebral infarction and the physical and cognitive disabilities it produces also need to be addressed (see Stroke).

- Most patients with vascular dementia have concomitant Alzheimer dementia, and dementia severity in such patients correlates more closely with neurofibrillary tangle than vascular pathology.

Frontotemporal Lobar Degeneration and Related Asymmetric Cortical Degeneration Syndromes

Clinical Description and Diagnostic Findings

Frontotemporal lobar degeneration (FTLD) encompasses the three main syndromes of progressive nonfluent aphasia, semantic dementia, and frontotemporal dementia (FTD). As with all degenerative diseases, symptom onset is insidious and progression gradual over the course of several years.

Progressive nonfluent aphasia is a striking disorder that is often mistaken for a stroke because of the obvious speech impairment produced. Semantic dementia might be better considered a form of progressive anomia with less obvious clinical impairment; it is best detected with formal neuropsychological testing.

FTD, the best known of the syndromes, is a progressive neuropsychiatric condition. Patients initially have behavioral and personality changes that range from apathy to social disinhibition. They fail to change their clothes, brush their teeth, pursue their former interests, or initiate many of their previous activities that constituted a normal day. They may fixate, in a seemingly idiosyncratic fashion, on a particular activity, such as going to the bathroom, sorting through a wallet, hoarding magazines, or watching television. Some patients have greater disinhibition and emotional lability (crying or laughing inappropriately).

The syndrome of progressive spasticity or primary lateral sclerosis, although not traditionally considered part of the FTLD spectrum, reflects degeneration of the posterior frontal lobe that includes the upper motoneurons. Cognitive impairment is mild but can include emotional lability and other frontal lobe features. In approximately 10% of patients with FTD and a smaller subset of those with progressive nonfluent aphasia, there is concurrent degeneration of lower motoneurons due to amyotrophic lateral sclerosis (ALS).

Pathology

Pathologically, FTLD primarily consists of nonspecific degenerative changes, such as lobar atrophy, neuronal loss, gliosis, and vacuolation of the neuropil, that predominantly affect the superficial cortical laminae. Pick disease is a pathologic subtype of FTLD; Pick bodies (rounded cytoplasmic masses) tend to predominate in the most severely atrophic cortical regions and in the hippocampi in Pick disease (although similarly appearing cells have been observed in other disorders).

Risk Factors

The major risk factor for any of the FTLD syndromes is a family history of a similar disorder in a first-degree relative. This may reflect an autosomal dominant mutation of either the *tau* or the progranulin gene on chromosome 17. A positive family history of dementia with onset before age 80 years occurs in 38% of patients with FTD, compared with 15% of controls. (The usual age of onset for the FTLD syndromes is closer to 60 years.) There is also an increased risk of FTD in patients with ALS.

Management

Management considerations for FTLD are similar to those for Alzheimer dementia, with the added caveat that patients presenting with FTD should be monitored for the development of ALS (and those with ALS for the development of FTD).

For management considerations in ALS, see Neuromuscular Disorders.

KEY POINTS

- The three main clinical syndromes of frontotemporal lobar degeneration are progressive nonfluent aphasia, semantic dementia, and frontotemporal dementia, with the last being the best known.
- Approximately 10% of patients with frontotemporal lobar degeneration, especially those with frontotemporal dementia, may have concurrent motoneuron disease.

Dementia with Lewy Bodies

Clinical Description and Diagnostic Findings

Dementia occurs in roughly 40% of patients with Parkinson disease. Although a terminologic controversy exists about the distinction between Parkinson disease with dementia and dementia with Lewy bodies, clinically (and pathologically) the distinction is not important except to highlight that dementia may precede or follow the onset of Parkinson disease. Dementia with Lewy bodies is characterized by dementia, parkinsonism, visual hallucinations, REM sleep behavior disorder, and a subcortical pattern of dementia that occurs at the onset or within 1 year of the onset of parkinsonism. The characteristic cognitive profile of dementia in patients with this disease includes impaired learning and memory, psychomotor slowing, constructional apraxia, and more profound visuospatial impairment than in similarly staged patients with Alzheimer dementia. Patients with dementia with Lewy bodies have greater extrapyramidal sensitivity to antipsychotic medications than do those with pure Alzheimer dementia. Mild parkinsonism can be an important diagnostic sign of this (and other extrapyramidal) disorder(s).

Pathology

Lewy bodies are intracytoplasmic inclusions composed of α-synuclein (**Figure 12**). A defining feature of Parkinson disease, Lewy bodies are concentrated in the catecholaminergic nuclei of the brainstem (substantia nigra, locus ceruleus, and dorsal motor nucleus of the vagus nerve) in that disease. In dementia with Lewy bodies, the Lewy bodies are found in these same regions but are also spread throughout the amygdala, entorhinal cortex, and neocortex. Most patients with this disorder have concomitant neuropathologic features of Alzheimer dementia.

Management

Management considerations for dementia with Lewy bodies are similar to those described for Alzheimer dementia. Intervention with dopaminergic medications can potentially create or worsen psychotic symptoms, particularly visual hallucinations in vulnerable patients. Treatment should therefore be reserved for those with clinically significant parkinsonism,

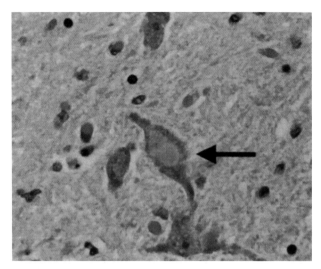

FIGURE 12.
Photomicrograph of Lewy bodies.
Substantia nigra neurons with intracytoplasmic inclusions (*arrow*) of aggregated α-synuclein (Lewy bodies).

Reprinted with permission from Caselli RJ, Beach TG, Sue LI, Connor DJ, Sabbagh MN. Progressive aphasia with Lewy bodies. Dement Geriatr Cogn Disord. 2002;14(2):57. [PMID: 12145451] Copyright 2002 S. Karger AG, Basel. (Photomicrograph courtesy of Dr. Thomas Beach.)

especially if balance becomes impaired and falls are a threat. Patients with dementia with Lewy bodies pose an additional challenge because of the co-occurrence of hallucinations and parkinsonism, as well as the controversy surrounding the efficacy and safety of atypical antipsychotic medications. Quetiapine has a low risk of producing parkinsonism and, unlike clozapine, is not associated with hematologic toxicity. Quetiapine is therefore often used for controlling hallucinations in patients with dementia with Lewy bodies who also have parkinsonism. Parkinsonism itself may require treatment with dopaminergic medications that may exacerbate hallucinations. REM sleep behavior disorder may be mistakenly reported by a caregiver as nocturnal hallucinations and so, in this context, be misinterpreted by an examiner as indicating an acute encephalopathy. However, careful history taking and examination should preclude this misdiagnosis.

KEY POINT

- Dementia with Lewy bodies is characterized by parkinsonism, visual hallucinations, rapid eye movement sleep behavior disorder, and a subcortical pattern of dementia that occurs at the onset or within 1 year of the onset of parkinsonism.

Bibliography

Dubinsky RM, Stein AC, Lyons K. Risk of driving and Alzheimer's disease (an evidence based review): report of the Quality Standards Subcommittee of the American Academy of Neurology. Neurology. 2000;54(12):2205-2211. [PMID: 10881240]

Ganguli M, Dodge HH, Stern C, Pandav RS, DeKosky ST. Alzheimer disease and mortality: a 15-year epidemiological study. Arch Neurol. 2005;62(5):779-784. [PMID: 15883266]

Hobson P, Meara J. Risk and incidence of dementia in a cohort of older subjects with Parkinson's disease in the United Kingdom. Mov Disord. 2004;19(9):1043-1049. [PMID 15372593]

Kalisvaart KJ, de Jonghe JF, Bogaards MJ, et al. Haloperidol prophylaxis for elderly hip surgery patients at risk for delirium: a randomized placebo-controlled study. J Am Geriatr Soc. 2005;53(10):1658-1666. [PMID: 16181163]

Knopman DS, DeKosky ST, Cummings JL, et al: Practice parameter: diagnosis of dementia (an evidence-based review). Report of the Quality Standards Subcommittee of the American Academy of Neurology. Neurology. 2001;56(9):1143-1153. [PMID: 11342678]

McKhann G, Drachman D, Folstein M, Katzman R, Price D, Stadlan EM. Clinical diagnosis of Alzheimer's disease: report of the NINCDS-ADRDA Work Group under the auspices of Department of Health and Human Services Task Force on Alzheimer's disease. Neurology. 1984;34(7):930-944. [PMID: 6610841]

Morris JC. The Clinical Dementia Rating (CDR): current version and scoring rules. Neurology. 1993;43(11):2412-2414. [PMID: 8232972]

Petersen RC, Stevens JC, Ganguli M, Tangalos EG, Cummings JL, DeKosky ST. Practice parameter: early detection of dementia: mild cognitive impairment (an evidence-based review). Report of the Quality Standards Subcommittee of the American Academy of Neurology. Neurology. 2001;56(9):1133-1142. [PMID: 11342677]

Poca MA, Mataro M, Matarin M, Arikan F, Junqué C, Sahuquillo J. Good outcome in patients with normal-pressure hydrocephalus and factors indicating poor prognosis. J Neurosurg. 2005;103(3):455-463. [PMID: 16235677]

Qaseem A, Snow V, Cross JT Jr, et al. Current pharmacologic treatment of dementia: a clinical practice guideline from the American College of Physicians and the American Academy of Family Physicians. Ann Intern Med. 2008;148(5):370-378. [PMID: 18316755]

Rasquin SM, Lodder J, Verhey FR. The effect of different diagnostic criteria on the prevalence and incidence of post-stroke dementia. Neuroepidemiology. 2005;24(4):189-195. [PMID: 15802923]

Saunders AM, Strittmatter WJ, Schmechel D, et al: Association of apolipoprotein E allele e4 with late onset familial and sporadic Alzheimer's disease. Neurology. 1993;43(8):467-472. [PMID: 8350998]

Schneider LS, Tariot PN, Dagerman KS, et al. Effectiveness of atypical antipsychotic drugs in patients with Alzheimer's disease. New Engl J Med. 2006;355(15):1525-1538. [PMID: 17035647]

Headache and Facial Pain

Approach to the Patient with Headache

The most important aspect of the evaluation of headache is to distinguish between primary and secondary headaches. Primary headaches (for example, migraine and tension-type headaches) are themselves diseases, whereas secondary headaches (for example, those caused by meningitis or giant cell arteritis) reflect an underlying structural, systemic, or infectious disorder. Most patients who are evaluated for headache have a primary headache disorder, and more than 90% of these patients have a type of migraine.

Features that suggest a secondary cause include the development of progressively frequent and severe headaches within 3 months or the presence of neurologic symptoms, focal or lateralizing neurologic signs, papilledema, headaches aggravated or relieved by postural changes, headaches precipitated by a Valsalva maneuver (cough, sneeze), systemic symptoms (for example, fever, night sweats, weight loss), a history of sudden-onset headache, and onset after age 50 years.

> **KEY POINT**
>
> - More than 90% of patients who present with recurrent primary headaches in the outpatient setting have migraine.

Role of Imaging

The American Academy of Neurology recommends neuroimaging in patients with headache and unexplained neurologic findings, atypical headache features, findings that do not fulfill the definition of migraine, or some additional risk factor, such as immune deficiency. Findings that significantly increase the odds of finding an abnormality on neuroimaging in a patient with nonacute headache include a history of rapidly increasing headache frequency, lack of coordination, localized neurologic signs or subjective numbness/paresthesia, and headache causing awakening from sleep.

CT of the head is the recommended imaging study in patients suspected of having acute subarachnoid hemorrhage or skull fracture. However, noncontrast head CT may miss serious intracranial causes of headache, and if these disorders are suspected, MRI of the head, magnetic resonance angiography, or CT angiography is recommended (**Table 10**).

> **KEY POINTS**
>
> - Neuroimaging is recommended in patients with headache and unexplained neurologic findings, atypical headache features, findings that do not fulfill the definition of migraine, and risk factors such as immune deficiency.
> - CT of the head is the recommended imaging study in patients with headache suspected of having acute subarachnoid hemorrhage or skull fracture; MRI, magnetic resonance angiography, or CT angiography is recommended if intracranial causes of headache are suspected.

Migraine

Clinical Features and Pathophysiology

The International Classification of Headache Disorders (ICHD) defines migraine as a recurrent headache disorder manifesting in attacks lasting 4 to 72 hours. Typical characteristics of migraine are unilateral location, pulsating quality, moderate or severe intensity, aggravation by routine physical activity, and association with nausea and/or photophobia and phonophobia. The ICHD also provides diagnostic criteria for the disorder (**Table 11**).

TABLE 10 Causes of Headache That Can Be Missed on Routine Noncontrast Head CT Scan

Vascular
Saccular aneurysms
Subarachnoid hemorrhage[a,b]
Acute cerebral infarction
Arteriovenous malformations[b,c]
Dural arteriovenous fistula[b,c]
Carotid or vertebral artery dissection[c]
Central nervous system vasculitis[a,b,c]
Reversible cerebral vasoconstriction[c]
Cerebral venous and cortical vein thrombosis[d]
Structural
Neoplasms (especially in the posterior fossa)[e]
Cerebral metastases[e]
Meningeal carcinomatosis[a,e]
Pituitary tumor or hemorrhage
Foramen magnum lesions
Arnold-Chiari malformations
Infections and Disorders of Intracranial Pressure
Paranasal sinusitis
Meningoencephalitis[f]
Meningitis[e,f]
Cerebrospinal fluid leak (pachymeningeal thickening and enhancement)[a,e]
Idiopathic intracranial hypertension[f]

[a]Lumbar puncture may be required.

[b]Conventional angiography is usually required.

[c]Magnetic resonance angiography or CT angiography is usually required.

[d]Magnetic resonance venography or CT venography is usually required.

[e]Gadolinium-enhanced imaging is usually required. (Lumbar puncture is recommended as the diagnostic procedure of choice in patients with suspected acute or chronic meningitis.)

[f]Lumbar puncture is required.

A neurologic aura occurs in up to one third of patients with migraine. The aura consists of such visual symptoms as spark photopsias (perceptions of flashes of light), fortification (arcs of flashing light that often form a zig-zag pattern), and scotoma (an area of loss of vision surrounded by a normal field of vision) in more than 90% of patients. Paresthesia involving the hands, arms, and face or expressive or receptive language dysfunction can also occur. The aura symptoms usually evolve over 5 minutes, last less than 60 minutes, and are followed within 60 minutes by a migraine headache.

Other common symptoms include sensitivity to odors, occipital-nuchal pain, and sinus pain or pressure. The latter two symptoms often lead to a misdiagnosis of tension-type and sinus headache. In two thirds of patients with migraine

TABLE 11 Diagnostic Criteria for Migraine Without Aura

A. At least five attacks fulfilling criteria B-D

B. Headache attacks lasting 4 to 72 hours (untreated or unsuccessfully treated)

C. Headache has at least two of the following characteristics:
1. Unilateral location
2. Pulsating quality
3. Moderate or severe pain intensity
4. Aggravation by or causing avoidance of routine physical activity (for example, walking or climbing stairs)

D. During headache at least one of the following:
1. Nausea and/or vomiting
2. Photophobia and phonophobia

E. Not attributed to another disorder

Data reprinted from Headache Classification Subcommittee of the International Headache Society. The International Classification of Headache Disorders: 2nd edition. Cephalalgia. 2004;24 Suppl 1:24-25. [PMID: 14979299] Copyright 2004 International Headache Society. Reprinted with permission from Blackwell Publishing Ltd.

with and without aura, the headache is preceded by a premonitory phase consisting of various symptoms, such as yawning, photophobia, mood alteration, fatigue, or neck stiffness or pain. The headache is then often followed by a postdromal phase of fatigue, difficulty concentrating, and sensitivity to movement. In up to three fourths of patients, attacks may be precipitated by triggers, such as alcohol, physical exertion, menstruation, emotional stress, weather changes, sleep deprivation, hunger, high altitude, and air travel.

Acute and Rescue Medications

The goals of acute migraine therapy are to achieve rapid and consistent relief of headache within 2 hours, to prevent recurrence within 48 hours, to restore the patient's ability to function, to minimize side effects and the use of back-up and rescue medications, and to avoid the overuse of acute headache medications.

Acute treatment strategies include administering medication while pain is still mild and individualizing therapy by using migraine-specific medication (triptans, ergot derivatives) in patients who have moderate or severe migraine that has not responded optimally to nonspecific medication (NSAIDs or acetaminophen). If the response to acute therapy is suboptimal, combining a nonspecific analgesic with a triptan may enhance the response. In patients who have severe and early nausea or vomiting, a nonoral route is preferable (nasal spray, suppository, or injection). For severe migraine, a self-administered rescue medication is needed when other treatments fail. Rescue medications include opioids, neuroleptic agents, and corticosteroids.

Preventive Medications

Approximately 38% of patients with migraine need preventive treatment, but preventive medications are prescribed to only 3% to 13% of such patients. More than 30 therapeutic agents

or approaches have been evaluated in clinical trials for the preventive treatment of migraine over the past two decades. Evidence-based guidelines for the preventive treatment of migraine have been developed by the American Academy of Neurology. There is level I evidence (that is, evidence from at least two randomized, double-blind, placebo-controlled studies) to support the use of eight drugs available in the United States (topiramate, valproic acid [divalproex sodium and sodium valproate], amitriptyline, metoprolol, propranolol, timolol, and extract of the plant Butterbur root *Petasites hybridus*) and two nonpharmacologic approaches (relaxation therapy and biofeedback). Methysergide is also proven effective for migraine prevention but is no longer available in the United States (because it was rarely prescribed, given its adverse events profile).

The comorbid conditions associated with migraine that affect its management include depression, anxiety disorders, epilepsy, and stroke. In patients with depression, a tricyclic antidepressant may be a useful preventive medication, whereas in patients with epilepsy, valproic acid or topiramate may be useful choices. In patients with hypertension or cardiovascular disease, a β-blocker may be appropriate for prevention. However, caution must be exercised not to undertreat a comorbid disorder by trying to treat two disorders with one medication.

The following principles, which are practice-based rather than evidence-based, can facilitate successful prevention:

- *Minimize side effects:* Start at a low dosage (for example, amitriptyline, 10 mg/d) and increase slowly by weekly equivalent dosage increments (amitriptyline, 10 mg/d week 1; 20 mg/d week 2) until therapeutic effects develop.

- *Set and reach target dosage:* Set initial target dosage (for example, amitriptyline, 50 mg/d), advising patient to stop earlier if partial efficacy or side effects occur. The ceiling dosage is reached when desired efficacy occurs or side effects become intolerable.

- *Accumulate efficacy over time:* Give each treatment a trial of at least 2 months at the target dosage; efficacy may begin within days to weeks, but the full benefit of a drug may not be realized until 6 months have elapsed.

- *Set expectations for success and side effects:* Success is defined as a 50% reduction in frequency of attacks, a significant decrease in their duration, or an improved response to acute medication. The most common side effects and rare (but serious) idiosyncratic side effects must be reviewed by the physician with the patient. Most side effects are self limited and dosage dependent, and patients should be encouraged to tolerate the early side effects that may develop when a new medication is started.

- *Select and maximize drug choice:* A drug may be selected (such as valproic acid in a patient with migraine who also has epilepsy) or avoided (such as a β-blocker in a patient with migraine who also has asthma) on the basis of the presence of a comorbid illness. The comorbid condition should not be undertreated, however, in an attempt to treat two conditions with one drug.

- *Avoid, if at all possible, preventive drugs in pregnant or lactating women:* Because migraine is most prevalent in women of childbearing age, the potential for adverse fetal effects should be discussed with the patient, who should be encouraged to discontinue drugs used for prevention if she is trying to become pregnant. Drugs with unequivocal teratogenic effects (valproic acid) should be avoided, if possible, in women of childbearing age.

- *Discontinue preventive therapy:* Therapy should be reevaluated and, if possible, the dosage tapered or the therapy discontinued after a sustained period (6 months) of remission.

Nonpharmacologic Therapy

Behavioral treatments for patients with migraines include relaxation training, biofeedback therapy, and cognitive-behavioral training (stress-management training). Evidence-based guidelines for the use of behavioral and physical therapies for the prevention of migraine have been developed by the American Academy of Neurology. These modalities are recommended especially in certain circumstances, including patient preference; poor tolerance, contraindications, or insufficient response to pharmacologic treatments; pregnancy, planned pregnancy, or nursing; history of excessive use of acute headache medications; or significant stress or deficient stress-coping skills. Physical treatments that have been evaluated include acupuncture, cervical manipulation, and mobilization therapy. Acupuncture is probably not effective, and there is inadequate evidence to support the use of hypnosis, transcutaneous electrical nerve stimulation, chiropractic or osteopathic cervical manipulation, or occlusal adjustment (corrections to the bite associated with loose or missing teeth) for prevention of migraine.

Migraine, Cardiovascular Disease, and Oral Contraception

Recent evidence from the Women's Health Study shows an increased risk of ischemic stroke in apparently healthy women older than 45 years who have migraine with aura when compared with unaffected women. Migraine with aura has been shown to be associated with a 14-fold increased risk for silent posterior circulation (cerebellar) infarctions compared with controls. The highest risk was in patients with migraine with aura with at least one attack per month. However, because the absolute occurrence of ischemic stroke among patients with migraine is rare, the absolute risks are low.

The Women's Health Study also demonstrated that among 27,840 apparently healthy women, migraine with aura was associated with a significantly increased risk for cardiovascular disease, myocardial infarction, coronary revascularization, angina, and death from cardiovascular disease when compared with women with migraine without aura and women with no history of migraine. However, the absolute risk increase was considerably low. Recent findings from the Physicians' Health Study in which 20,084 apparently healthy U.S. male physicians were followed for a mean of 15.7 years indicate an association between migraine and cardiovascular disease, which was driven by a significant increase in the risk of myocardial infarction.

There is no evidence that therapy with triptans increases the risk for ischemic vascular events in patients with migraine with or without aura. However, in patients with existing cardiovascular disease or for those at high risk for ischemic vascular events, medication such as triptans and ergotamine should be avoided. With regard to primary prevention, there are no data available from controlled studies on preventing first strokes in patients with migraines with aura with or without additional risk factors for stroke. There is no evidence for the use of low-dose aspirin therapy in these patients, especially because of the low attributable risk associated with migraine. Some, but not all, studies have suggested that young women who use oral contraceptives are at particularly increased risk for ischemic stroke. The World Health Organization recommends that women who have migraine without aura and are age 35 years or older and women who have migraine with aura at any age should not use combined (estrogen-progestin) oral contraceptives.

Treatment of Menstrual Migraine

Menstrually related migraine is defined as headaches that occur between 2 days before and 2 days after the onset of menses in at least two of three menstrual cycles and additionally at other times in the cycle. The first day of the menstrual cycle is considered day 1, and the day before menses is day −1; there is no day 0. Pure menstrual migraine is defined as headache occurring exclusively on the day of the onset of menses or the following day in at least two of three menstrual cycles and at no other times of the menstrual cycle.

The treatment of menstrually related migraine and pure menstrual migraine consists of acute therapy at the time of the migraine and preventive therapy perimenstrually for several days to prevent the migraine. The same treatment goals, principles, and medications used for the acute treatment of nonmenstrual migraine apply to the treatment of menstrually related migraine. For patients with a suboptimal acute treatment response or whose attacks continue to recur over several days despite an initial response to acute medication, short-term migraine prevention may be useful. Predictable menstrual periods and a predictable relationship between the onset of migraine and menses are important for this strategy to succeed. Treatment usually begins 2 days before the onset of menses or 1 day before the expected onset of the migraine in relationship to the onset of menses; treatment is continued for 5 to 7 days. Medications that are used and for which there is evidence of efficacy include naproxen sodium, mefenamic acid, frovatriptan, naratriptan, and percutaneous estradiol.

Treatment of Migraine During Pregnancy

Behavioral management of headache, including relaxation training, biofeedback training, and cognitive behavioral therapy, should be recommended as a standard treatment for all women with migraine who are pregnant or planning pregnancy.

Although drug therapy should be avoided during pregnancy, migraine may worsen during the first and second trimesters, and pharmacologic therapy is, therefore, unavoidable for some women. Intermittent acute treatment may be sufficient, but preventive medications may be necessary for women who have severe daily or near-daily migraine. Patients should be informed of any known possible treatment-related adverse pregnancy outcome associated with a particular medication and told that definitive information about the safe use of many drugs in pregnancy is lacking.

The U.S. Food and Drug Administration (FDA) has five categories of labeling for drug use in pregnancy. An alternative rating system is the Teratogen Information System (TERIS), a resource based on a thorough review of published clinical and experimental literature. The American Academy of Pediatrics (AAP) has also reviewed and categorized drugs for lactating women. The FDA and TERIS categories and the AAP lactation ratings for drugs used for acute treatment and prophylaxis for migraine are shown in **Table 12**.

Acute Treatment

Initial attempts to treat mild or moderate attacks should emphasize rest, icing of the painful area, relaxation strategies, and other nonpharmacologic methods. For moderate or severe headaches that do not respond, acute medications are often necessary. The choice of drug depends on the stage of pregnancy.

Acetaminophen (alone or with an opioid) or opioids alone can be used throughout pregnancy. Opioid use should be intermittent and limited to avoid dependence in the mother and withdrawal symptoms in the newborn. Metoclopramide, chlorpromazine, prochlorperazine, and promethazine are available orally, parenterally, and by suppository and can all be used safely throughout pregnancy. Most NSAIDs may be taken safely for pain during the first trimester of pregnancy.

Evidence from the prospective sumatriptan pregnancy registry and other complementary sources of information shows no sign of teratogenicity with first-trimester exposure to the drug, but the number of pregnancies studied is too small to exclude with confidence an associated increased risk

for common birth defects or a modest increase in risk for rare birth defects.

Preventive Therapy

The threshold for initiating preventive treatment should be higher in the pregnant patient with migraine, and such therapy is usually not implemented unless the patient has at least two severe episodes per week. If possible, treatment should be delayed until the second trimester when the fetus's major organ systems have formed and the risk of adverse effects is probably less.

Valproic acid is a known teratogen. First-trimester exposure to this drug is associated with neural tube defects in approximately 17% of exposed fetuses. Its use should be avoided in women who are planning to become pregnant and during the first trimester of pregnancy.

KEY POINTS

- Occipital-nuchal pain and sinus pain/pressure are common during migraine attacks and often lead to a misdiagnosis of tension-type headache or sinus headache.

- Acute treatment of migraine includes migraine-specific medication (triptans, ergot derivatives) in patients who have moderate or severe migraine that has not responded optimally to nonspecific analgesics (NSAIDs or acetaminophen)

- Level 1 evidence supports the use of valproic acid, topiramate, propranolol, timolol, metoprolol, amitriptyline, and *Petasites hybridus* extract for the preventive drug treatment of migraine.

- Persons with migraines with aura have up to an 8-fold increased risk of ischemic stroke; the absolute risk of stroke in migraine with aura is low, with an attributable risk of 18 to 40 additional ischemic stroke cases per 100,000 women per year, but this risk is tripled by smoking and quadrupled by oral contraceptive use.

- Naproxen, mefenamic acid, frovatriptan, naratriptan, and percutaneous estradiol are effective for the short-term prevention of menstrual migraine.

Tension-Type Headache

Tension-type headache is a dull, bilateral, or diffuse headache, often described as a pressure or squeezing sensation of mild to moderate intensity. It has no accompanying migraine features (nausea, emesis, photophobia, phonophobia), and its pain is not worsened with movement and does not prohibit activity. In patients with a new headache at presentation, especially patients older than 50 years, tension-type headache should be considered a diagnosis of exclusion because it is the type of headache most frequently mimicked by brain tumors and other organic causes.

Chronic Daily Headache

Chronic daily headache is a nonspecific term that refers to both primary (including migraine) and secondary headache disorders in which headache is present on more than 15 days per month for at least 3 months. Risk factors for chronic daily headache include obesity, a history of frequent headache (more than 1 per week), caffeine consumption, and overuse (>10 days per month) of acute headache medications, including analgesics, ergots, triptans, and opioids. In addition, more than half of all patients with chronic daily headache have sleep disturbance and mood disorders, such as depression and anxiety.

The clinical features of the common disorders causing chronic daily headache are shown in **Table 13**. These disorders are classified (on the basis of the usual length of each headache episode) as long-lasting (4 hours or longer) and short-lasting (less than 4 hours) disorders. Chronic migraine and medication overuse headache overwhelmingly represent the most common and challenging of the chronic daily headache disorders in clinical practice.

Chronic migraine (previously referred to as transformed migraine) is defined as headaches that occur on more than 15 days per month of which at least 8 headache days must meet the diagnosis of migraine without aura and/or respond to migraine-specific drugs (ergots or triptans). In general, patients with chronic migraine have headache 20 to 25 days per month, and almost all headaches meet the ICHD criteria for migraine without aura. The diagnoses of chronic migraine and medication overuse headache can be missed because patients may report only their most severe headaches. In addition, they may not report use of over-the-counter analgesics for headache that they do not consider to be migraine. Therefore, patients with migraine should be asked how many days in an average month they have a headache of any type and how many days in an average month they use any acute medication for headache.

Medication overuse headache (previously referred to as rebound headache) is defined as daily or near-daily headache (at least 15 days per month) that occurs in patients with a primary headache disorder who frequently and regularly use symptomatic or acute medications, often in excessive amounts. Overuse is defined as the use of acute headache medications on more than 10 days per month (more than 15 days for simple analgesics, such as acetaminophen, or the use of two or more acute medications [for example, 7 days of a triptan and 9 days of a simple analgesic agent]). The most frequently overused acute headache medications include analgesics, opioids, ergotamine, and triptans. Patients who overuse triptans develop overuse headache faster but respond more quickly and more completely to withdrawal than do patients who overuse opioids or combination analgesics, especially those that contain butalbital, caffeine, and acetaminophen. Moreover, the relapse rate in patients who overuse triptans is significantly lower than that of patients overusing opioids and combination analgesics.

Patients with migraine, especially those with several attacks per month, should be cautioned about the risk of medication overuse headache and advised to limit acute medication use to no more than 2 days per week. Although it is often difficult to be certain whether the overuse of acute headache medication is the cause or the consequence of the daily headache disorder, accurate diagnosis and management require the withdrawal of overused headache medications in all patients.

Medication overuse headache and chronic migraine are managed similarly, with the obvious exception of the need to discontinue the overuse of acute medications in medication overuse headache (**Table 14**). Most patients can be managed as outpatients, except for those in whom the overuse of opioids or butalbital-containing analgesics is excessive, which makes outpatient withdrawal unsafe because of the risk of withdrawal syndromes and seizures. Patients in this population should, in general, be referred to a headache medicine specialist.

KEY POINTS

- Risk factors for chronic daily headache include obesity, a history of more than one headache per week, caffeine consumption, and overuse of acute headache medications.

- Chronic migraine is defined as headaches that occur on more than 15 days per month of which at least 8 headache days must meet the diagnosis of migraine without aura and/or respond to migraine-specific drugs.

- Medication overuse headache is defined as more than 15 days per month with a headache and more than 10 days of use of acute headache medication per month.

- Medication overuse headaches due to opioid or combination analgesics are less responsive to treatment and are associated with a higher relapse rate after drug withdrawal.

Cluster Headache and Other Trigeminal Autonomic Cephalalgias

The trigeminal autonomic cephalalgias are a group of primary headache disorders characterized by excruciating unilateral headache that occurs in association with prominent cranial autonomic features such as lacrimation, nasal congestion, rhinorrhea, and conjunctival injection. These disorders include cluster headache, paroxysmal hemicrania, and Short-lasting

TABLE 12 FDA and TERIS Pregnancy Ratings and AAP Lactation Ratings of Commonly Used Acute and Prophylactic Migraine Drugs

Acute Medication	FDA Pregnancy Rating Categories[a]	TERIS	AAP Lactation Rating
Simple Analgesics			
Acetaminophen	B	N	Caution
Aspirin	C[b]	Min	Compatible
Caffeine	B	N	Compatible
NSAIDs			
Ibuprofen	B[b]	Min	Compatible
Ketorolac	C[b]	U	Compatible
Naproxen	B[b]	U	Compatible
Ergots			
Ergotamine	X	U	Contraindicated
Dihydroergotamine	X	Min	Contraindicated
Triptans			
Almotriptan	C	U	Probably compatible
Eletriptan	C	U	Probably compatible
Frovatriptan	C	U	Compatible
Naratriptan	C	U	Probably compatible
Sumatriptan	C	Unl	Compatible
Rizatriptan	C	U	Probably compatible
Zolmitriptan	C	U	Probably compatible
Opioids			
Butorphanol	B[c]	U	Compatible
Codeine	C[c]	Unl	Compatible
Propoxyphene	C[c]	N	Compatible
Others			
Prednisone	C	N – Min	Compatible
Dexamethasone	C	Min	Compatible
Butalbital	C[c]	Unl	Caution
Neuroleptics and antiemetics			
Metoclopramide	B	Unl	Concern
Prochlorperazine	C (D if third trimester; D[c] if prolonged or at term)	N	Concern
Anticonvulsants			
Gabapentin	C	U	Probably compatible
Valproic acid	D	Mod	Compatible
Topiramate	C	U	Caution
Lamotrigine	C	Min – S	Concern
Antihypertensive Medications			
Atenolol	D	U	Caution
Metoprolol	C[b]	U	Compatible

TABLE 12 FDA and TERIS Pregnancy Ratings and AAP Lactation Ratings of Commonly Used Acute and Prophylactic Migraine Drugs (continued)

Acute Medication	FDA Pregnancy Rating Categories[a]	TERIS	AAP Lactation Rating
Antihypertensive Medications (continued)			
Nadolol	C[b]	U	Compatible
Propranolol	C[b]	U	Compatible
Timolol	C[b]	U	Compatible
Verapamil	C	U	Compatible
Antidepressants			
Amitriptyline	C	Unl	Concern
Nortriptyline	C	U	Concern
Fluoxetine	C	Unl	Concern
Venlafaxine	C	Unl	Concern
Others			
Magnesium sulfate	B	Unl	Compatible
Melatonin	C	U	Probably compatible
Riboflavin	A[c]	U	Compatible

AAP = American Academy of Pediatrics; FDA = U.S. Food and Drug Administration; Min = minimal; Min – S = minimal – small; N = none; N – Min = none – minimal; TERIS, Teratogen Information System; U = undetermined; Unl = unlikely.

[a]FDA risk categories for drugs used during pregnancy: Category A, controlled human studies show no risk; Category B, no evidence of risk in humans but there are no controlled human studies; Category C, risk to humans has not been ruled out; Category D, positive evidence of risk to humans from human and/or animal studies; Category X, contraindicated for use in pregnancy.

[b]Second or third trimester.

[c]If dosage is above recommended daily allowance.

Unilateral Neuralgiform headache attacks with Conjunctival injection and Tearing (SUNCT) syndrome.

The trigeminal autonomic cephalalgias differ in duration and frequency of episodes and in their response to therapy. Cluster headache lasts longest (mean duration, 1 hour), has relatively low episode frequency (one to three per day), and responds best to verapamil. Paroxysmal hemicrania has an intermediate duration (mean, 15 minutes), has an intermediate episode frequency (mean, 11 per day), and responds best to indomethacin. SUNCT syndrome has the shortest duration (mean, 60 seconds), has the highest frequency (30 to 200 per day), and may respond best to lamotrigine (although controlled trials are lacking). It is important to recognize these syndromes because of their highly selective response to treatment.

Cluster headache is the most common trigeminal cephalalgia and is three times more common in men than in women. Guidelines for the treatment of cluster headache and other trigeminal autonomic cephalalgias have been recently developed (**Table 15**).

Treatment usually consists of a transitional therapy for 1 or 2 weeks to rapidly suppress episodes and preventive treatment, which may take 1 to 2 weeks to become effective but is then usually maintained for at least 2 weeks beyond the usual duration of a cluster episode. Cluster episodes usually last 6 to 8 weeks and remission periods usually last 2 to 6 months, but the duration of episodes and remission varies greatly among patients. In patients with chronic cluster headache, which occurs in up to 20% of patients, remission does not last more than 1 month. Typically, a brief course of oral corticosteroids (1 to 3 weeks) or an occipital nerve block is started in conjunction with verapamil as the preventive drug of choice. Oxygen delivered by face mask at 7 to 15 L/min or subcutaneous sumatriptan are first-line acute treatments for breakthrough attacks.

KEY POINTS

- The trigeminal autonomic cephalalgias are a group of primary headache disorders that differ in the duration of each headache episode, the 24-hour frequency of episodes, and their response to treatment.

- Oxygen, subcutaneous sumatriptan, and verapamil are the treatments of choice for cluster headache.

Trigeminal Neuralgia

Trigeminal neuralgia is a unilateral condition characterized by brief episodes of lancinating pain in the distribution of one or more divisions of the trigeminal nerve, invariably V2 and/or V3. The pain is excruciating and often described as sudden,

TABLE 13 Primary Chronic Daily Headache Disorders

Disorder	Clinical Features	Recommended Treatments
Chronic migraine	Migraine with or without aura on >15 days per month for >3 months	Approved medications for episodic migraine (propranolol, topiramate, valproic acid)
Chronic tension-type headache	Mild to moderate severity; no migraine symptoms; bilateral	Amitriptyline
New daily persistent headache	Bilateral, persistent, moderately severe; may be preceded by viral infection; may resemble migraine or tension-type headache	Amitriptyline
Hemicrania continua	Rare, unilaterally constant exacerbations of severe headache, cranial autonomic symptoms, and "ice-pick" pain; completely responsive to indomethacin	Indomethacin
Cluster headache	Cluster periods of 4-8 weeks, 1-3 times per year; daily headaches, frequently nocturnal, occurring 1-8 times per day, each lasting about 1 hour on average; extremely severe, mostly periorbital/temporal, and associated with motor restlessness and autonomic symptoms (tearing, rhinorrhea)	Verapamil, prednisone, gabapentin; acute: sumatriptan by NS or SC injection; zolmitriptan by NS; 100% oxygen
Hypnic headache	Occurs daily but only during sleep; moderately severe; often bilateral; lasts about 1 hour; not associated with autonomic symptoms	Caffeine; lithium; indomethacin
Paroxysmal hemicrania	Headaches identical to cluster headache except that attacks occur more frequently (>5 and up to 24 per day) and are shorter in duration (8-25 min); usually completely responsive to indomethacin	Indomethacin
SUNCT syndrome	Headaches resemble cluster and paroxysmal hemicranias except that attacks occur more frequently (30-100 per day) and are much shorter in duration (20-120 seconds). These headaches may be mistaken for trigeminal neuralgia except that patients have strictly periorbital (cranial nerve V1) pain and cranial autonomic symptoms.	Lamotrigine, gabapentin, topiramate, carbamazepine

Note: Secondary causes require careful consideration and exclusion. These include medication overuse headache, cervicogenic headache, intracranial hypertension or hypotension, intracranial infection (meningitis or sinusitis), space-occupying lesions, posttraumatic headache, arterial dissection, venous sinus thrombosis, and giant-cell arteritis.

NS = nasal spray; SC = subcutaneous; SUNCT = short lasting unilateral neuralgiform pain with conjunctival injection and tearing.

Source: Dodick DW. Clinical practice. Chronic daily headache [erratum in N Engl J Med. 2006;354(8):884]. N Engl J Med. 2006;354(2):160. [PMID: 16407511]

TABLE 14 Treatment of Chronic Migraine and Medication Overuse Headache

Education, support, and close follow-up for 8 to 12 weeks

Lifestyle modifications (quitting smoking, eliminating caffeine, exercising, eating regular meals, and establishing a regular sleep schedule)

Behavioral therapy (relaxation therapy, biofeedback, cognitive behavioral therapy)

Abrupt withdrawal of overused medications for acute headache, except barbiturates or opioids[a]

Standard acute headache treatment (for moderate or severe headache; such therapy is generally not associated with medication overuse headache)

NSAIDs (such as naproxen sodium, 550 mg)

Dihydroergotamine (1 mg intranasally, subcutaneously, or intramuscularly)

Antiemetics (metoclopramide, 10-20 mg; prochlorperazine, 10 mg)

Preventive therapy
  Topiramate, 50-100 mg twice daily
  Valproic acid, 250-500 mg twice daily
  Amitriptyline, 50-100 mg at bedtime

[a]For butalbital overuse, taper the drug over a period of 2 to 4 weeks; if there is concern about the possibility of withdrawal syndrome, provide a tapering course of phenobarbital (30 mg twice daily for 2 weeks, followed by 15 mg twice daily for 2 weeks). For opioid overuse, taper the drug over a period of 2 to 4 weeks; if there is concern about the possibility of withdrawal syndrome, provide clonidine (transdermal therapeutic system patch for 1 to 2 weeks).

Source: Dodick DW. Clinical practice. Chronic daily headache [erratum in N Engl J Med. 2006;354(8):884]. N Engl J Med. 2006;354(2):163. [PMID: 16407511]

TABLE 15 Treatment Guidelines for the Trigeminal Autonomic Cephalalgias

	Treatment of Choice		
Therapy	**Cluster Headache**	**Paroxysmal Hemicrania**	**SUNCT Syndrome**
Acute	100% oxygen, 15 L/min (A)	None	None
	Sumatriptan, 6 mg subcutaneously (A)		
	Sumatriptan, 20 mg nasally (A)		
	Zolmitriptan, 5 mg nasally (A/B)		
	Zolmitriptan, 10 mg nasally (A/B)		
	Zolmitriptan, 5 mg orally (B)		
	Zolmitriptan, 10 mg orally (B)		
	Lidocaine intranasally (B)		
	Octreotide (B)		
Preventive	Verapamil (A)	Indomethacin (A)	Lamotrigine (C)
	Corticosteroids (A)	Verapamil (C)	
	Lithium carbonate (B)	NSAIDs (C)	
	Methysergide (B)		
	Topiramate (B)		
	Ergotamine tartrate (B)		
	Valproic acid (C)		
	Melatonin (C)		
	Baclofen (C)		

A = effective; B = probably effective; C = possibly effective; SUNCT = short lasting unilateral neuralgiform pain with conjunctival injection and tearing.

Reprinted from May A, Leone M, Afra J, et al; EFNS Task Force. EFNS guidelines on the treatment of cluster headache and other trigeminal-autonomic cephalalgias. Eur J Neurol. 2006;13(10):1070. [PMID: 16987158] Copyright 2006 The European Federation of of Neurological Societies. Reproduced with permission from Blackwell Publishing Ltd.

sharp, superficial, and stabbing or burning in quality. The pain is paroxysmal and usually lasts 2 to 3 seconds and may occur in volleys of jabs or stabs of pain. The paroxysms are often punctuated by pain-free periods lasting seconds to hours. Characteristically, the painful episodes are associated with trigger zones, particularly around the mouth and nostrils, and the pain may be triggered by trivial stimuli, such as wind on the face, brushing the teeth, shaving, chewing, or even talking.

Although most cases are idiopathic, there are features that may suggest a secondary cause. Pain that spreads to involve the ear, occiput, neck, or chest is likely the result of another cause. Bilateral pain is invariably associated with a secondary cause, such as nasopharyngeal carcinoma, leptomeningeal carcinomatosis, brainstem lesion, or connective tissue disease (such as Sjögren syndrome). Although a dull aching discomfort may persist for several hours following an especially long or intense episode of pain, suspicion of a secondary cause should arise when chronic continuous pain is present or when sensory symptoms, such as paresthesia or numbness, are present. Because more than 90% of patients present after age 40 years, a diagnosis in a younger patient should prompt an extensive evaluation for secondary causes, such as multiple sclerosis, posterior fossa tumors, and vascular or aneurysmal compression of the trigeminal nerve.

Up to 10% of patients with trigeminal neuralgia may harbor an intracranial lesion; therefore, an MRI should be obtained for every patient with trigeminal neuralgia, even those who respond to medication and whose examination findings are normal.

Spontaneous remissions are the rule in trigeminal neuralgia. More than 50% of affected patients have a remission of at least 6 months. Therefore, after approximately 8 weeks of successful therapy with complete remission of pain, a slow drug taper over a similar time period may be considered.

All medications should be started at a low dosage and titrated slowly until the desired effect is achieved or dose-limiting side effects occur. Monotherapy is a treatment goal, but in some patients, combination therapy with two drugs used in smaller dosages may be more effective and better tolerated. The drug of first choice is carbamazepine or oxcarbazepine, but caution must be exercised in the use of these drugs in patients of Asian origin. Oxcarbazepine may be preferred because carbamazepine may cause hematologic and hepatic toxicity, although both drugs may cause symptomatic hyponatremia. Serum sodium concentration should be monitored during treatment with either of these medications. Other potentially useful medications include gabapentin, clonazepam, lamotrigine, baclofen, valproic acid, and phenytoin.

Approximately 30% of patients with trigeminal neuralgia do not respond to medical therapy and may require a surgical or ablative procedure. Microvascular decompression is the definitive procedure for idiopathic trigeminal neuralgia, but it is often reserved for intractable cases because of the need for a craniotomy. MRI of the head with high-resolution images of the posterior fossa obtained to evaluate for vascular compression of the trigeminal nerve is recommended before surgery. The procedure involves an occipital craniotomy and separation of the trigeminal nerve from a juxtaposed or adherent vessel using a synthetic material. The success rate is approximately 90%. Other procedures involve ablation of the trigeminal nerve or root with either radiation (gamma knife) or a percutaneous radiofrequency lesion; balloon compression; or glycerol injection of the trigeminal ganglion at the skull base. Each procedure has similar long-term success rates (60% to 85%), but facial sensory loss may occur; corneal anesthesia, anesthesia dolorosa (severe spontaneous pain occurring in an anesthetic zone), dysesthesias, and masseter muscle weakness can also occur.

KEY POINTS

- The pain associated with trigeminal neuralgia is most commonly referred to the second and third division of the trigeminal nerve.

- MRI should be performed in all patients with trigeminal neuralgia to exclude vascular or structural compression of the trigeminal nerve.

- Oxcarbazepine or carbamazepine is the treatment of choice for trigeminal neuralgia.

Headaches Due to Disorders of Intracranial Pressure or Volume

Orthostatic Headache

Spontaneous leak of cerebrospinal fluid (CSF) may cause orthostatic headache, which mimics the headache that occurs after a traumatic lumbar puncture. Many patients report a history of trivial trauma, which might have started a leak, especially in patients with an inherited connective tissue disorder or weakened and attenuated dura or meningeal diverticula.

Headache is the main clinical feature of a CSF leak. It is typically an orthostatic headache that is present when the patient is upright and relieved when the patient is supine. In some patients, the orthostatic features may diminish over weeks or months, and the headache may become chronic, daily, and continuous. Muffled hearing is common, and some patients may experience cranial nerve palsies, stupor, encephalopathy, parkinsonism, ataxia, and bulbar weakness, most likely due to sagging of the brain within the cranial vault.

Although most patients with CSF leak have reduced pressure on lumbar puncture, the opening pressure may be normal in up to one third of these patients. The CSF protein concentration is often normal or less than 100 mg/dL (1000 mg/L), but it may be as high as 1000 mg/dL (10,000 mg/L). The erythrocyte and leukocyte counts may be normal or as high as 200/µL (200 × 10⁶/L). An MRI with gadolinium may show diffuse, homogeneous, pachymeningeal thickening and enhancement; engorgement of the dural venous sinuses; enlargement and enhancement of the pituitary gland; and evidence of "brain sag," including subdural fluid collections, buckling of the optic chiasm, compression of the midbrain, crowding of the posterior fossa, and descent of the cerebellar tonsils, mimicking a Chiari malformation (**Figure 13**). In patients in whom the disorder is suspected but the imaging and CSF findings are absent, indium-111–labeled isotope cisternography may show the presence of a leak. CT myelography is the most sensitive diagnostic test for determining the location of the leak.

Conservative treatment, including bed rest and hydration, is effective for many patients. If symptoms persist, an autologous epidural blood patch is the treatment of choice, which involves withdrawing a 15- to 40-mL sample of the patient's own blood, inserting a spinal needle into the epidural space, and injecting the blood slowly over minutes because some patients may develop radicular or back pain with more rapid injections. In the few patients who do not respond to the first epidural blood patch, a second blood

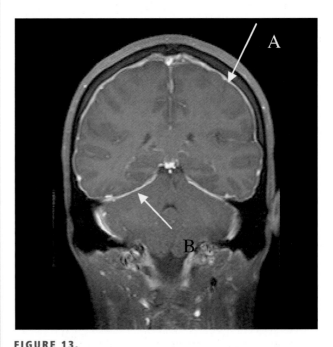

FIGURE 13.
Coronal gadolinium-enhanced MRI of the brain.
Coronal T1-weighted MRI with gadolinium showing the smooth and continuous enhancement of the dura mater over the supratentorial pachymeninges (*A arrow*) and tentorium cerebelli (*B arrow*) in a patient with low cerebrospinal fluid (CSF) pressure secondary to a spinal CSF leak.

patch is usually effective. Some patients may require up to six blood patches before complete relief is obtained. Autologous blood patches may be effective when delivered at the lumbar epidural space, even when the leak is at the level of the thoracic or cervical spine. In unusually refractory cases, an autologous blood patch and/or CT-guided injections of fibrin glue at the site of the leak may be effective. In rare cases, open surgical repair may be necessary.

Idiopathic Intracranial Hypertension (Pseudotumor Cerebri)

Idiopathic intracranial hypertension is primarily a disorder of young obese women. The diagnosis rests on documenting elevated CSF opening pressure (>250 mm H_2O) during lumbar puncture measured in the lateral decubitus position, normal CSF composition, and normal mental status, as well as on evidence from MRI and venography of the brain and dural venous sinuses. Other factors associated with increased intracranial pressure include systemic retinoid therapy, tetracyclines, a subdermal implant of levonorgestrel (Norplant®), corticosteroid withdrawal, human growth hormone, cerebral venous sinus thrombosis, mastoiditis, Behçet disease, renal failure, and obstructive sleep apnea. Intracranial hypertension may develop during pregnancy, although pregnancy is not an independent risk factor for the disorder. The onset of idiopathic intracranial hypertension in the peripartum period or after fetal loss should prompt an evaluation for cerebral venous sinus thrombosis.

The most common presenting symptom of idiopathic intracranial hypertension is headache, which occurs in more than 90% of patients. Photophobia, blurred vision, diplopia, and visual field loss commonly accompany the headache. Transient visual obscurations are also common and are described as partial or complete episodes of visual loss lasting seconds to minutes, are often precipitated by rising from a stooped position or rolling the eyes, and reflect brief episodes of optic nerve head ischemia caused by papilledema. Visual loss may be acute and dramatic, leading to profound visual loss or blindness. Pulsatile tinnitus occurs in 60% of patients and is often described as "hearing my heartbeat in my head" or a whooshing sound in one or both ears. The hallmark of idiopathic intracranial hypertension is papilledema that may be asymmetric and, rarely, unilateral. Mild papilledema may be difficult to discern with the direct ophthalmoscope; stereoscopic viewing with indirect ophthalmoscopy or slit lamp bimicroscopy is helpful to detect subtle disc edema.

The treatment of idiopathic intracranial hypertension is generally coordinated by a neurologist (or neuro-ophthalmologist) and an ophthalmologist. The goals of treatment are to preserve vision and to alleviate symptoms. All treatment recommendations are based on case series and clinical experience. Asymptomatic patients with mild papilledema may be followed closely without specific treatment. Weight loss is generally advised for obese patients but is not always successful

in reducing intracranial pressure or alleviating symptoms. Acetazolamide is the most common medication used; side effects include paresthesias, taste perversion, somnolence, and depression. Rare but serious side effects are hypersensitivity reaction, renal stones, and aplastic anemia. Furosemide therapy may also lower intracranial pressure, but the patient must be monitored to prevent dehydration and hypokalemia. Topiramate, which is commonly used for migraine prevention, is associated with weight loss and may be useful as treatment of idiopathic intracranial hypertension, especially because migraine and tension-type headaches commonly occur in such patients. Corticosteroid therapy should be avoided because it causes weight gain and fluid retention and may cause rebound intracranial hypertension as therapy is withdrawn.

Surgery may be indicated when severe optic neuropathy is present early in the course of the illness, when there is rapid deterioration of vision, or when other forms of therapy fail to prevent visual loss. Surgery is not recommended for the treatment of headaches alone. Optic nerve sheath fenestration generally stabilizes or improves vision and sometimes relieves headaches; risks include transient or permanent visual loss, diplopia, and infection. Shunts (ventriculoperitoneal or lumboperitoneal) lower intracranial pressure and may spare vision and relieve headache, but they have a very high failure rate, with over half of patients ultimately requiring one or more revisions. Other complications of shunting include low CSF pressure, infection, obstruction, and migration of the shunt catheter. Patients with a sudden decline in vision often have an ischemic component to their visual loss and may fail to improve even after aggressive medical and surgical intervention.

KEY POINTS

- Pachymeningeal thickening and enhancement and evidence of brain sag are the most common MRI features of orthostatic headache associated with spontaneous cerebrospinal fluid leaks.

- Headache, pulsatile tinnitus, and transient visual obscurations are the most common symptoms of idiopathic intracranial hypertension.

Thunderclap Headache

A thunderclap headache is a severe and explosive headache that is maximal in intensity at or within 60 seconds of onset. Every thunderclap headache must be immediately evaluated to detect potentially catastrophic conditions, especially subarachnoid hemorrhage. An underlying disorder, most commonly vascular, is detected in 30% to 80% of patients. Thunderclap headache may occur in isolation, may be recurrent over days to weeks, and may begin spontaneously or be triggered by Valsalva maneuvers, physical effort, or sexual intercourse.

CT of the head without enhancement is the most sensitive test for subarachnoid hemorrhage. A lumbar puncture is necessary if CT scan results are normal. If results of both the CT scan and lumbar puncture are normal, the patient still requires urgent investigation for other serious neurologic causes of thunderclap headache, including cerebral venous sinus thrombosis, arterial dissection, unruptured intracranial aneurysm, and reversible cerebral vasoconstriction. Therefore, neurovascular imaging is indicated in these patients and should include magnetic resonance or CT angiography (or venography). If all investigations are negative, the patient may have primary (idiopathic) thunderclap headache or another primary headache disorder, such as primary sexual headache.

KEY POINTS

- A thunderclap headache is a severe and explosive headache that is maximal in intensity at or within 60 seconds of onset.

- All patients with thunderclap headache with normal results on a CT scan and lumbar puncture should undergo neurovascular imaging with magnetic resonance or CT angiography (or venography).

Bibliography

Boes CJ, Swanson JW. Paroxysmal hemicrania, SUNCT, and hemicrania continua. Semin Neurol. 2006;26(2):260-270. [PMID: 16628536]

Dodick DW. Clinical practice. Chronic daily headache [erratum in N Engl J Med. 2006;354(8):884]. N Engl J Med. 2006;354(2):158-165. [PMID: 16407511]

Headache Classification Subcommittee of the International Headache Society. The International Classification of Headache Disorders: 2nd edition. Cephalalgia. 2004(24 Suppl 1):9-160. [PMID: 14979299]

Kurth T, Slomke MA, Kase CS, et al. Migraine, headache, and the risk of stroke in women: a prospective study. Neurology. 2005;64(6):1020-1026. [PMID: 15781820]

May A, Leone M, Afra J, et al. EFNS guidelines on the treatment of cluster headache and other trigeminal-autonomic cephalalgias. Eur J Neurol. 2006;13(10):1066-1077. [PMID: 16987158]

Practice parameter: the utility of neuroimaging in the evaluation of headache in patients with normal neurologic examinations (summary statement). Report of the Quality Standards Subcommittee of the American Academy of Neurology. Neurology. 1994;44(7):1353-1354. [PMID: 8035948]

Schwedt TJ, Matharu MS, Dodick DW. Thunderclap headache. Lancet Neurol. 2006;5(7):621-631. [PMID: 16781992]

Head Injury

Concussive Head Injury

A concussion is a trauma-induced alteration in mental status that is sometimes associated with a loss of consciousness. Confusion and amnesia, the hallmarks of concussion, can occur immediately after a blow to the head or several minutes later. The most frequently observed symptoms of patients with concussion are listed in **Table 16**.

Grades of Concussion

Because internists may frequently encounter symptoms of concussive head injury in patients (for example, in young athletes), they must be able to determine the seriousness of the injury. The usefulness of a grading scale to determine concussion severity has been well established in sports medicine, and several groups have developed guidelines. For example, the American Academy of Neurology has established a practice parameter for the management of concussion in sports that uses the following grading scale:

- *Grade 1*: The most common yet most difficult form of concussion to recognize. An affected athlete is not rendered unconscious and has only momentary confusion (for example, inattention, poor concentration, or an inability to process information or sequence tasks) or mental status alterations (colloquially referred to as having been "dinged" or having one's "bell rung").

TABLE 16 Symptoms of Concussion

Onset of Concussion Symptoms After Injury	
Early (Minutes and Hours Later)	**Late (Days to Weeks Later)**
Headache	Persistent low-grade headache
Dizziness or vertigo	Light-headedness
Lack of awareness of surroundings	Poor attention and concentration
Nausea or vomiting	Memory dysfunction
	Easy fatigability
	Irritability and low tolerance of frustration
	Intolerance of bright lights or difficulty focusing vision
	Intolerance of loud noises, sometimes with ringing in the ears
	Anxiety and/or depressed mood
	Sleep disturbance

- *Grade 2*: No loss of consciousness, but an affected athlete experiences symptoms or exhibits signs of concussion or mental status abnormalities (such as poor concentration or posttraumatic amnesia) on examination that last longer than 15 minutes. Any persistent grade-2 symptoms (lasting longer than 1 hour) warrant medical observation.
- *Grade 3*: Any loss of consciousness, either brief (seconds) or prolonged (minutes).

Although originally designed for subjects with sports-related injuries, this scale can and is used to grade all concussive head injuries, regardless of how the trauma occurred.

Returning to Play or Work in Patients with Concussive Head Injury

There is general agreement that all athletes who sustain a concussion, regardless of grade, require an on-site evaluation and should not return to play during the sporting event. The American Academy of Neurology further states that all athletes with grade-2 or grade-3 concussions also require a neurologic evaluation and recommends a period away from competitive play for a minimum of 1 week. Multidisciplinary consensus recommendations from the American College of Sports Medicine similarly indicate that the athlete be asymptomatic at rest before resuming any exertional activity and complete a progressive aerobic and resistance exercise challenge before full return to play; return to play on the same day is contraindicated if any loss of consciousness, posttraumatic amnesia, or retrograde amnesia has occurred. Although some controversy and a lack of evidence exist about same-day return to play in athletes with lesser-severity grade-2 injuries whose symptoms have fully resolved or are persistently mild, the American College of Sports Medicine indicates that the duration and severity of symptoms are the determining factors and that the safest course of action is to disallow same-day return to play when in doubt about subjects with a grade-2 concussion.

Guidelines for determining when an athlete may return to play after a concussive headache injury are based on the grade of the concussion (**Table 17**). These guidelines should be closely followed in practice and can be applied in nonathletes as return-to-work recommendations, especially because one of the most frequent and disabling symptoms after a concussive head injury is cognitive impairment.

KEY POINTS

- All athletes with a grade-2 or grade-3 concussion should not return to play during the sporting event.
- For athletes with a grade-2 or grade-3 concussion, the American Academy of Neurology recommends a neurologic evaluation and a minimum of 1 week away from competitive play.
- For athletes with a grade-2 or grade-3 concussion, the American College of Sports Medicine states that return to play on the same day is contraindicated if any loss of consciousness, posttraumatic amnesia, or retrograde amnesia has occurred.

Subdural Hematomas

Acute subdural hematomas usually occur after severe, high-impact head trauma and may be associated with contusions of adjacent brain tissue. At presentation, patients with subdural hematomas typically have symptoms of headache, an altered level of awareness or consciousness, and/or focal neurologic symptoms and signs, which may be transient or persistent. Neurosurgical consultation should be available in the event of an acute intracranial hemorrhage.

Chronic subdural hematomas may occur as a result of the gradual accumulation of liquefied hematoma over weeks or months. Chronic subdural hematomas occur after mild or seemingly trivial head trauma, which the patient may not even recall. Affected patients have the same symptoms as those with acute subdural hematoma, but the symptoms are more gradual in onset and more indolent in their progression. Neurosurgical drainage of the hematoma may be required because the hemorrhage, which has collected over weeks, behaves as a mass with displacement and mass effect on adjacent brain structures.

TABLE 17 American Academy of Neurology Guidelines on When to Return to Play or Work After a Concussion

Grade of Concussion	Time Until Return to Play or Work[a]
Single or multiple grade-1 concussions	1 week
Grade-2 concussion	1 week
Multiple grade-2 concussions	2 weeks
Grade-3 concussion with brief (seconds) loss of consciousness	1 week
Grade-3 concussion with prolonged (minutes) loss of consciousness	2 weeks
Multiple grade-3 concussions	1 month or longer, based on the clinical determination of the evaluating physician

[a]Only if asymptomatic, with a normal neurologic assessment at rest and with exercise.

Imaging in Traumatic Brain Injury

The imaging modality of choice in patients who have experienced a traumatic brain injury is CT of the head. CT scans are very sensitive for detecting acute intracranial hemorrhage and skull fractures. Patients with symptoms of a subdural hematoma must undergo urgent imaging with noncontrast CT. All patients with traumatic brain injury who are on anticoagulation or have a hemorrhagic diathesis (such as those with severe hepatic disease) should undergo imaging. In addition, patients who experience persistent headache (>72 hours); a change in the level of behavior, consciousness, or alertness; or focal or lateralizing neurologic symptoms or signs should undergo emergent CT without contrast.

KEY POINTS

- All patients with traumatic head injury who have a hemorrhagic diathesis or are on anticoagulation should undergo noncontrast CT of the head.
- Noncontrast CT head imaging should be performed in persons who experience traumatic head injury if they have a persistent headache (>72 hours); if there is a change in their level of consciousness, awareness, or behavior; or if focal or lateralizing neurologic symptoms or signs develop.

Concussive Head Injury and Traumatic Brain Injury in an Elderly Population

Concussive head injury and mild traumatic brain injury are common in elderly patients because of the dysequilibrium that occurs as a result of age and because of other diseases that affect spatial orientation and gait. Such diseases are more common in elderly persons, particularly vestibular disorders (such as benign paroxysmal positional vertigo) and neurodegenerative diseases. Because of age-related brain atrophy, subdural hematomas can occur more commonly in elderly persons with a head injury, most likely because of traction on bridging dural veins. Additionally, anticoagulation with warfarin or antiplatelet therapy, which is very common in elderly persons because of the increasing prevalence of cardiovascular risk factors and disease, increases the risk of intracranial hemorrhage, particularly subdural hematomas.

Concussive Head Injury and Traumatic Brain Injury in the Military

Head and neck injuries, including severe brain trauma, have been reported in one quarter of service members who have been evacuated from Iraq and Afghanistan, and traumatic brain injury has been labeled a signature injury of these wars. Nearly 15% of these soldiers have reported an injury during deployment that involved loss of consciousness or altered mental status. Soldiers with mild traumatic brain injury are significantly more likely to experience physical and mental health problems and to report poor general health, headache, missed days at work, medical visits, and more somatic and postconcussive symptoms, including mood alteration and cognitive impairment. Those with more serious traumatic brain injury with loss of consciousness are more likely to have symptoms of posttraumatic stress disorder and depression. The high prevalence of traumatic brain injury, somatic symptoms, affective disorders, and significant disability emphasizes the need for aggressive, multidisciplinary care of these patients.

Bibliography

Concussion (mild traumatic brain injury) and the team physician: a consensus statement. Med Sci Sports Exerc. 2006;38(2):395-399. [PMID: 16531912]

Hoge CW, McGurk D, Thomas JL, Cox AL, Engel CC, Castro CA. Mild traumatic brain injury in U.S. soldiers returning from Iraq. N Engl J Med. 2008;358(5):453-463. [PMID: 18234750]

Practice parameter: the management of concussion in sports (summary statement). Report of the Quality Standards Subcommittee. Neurology. 1997;48(3):581-585. [PMID: 9065530]

Movement Disorders

Approach to the Patient with a Movement Disorder

A careful neurologic history and thorough neurologic examination are essential in the correct identification of a movement disorder. These disorders are diagnosed primarily by their clinical features. General categories of abnormal movements include tremor, dystonia, chorea, ataxia, myoclonus, and parkinsonism. Recognition of the presence (and absence) of these movements allows the practitioner to arrive at a specific clinical diagnosis.

Tremor refers to the rhythmic oscillation of a body part. Tremor frequency, distribution, and presence at rest, with movement, or with sustained posture should be noted. A unilateral, low-frequency resting tremor is typical of Parkinson disease, whereas a bilateral, high-frequency, kinetic, and postural tremor (with both limb movement and sustained posture) is typical of essential tremor.

Dystonia is characterized by the sustained contraction of agonist and antagonist muscles; can be generalized, focal, or segmental; and can involve virtually any body part. Chorea refers to brief, irregular, nonstereotypical, nonrhythmic movements and can involve the extremities, head, trunk, and face. Cerebellar ataxia is characterized by impaired initiation and coordination of movements and can involve speech, gait, and the extremities. Myoclonus refers to abnormal lightning-like jerking extremity movements.

Parkinsonism refers to a set of clinical features that include rigidity, resting tremor, bradykinesia, and postural instability. This term is generally used to describe such clinical features in either a patient with an established secondary cause (such as drug-induced parkinsonism) or a patient with an unknown condition causing the symptoms. Many of the diseases discussed in this section can be associated with parkinsonism. Parkinson disease is a specific clinical parkinsonian disorder characterized by its distinct clinical and pathologic features and by its robust therapeutic response to dopaminergic medication.

Evaluation of the Patient with Gait Unsteadiness

Gait unsteadiness is a common symptom, particularly in elderly persons. Because many conditions affect gait in characteristic patterns, careful observation can permit the identification of an underlying neurologic disorder. Gait analysis should ideally occur over a distance of 20 or more feet.

Many different systems are involved in the control of posture and ambulation. The musculoskeletal system provides mechanical stability and, if perturbed, can cause pain, weakness, and gait unsteadiness. Maintenance of an upright posture is dependent on postural reflexes and a dynamic interplay of visual, vestibular, and somatosensory systems. Impairment in any of these systems can result in postural and gait instability. Impairment in proprioception (joint position sense) or a positive Romberg sign suggests somatosensory impairment. A history of vertigo (the illusion of self- or environmental motion) can suggest vestibular impairment.

Recognition of the clinical features of the major gait disorders is helpful. The spastic gait pattern found in patients with corticospinal tract problems is characterized by circumduction of the involved leg such that the stiffly extended knee is swung laterally and forward from the hip, which often results in dragging the foot on the ground. Cerebellar ataxia is recognized by a wide-based stance and lurching, irregular steps that are worse with turning. Patients with a sensory ataxia adopt a wide-based stance and may have a foot slap. The akinetic rigid (parkinsonian) gait is characterized by poor initiation of gait, freezing or complete cessation of gait, postural instability, and a slow, shuffling gait pattern.

Cerebellar Ataxia

Approach to the Patient with Ataxia

Ataxic disorders can affect posture, gait, the extremities, and speech and can manifest as gait unsteadiness, extremity incoordination, and slurred speech. Because many acquired and hereditary disorders can cause cerebellar ataxia, a thoughtful approach based on the mode and timing of symptom onset is necessary to guide diagnostic evaluation (**Table 18**).

TABLE 18 Approach to Ataxia Based on Mode of Onset
Acute Onset
Ischemic stroke of the cerebellum, brain stem
Hemorrhagic stroke of the cerebellum, brain stem
Medication induced
Subacute Onset
Thiamine deficiency
Multiple sclerosis
Hydrocephalus
Posterior fossa tumor
Posterior fossa abscess
Paraneoplastic disorder
Toxins
Miller-Fisher form of Guillain-Barré syndrome
Chronic Progressive
Primary progressive multiple sclerosis
Alcoholic cerebellar degeneration
Paraneoplastic disorder
Hydrocephalus
Vitamin E deficiency
Hypothyroidism
Celiac disease
Creutzfeldt-Jakob disease
Posterior fossa tumor
Inherited ataxias
Multiple system atrophy

Symptom distribution is also an important consideration. Unilateral ataxia suggests a structural cause due to stroke, tumor, or demyelinating disease. Chronic alcohol abuse can result in gait unsteadiness due to truncal and leg ataxia, with the arms left unaffected. Identification of involvement of other neurologic systems can suggest particular conditions. A history of rapidly progressive ataxia in conjunction with signs of progressive cognitive dysfunction most typically indicates Creutzfeldt-Jakob disease or a paraneoplastic disorder. The presence of parkinsonism or dysautonomia in a patient with chronic, progressive cerebellar ataxia suggests multiple system atrophy. The primary inherited cerebellar ataxic disorders in adults include spinocerebellar ataxia, Friedreich ataxia, and fragile X tremor ataxia syndrome.

Acquired Ataxic Disorders

In general clinical practice, ataxia is more likely to be due to an acquired disorder. Ischemic or hemorrhagic stroke in the brain stem, cerebellum, or thalamus can cause cerebellar ataxia. Patients with the disorder report abrupt symptom onset, with ataxia that typically affects the extremities, speech, and gait. Cerebellar ataxia is a frequent manifestation of multiple sclerosis lesions involving the spinal cord or brainstem. Primary brain tumors or metastatic brain tumors can also involve the cerebellar pathways and cause chronic progressive cerebellar ataxia.

In addition to chronic alcohol abuse, cerebellar ataxia may also occur in association with phenytoin, 5-fluorouracil, and cytosine arabinoside administration. Wernicke encephalopathy characteristically results in ataxia but is also associated with ophthalmoplegia (paresis of eye muscles), confusion, peripheral neuropathy, and even seizures. Wernicke encephalopathy is caused by thiamine (vitamin B_1) deficiency; it most commonly occurs in persons with alcoholism but has also been reported in patients who have undergone bariatric surgery, have had a prolonged period of fasting, have had repeated episodes of vomiting, or have been on prolonged parenteral nutrition without adequate vitamin supplementation. Immediate treatment with parenteral thiamine is necessary, or a chronic amnestic state (Korsakoff psychosis) may develop. Acquired vitamin E deficiency may also result in gait ataxia and sensory neuropathy, most typically in patients with a history of malabsorption due to gastrointestinal disease.

A severe, rapidly progressive cerebellar ataxia may occur as a paraneoplastic manifestation in a patient with a known or occult cancer. Patients with paraneoplastic ataxia often have other neurologic manifestations, including peripheral neuropathy or encephalomyelitis. For further discussion, see Neuro-oncology.

Hypothyroidism is a very rare cause of ataxia. The ataxia resolves completely with thyroid hormone replacement. Celiac disease can (rarely) be associated with ataxia, and most patients will have concomitant sensory peripheral neuropathy.

KEY POINTS

- Ischemic or hemorrhagic stroke in the brain stem, cerebellum, or thalamus can cause a cerebellar ataxia that affects the extremities, speech, and gait.

- Wernicke encephalopathy can occur in persons who have alcoholism, have undergone bariatric surgery, had a prolonged period of fasting, had repeated episodes of vomiting, or have been on prolonged parenteral nutrition without adequate vitamin supplementation

- Immediate treatment with parenteral thiamine can prevent irreversible neurologic dysfunction in persons with Wernicke encephalopathy.

Inherited Ataxias

The hereditary ataxic disorders are a heterogeneous group of diseases that manifest primarily as chronic, progressive ataxia. Degeneration occurs in the cerebellum and, in many of these disorders, also in the spinal cord. These conditions are typically either autosomal dominant or autosomal recessive.

Although the responsible genetic defect is known in several of these disorders, the only treatable conditions are Refsum disease, cerebrotendinous xanthomatosis, and ataxia with isolated vitamin E deficiency. In the other disorders, treatment is supportive.

Fragile X Tremor Ataxia Syndrome

Fragile X tremor ataxia syndrome is a recently recognized disorder that develops in later life, primarily with symptoms of ataxia and intention tremor. Other reported symptoms include dementia, psychiatric symptoms, peripheral neuropathy, and dysautonomia. Diagnosis is established by demonstrating allele expansion of the *FMR1* gene.

Friedreich Ataxia

Friedreich ataxia is the most common autosomal recessive ataxic disorder, with an estimated prevalence of 2 to 3 per 100,000 persons. The mean age of onset is approximately 15 years, but onset into the sixth decade of life is seen. Typical symptoms include ataxia involving gait, limbs, and speech. Neurologic examination shows absent deep tendon reflexes in the lower limbs and impaired proprioception. Cardiomyopathy develops in most patients, and diabetes mellitus is present in some. Diagnosis is established by demonstrating a trinucleotide (GAA) repeat in the *X25* gene. Treatment is supportive.

Spinocerebellar Ataxias

The spinocerebellar ataxias are a clinically and genetically heterogeneous group of disorders. Estimated prevalence of the spinocerebellar ataxias is approximately 1 per 100,000 persons. The spinocerebellar ataxias have an autosomal dominant pattern of inheritance and are associated with chronic, progressive cerebellar ataxia, with a mean age of onset in the fourth and fifth decades.

Parkinson Disease

Epidemiology and Genetics

One of the more common neurodegenerative disorders, Parkinson disease is estimated to affect 1% of persons older than 65 years and 2.5% of persons older than 80 years. Estimated prevalence is 100 to 200 per 100,000 persons. Peak onset is in the sixth and seventh decades of life. The disease is more prevalent in men, with a ratio of 1.5-2:1. A chronic, progressive disease course is expected, with significant disability approximately 10 to 15 years after onset. It is now thought that as many as 10% to 15% of cases may be familial, although genetic testing is currently performed only for research purposes.

Clinical Features and Diagnosis

Parkinson disease remains a clinical diagnosis that is based on a cardinal set of clinical features, including resting tremor, bradykinesia, rigidity, and postural instability; the tremor, bradykinesia, and rigidity are asymmetric. Sustained levodopa responsiveness is expected in Parkinson disease and helps confirm the clinical diagnosis. Signs suggesting an alternative condition include symmetric symptoms or signs, early falls, rapid progression, poor or waning response to levodopa, dementia, early autonomic failure, and ataxia. Parkinsonism can be a presenting feature of a number of other conditions (**Table 19**).

The diagnostic evaluation of suspected Parkinson disease should include a careful review of a patient's medication history to exclude drug-induced parkinsonism. A history of repeated head trauma or toxin exposure should also be explored. Although findings are normal in Parkinson disease, MRI is indicated to exclude other disease processes, such as vascular disease, hydrocephalus, and other degenerative diseases.

KEY POINTS

- The cardinal clinical features of Parkinson disease are a resting tremor, bradykinesia, rigidity, and postural instability; early falls, rapid progression, poor or waning response to levodopa, dementia, early autonomic failure, and ataxia suggest other disorders.

- The tremor, bradykinesia, and rigidity of Parkinson disease are characteristically asymmetric.

Treatment of Parkinson Disease

To date, no treatment exists to slow the loss of dopamine-producing neurons in Parkinson disease. Both pharmacologic

TABLE 19 Differential Diagnosis of Parkinsonism

Disorder	Notes
Parkinson Disease[a]	
Degenerative parkinsonism	
Multiple system atrophy	Ataxia, dysautonomia
Progressive supranuclear palsy	Early falls, impaired vertical eye movement
Corticobasal degeneration	Asymmetric spasticity and rigidity, alien limb movement, myoclonus
Dementia with Lewy bodies	Dementia and hallucinations
Secondary parkinsonism	
Drugs (antipsychotics, antiemetics, metoclopramide, reserpine, lithium, tetrabenazine, flunarizine)	Exposure history
Toxins (manganese, MPTP, mercury, methanol, ethanol, carbon monoxide)	Exposure history
Vascular	History and MRI showing stroke
Trauma (including pugilistic encephalopathy)	History of head trauma
Hydrocephalus	MRI suggestive of contusion, lower body parkinsonism
Creutzfeldt-Jakob disease	Rapidly progressive; signs and symptoms of ataxia, dementia, myoclonus, and dystonia
Paraneoplastic syndrome	Rapidly progressive; signs and symptoms of ataxia, encephalopathy, and myoclonus
Hepatocerebral degeneration	History of liver disease; MRI changes in basal ganglia
Hypothyroidism	Rare; resolves with treatment
Hereditary Disorders Associated with Parkinsonism[b]	
Wilson disease	Must be ruled out in patients less than age 50 years; Hepatic and psychiatric disease; tremor; dystonia; ataxia
Familial amyotrophy-dementia-parkinsonism	Cognitive/behavioral change; extremity weakness, atrophy; rigidity, bradykinesia
Spinocerebellar ataxias	Autosomal dominant; begin in early life; Ataxia predominates
Huntington disease	Chorea, dystonia, psychiatric symptoms, dementia, ataxia
Fragile X tremor ataxia syndrome	Ataxia, tremor, dementia

MPTP = methylphenyltetrahydropyridine.

[a]Characterized by asymmetric tremor, rigidity, and brandykinesia.

[b]Not a complete list.

therapy and nonpharmacologic therapy are tailored to patient age, the nature of the symptoms, and symptom severity.

General Pharmacotherapy

The mainstay of drug therapy is targeted toward dopamine replacement with levodopa or dopamine agonists. Drug treatment can be delayed until the patient's symptoms interfere with employment or social activities. The choice of pharmacotherapy in early Parkinson disease remains somewhat controversial because of concerns about levodopa-induced motor complications. Levodopa is the most effective medication used in the treatment of Parkinson disease but is associated with motor fluctuations, such as dyskinesias and a "wearing-off" effect, which refers to enhanced parkinsonian symptoms due to ineffective dopamine therapy. These motor fluctuations develop at a rate of 10% annually in patients older than 60 years but seem to develop more rapidly and are more severe in younger patients. Therefore, most clinicians will initiate therapy with a dopamine agonist in patients younger than 65 years. At some point, however, all patients will require the addition of levodopa therapy. Levodopa is the drug of choice in older patients.

Levodopa is administered in conjunction with carbidopa, which prevents the peripheral conversion of levodopa to dopamine, in a three-times daily dosing regimen at least 1 hour before meals. The dopamine agonists ropinirole and pramipexole are also administered in a three-times daily dosing regimen, starting at a low dose and titrating up on the basis of treatment effect. Involvement of physical therapists can benefit patients with significant gait freezing and postural instability.

Management of Motor Fluctuations in Parkinson Disease

At some point, most patients with Parkinson disease develop motor complications, such as dyskinesias and "wearing off" (also called "off-time"). Dyskinesias are recognized as choreiform and dystonic movements, which are involuntary and related to dopamine therapy. If these are mild and do not disturb the patient, they should not be treated. Risk factors for motor fluctuations include younger age of onset, increasing disease severity, higher levodopa dosage, and longer disease duration.

Patients with disabling dyskinesias on levodopa monotherapy may benefit from the addition of a dopamine agonist. Amantadine can also be used to reduce dyskinesias. In patients with wearing-off phenomena, the initial strategy is to increase either individual levodopa dosage or the frequency of levodopa administration. If dyskinesias then become problematic or the duration of levodopa effect becomes too short, coadministration of a dopamine agonist is often beneficial. Administration of entacapone or rasagiline has also been shown to reduce the wearing-off effect. Additionally, deep brain stimulation has been shown to improve motor function, reduce the wearing-off effect, and reduce dyskinesias. Patients with severe motor fluctuations despite optimal pharmacotherapy should be referred for consideration of deep brain stimulation.

Treatment of Neuropsychiatric and Sleep Disturbances in Parkinson Disease

Approximately 60% of patients with Parkinson disease develop psychiatric symptoms during the course of their disease. Depression and anxiety are common manifestations and can occur at any stage of the disease. The first step in such patients is to optimize dopaminergic therapy. Selective serotonin reuptake inhibitors and serotonin-norepinephrine reuptake inhibitors are first-line agents for those requiring drug treatment. Other patients may benefit from a subset of these medications that also have antianxiolytic properties (paroxetine, sertraline, venlaflaxine). A number of controlled trials have demonstrated the efficacy of antidepressant agents, including paroxetine, sertraline, bupropion, and the tricyclic nortriptyline, for the treatment of depression in Parkinson disease.

Neuropsychiatric symptoms, including psychosis, commonly occur in patients with advanced Parkinson disease. Before initiation of neuroleptic therapy for treatment of psychosis in such patients, medical conditions—such as urinary tract and pulmonary infections, metabolic disturbances, and adverse effects of medications—must be excluded. Polypharmacy, in particular, has been shown to be an independent risk factor for the development of psychosis in Parkinson disease. Therefore, in patients with persistent psychosis, reduction or elimination of medications should be considered, including parkinsonian medications. Such changes are usually best made in consultation with a neurologist. Psychological approaches to the management of psychosis, such as cognitive-behavioral therapy, supportive therapy, and psychoeducation, should also be considered. Pharmacotherapy is occasionally necessary in the treatment of psychosis. Cholinesterase inhibitors may be beneficial in some patients and are usually well tolerated. Quetiapine, an atypical antipsychotic medication that typically does not worsen motor function, is used by many experts as first-line therapy.

Sleep disorders affect 60% to 98% of patients with Parkinson disease. Motor manifestations of these disorders are common causes of sleep disturbance and can manifest as stiffness, inability to move, dystonia, cramps, or pain. Therapy with an extended-release carbidopa-levodopa preparation should be considered. Restless legs syndrome and periodic limb movements of sleep are also common and may require additional dopaminergic medication before bedtime. Rapid eye movement sleep behavior disorder may occur in up to one third of patients with Parkinson disease, manifesting as kicking, grabbing, yelling, and falling or even jumping out of bed. A sleep study may facilitate the recognition of these disorders. Clonazepam before bedtime may be indicated if these events disrupt sleep or are dangerous to the patient (or their sleeping partner).

- Levodopa is the drug of choice to treat Parkinson disease in older patients, whereas dopamine agonists are often used first in patients younger than 65 years.
- Patients with Parkinson disease who have disabling dyskinesias on levodopa monotherapy may benefit from the addition of a dopamine agonist.
- Approximately 60% of patients with Parkinson disease develop psychiatric symptoms, and more than 60% develop a sleep disorder.

Other Parkinsonism Disorders

Drug-Induced Parkinsonism

Parkinsonism is an established side effect of many medications, particularly those that interfere with the storage, synthesis, and release of dopamine or cause blockade of dopaminergic receptors. Neuroleptic medications are frequently associated with parkinsonian side effects; however, many others have been associated with the development of drug-induced parkinsonism (see Table 19). The parkinsonism is bilateral, with evident bradykinesia, rigidity, and tremor. Tremor in drug-induced parkinsonism is often postural and may be higher in frequency than in Parkinson disease.

- Neuroleptic medications are frequently associated with drug-induced parkinsonism.

Multiple System Atrophy

Multiple system atrophy is a heterogeneous degenerative disorder that can be associated with parkinsonism, ataxia, and autonomic nervous system impairment. It has an estimated prevalence of 4.4 per 100,000 persons and seems to affect men and women equally. Multiple system atrophy is generally considered to be a sporadic disease of unknown cause. Mean age of onset is in the sixth decade of life, and median survival is 9.5 years. There are different forms of multiple system atrophy, and its classification has historically been based on the predominant neurologic system involved. However, most patients will have a combination of symptoms, reflecting degeneration of multiple neurologic systems.

Parkinsonian symptoms, such as rigidity, bradykinesia, and postural instability, occur in conjunction with ataxia or symptoms of dysautonomia. Signs and symptoms of dysautonomia include erectile dysfunction, constipation, diarrhea, urinary incontinence, and orthostatic hypotension. A history of voice change or breathing difficulties should prompt ear, nose and throat evaluation to look for vocal cord abnormalities.

Treatment of multiple system atrophy is symptomatic only. Carbidopa-levodopa should be administered to affected patients with significant parkinsonism; 25% of these patients will have an initial beneficial response to this drug. Orthostatic hypotension is treated with a combination of conservative and pharmacologic measures. Patients should be instructed to elevate the head of the bed, increase their salt intake, and use compression stockings. Medications used to treat orthostatic hypotension include midodrine, fludrocortisone, and pyridostigmine.

- Multiple system atrophy is a heterogeneous degenerative disorder that can be associated with parkinsonism, ataxia, and autonomic nervous system impairment.

Progressive Supranuclear Palsy

Progressive supranuclear palsy is a progressive neurodegenerative disorder with an estimated prevalence of 6.5 per 100,000 persons. Occurring equally in men and women, it is a sporadic condition. Patients typically present in their sixties with symptoms of gait impairment, falls, and bulbar abnormalities, including slurred speech and dysphagia. Examination shows parkinsonism, impaired vertical eye movements, dysarthria, and a reduction in facial expression and blink frequency. The presence of symmetric bradykinesia and axial muscle rigidity, the lack of a significant resting tremor, and the restriction of vertical saccades help distinguish progressive supranuclear palsy from Parkinson disease. Treatment of progressive supranuclear palsy is limited. A levodopa trial can be considered in patients with significant parkinsonism, although the effects are typically modest and are not sustained. Involvement of physical and occupational therapists can help to prevent contractures and provide gait aid.

Corticobasal Degeneration

Corticobasal degeneration is a rare, sporadic, degenerative condition. Clinical manifestations include gait impairment, dystonia, myoclonus, tremor, and slurred speech. Neurologic examination shows asymmetric rigidity, bradykinesia, and dystonia in most patients. The presence of alien limb phenomenon, by which an extremity moves independent of conscious voluntary control, in conjunction with these signs suggests corticobasal degeneration. Tremor is less frequently seen than in patients with Parkinson disease. Diagnosis is based on clinical features, and therapy is symptomatic, similar to that for progressive supranuclear palsy.

Essential Tremor

Essential tremor affects between 1% and 6% of the population and has a bimodal age of onset, peaking in the third and sixth decades. Both sexes are affected equally. Although there is no evidence of increased mortality in patients with essential tremor, the tremor can become disabling. Approximately 50% to 70% of patients with essential tremor have a family history of such tremor. A person with a first-degree relative with essential tremor is five times more likely to develop the disorder.

Essential tremor is characterized by an upper extremity high-frequency tremor, which is present with both limb movement and sustained posture of the involved extremities. The tremor is characteristically bilateral, but there can be mild to moderate asymmetry. Tremor amplitude over time typically increases and can be so severe as to interfere with writing, drinking, and other activities requiring smooth, coordinated upper limb movements. Head tremor is seen in 50% of patients, voice tremor in 30%, and a tremor involving the legs or chin in 15%. Many patients report improvement in the tremor with ingestion of alcohol.

Diagnosis of essential tremor is based on clinical features. It is distinguished from Parkinson disease by the lack of rigidity, bradykinesia, postural instability, and resting tremor. Medication history should be reviewed to exclude medication-induced (such as corticosteroid-, valproate-, and lithium-induced) tremor. Enhanced physiologic tremor due to anxiety, stress, and metabolic disturbances, such as hypoglycemia and hyperthyroidism, should be considered and excluded. Wilson disease should be considered in a patient younger than 40 years who has a kinetic or postural tremor.

Patients with mild tremor may not require treatment. For more serious tremors, propranolol and primidone are first-line agents (**Table 20**). Either drug may be initiated when tremor interferes with activities of daily living or causes psychological distress. Alternative medication options include gabapentin, topiramate, alprazolam, and sotalol. Injection of botulinum toxin can be considered in patients with head tremor because oral medications are less effective in treating this type of tremor. Botulinum toxin has also been used in some patients with severe extremity tremor. The 15% of patients with severe, disabling essential tremor should be considered for deep brain stimulation, which is generally safe, results in 60% to 90% improvement, and has been reported to improve quality of life.

KEY POINTS

- Essential tremor is distinguished from Parkinson disease by the lack of rigidity, bradykinesia, postural instability, and resting tremor; approximately 50% to 70% of patients have a family history of the disorder.

- Propranolol and primidone are first-line agents when essential tremor interferes with activities of daily living or causes psychological distress.

Dystonia

Drug-Induced Dystonia

All medications that block D_2 dopamine receptors can cause acute dystonic reactions. Dystonic movements are due to sustained contraction of agonist and antagonist muscles, which results in twisting and repetitive movements or sustained abnormal postures. These movements most frequently affect the ocular muscles (oculogyric crisis) and the face, jaw, tongue, neck, and trunk. The limbs are rarely affected. Neuroleptic, antiemetic, and serotoninergic agents have been implicated. Treatment consists of parenteral diphenhydramine, benztropine mesylate, or biperiden.

Cervical Dystonia

Cervical dystonia, formerly known as torticollis, is a focal dystonia that involves the cervical musculature and causes abnormal postures of the head, neck, and shoulders. Quick, non-rhythmic, repetitive movements can also occur and can be mistaken for tremor. The prevalence of cervical dystonia is approximately 33 per 100,000 persons. The diagnosis is based on clinical features. MRI of the brain and cervical spine to rule out structural disease is indicated in those with cervical dystonia that is acute in onset and is associated with restricted range of motion about the neck.

Mild, nondisabling symptoms of cervical dystonia may not require therapy. However dystonic movements that interfere with social or occupational functioning should be

TABLE 20 Treatment of Essential Tremor	
Treatment	**Potential Adverse Effects**
Propranolol	Reduced blood pressure and/or heart rate, impotence, drowsiness, dyspnea
Primidone	Drowsiness, fatigue, ataxia, vertigo, vomiting, nausea
Gabapentin	Lethargy, fatigue, dizziness, depression, cognitive impairment
Topiramate	Weight loss, paresthesias, cognitive impairment, glaucoma
Atenolol	Lightheadedness, nausea, sleepiness
Nadolol	Hypotension, dizziness
Sotalol	Drowsiness, arrhythmia, palpitations, fatigue, nausea, vomiting
Botulinum toxin	Hand/neck weakness
Deep brain stimulation	Infection, hematoma, seizures, visual disturbances

considered for pharmacotherapy or botulinum toxin therapy. Botulinum toxin therapy, which has been reported to be beneficial in 60% to 85% of patients with cervical dystonia, is the treatment of choice. Therapy with anticholinergic medications results in improvement in 39% of patients with this disorder.

Spasmodic Dysphonia

Characterized by spasmodic interruptions in the voice, spasmodic dysphonia is classified as a task-specific focal dystonia of the voice caused by inappropriate vocal cord spasm. Diagnosis is based on the presence of appropriate clinical features. Other disorders, such as vocal cord paralysis, gastroesophageal reflux, and vocal fold polyps, nodules, and cysts, should be excluded by laryngeal evaluation. Botulinum toxin injection, typically into the thyroarytenoid muscles, is the treatment of choice.

Chorea

Acquired Causes of Chorea

Chorea may result from medications, systemic metabolic disorders, immunologic disease, brain tumor, or cerebrovascular disease. Substances associated with chorea include oral contraceptive agents, lithium, digoxin, tricyclic medications, anticonvulsant agents, amphetamines, cocaine, and dopaminergic medications. Hyper- and hypoparathyroidism, hyper- and hypoglycemia, and pregnancy have been associated with chorea. Systemic lupus erythematosus and primary antiphospholipid antibody syndrome should be excluded by checking serum levels of antinuclear and anticardiolipin antibodies. Children and adolescents with chorea should be checked for recent streptococcal infection (Sydenham chorea).

Huntington Disease

Huntington disease is a hereditary, progressive, neurodegenerative disorder characterized by increasingly severe motor impairment, cognitive decline, and psychiatric symptoms. In addition to chorea, other motor symptoms include ataxia, dystonia, slurred speech, swallowing impairment, and myoclonus. Various psychiatric symptoms, such as dysphoria, agitation, irritability, anxiety, apathy, disinhibition, delusions, and hallucinations, are commonly seen. Symptoms typically begin in the fourth and fifth decade, but 10% of patients have symptoms in the second decade. Average illness duration (diagnosis to death) is approximately 15 years but is shorter in patients younger than 20 years and older than 50 years.

Huntington disease is an autosomal dominant disorder caused by a CAG repeat within the gene on chromosome 4.

Genetic testing is commercially available and should always be offered with genetic counseling. There is, however, no definitive therapy, and treatment is symptomatic. Quetiapine, olanzapine, or risperidone can be considered in the treatment of severe chorea. Speech, physical, and occupational therapy can be helpful for some of the other motor manifestations of the disease. Selective serotonin reuptake inhibitors can be used to treat depression, and quetiapine, risperidone, or olanzapine can be used to treat psychotic symptoms.

Restless Legs Syndrome and Periodic Limb Movements of Sleep

Restless legs syndrome is a common condition, with an estimated prevalence between 6% and 12%. A positive family history is present in at least 50% of patients with the disorder. Genetic studies in familial restless leg syndrome have suggested linkage to chromosomes 12 and 14, typically with an autosomal dominant pattern of inheritance.

Restless legs syndrome can be divided into primary and secondary forms. The primary form refers to patients without another condition known to be associated with restless legs syndrome. Well-established conditions that can be labeled as secondary restless legs syndrome include pregnancy, end-stage renal disease, and iron deficiency. Symptoms resolve with resolution of these conditions.

Restless legs syndrome remains a clinical diagnosis. Besides an urge to move the legs, there are four other criteria for making the diagnosis: (1) an uncomfortable or unpleasant sensation in the legs; (2) an unpleasant sensation in the legs that begins or worsens during periods of rest or inactivity; (3) an unpleasant sensation in the legs that is partially or totally relieved by movement, as long as activity continues; and (4) an unpleasant sensation that is worse in the evening or night or is present only at night.

Physical examination typically shows normal findings in affected patients, although associated peripheral neuropathy is common in patients with late-onset restless legs syndrome. Evaluation for iron deficiency anemia by measurement of serum ferritin levels and percent iron saturation should be performed in all patients suspected of having the disease. Periodic limb movements of sleep occur in 85% of patients with restless legs syndrome and, when present, help confirm the diagnosis; they are described as involuntary jerking (clonic) movements of the legs during sleep. A positive family history of restless legs syndrome and response to dopaminergic therapy also help confirm the diagnosis.

Both pharmacologic and nonpharmacologic therapies should be considered in the treatment of restless legs syndrome and are tailored to symptom severity (**Table 21**). Dopamine agonists, such as ropinirole and pramipexole, are first-line agents used to treat daily symptoms. Gabapentin, clonazepam, and opioid medications can also be helpful either as combination therapy with a dopamine agonist or as

TABLE 21 Management of Restless Legs Syndrome

Nonpharmacologic Management

Avoiding medications/substances that exacerbate restless legs syndrome
  Antidepressant medications (selective serotonin reuptake inhibitors, tricyclic antidepressants
  Neuroleptic medications
  Antihistamine medications
  Antinausea medications, promotility agents (metoclopramide, chlorpromethazine)
  Caffeine
  Alcohol

Sleep hygiene
  Regular sleep and wake times
  Restricting bed to sleep and intimacy
  Avoiding perturbing activities before sleep

Behavioral interventions
  Brief walks before bedtime
  Hot baths or cold showers
  Massaging of limbs

Pharmacotherapy

For daily symptoms
  Dopamine agonists
    Ropinirole
    Pramipexole
  Anticonvulsant agents
    Gabapentin
    Clonazepam
  Opioids (low potency)
    Tramadol
    Hydrocodone
    Oxycodone
For refractory symptoms
  Switch to a different dopamine agonist.
  Switch to a low-potency opioid or gabapentin if currently using a dopamine agonist.
  Add a second medication.
  Use a high-potency opioid (such as methadone).

monotherapy. Changing to a different dopamine agonist, switching to an opioid or gabapentin, combining therapies, and using high-dose opioid therapy with another medication (such as methadone) are all treatment options in patients with refractory restless legs syndrome.

KEY POINTS

- Restless legs syndrome may be familial or associated with pregnancy, end-stage renal disease, iron deficiency anemia, or peripheral neuropathy.
- Dopamine agonists, such as ropinirole and pramipexole, are first-line agents used to treat daily symptoms of restless legs syndrome.

Bibliography

Benito-León J, Louis ED. Clinical update: diagnosis and treatment of essential tremor. Lancet. 2007;369(9580):1152-1154. [PMID: 17416247]

Chen H, O'Reilly E, McCullough ML, et al. Consumption of dairy products and risk of Parkinson's disease. Am J Epidemiol. 2007; 165(9):998-1006. [PMID: 17272289]

Diamond A, Jankovic J. The effect of deep brain stimulation on quality of life in movement disorders. J Neurol Neurosurg Psychiatry. 2005; 76(9):1188-1193. [PMID: 16107348]

Ferreri F, Agbokou C, Gauthier S. Recognition and management of neuropsychiatric complications in Parkinson's disease. CMAJ. 2006; 175 (12):1545-1552. [PMID: 17146092]

Haehner A, Hummel T, Hummel C, Sommer U, Junghanns S, Reichmann H. Olfactory loss may be a first sign of idiopathic Parkinson's disease. Mov Disord. 2007;22(6):839-842. [PMID: 17357143]

Hauser RA, Zesiewicz TA. Advances in the pharmacologic management of early Parkinson disease. Neurologist. 2007;13(3):126-132. [PMID: 17495756]

Pahwa R, Factor SA, Lyons KE, et al. Practice Parameter: treatment of Parkinson disease with motor fluctuations and dyskinesia (an evidence-based review): report of the Quality Standards Subcommittee of the American Academy of Neurology. Neurology. 2006;66(7):983-995. [PMID: 16606909]

Demyelinating Diseases

Spectrum, Pathophysiology, and Epidemiology of Demyelinating Diseases

The idiopathic inflammatory demyelinating diseases of the central nervous system (CNS) are defined by their distribution, clinical symptoms, severity, and tendency to relapse (**Table 22**).

Multiple sclerosis (MS), the most common of these disorders, is a putative autoimmune disease characterized by episodic neurologic symptoms and signs caused by focal demyelinating lesions (plaques) involving the white matter of the brain, spinal cord, and optic nerves. The pathologic hallmarks of MS plaques are inflammation and demyelination, with relative sparing of nerve axons. However, axonal loss and degenerative processes, major contributors to neurologic disability, may begin early in this disease. Moreover, contemporary immunopathologic studies show that MS is heterogeneous. Four different pathologic patterns have been described, each with distinctive characteristics, such as complement activation and immunoglobulin deposition, loss of oligodendrocytes (myelin-supporting cells), or apoptosis. Lesions from individual patients with MS appear restricted to one pattern, suggesting that the term "multiple sclerosis" encompasses several distinct disorders that follow different mechanisms toward the final common pathway of inflammatory demyelination. Each mechanism may require a specific therapeutic strategy; this is an area of active research.

MS is the most common cause of nontraumatic neurologic disability in young and middle-aged adults in the United

TABLE 22 Spectrum of Inflammatory Demyelinating Diseases of the Central Nervous System

Disorder	Distribution	Course	Relapse Severity
Multiple sclerosis	Multifocal	Relapsing or progressive	Mild to moderate
Neuromyelitis optica	Optic nerve and spinal cord	Relapsing	Severe
ADEM	Multifocal	Monophasic	Moderate to severe
Transverse myelitis	Focal	Monophasic or relapsing	Moderate to severe

ADEM = acute disseminated encephalomyelitis.

States; it affects 0.1% to 0.2% of the population or 400,000 people. Disease onset is usually between age 20 and 40 years; however, MS may occur at virtually any age, including during childhood. Epidemiologic studies demonstrate a female-to-male predominance of approximately 2:1, and recent data indicate that the female preponderance has increased over the past several decades, nearing 3:1.

The cause of MS is unknown, but genetic and environmental factors each contribute to individual risk. Approximately 15% of people with MS have a family history of the disease. There are strong racial and ethnic predilections; the highest rates occur in Northern Europeans, whereas in other groups, such as North American aboriginal people and black Africans, typical MS is virtually unknown.

Environmental factors are also necessary to allow disease expression in a genetically susceptible individual. These as yet unidentified factors are postulated to act early in life. Migration studies show that moving prior to adulthood from a low-prevalence (<5 cases per 100,000 population) to a high-prevalence (>30 cases per 100,000 population) region increases MS risk. However, migration during adulthood from a low-prevalence to a high-prevalence region does not increase risk. These findings, together with evidence of possible MS "outbreaks" in certain areas, suggest that an infective agent or agents might be involved. The "molecular mimicry" concept hypothesizes that sequence similarities between foreign peptides (from viruses or other infective agents) and self-peptides (such as myelin) are sufficient to activate autoreactive T or B cells that trigger autoimmune disease. No single agent has been proved responsible, but serologic evidence indicates that an immune response against Epstein-Barr virus early in life is a risk factor for later development of MS.

The prevalence of MS escalates with increasing geographic latitude, a fact only partially explained by genetic factors and population migration patterns. Additional influences might include climate, sunlight exposure, or other factors. Vitamin D has been implicated in MS pathogenesis because many patients with the disease are vitamin D deficient, and dietary supplementation with vitamins, including vitamin D, is associated with a lower future risk of MS; vitamin D also has immunologic effects. Reduced sunlight exposure during winter months in high-latitude regions may result in vitamin D deficiency and subsequent MS risk.

A notable recent advance is the discovery of an autoantibody marker, NMO-IgG, which distinguishes neuromyelitis optica (Devic disease) from MS. Neuromyelitis optica is now recognized as a distinct demyelinating disease with a predilection for the optic nerves and spinal cord. NMO-IgG targets the water channel aquaporin-4, and growing evidence suggests it may be the primary cause of neuromyelitis optica.

KEY POINTS

- Genetic and environmental factors contribute to multiple sclerosis susceptibility.
- The cause of multiple sclerosis (MS) is unknown, but approximately 15% of people with MS have a family history of the disease.
- Moving before adulthood from a low- to a high-prevalence geographic region of multiple sclerosis increases risk of the disease.

Presenting Signs and Symptoms of Multiple Sclerosis

Symptoms of MS typically emerge as discrete events called attacks (also known as relapses, flare-ups, or exacerbations). Attacks are subacute episodes of neurologic dysfunction that progress over days to weeks, plateau, and then improve partially or completely over subsequent days to months. Demyelinating plaques are the pathologic basis for attacks and cause symptoms by interrupting electrical conduction along neural pathways.

Virtually any CNS symptom can occur in MS. Sensory symptoms, such as paresthesias of the limbs or face, are particularly common. Typical sensory patterns include ascending numbness of the distal limb with gradual proximal spread to involve the trunk with a sensory level, a "useless hand" syndrome in which impaired dexterity occurs with reduced proprioceptive function, or a "tight band" sensation around the trunk or limb. Optic neuritis is common and consists of monocular loss of vision (partial or complete) associated with orbital pain, pain with eye movement, and impaired color vision. Examination usually reveals a scotoma and a relative afferent pupillary defect in which the affected pupil fails to constrict normally with direct light stimulation but shows a normal "indirect" constrictive response when the contralateral eye is illuminated. Oculomotor dysfunction causes diplopia or oscillopsia (perception of involuntary eye movements), and internuclear ophthalmoplegia (one eye fails to adduct normally with contralateral gaze) on examination is strongly suggestive of MS. Motor weakness, imbalance, bladder or bowel dysfunction (especially urinary urgency, frequency, and incontinence and constipation), and facial pain (trigeminal neuralgia) are other common symptoms. Characteristic symptoms include Lhermitte sign (spinal or limb paresthesias elicited by neck flexion), diurnal fatigue (typically worst in the early afternoon), and sensitivity to heat exposure or exercise (which may cause temporary worsening of fatigue or neurologic symptoms). Memory loss or other cognitive symptoms, chronic neuropathic pain, and mood disorders are also prevalent but usually develop gradually rather than as a relapse.

KEY POINT

- Optic neuritis, Lhermitte sign, diurnal fatigue, heat sensitivity, and internuclear ophthalmoplegia are characteristic features of multiple sclerosis.

Diagnosis of Multiple Sclerosis

Brain MRI is the most useful test for diagnosing MS. In addition to excluding other structural causes of a patient's symptoms and signs, brain MRI reveals white matter lesions supportive of a diagnosis of MS (**Figure 14**). Such lesions are characteristically ovoid in shape, are distributed in periventricular regions and in the posterior fossa, and are oriented perpendicular to the lateral ventricles and corpus callosum. Recent lesions (<12 weeks) may enhance after gadolinium administration because they are associated with an inflammatory breach of the blood-brain barrier. In a young adult with typical symptoms and signs of MS and recurrent attacks, brain MRI alone may be sufficient to confirm the diagnosis. After a first-ever attack (such as the occurrence of optic neuritis with no prior neurologic history), brain MRI also provides the strongest prognostic information about the future risk of MS and may be used to confirm the diagnosis if serial scans done several months later demonstrate new lesions. However, expert MRI interpretation and integration with the clinical scenario are mandatory because numerous other conditions, such as migraine, established cerebrovascular disease or presence of vascular risk factors (age >50 years, hypertension, smoking, diabetes mellitus, hyperlipidemia), and head trauma, are also associated with white matter abnormalities on brain MRI. The morphology of the white matter lesions associated with these conditions differs from that of typical MS; the lesions are usually small or punctate, somewhat irregular, and subcortical (nearer to the cortex or brain surface). Misinterpretation of white matter abnormalities discovered incidentally in a patient with nonspecific symptoms is a leading cause of MS misdiagnosis.

Additional neuroimaging may be used to establish the presence of subclinical lesions that confirm involvement of multiple CNS regions (dissemination in space). Lesions detected by spinal cord MRI have high specificity for MS and do not occur in association with migraine or cerebrovascular disease. Orbital MRI with gadolinium obtained during an

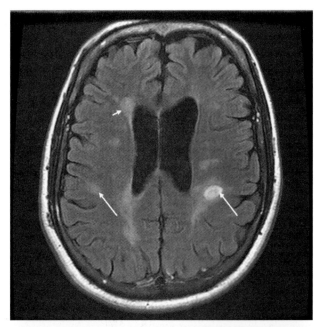

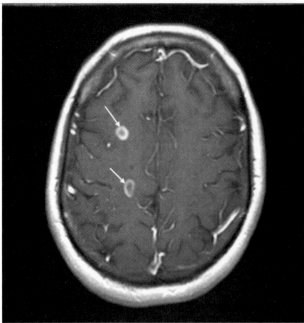

FIGURE 14.
Brain MRI of a patient with multiple sclerosis.
Top, axial brain MRI, fluid-attenuated inversion recovery sequence, shows numerous typical ovoid lesions of MS (*long arrows*), many in a periventricular location (*short arrow*). Bottom, axial T1-weighted brain MRI with gadolinium reveals multiple enhancing lesions (*arrows*) that indicate active MS.

attack of optic neuritis may reveal optic nerve enhancement, which confirms an inflammatory process.

Cerebrospinal fluid (CSF) analysis is useful if the clinical features are suggestive of MS but neuroimaging is inconclusive. About 85% of patients with MS have abnormal CSF findings. A mild lymphocytic pleocytosis, generally 10 to 30 cells/μL, may be present, although in most patients the cell count is normal. More specific findings include the presence of CSF oligoclonal bands not detectable in serum samples collected at the time of lumbar puncture and indices that show intrathecal immunoglobulin production (elevation of the IgG index and synthesis rate).

Neurophysiologic studies can detect subclinical lesions in visual pathways (visual evoked potentials) or sensory tracts (somatosensory evoked potentials) and therefore demonstrate dissemination of lesions in space when results of MRI studies are normal.

KEY POINTS

- In multiple sclerosis, brain MRI reveals ovoid lesions in the periventricular white matter that sometimes enhance with gadolinium; misinterpretation of brain MRI white matter abnormalities discovered in patients with nonspecific symptoms is a leading cause of misdiagnosis of multiple sclerosis.

- Cerebrospinal fluid analysis is useful when the clinical setting is suspicious for multiple sclerosis but neuroimaging is inconclusive because approximately 85% of patients with MS have abnormal findings.

Differential Diagnosis of Multiple Sclerosis

Patients referred to MS clinics may be categorized as having MS, another CNS demyelinating disease, a different neurologic disease, a medical or psychiatric disorder, or no disease. More than half of patients referred to tertiary MS clinics for diagnostic purposes receive a final diagnosis other than MS. The primary reasons for this include the overlap of MS symptomatology with that of other disorders and the strong suspicion of MS in patients with vague neurologic symptoms who have nonspecific brain MRI results. The emergence of new disease-modifying therapies for MS, which are becoming increasingly powerful and are associated with uncommon but serious toxicities, mandates accurate and early diagnosis, preferably by an experienced neurologist.

Although MS is the most common sporadic inflammatory demyelinating CNS disease, there are others. Neuromyelitis optica causes attacks of recurrent optic neuritis and myelitis with relative sparing of the brain and is associated with severe disability early in the disease course. Neuromyelitis optica comprises a greater proportion of demyelinating disease in non-white populations (blacks, Hispanics, Asians), has a 9:1 female-to-male predominance, and is associated with

coexisting systemic autoimmunity, such as thyroid or connective tissue disorders or serum autoantibodies, including antinuclear antibody. Early detection is paramount because the treatment strategy differs from that of MS, as explained later. In addition, the monophasic disorder acute disseminated encephalomyelitis is more common in childhood but can occur as a postinfectious disorder in adults, typically presenting as a meningoencephalitic syndrome with multifocal neurologic symptoms and signs, numerous enhancing brain lesions, and inflammatory CSF. Caution is warranted in applying this diagnosis because many patients ultimately relapse and follow a course typical for MS.

A partial list of other neurologic diseases that can mimic features of MS is provided in **Table 23**. Finally, some patients have nonspecific (but numerous) neurologic symptoms in the setting of major depression, anxiety or panic disorder, or other psychiatric disorders that, after excluding other causes, seem to best explain their syndrome (see MKSAP 15 General Internal Medicine).

Clinical Course in Multiple Sclerosis

The clinical course of MS is used to describe its behavior over time but also to establish prognosis and treatment options. Multiple sclerosis begins with a clinical attack in 85% of patients. Patients presenting at this stage are diagnosed with a "clinically isolated syndrome," which implies that if their brain MRI shows lesions consistent with demyelination, they have a risk of experiencing another attack over the next 10 to 15 years (and, therefore, of having confirmed MS) that approaches 90%. If their brain MRI is normal and no other cause is found, the risk of future confirmed MS is low but still approaches 20%. Therefore, neurologic follow-up is required for all such patients.

Once there is evidence of "dissemination in time," either by occurrence of a second clinical attack or by development of new demyelinating lesions on serial brain MRIs, a diagnosis of relapsing-remitting MS is confirmed (**Figure 15**). Individual relapses tend to be mild to moderate in severity and recover completely (or nearly so) with or without acute therapies. Relapses may be triggered by viral or bacterial infections but most occur without an obvious precipitant. Women experience a reduced relapse rate during pregnancy and a transient increased rate in the first several postpartum months. Over time, relapse frequency declines but so does the degree of recovery from individual relapses. Therefore, the risk of residual neurologic impairment from attacks increases with disease duration.

The course of relapsing-remitting MS is notoriously heterogeneous; early in the disease, the mean relapse frequency is one event every 12 to 14 months. However, some patients will experience a series of severe relapses during the first year despite aggressive treatment, whereas others will maintain clinical remission for several years without preventive therapy.

TABLE 23 Differential Diagnosis of Multiple Sclerosis

Disorder	Notes
Structural or compressive lesions of the brain or spinal cord 　Spinal cord compression by cervical spondylosis or compressive disk disease 　Durally based arteriovenous fistula 　Meningioma 　Primary CNS neoplasm (glioma, lymphoma)	These disorders typically progress subacutely and do not remit. They can usually be differentiated from MS with an MRI.
Paraneoplastic syndrome	This manifests as a progressive, severe ataxia or myelopathy in the setting of cancer, especially lung or breast carcinoma.
Metabolic disorders 　Vitamin B_{12} deficiency 　Vitamin E deficiency 　Copper deficiency	Spasticity, weakness, and dorsal column dysfunction (vibratory and proprioception loss) in the setting of malabsorption suggest vitamin B_{12} or copper deficiency; vitamin E deficiency causes ataxia.
Vascular diseases 　Sporadic and genetic stroke syndromes 　CNS vasculitis	Nonspecific white matter lesions are associated with increased age and vascular risk factors. Family history of migraine, early stroke, dementia, and mood disorders suggests CADASIL, which can be detected with skin biopsy or genetic analysis.
Multisystem inflammatory diseases 　Systemic lupus erythematosus 　Sjögren syndrome 　Sarcoidosis 　Behçet syndrome	Known coexisting disease or systemic clues (arthritis, rash, sicca syndrome, lymphadenopathy, orogenital ulceration) are evident.
Infections 　HIV 　Lyme disease 　Human T-lymphotropic virus type 1 　Syphilis	These infections are associated with myelopathy and can be excluded with appropriate laboratory and CSF testing.
Migraine	This is associated with nonspecific brain MRI white matter abnormalities, which sometimes lead to concern about MS
Medical disorders that cause transient neurologic dysfunction (diabetes mellitus, thyroid disorders)	Such diseases cause symptoms (fatigue, paresthesias) that sometimes lead to investigations for MS.

CADASIL = cerebral autosomal dominant arteriopathy with subcortical infarcts and leukoencephalopathy; CNS = central nervous system; CSF = cerebrospinal fluid; MS = multiple sclerosis.

Unfortunately, there is no validated method to predict outcome for an individual patient at an early disease stage. From a population standpoint, adverse prognostic factors include the involvement of more than one neurologic system at onset and a relatively high attack frequency in the first few years after onset. Disability rating at 5 years after clinical onset is an independent predictor of the future disability accrual. Other long-held negative prognostic factors, such as male sex and older age at disease onset, have recently been challenged.

More than two thirds of patients with relapsing-remitting MS eventually develop a secondary progressive course, which is defined as the development of gradual neurologic worsening without remission. Typically, this manifests as a gradually worsening gait disorder. Documentation of objective decline for more than 1 year is required to confidently declare the onset of secondary progressive MS. This is an important turning point in the disease because once the secondary progressive phase is established, the risk of accumulating permanent disability increases markedly, and the effectiveness of current preventive therapies is minimal. The rate of progression varies enormously between patients, but important changes are usually noted over years rather than weeks or months.

Fifteen percent of patients with MS experience a gradually progressive disorder, rather than an attack, at disease onset (see Figure 15). They are classified as having primary progressive MS. This diagnosis may be more difficult to make because the lack of clinical relapses and relative paucity of MRI lesions make it harder to establish dissemination in time and space. However, diagnostic criteria address this problem by using serial MRI studies and ancillary laboratory studies, including CSF analysis and evoked potentials, to provide supportive evidence and exclude other disorders. Primary progressive MS develops at a later age (fifth to sixth decade) and follows an unremitting course that is remarkably similar to secondary progressive disease in pace and clinical phenotype.

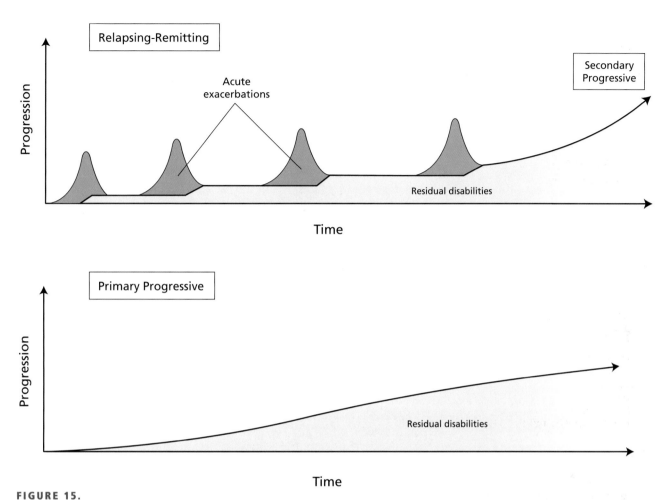

FIGURE 15.

Clinical course of multiple sclerosis.

Top, course of relapsing-remitting multiple sclerosis (MS). A representation of the intermittent, unpredictable, self-limited attacks or exacerbations of neurologic dysfunction lasting days to weeks is shown by the darkly shaded areas. Recovery is usually complete (or nearly so) early in the course of the disease, as illustrated by the initially slight rise in the lightly shaded ("Residual disabilities") area; repeated attacks ("Acute exacerbations") typically result in accrual of permanent neurologic dysfunction, but the remission phase between attacks is defined by clinical stability. About two thirds of patients go on to develop secondary progressive MS, defined by a transition to a gradually progressive (unremitting) course of increasing disability (steeper rise in the lightly shaded area). Acute relapses may still be superimposed on progression but are less frequent than during the relapsing-remitting phase. *Bottom*, course of primary progressive MS. There is a later age of onset of the disease, which begins, by definition, as a progressive disorder rather than with a clinical attack. The course of the disease is remarkably similar to that of secondary progressive MS.

Permanent neurologic disability in progressive MS can take many forms, including dementia, visual loss, or ataxia, but in most instances manifests as a gait disorder with weakness and ataxia. Most patients who require gait assistance or a wheelchair reach those points as a result of progressive disease. The median time from MS onset until conversion to the secondary progressive phase ranges from 10 to 15 years, and to reach the point that unilateral gait assistance (cane) is required, 15 to 25 years. However, many patients are able to walk with some type of assistance for more than 20 years after the progressive phase begins. Multiple sclerosis has a minimal effect on expected life-span, but, notably, the risk of suicide is approximately 7 times higher in those with MS than in control populations.

Those patients with a diagnosis of MS who do not experience progressive disease have a greater chance of being categorized as having "benign MS." This category, which is defined loosely as no or minimal neurologic impairment 15 or more years after MS onset, may encompass as many as 20% of all patients. The definition of benign MS is controversial because continued follow-up of such patients often uncovers late progressive disease and disability accrual. However, there is little doubt that a small minority of patients with MS live a long and essentially unrestricted life.

- Multiple sclerosis begins with a clinical attack in 85% of patients; if the brain MRI at presentation shows lesions consistent with demyelination, the risk of experiencing a second attack (confirmed multiple sclerosis) approaches 90% over the next 10 to 15 years.

- At least two thirds of patients with relapsing-remitting multiple sclerosis develop a secondary progressive disease course; the median time from onset until such progression ranges from 10 to 15 years.

- Multiple sclerosis begins as a primary progressive disorder in 15% of patients.

Treatment of Multiple Sclerosis

Lifestyle Modifications and General Health Care

Because many people with MS are deficient in vitamin D and may be at risk for bone loss because of reduced mobility, encouragement of dietary supplementation with vitamin D (the optimal dose is not established, but 800 U daily is safe) and calcium (1500 mg daily) is reasonable. Physical activity, including cardiovascular exercise, strengthening, and stretching, is to be encouraged because it increases aerobic fitness and health self-perception and reduces fatigue. Temporary reemergence or worsening of neurologic symptoms with exercise (Uhthoff phenomenon) is common, and patients should be told that this physiologic phenomenon does not worsen nerve injury or trigger exacerbations. Cooling vests or collars may reduce heat-related symptoms in patients who are particularly sensitive to temperature. Planned rest or nap periods may assist in fatigue management.

Patients with MS should follow Centers for Disease Control and Prevention indications for routine immunizations, including those for influenza, hepatitis B, varicella, and tetanus; there is insufficient evidence for other vaccinations, but clinical experience suggests that they are also safe. It is advised to delay immunization for 4 to 6 weeks after an acute MS attack, and live vaccines should not be administered to patients with MS who are on immunosuppressive therapies, such as mitoxantrone.

- Immunizations should be delayed for 4 to 6 weeks after an acute attack of multiple sclerosis, and live vaccines should not be administered to patients on immunosuppressive therapies, such as mitoxantrone.

Treatment of Acute Exacerbations

Patients should be educated about the typical symptoms and temporal profile of relapses. Pseudorelapses, or temporary worsening of neurologic symptoms, may occur in the setting of systemic infection, possibly because of the effects of fever. If there is uncertainty about whether new symptoms represent a true MS relapse or a pseudorelapse, investigation for occult infection is warranted with evaluation for urinary tract infection and history- and examination-directed laboratory tests, if deemed necessary. Successful treatment of the infection or supportive care, such as antipyretics for a viral upper respiratory tract infection, will be followed by neurologic improvement. True MS relapses that have no or minimal impact on function may simply be observed. If functional status (vision, strength, balance, or coordination) is impaired, intravenous methylprednisolone, 1 g/d for 3 to 5 days, may be used to speed recovery, although it does not alter the ultimate degree of recovery. A 10- to 14-day oral prednisone taper is optional after completion of intravenous therapy. Severe corticosteroid-refractory relapses of demyelinating disease (MS or neuromyelitis optica) may respond to rescue therapy with plasmapheresis. Physical, occupational, or speech therapy may be necessary to enhance adaptation during the recovery period, depending on the type, severity, and therapeutic responsiveness of the relapse.

- Pseudorelapses (worsening of neurologic symptoms due to another cause, such as systemic infection, that requires antibiotic treatment or supportive care) should be differentiated from true multiple sclerosis relapses (which may require corticosteroid treatment).

- Intravenous methylprednisolone, 1 g/d for 3 to 5 days, may be used to speed recovery from multiple sclerosis relapses that impair vision, strength, balance, or coordination, and severe corticosteroid-refractory relapses may respond to rescue therapy with plasmapheresis.

Disease-Modifying Therapies

There are currently six disease-modifying MS therapies approved by the U.S. Food and Drug Administration (**Table 24**). All have immunomodulatory or immunosuppressive properties and reduce relapse rate, relapse severity, and the accumulation of lesions as determined by MRI. These therapies vary substantially regarding route and frequency of administration and potential toxicity, factors which influence patients' preferences and initial choice of therapy. There are no predefined treatment durations, except for mitoxantrone, which is limited by cumulative dose-related cardiotoxicity. Therefore, most patients continue on a preventive therapy as long as they tolerate it well and experience little or no breakthrough disease activity.

Three of the drugs are interferon preparations that, among other effects, appear to protect the blood-brain barrier. Interferon beta-1a is administered intramuscularly once weekly (Avonex®) or subcutaneously three times weekly (Rebif®), whereas interferon beta-1b (Betaseron®) is administered subcutaneously every other day. More frequently

TABLE 24 Drug Treatment for Multiple Sclerosis

Agent	Notes
Interferon beta-1a and interferon beta-1b	Immunomodulatory
	Reduction in relapse rate and accrual of neurologic disability
	Flu-like symptoms, fatigue, injection site reactions, liver chemistry abnormalities, depression
	Dosing depends on specific agent used
	Pre- and postinjection acetaminophen or NSAIDs may reduce flu-like symptoms.
	Monitoring of CBC and liver chemistry is required every 6 months
	FDA class C drug—should not be used during pregnancy or lactation
Glatiramer acetate	Immunomodulatory
	Reduction in relapse rate
	Injection site reactions
	Rare systemic symptoms (dyspnea/panic attack–like syndrome)
	No laboratory monitoring is required
	FDA class B drug—safety in pregnancy or lactation is not established
Natalizumab	Selective adhesion molecule inhibitor
	Reduction in relapse rate
	Boxed warning: indeterminate risk of progressive multifocal leukoencephalopathy
	Headache, back pain, 1.3% incidence of infusion reaction, 0.8% incidence of anaphylactoid reaction
	Only patients, treating physicians, infusion centers, and pharmacies that are enrolled in a restricted distribution prescribing program known as TOUCHE are authorized to prescribe, distribute, or infuse natalizumab
	FDA class C drug—should not be used during pregnancy or lactation
Mitoxantrone	Immunosuppression
	Reduction in relapse rate; disease stabilization in rapidly progressive disease
	Boxed warnings: cardiotoxicity and secondary acute myeloid leukemia
	Immunosuppression risks, infection, nausea, mouth sores, mild alopecia, menstrual irregularities; urine may temporarily be colored blue
	Monitoring of cardiac ejection fraction (with echocardiography or multigated radionuclide angiography) is required before each dose
	FDA class D drug—has well-documented fetal risk
Corticosteroid	Immunomodulatory
	Speeds recovery from MS exacerbations
	Insomnia, flushing, metallic taste, fluid retention, electrolyte abnormalities, hyperglycemia

CBC = complete blood (cell) count; FDA = U.S. Food and Drug Administration; MS = multiple sclerosis.

Adapted from Wingerchuk DM. Multiple sclerosis. pier.acponline.org/physicians/diseases/d468/drug.tx/d468-s7.html. In PIER (online database). Philadelphia: American College of Physicians, 2008. Accessed January 15, 2009.

administered preparations may have somewhat greater efficacy, according to MRI findings. Each of the drugs reduces the risk of relapse by about one third and modestly slows disability progression. Interferon beta-1a and interferon beta-1b are also indicated for delay of a second clinical attack in patients with a clinically isolated syndrome and brain lesions on MRI. The development of persistent neutralizing antibodies likely interferes with interferon efficacy, but there is not yet consensus regarding use of this information in clinical decision-making.

Glatiramer acetate (Copaxone®) is administered by daily subcutaneous injection; it consists of the acetate salts of four amino acids and is thought to modulate immune responses relevant to MS pathophysiology. Glatiramer acetate is well tolerated and reduces the relapse rate by approximately one third.

Mitoxantrone, a general immunosuppressant, is approved for worsening relapsing-remitting or secondary progressive MS. There is a risk of cumulative dose-dependent cardiotoxicity, limiting treatment to 2 years with the standard protocol of quarterly infusions. Mitoxantrone should not be used in patients with a baseline ejection fraction of less than 50% and should be discontinued if cardiac symptoms or signs emerge during therapy or if the ejection fraction decreases by more than 10% or goes below 50%. Posttherapy leukemia risk has been reported to be as high as 0.4%. Mitoxantrone is typically used for rapidly worsening disease that has not responded to other therapies.

Natalizumab (Tysabri®) is a monoclonal antibody that targets α4 integrin and interferes with the transendothelial migration of lymphocytes into the CNS. Administered intravenously every 4 weeks, natalizumab is associated with a two-thirds reduction in relapse rate and a 40% reduction in disability progression rate. However, the emergence of three cases of progressive multifocal leukoencephalopathy, an often fatal opportunistic JC-virus CNS infection, in MS and Crohn disease trials that included approximately 3000 patients (risk of one case of progressive multifocal leukoencephalopathy per 1000 treated patients over 18 months of treatment) led to brief market withdrawal of the drug. It was reapproved in 2006 with a rigorous surveillance plan and guidelines for use, including restriction to relapsing-remitting disease and avoidance of concomitant immunosuppressive therapies. Natalizumab is generally used as a second-line agent for significant breakthrough disease despite use of other therapies or when there is an inability to tolerate such therapies.

Treatments for progressive forms of MS have limited or no efficacy. Interferon drugs appear to influence the course of secondary progressive MS for patients who continue to have superimposed relapses, but trials of interferons and glatiramer acetate for primary progressive MS have shown no benefit. These progressive forms of MS require different therapeutic strategies aimed at slowing neurodegenerative mechanisms. Preventive therapy for neuromyelitis optica involves immunosuppression with agents such as azathioprine or rituximab.

KEY POINTS
- Three interferons, glatiramer acetate, and natalizumab are approved for reducing the relapse rate in relapsing-remitting multiple sclerosis.
- Natalizumab is associated with a small risk of developing progressive multifocal leukoencephalopathy, and treatment requires participation in a safety surveillance program.
- No therapies have had convincing effects on the neurodegenerative processes that underlie progressive forms of multiple sclerosis.

Symptomatic Management

At all stages of MS, effective symptom management can provide improved quality of life. Specific drugs used to treat disease-associated symptoms are generally empiric and not based on randomized controlled studies, except in a few cases.

Fatigue is a common but nonspecific symptom. Exclusion of anemia, sleep disorders, hypothyroidism, and other medical conditions is required. Adequate rest, regular physical exercise, and treatment with stimulant drugs, such as amantadine or modafinil, can be helpful.

Depression commonly coexists with MS, and the risk of suicide is elevated compared with the general population. Mood should be regularly assessed with a standard screening instrument, and contributing factors (such as medications) should be eliminated, if possible. Psychological support and pharmacologic therapy may be required.

Neuropathic pain, especially involving the lower extremities, is very common and may require tricyclic antidepressants, gabapentin, pregabalin, duloxetine, analgesics, or other agents. Trigeminal neuralgia responds to carbamazepine or gabapentin, but patients with refractory pain may require surgical intervention, such as glycerol or radiofrequency rhizotomy.

Spasticity, spasms, and cramping usually respond to a combination of physical therapy (stretching) and oral antispasticity drugs, such as baclofen, tizanidine, or clonazepam. Patients with severe and refractory symptoms may require trials of botulinum toxin injections or an intrathecal baclofen pump.

Urinary urgency and frequency with occasional incontinence may be managed with timed voiding, avoidance of caffeine, and judicious use of anticholinergic drugs, such as oxybutynin or tolterodine, as long as the postvoid residual urine volume is less than 100 mL. Patients with mixed symptoms (urgency and incomplete bladder emptying), pelvic or bladder pain, or hematuria should be referred to a urologist.

KEY POINTS
- Adequate rest and regular physical exercise may reduce fatigue related to multiple sclerosis, but many patients require treatment with stimulants, such as amantadine or modafinil.
- Multiple sclerosis is associated with a high prevalence of depression and an elevated risk of suicide, so mood should be assessed regularly.
- Spasticity in patients with multiple sclerosis is best managed by physical therapy interventions that include stretching, with or without antispasticity medications.

Bibliography
Frohman EM, Racke MK, Raine CS. Multiple sclerosis—the plaque and its pathogenesis. N Engl J Med. 2006;354(9):942-955. [PMID: 16510748]

Goodin DS, Frohman EM, Garmany GP Jr, et al. Disease modifying therapies in multiple sclerosis: report of the Therapeutics and Technology Assessment Subcommittee of the American Academy of Neurology and the MS Council for Clinical Practice Guidelines [erratum in Neurology. 2002;59(3):480]. Neurology. 2002;58(2):169-178. [PMID: 11805241]

Goodin DS, Frohman EM, Hurwitz B, et al. Neutralizing antibodies to interferon beta: assessment of their clinical and radiographic impact: an evidence report: report of the Therapeutics and Technology Assessment Subcommittee of the American Academy of Neurology [erratum in Neurology. 2007;69(7):712]. Neurology. 2007:68(13): 977-984. [PMID: 17389300]

Kappos L, Bates D, Hartung HP, et al. Natalizumab treatment for multiple sclerosis: recommendations for patient selection and monitoring. Lancet Neurol. 2007;6(5):431-441. [PMID: 17434098]

Munger KL, Leven LI, Hollis BW, Howard NS, Ascherio A. Serum 25-hydroxyvitamin D levels and risk of multiple sclerosis. JAMA. 2006;296(23):2832-2838. [PMID: 17179460]

Noseworthy JH, Lucchinetti C, Rodriguez M, Weinshenker BG. Multiple sclerosis. N Engl J Med. 2000;343(13):938-952. [PMID: 11006371]

Polman CH, Reingold SC, Edan G, et al. Diagnostic criteria for multiple sclerosis: 2005 revisions to the "McDonald Criteria". Ann Neurol. 2005;58(6):840-846. [PMID: 16283615]

Rolak LA, Fleming JO. The differential diagnosis of multiple sclerosis. Neurologist. 2007;13(2):57-72. [PMID: 17351525]

Sayao AL, Devonshire V, Tremlett H. Longitudinal follow-up of "benign" multiple sclerosis at 20 years. Neurology. 2007;68(7):496-500. [PMID: 17296915]

Wingerchuk DM, Lennon VA, Lucchinetti CF, Pittock SJ, Weinshenker BG. The spectrum of neuromyelitis optica. Lancet Neurol. 2007; 6(9):805-815. [PMID: 17706564]

Neuromuscular Disorders

Peripheral Neuropathies

Peripheral neuropathies are common disorders that may involve a single nerve (mononeuropathy), two or more nerves in different sites (mononeuropathy multiplex), or many nerves over a wide area, which causes a more generalized disorder (polyneuropathy).

General Findings and Diagnosis

At presentation, patients with a peripheral neuropathy typically have sensory symptoms, such as numbness and tingling, burning or lancinating pain, weakness, and unsteady gait. Symptoms most commonly involve the distal extremities, particularly the feet. With increasing disease severity, signs and symptoms may become more profound and progress to involve the proximal extremities. The most common categories of peripheral neuropathies are listed in **Table 25**.

Evaluation requires a review of symptom distribution; time course; medical, medication, and family history; and any

TABLE 25 Clinical Correlates of Peripheral Neuropathy

Classification	Signs and Symptoms	Major Diagnostic Considerations
Mononeuropathy multiplex	Subacute asymmetric motor and sensory impairment	Vasculitis
		Diabetes mellitus
Sensory neuropathy	Severe pansensory loss (sensory ataxia)	Sjögren syndrome
		Paraneoplastic syndrome
		Copper deficiency
		Celiac disease
Autonomic neuropathy	Orthostatic hypotension	Amyloidosis
	Constipation	Diabetes mellitus
	Early satiety	Paraneoplastic syndrome
	Erectile dysfunction	
Small-fiber neuropathy	Burning extremity pain without weakness	Diabetes mellitus
	Normal reflexes	Impaired glucose tolerance
		Sjögren syndrome
		Familial burning feet syndrome
Acquired sensorimotor neuropathy	Distal sensory loss and diminished reflexes	Diabetes mellitus
	Distal extremity weakness	Monoclonal gammopathy
		Toxic (chemotherapy)
Hereditary sensorimotor neuropathy	High arches	Charcot-Marie-Tooth disease
	Hammer toes	Familial amyloidosis
	Family history	
Polyradiculoneuropathy	Severe weakness	Guillain-Barré syndrome
	Sensory loss	Chronic inflammatory demyelinating polyradiculoneuropathy
	Areflexia	Amyloidosis
Motor neuropathy	Asymmetric weakness	Multifocal motor neuropathy
	Muscle atrophy	Motoneuron disease

associated autonomic symptoms, such as orthostatic hypotension, constipation, and early satiety. Typical findings on neurologic examination include sensory loss, muscle weakness, and reduced or absent deep tendon reflexes in the distal extremities. The history and neurologic examination help determine the cause of a suspected peripheral neuropathy and guide the diagnostic evaluation.

Routine laboratory studies include a complete blood count, measurement of erythrocyte sedimentation rate and serum vitamin B_{12} and fasting plasma glucose levels, and serum immunofixation. Electromyography (EMG) helps confirm the diagnosis and characterize the type (axonal or demyelinating), severity, and distribution of the neuropathy. Additional laboratory studies, such as cerebrospinal fluid (CSF) examination and nerve or skin biopsies, may be necessary. CSF examination should be considered in patients with acute, severe, or rapidly progressive neuropathy and in those with a demyelinating neuropathy. Sural nerve biopsy is most typically performed in patients with suspected vasculitis or amyloidosis. Skin biopsy may be necessary to diagnose a small-fiber neuropathy, given that EMG is often normal in this condition. Small fiber neuropathies often present with painful sensory symptoms, such as burning, dysesthesias, paresthesias, and autonomic symptoms and signs, without significant motor weakness. Autonomic testing may also be performed in patients with a suspected small-fiber neuropathy or in patients with symptoms suggestive of dysautonomia. This testing typically includes tests of sudomotor (sweating), cardiovagal (heart rate change with Valsalva or deep breathing), and cardiovascular adrenergic (blood pressure response with tilt-table testing) function.

KEY POINTS

- Typical findings on neurologic examination in patients with a peripheral neuropathy include sensory loss, muscle weakness, and reduced or absent deep tendon reflexes in the distal extremities.

- Small-fiber nerves cannot be detected by routine electromyography and may be best assessed with skin biopsy or autonomic nerve studies.

Mononeuropathies

Median and ulnar neuropathies are the most common mononeuropathies and are typically due to compression of these nerves at the wrist and elbow, respectively. Carpal tunnel syndrome, for example, refers to median nerve compression at the wrist in the carpal tunnel. This syndrome is associated with paresthesias and occasionally with pain or weakness involving the fingers. Examination may show sensory loss over the palmar surface of the first three digits and weakness of abduction and opposition of the thumb. The paresthesias are often worse at night or when holding a book or steering a car.

EMG is essential to confirm the diagnosis, to exclude other subclinical disorders, and to establish disease severity. Conservative treatment options include wrist splints and corticosteroid injections. Surgery should be considered in patients with severe sensory loss, hand weakness, moderate to severe EMG findings, or failure to respond to conservative therapy.

Ulnar neuropathy causes numbness of the fourth and fifth fingers and, when severe, may cause weakness of interosseous muscles. EMG should be performed to localize the site of ulnar nerve impairment and to document severity. The elbow is the most frequent site of compression. Patients are initially managed conservatively with a splint that can be used during sleep and instructions to avoid resting the elbow on furniture and other objects or to use an elbow pad. When conservative measures fail, surgical options include either decompression or translocation of the ulnar nerve.

Bell palsy refers to paralysis of the facial nerve causing weakness of ipsilateral facial muscles. Mounting evidence implicates human herpesvirus 1 in the pathogenesis of this condition. Symptoms typically begin suddenly and peak over 1 to 2 days. Paralysis of the upper and lower face distinguishes Bell palsy from stroke, which affects only lower facial muscles (sparing the forehead and eye) when associated with facial paralysis. Most patients experience excellent recovery, although as many as 30% of patients may have poor recovery. Treatment involves eye patching and lubrication to protect the cornea. A recently reported randomized, double-blind, placebo-controlled trial showed improved outcome in patients treated with prednisone within 72 hours of symptom onset. Evidence-based studies have not clearly demonstrated benefit with antiviral therapy.

KEY POINTS

- In patients with suspected median and ulnar neuropathy, electromyographic studies are necessary to establish the diagnosis, determine severity, and diagnose other diseases (such as cervical radiculopathy) that may be subclinical.

- Ulnar neuropathy causes numbness of the fourth and fifth fingers and, occasionally, weakness of the hand.

- Treatment of Bell palsy should include corneal protection and, if the patient is seen within 72 hours of symptom onset, oral prednisone.

Brachial Plexopathy

The brachial plexus is responsible for sensory and motor innervation of the entire upper limb. Conditions that can impair brachial plexus function include trauma, radiation, carcinomatous infiltration, and neuralgic amyotrophy. Neuralgic amyotrophy, or Parsonage-Turner syndrome, is a self-limited, idiopathic, inflammatory disorder of the brachial plexus. Severe shoulder and arm pain is typically followed by sensory loss and weakness of the upper limb. EMG studies confirm the diagnosis. Corticosteroid therapy can be helpful for pain.

Polyneuropathies

Neuropathies of Diabetes Mellitus and Impaired Glucose Tolerance

Diabetes mellitus is associated with several different neuropathies (**Table 26**). More than one type may exist in the same patient. The most common is a distal sensorimotor peripheral neuropathy. Patients may be asymptomatic but typically report numbness, tingling, and often lancinating or burning foot pain. Median and ulnar mononeuropathies are also common in patients with diabetes. Involvement of autonomic nerves can occur in patients with long-standing diabetes.

Diabetic lumbosacral radiculoplexus neuropathy (diabetic amyotrophy) is a severe form of neuropathy in patients with mild or early diabetes and may even occur in those with previously undiagnosed diabetes. Patients typically present with weight loss, unilateral leg pain (often severe), numbness, proximal weakness, and atrophy. Signs and symptoms develop over weeks, may progress over several months, and may later involve the contralateral leg or even the arms.

Small-fiber peripheral neuropathy frequently develops in patients with diabetes and in those with impaired glucose tolerance. Symptoms include numbness, tingling, and burning or lancinating foot pain. All patients with a small-fiber peripheral neuropathy should be screened for diabetes. This should include measurement of fasting plasma glucose level, hemoglobin A_{1c} determination, and (if these values are normal or only minimally elevated) a 2-hour glucose tolerance test.

Hereditary Neuropathies

Although hereditary neuropathies are a common cause of peripheral neuropathy, establishing a diagnosis is often challenging. Patients are frequently unaware of their family medical history; neuropathy in family members may have been misdiagnosed, or family members may have died before a hereditary neuropathy was recognized. De novo mutations are also common. The hereditary neuropathies can be broadly categorized as hereditary small-fiber neuropathies, Charcot-Marie-Tooth disease, and familial amyloidosis.

Patients with hereditary small-fiber neuropathy typically have burning or lancinating pain in the feet, which can progress to involve the legs and hands. They may also have signs and symptoms of dysautonomia. EMG findings are often normal. Conditions to consider include autosomal dominant burning feet syndrome, hereditary sensory autonomic neuropathies, and Fabry disease.

Patients with Charcot-Marie-Tooth disease typically present with distal extremity weakness, an unsteady gait, and numbness. These patients do not develop neuropathic pain symptoms and typically have high arches, hammer toes, and distal leg atrophy (**Figure 16**). EMG is important to determine whether axonal or demyelinating neuropathy is present because genetic testing is generally commercially available for the demyelinating but not the axonal forms of Charcot-Marie-Tooth disease. Treatment is supportive, including bracing (for example, an ankle-foot orthosis) when indicated.

TABLE 26 Peripheral Nerve Manifestations of Diabetes Mellitus	
Classification	**Signs and Symptoms**
Sensorimotor peripheral neuropathy	Distal sensory loss and weakness
	May cause pain
	May be asymptomatic
Radiculopathy	Sensory loss
	Weakness in distribution of nerve root(s)
Mononeuropathy	Sensory loss
	Weakness in distribution of single nerve, most often the median or ulnar nerve
Autonomic neuropathy	Orthostatic hypotension
	Constipation
	Early satiety
	Erectile dysfunction
Diabetic lumbosacral radiculoplexus neuropathy (diabetic amyotrophy)	Severe pain, weakness, and sensory loss
	Weight loss
	Autonomic symptoms common
Small-fiber neuropathy	Burning extremity pain without weakness

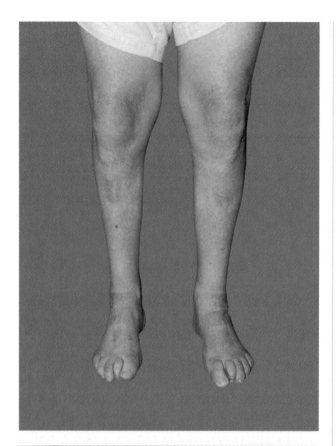

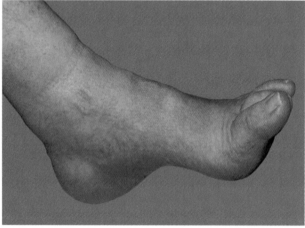

FIGURE 16.
Inherited neuropathy.
Distal leg atrophy (top) and a high arch and hammer toe (bottom) in a patient with an inherited neuropathy, in this case Charcot-Marie-Tooth disease, are shown.

Polyradiculoneuropathies

Guillain-Barré syndrome and chronic inflammatory demyelinating polyradiculoneuropathy (CIDP) involve an inflammatory process directed against both nerve roots and peripheral nerves. Guillain-Barré syndrome is an acute disorder (symptoms peak within 4 weeks), and CIDP is more chronic (symptoms must be present for at least 8 weeks for a diagnosis). The distinction between acute and chronic forms is important

because Guillain-Barré syndrome is a self-limited disorder, whereas patients with CIDP require ongoing immune-modulating therapy.

Guillain-Barré Syndrome

At presentation, patients with Guillain-Barré syndrome have numbness, weakness, unsteady gait, and often neuropathic pain in the extremities. Most patients have a preceding history of infection, trauma, or surgery. The most frequent precipitating factor is *Campylobacter jejuni* infection that causes a diarrheal syndrome. Findings on neurologic examination typically include limb weakness, sensory loss, and reduced or absent deep tendon reflexes. Bulbar and respiratory muscle weakness may impair speaking and swallowing functions and result in respiratory failure. Dysautonomia develops in 20% of patients, most often in those with severe, generalized weakness and respiratory failure. Signs and symptoms of dysautonomia include cardiac arrhythmias, marked blood pressure instability, and constipation.

All patients with suspected Guillain-Barré syndrome should be hospitalized for urgent evaluation and ongoing observation. Initial evaluation requires EMG, CSF examination, and pulmonary function testing (including measurement of maximal inspiratory and expiratory pressures). The EMG typically shows a predominantly demyelinating process. Typical CSF findings include a normal glucose level and cell count and an elevated protein concentration; presence of CSF pleocytosis in patients with suspected Guillain-Barré syndrome should prompt consideration of other diagnoses, such as HIV, cytomegalovirus, West Nile virus infection, or other infectious or inflammatory processes.

Treatment of Guillain-Barré syndrome includes either intravenous immune globulin or plasma exchange. Intravenous immune globulin, 0.4 g/kg, is given once daily for 5 consecutive days, and plasma exchange involves five exchanges of 200 mL/kg over 10 days. Both treatments are equally effective. Corticosteroids are not effective. Supportive therapies are crucial, including respiratory and cardiovascular monitoring, venous thrombosis prophylaxis, physical and occupational therapy, and bowel care.

The overall prognosis in patients with Guillain-Barré syndrome is good, with 80% of patients achieving recovery with little or no disability. Poor prognostic features include the need for mechanical ventilation, axonal findings on EMG, and rapidly progressive weakness.

Chronic Inflammatory Demyelinating Polyradiculoneuropathy

At presentation, patients with CIDP have symptoms similar to those of patients with Guillain-Barré syndrome, but the symptoms are chronic (of at least 8 weeks in duration). Symptoms may be progressive or relapsing-remitting. Diagnostic evaluation includes EMG, CSF examination, and, occasionally, nerve biopsy.

Patients require long-term immune-modulating therapy with prednisone, mycophenolate mofetil, azathioprine, or cyclosporine. A brief or ongoing course of intravenous immune globulin may also be helpful. Plasma exchange may be tried in patients with severe CIDP to attempt to induce or sustain remission.

Critical Illness Neuropathy

Neuropathy develops in as many as 50% to 70% of patients with sepsis. Critical illness neuropathy is typically recognized when a patient is unable to be weaned from mechanical ventilation or when severe, generalized weakness of the extremities develops during or after recovery from a critical illness.

A complete history, neurologic examination, and EMG are required to exclude other disorders that can present similarly, particularly given that the neurologic examination in these critically ill, often encephalopathic patients may be limited. The specific EMG finding in critical illness neuropathy is an axonal sensorimotor peripheral neuropathy. There is growing consensus that most patients with critical illness neuropathy also have a myopathy of critical illness or a critical illness neuromyopathy.

Once the diagnosis of critical illness neuropathy is suspected, corticosteroids and neuromuscular junction–blocking agents are contraindicated because they may play a role in pathogenesis. Treatment is supportive and includes ongoing physical and occupational therapy.

The severity of critical illness neuropathy is associated with length of stay in the intensive care unit, elevated plasma glucose levels, and decreased serum albumin levels. Prognostic data are limited, but at least one third of patients may have significant residual weakness.

> **KEY POINTS**
>
> - Distal sensorimotor peripheral neuropathy is the most common type of neuropathy in patients with diabetes mellitus.
> - All patients with small-fiber peripheral neuropathy should be screened for diabetes mellitus by measurement of their fasting plasma glucose level and, if normal or minimally elevated, a 2-hour glucose tolerance test.
> - Patients with Guillain-Barré syndrome, characterized by limb weakness, sensory loss, and reduced or absent deep tendon reflexes on neurologic examination, require treatment with either intravenous immune globulin or plasma exchange; corticosteroids are not effective.
> - Patients with chronic inflammatory demyelinating polyradiculoneuropathy have chronic symptoms and signs similar to the acute ones of Guillain-Bathé syndrome and require long-term immune-modulating therapy.
> - Corticosteroids and neuromuscular junction–blocking agents should be avoided in patients with critical illness neuropathy.

Treatment of Neuropathic Pain

Neuropathic pain is common in patients with peripheral neuropathy. It is usually described as a burning or lancinating pain that typically affects the distal extremities and is often worse at night.

Physical measures, such as soaking the affected area in warm or cold water, may be helpful. Many different medications are used to treat neuropathic pain. Topical agents, such as lidocaine patches and capsaicin cream, may be helpful and do not cause systemic side effects. Tricyclic antidepressants, such as amitriptyline and nortriptyline, are first-line agents but can cause excessive sedation, orthostatic hypotension, and weight gain. Gabapentin, pregabalin, and duloxetine are newer agents that may be helpful and are now considered first-line agents. Tramadol is a nonnarcotic, centrally acting, second-line agent that is often used adjunctively to decrease pain. Mexiletine, carbamazepine, and lamotrigine are third-line agents. Some patients may require more than one drug for pain control. Although somewhat controversial, opioid medications may be needed to treat some patients. Patients with refractory pain may benefit from oral medications that have a different mechanism of action (such as a tricyclic antidepressant in conjunction with an anticonvulsant agent).

> **KEY POINT**
>
> - Neuropathic pain, which is common in patients with peripheral neuropathy, typically affects the distal extremities and is often worse at night.

Amyotrophic Lateral Sclerosis

Amyotrophic lateral sclerosis (ALS) is a relentlessly progressive motoneuron disorder with an estimated incidence of two cases per 100,000 persons. Most cases are acquired or sporadic, but some (about 10%) are inherited. Approximately 20% of patients with inherited ALS have a mutation in the superoxide dismutase gene. Superoxide dismutase is an important mediator in free-radical pathways, and mutations in this gene may lead to excessive free-radical damage to anterior horn cells.

Patients with ALS typically report progressive painless weakness, atrophy, and fasciculations beginning in an arm or leg. Patients do not have sensory loss, pain, or impairment in bowel and bladder function. In addition to lower motoneuron signs of atrophy and fasciculations, upper motoneuron signs, such as hyperreflexia and extensor plantar responses, are also typically seen. Approximately 20% of patients have bulbar-onset ALS, characterized by slurred speech, difficulty swallowing, and emotional lability. As ALS progresses, patients develop weight loss and respiratory insufficiency. The presence of cognitive impairment, specifically frontotemporal dementia, is being increasingly recognized in some patients (see Dementia).

Findings on neurologic examination include limb weakness, fasciculations, atrophy, brisk deep tendon reflexes, and extensor plantar responses. Signs of bulbar impairment (such as slurred speech), tongue atrophy, and fasciculations may also be evident.

MRI of the brain and spinal cord should be performed to exclude a structural lesion. EMG is essential to rule out other disorders and to establish the extent and severity of denervation. Pulmonary function tests and overnight pulse oximetry studies can establish the presence of respiratory insufficiency. Patients with bulbar signs or symptoms require evaluation of swallowing function.

Management is symptom based, and referral to a multidisciplinary ALS clinic for ongoing care and support is beneficial. Riluzole, a glutamate antagonist, is the only medication approved by the U.S. Food and Drug Administration for treatment of ALS and has been shown in clinical trials to slow the decline of muscle weakness and prolong survival by a median of 83 days.

Use of noninvasive positive-pressure ventilation with bilevel positive airway pressure has also been shown to prolong survival and improve quality of life. In addition to symptoms of nocturnal hypoventilation, indications for ventilatory support include a forced vital capacity of less than 50%, nocturnal oxygen saturation of less than 90% for more than 1 minute, maximal inspiratory pressure of less than 60 cm H_2O, and maximal expiratory pressure of less than 30 cm H_2O. Placement of a percutaneous endoscopic gastrostomy tube has also been shown to improve the quality of life in patients with ALS. Such tube placement should be considered when patients experience a 10% or greater weight loss, require 30 minutes or more to finish a meal, or have episodes of coughing and choking when eating.

Excessive salivation can be treated symptomatically with anticholinergic agents, such as glycopyrrolate, amitriptyline, and benztropine. When oral medications are ineffective, injection of botulinum toxin into the parotid or submandibular glands can be considered. Excessive emotional lability can be treated with either tricyclic antidepressants or selective serotonin reuptake inhibitors. Augmentative and alternative communication devices can help preserve communication when speech becomes unintelligible.

KEY POINTS

- Both upper and lower motoneuron findings are present in patients with amyotrophic lateral sclerosis.
- Bilevel positive airway pressure and percutaneous endoscopic gastrostomy tube placement, when indicated, have been shown to prolong survival and improve quality of life in patients with amyotrophic lateral sclerosis.

Neuromuscular Junction Disorders

Disorders of neuromuscular junction transmission should be considered in patients with painless proximal limb weakness and in those with bulbar symptoms, such as diplopia, ptosis, dysarthria, and dysphagia. Myasthenia gravis and Lambert-Eaton myasthenic syndrome are the primary neuromuscular junction disorders.

Myasthenia Gravis

Myasthenia gravis is caused by an immune-mediated attack on postsynaptic neuromuscular junctions. Approximately 85% of patients have antibodies directed against the acetylcholine receptor. Among patients without acetylcholine receptor antibodies, approximately 50% have antibodies directed against muscle-specific kinase receptors. Patients with the disease but without detectable antibodies against any of these receptors are considered to have seronegative myasthenia gravis.

Myasthenia gravis is estimated to occur in 140 per million persons in the United States. There are two recognized forms: ocular and generalized. The ocular disorder is less common and occurs in approximately 10% of patients. Some patients who initially have only ocular symptoms ultimately develop the generalized disorder. Generalized myasthenia gravis can affect either sex at any age but typically begins in the third and fourth decades in women and after age 50 in men.

Signs and symptoms in patients with ocular myasthenia gravis include fatigable blurring of vision, binocular diplopia, and ptosis. Patients with generalized myasthenia gravis typically report limb weakness, diplopia, slurred speech, dysphagia, and dyspnea. Findings on neurologic examination include ptosis, impaired ocular motility, and limb weakness that increases with repeated testing (fatigable weakness). Deep tendon reflexes and the sensory examination are normal.

Diagnostic evaluation includes screening assays for acetylcholine antibodies and, if negative, testing for muscle-specific kinase antibodies. Serum thyroid-stimulating hormone levels should also be measured because of the association of myasthenia gravis with autoimmune thyroid disorders. EMG studies, including repetitive nerve stimulation studies, help to exclude other conditions and confirm the diagnosis. Single-fiber EMG is the most sensitive diagnostic test. Once the diagnosis is confirmed, a CT scan of the chest should be performed to exclude a thymoma, which is present in up to 15% of patients.

Treatment of myasthenia gravis is based on symptom distribution and severity. Pyridostigmine, an acetylcholinesterase inhibitor, is usually given as first-line therapy (**Table 27**). Patients with mild ocular or generalized myasthenia gravis may not require additional immune-modulating agents, at least initially. Some patients may experience a transient worsening of myasthenic symptoms when first placed on corticosteroids. Prednisone plus mycophenolate mofetil, azathioprine, cyclosporine, or rituximab is used to induce or

TABLE 27 Treatment of Myasthenia Gravis

Drug Classification[a]	Medication or Procedure
Immediate	Pyridostigmine
Intermediate	Plasma exchange
	Intravenous immune globulin
	Prednisone
Long-term	Mycophenolate mofetil
	Azathioprine
	Rituximab
	Cyclosporine
	Thymectomy

[a]Medications are classified on the basis of the time to clinical effect.

sustain remission. Those with significant bulbar dysfunction, respiratory impairment, or severe limb weakness may benefit from plasma exchange, given as five exchanges over 10 days. Thymectomy is indicated in patients with CT evidence of thymoma and may be considered in patients younger than 50 years of age without thymoma.

KEY POINTS

- Approximately 85% of patients with myasthenia gravis have antibodies directed against the acetylcholine receptor.

- CT scan of the chest should be performed in patients with myasthenia gravis to exclude the presence of a thymoma.

- Treatment of patients with myasthenia gravis is based on symptom distribution and severity and includes pyridostigmine and usually the addition of immune-modulating agents.

Lambert-Eaton Myasthenic Syndrome

Lambert-Eaton myasthenic syndrome is a rare neuromuscular junction transmission disorder caused by antibodies directed against presynaptic voltage-gated P/Q-type calcium channels. This syndrome occurs in 5% of patients who have small cell lung cancer and also in patients with other cancers. The diagnosis of a cancer frequently follows the diagnosis of Lambert-Eaton myasthenic syndrome.

Patients typically report progressive proximal limb weakness, and most have symptoms of dysautonomia, such as dry eyes, dry mouth, constipation, and erectile dysfunction. Lambert-Eaton myasthenic syndrome should be considered in any patient with findings of proximal limb weakness and absent deep tendon reflexes on neurologic examination. Facilitation (improvement of deep tendon reflexes and muscle strength after brief isometric exercise) may also be noted on neurologic examination. EMG testing

and positive assays for P/Q-type calcium channel antibodies establish the diagnosis.

Patients with newly diagnosed Lambert-Eaton myasthenic syndrome but without a known malignancy should undergo evaluation for occult cancer, because at least 50% will ultimately develop a malignancy (mostly small cell lung cancer). CT scans of the chest, abdomen, and pelvis should be performed in all patients, and if results are normal, whole-body positron emission tomography should be performed. Treatment consists of pyridostigmine and 3,4-diaminopyridine; the latter is available on a compassionate-use basis at some institutions in the United States.

KEY POINT

- At least 50% of patients diagnosed with Lambert-Eaton myasthenic syndrome ultimately develop a malignancy, most commonly small cell lung cancer.

Myopathy

Myopathy should be suspected in patients with a history of progressive limb weakness but without signs or symptoms of sensory loss. Most myopathies primarily affect proximal limb muscles, but some myopathic disorders may severely affect specific muscle groups (for example, finger flexor and quadriceps muscle weakness in inclusion-body myositis). Whereas motoneuron disorders typically begin asymmetrically, most myopathies cause symmetric limb weakness. Although many patients with a myopathy report fatigue, the presence of markedly fluctuating, fatigue-induced weakness is not typical and should suggest a neuromuscular junction disorder.

Muscle pain is not typical in most myopathic disorders and should prompt consideration of other conditions. However, specific myopathic disorders that may be associated with muscle pain include toxic myopathies, myotonic dystrophy, metabolic myopathies, infectious myositis, and infiltrative myopathies, such as amyloidosis and sarcoidosis. Because acquired myopathies do not typically cause significant facial muscle dysfunction, a neuromuscular junction disorder should be considered in a patient with a history of ocular symptoms or facial muscle weakness. Certain inherited myopathic disorders, including oculopharyngeal muscular dystrophy, facioscapulohumeral dystrophy, and certain mitochondrial myopathies, can prominently affect ocular or facial muscles.

Age of symptom onset and rate of progression are important historical features. A rapidly progressive myopathic disorder suggests an inflammatory myopathy, such as polymyositis or dermatomyositis, whereas a chronic, slowly progressive disorder is typical of an inherited myopathy.

Myopathic disorders are frequently associated with involvement of other organ systems. For example, the presence of a typical rash in conjunction with proximal limb weakness suggests dermatomyositis. Cardiac disease, including arrhythmias and cardiomyopathy, is also common in many types of muscular dystrophy, and patients with a myopathy known to cause cardiac disease require screening. Cataracts and frontal balding are common features in patients with myotonic dystrophy.

EMG is necessary to help confirm the presence of a myopathy, exclude neuromuscular junction disorders, and establish the distribution and severity of disease. EMG is helpful to guide the selection of a site for muscle biopsy and can be used to monitor response to treatment.

Muscle biopsy should be performed in patients with significant muscle weakness or elevated serum creatine kinase levels and in those with EMG findings of significant myopathy. Genetic testing should be considered in patients with a suspected inherited myopathy and can obviate the need for muscle biopsy in many of them.

Inflammatory Myopathies

The inflammatory myopathic disorders, which include polymyositis, dermatomyositis, and inclusion-body myositis, are discussed in detail in MKSAP 15 Rheumatology.

Endocrine-Related Myopathies

Corticosteroid-Induced Myopathy

Corticosteroid-induced myopathy is the most common endocrine-related muscle disorder. Patients report proximal limb weakness, most often in the lower limbs. Most patients have a cushingoid appearance. Ocular, facial, and distal extremity muscle strength and deep tendon reflexes are normal. Women are affected nearly twice as often as men. Prednisone dosages of 30 mg/d or higher seem to confer the greatest risk. Pulsed and alternate-day corticosteroid regimens are less likely to induce myopathy.

Although EMG findings and serum creatine kinase levels are normal in patients with corticosteroid-induced myopathy, these studies should be obtained to rule out other conditions, such as neuromuscular junction disorders or other neurogenic processes. Muscle biopsy results show only atrophy of type IIb muscle fibers. Treatment involves discontinuing or tapering corticosteroid therapy.

Thyrotoxic Myopathy

Although most patients with hyperthyroidism do not report limb weakness as a presenting symptom, symmetric proximal limb weakness is typically found on examination. Other signs and symptoms of hyperthyroidism are present, including anxiety, tremor, heat intolerance, insomnia, and weight loss. Myalgia and fatigue are also commonly reported. Serum creatine kinase measurement and EMG findings are typically normal. After treatment of the thyrotoxic state, the myopathy usually resolves over several months.

Hypothyroid Myopathy

Proximal limb weakness develops in one third of patients with hypothyroidism. Myalgia, cramps, and muscle hypertrophy are also common. Neurologic examination findings show proximal limb weakness and delayed relaxation of deep tendon reflexes. Serum creatine kinase levels may be normal or slightly elevated. EMG findings are usually normal, although minor myopathic changes are occasionally seen. Gradual improvement in myopathic symptoms occurs with correction of the hypothyroidism.

Myopathy Associated with Hyperparathyroidism and Vitamin D Deficiency

Myopathy occurs in patients with both primary and secondary hyperparathyroidism and causes proximal limb weakness, particularly of the lower extremities. Serum parathyroid hormone levels are elevated, and serum calcium levels are also usually increased. Serum creatine kinase measurement and EMG findings are typically normal, although minor myopathic changes may be seen on EMG. Myopathy improves or resolves following medical or surgical treatment of the hyperparathyroidism.

Vitamin D deficiency has been associated with osteomalacia and proximal muscle weakness. There is strong evidence that vitamin D deficiency, even in the absence of osteomalacia, is associated with myalgia and proximal limb weakness. Low serum 25-hydroxyvitamin D levels suggest the diagnosis. Serum creatine kinase measurement and EMG findings are usually normal, and myopathic symptoms typically improve following vitamin D supplementation.

KEY POINTS

- Corticosteroid-induced myopathy is the most common endocrine-related muscle disorder.
- Electromyography findings and serum creatine kinase levels are normal in patients with corticosteroid-induced myopathy.
- Proximal limb weakness is a common but correctable finding in patients with myopathy and hyperthyroidism, hypothyroidism, hyperparathyroidism, or vitamin D deficiency.

Inherited Myopathies

The inherited myopathies are a diverse group of disorders that include congenital myopathies, muscular dystrophies, myotonic disorders, and metabolic myopathies (**Table 28**). Inheritance patterns are autosomal dominant, autosomal recessive, or, rarely, X-linked or maternal. Age of onset, rate of disease progression, and severity of disease are often quite variable. The genetic and molecular abnormalities have been identified in some disorders and are unknown in others.

Critical Illness Myopathy

Myopathy is a common complication of critical illness and most likely occurs more frequently than does critical illness neuropathy (see Critical Illness Neuropathy). As in critical illness neuropathy, critical illness myopathy should be suspected

TABLE 28 Inherited Myopathies

Myopathy Type	Notes
Congenital	
Central core disease	Allelic with malignant hyperthermia Mutation of ryanodine receptor gene
Nemaline myopathy	Can present in infancy, childhood, or adulthood
Centronuclear myopathy	May have elongated face, high-arched palate, and scoliosis
Myofibrillar myopathy	In addition to proximal myopathy, may have polyneuropathy and cardiomyopathy
Congenital fiber-type disproportion myopathy	May have dysmorphic facial and skeletal features
Muscular Dystrophies[a]	
Limb-girdle muscular dystrophy	Proximal greater than distal weakness
Duchenne muscular dystrophy	X-linked
Becker muscular dystrophy	Limb-girdle weakness with cardiomyopathy
Emery-Dreifuss muscular dystrophy	X-linked Proximal greater than distal weakness Cardiac conduction defects and muscle contractures
Facioscapulohumeral muscular dystrophy	Asymmetric facial, scapular and proximal upper limb weakness
Distal myopathy	Asymmetric distal extremity weakness
Myotonic dystrophy	Myotonia and weakness of the forearm and peroneal muscular groups Balding Cataracts Cardiac dysrhythmia
Proximal myotonic myopathy	Myotonia Proximal weakness and pain Cardiac dysrhythmia
Oculopharyngeal muscular dystrophy	Ptosis Dysphagia Proximal limb weakness
Metabolic Myopathies	
Glycogen metabolism disorders	Cramping, stiffness, and pain shortly after exertion
Lipid metabolism disorders	Cramping, stiffness, pain shortly after exertion
Mitochondrial myopathies	Exercise intolerance Various other neurologic and systemic symptoms

[a]Not a comprehensive list.

in patients who cannot be weaned from mechanical ventilation. Diffuse, flaccid weakness involving the limb, neck, diaphragm, and even facial muscles is noted on examination. Serum creatine kinase levels are often normal but may be elevated in patients with acute necrotizing myopathy. Muscle biopsy is generally not needed for diagnosis. The prognosis is favorable in patients without an elevated serum creatine kinase level or necrosis on muscle biopsy.

Toxic Myopathies

Prompt recognition of toxic myopathies is essential because of the potential for reversibility. Statin medications may cause an acute or subacute painful proximal myopathy with rhabdomyolysis. Myalgia, with or without a slight increase in the serum creatine kinase level, is more commonly reported. Other substances with established myotoxic potential include corticosteroids (see Corticosteroid-Induced Myopathy), alcohol, chloroquine, hydroxychloroquine, interferon alfa, colchicine, and procainamide.

Bibliography

Bolton CF. Neuromuscular manifestations of critical illness. Muscle Nerve. 2005;32(2):140-163. [PMID: 15825186]

Dyck PJB, Windebank AJ. Diabetic and nondiabetic radiculoplexus neuropathies: new insights into pathophysiology and treatment. Muscle Nerve. 2002;25(4):477-491. [PMID: 11932965]

Hoffman-Snyder C, Smith BE, Ross MA, Hernandez J, Bosch EP. Value of the oral glucose tolerance test in the evaluation of chronic idiopathic axonal polyneuropathy. Arch Neurol. 2006;63(8):1075-1079. [PMID: 16769858]

Holick MF. High prevalence of vitamin D inadequacy and implications for health. Mayo Clin Proc. 2006;81(3):353-373. [PMID: 16529140]

Hughes RAC, Wijdicks EFM, Benson E, et al. Supportive care for patients with Guillain-Barré syndrome. Arch Neurol. 2005;62(8): 1194-1198. [PMID: 16087757]

Oh SJ, Kurokawa K, de Almeida DF, Ryan HF Jr, Claussen GC. Subacute inflammatory demyelinating polyneuropathy. Neurology. 2003;61(11):1507-1512. [PMID: 14663033]

Simmons Z. Management strategies for patients with amyotrophic lateral sclerosis from diagnosis through death. Neurologist. 2005; 11(5):257-270. [PMID: 16148733]

Sullivan FM, Swan IR, Donnan PT, et al. Early treatment with prednisolone or acyclovir in Bell's palsy. N Engl J Med. 2007;357(16): 1598-1607. [PMID: 17942873]

Neuro-oncology

Introduction

Neuro-oncologic disorders are classified as primary tumors, metastatic tumors, and paraneoplastic syndromes. Patients with primary and metastatic brain lesions typically present with seizures, nonfocal neurologic findings (such as headache and behavioral and cognitive changes), or subacute progression of a focal neurologic deficit (such as hemiparesis). Neurologic deficits result from edema, compression, or infiltration of the brain and spinal cord and vary according to tumor location. Definitive treatment depends on tumor type and may include resection, radiation therapy, and chemotherapy. Corticosteroids can provide symptomatic relief when tumor-associated edema is present. Seizures should be treated with anticonvulsant agents. However, primary prophylaxis for seizures is not of proven benefit.

KEY POINT

- Common presenting symptoms of brain malignancy include seizures, headaches, behavioral changes, and subacute progressive focal neurologic deficits.

Primary Central Nervous System Tumors

Primary central nervous system (CNS) tumors develop from nervous system cells or their embryonic precursors. The most common of these neoplasms are gliomas and meningiomas, followed by CNS lymphomas.

Gliomas

Gliomas account for 50% of all primary brain tumors. The most common subtypes are astrocytomas, oligodendrogliomas, mixed gliomas, and ependymomas. In the World Health Organization histopathologic classification system, gliomas are classified from grade 1 to 4, with higher grades correlating with more aggressive behavior and poorer prognosis. The most common glial tumor, the grade-4 glioblastoma multiforme, is also the most malignant.

Low-grade gliomas (grades 1 and 2) occur most often in the fourth to sixth decade of life. Seizures are the most common presenting symptom. Although grade-2 gliomas grow slowly, they almost inevitably transform into a higher grade if left untreated. High-grade gliomas (grades 3 and 4) are most often diagnosed in patients in their forties to sixties.

On an MRI, which is the imaging modality of choice for detecting gliomas, low-grade gliomas appear as poorly marginated lesions with minimal contrast enhancement and little or no edema (**Figure 17**). Ninety percent of oligodendrogliomas are calcified. Higher-grade tumors are more likely to show irregular contrast enhancement and surrounding edema. Glioblastoma multiforme is further characterized by areas of necrosis and hemorrhage (**Figure 18**). Tissue diagnosis by brain biopsy or craniotomy resection is required. Specialized genetic testing is sometimes used for additional classification and prognosis. For example, loss of heterozygosity at chromosomes 1p and 19q in patients with an oligodendroglioma correlates with improved response to chemotherapy and prolonged survival.

Surgical resection is curative for grade-1 gliomas. Grade-2 and -3 gliomas require maximally safe surgical resection followed by radiation therapy or chemotherapy, or both. Glioblastoma multiforme is refractory to treatment; however, radiation therapy and chemotherapy with temozolomide have a small, proved therapeutic benefit. Median survival is 9 years for grade-2 lesions, 3 years for grade-3 lesions, and 1 year for glioblastoma multiforme.

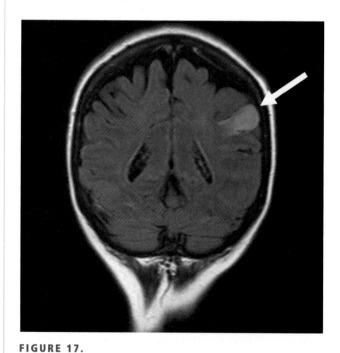

FIGURE 17.
Low-grade glioma.
Coronal flair MRI showing an infiltrating lesion (*arrow*) enlarging the postcentral gyrus.

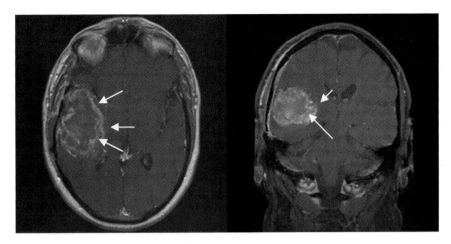

FIGURE 18.
Glioblastoma multiforme.
Axial (*left*) and coronal (*right*) postcontrast T1-weighted MRI showing a large right temporal mass (*arrows*) with central necrosis and peripheral nodular enhancement.

KEY POINTS

- Gliomas account for 50% of all primary brain tumors.

- Surgical resection is curative in patients with grade-1 gliomas; median survival is 9 years for grade-2 lesions, 3 years for grade-3 lesions, and 1 year for glioblastoma multiforme.

Meningiomas

Meningiomas are benign, slow-growing, dura-based tumors. The second most common primary brain tumor in adults (after gliomas), meningiomas account for 20% of all primary brain tumors. Incidence increases with age and female sex. Most meningiomas are estrogen receptor– and progesterone receptor–positive, and approximately 50% are positive for androgen receptors. Exposure to exogenous hormones may be a risk factor for the development of meningioma.

Meningiomas are often found incidentally during neuroimaging studies. At diagnosis, patients may be asymptomatic or have subtle signs and symptoms. Seizure is the most common presentation and is reported in greater than 50% of symptomatic patients. Meningiomas characteristically appear on CT scans and MRIs as a well-delineated, partially calcified, dura-based mass with strong homogeneous contrast enhancement (**Figure 19**).

Treatment depends on tumor size and location and age of the patient. Older adults with small, asymptomatic tumors can be managed conservatively with observation and serial neuroimaging studies. Surgical resection is the treatment of choice for younger patients with and without symptoms and for symptomatic older adults and is curative when complete. Radiation therapy or stereotactic radiosurgery may benefit patients with unresectable or rare aggressive meningiomas.

KEY POINTS

- Meningiomas appear on CT scans and MRIs as well-delineated, partially calcified, dural-based masses with strong homogeneous contrast enhancement.

- Small, asymptomatic meningiomas in older adults can be managed by serial clinical evaluations and radiographic follow-up studies.

- Surgical resection is the treatment of choice for meningiomas in younger patients with and without symptoms and in symptomatic older adults and is curative when complete.

Primary Central Nervous System Lymphoma

Primary central nervous system lymphoma is a rare form of non-Hodgkin lymphoma that is limited to the brain, meninges, spinal cord, and eyes; 90% of such tumors are large B-cell lymphomas. The prevalence has increased in recent decades but appears to be stabilizing at 3% to 4% of newly diagnosed primary CNS tumors. Severe immunosuppression is a risk factor, and the incidence is significantly increased in patients with congenital immunodeficiency and in patients who have received transplants. In immunocompromised patients, primary central nervous system lymphoma is associated with Epstein-Barr virus infection.

Primary central nervous system lymphoma can occur at any age but peaks at ages 60 to 70 years in immunocompetent patients. Unlike patients with systemic lymphoma, those with primary central nervous system lymphoma present with neurologic deficits or seizures rather than "B" symptoms (fever and chills, drenching night sweats, fatigue,

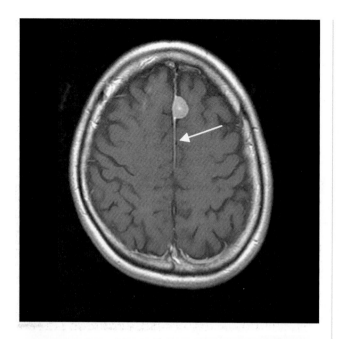

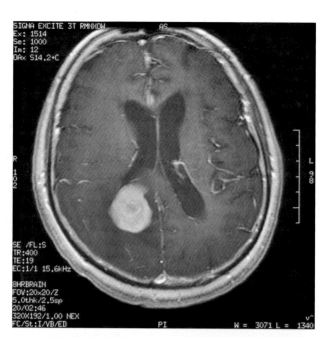

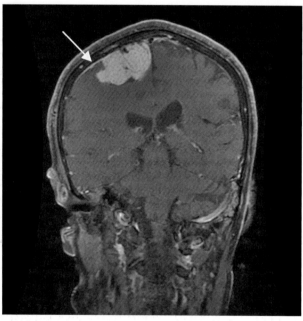

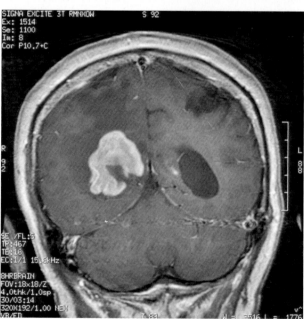

FIGURE 19.
Meningiomas.
Top, axial postcontrast T1-weighted MRI showing a meningioma arising from the falx cerebri. *Bottom*, coronal postcontrast T1-weighted MRI demonstrating a larger parafalcine meningioma with associated edema and mass effect. Note the homogeneous enhancement and "dural tail" (*arrow*) in both images.

FIGURE 20.
Primary central nervous system lymphoma.
Axial (*top*) and coronal (*bottom*) T1-weighted MRI of the head with gadolinium enhancement in a patient with a primary central nervous system lymphoma. Note the homogeneous enhancement and periventricular location.

pruritus, and weight loss). Twenty percent of these patients have ocular involvement and report floaters, blurred vision, or eye pain.

MRI with contrast is the recommended diagnostic imaging study. The classic finding is a single, rounded, contrast-enhancing lesion involving the deep white matter or basal ganglia (**Figure 20**). Meningeal spread is the rule but may be

difficult to detect on imaging studies. It is best assessed by cerebrospinal fluid examination, including cytology and flow cytometry studies that look for a monoclonal B-cell population. When cerebrospinal fluid analysis is nondiagnostic, stereotactic biopsy of the brain lesion is generally required to establish the diagnosis. Ocular involvement may be seen on slit lamp examination, and vitreal biopsy may also be used for diagnosis. Corticosteroid administration may cause primary central nervous system lymphoma to "vanish" temporarily and reduce the yield of tissue diagnosis. Withholding corticosteroids is therefore recommended, when feasible, until after tissue diagnosis. In severely immunosuppressed patients, the differential diagnosis of primary central nervous system lymphoma includes toxoplasmosis and progressive multifocal leukoencephalopathy. Polymerase chain reaction of the cerebrospinal fluid to detect Eptein-Barr virus and JC virus (causing progressive multifocal leukoencephalopathy) and serologic studies for toxoplasmosis may help distinguish between these causes, but tissue diagnosis is still the gold standard.

Because primary central nervous system lymphoma is rare, determining the optimal treatment has been difficult. Surgery is seldom indicated and does not improve survival. Treatment for most patients involves high-dose systemic or intrathecal methotrexate followed by whole-brain radiation therapy. Chemotherapy alone is often recommended for patients over age 60 years because of the excessive neurotoxicity from radiation therapy in this age group. The 5-year survival rate after combined therapy is 25% to 40%. Even with treatment, however, local recurrence or progression is common.

KEY POINTS

- Primary central nervous system lymphoma is diagnosed by detection of a clonal B-cell population in serum or cerebrospinal fluid or by brain biopsy.

- Treatment for most patients with primary central nervous system lymphoma involves high-dose systemic or intrathecal methotrexate followed by whole-brain radiation therapy.

Metastatic Brain Tumors

Metastases to the central nervous system are more common than primary brain tumors and occur in 10% to 30% of all patients with cancer. In adults, the malignant tumors most likely to spread to the brain are lung cancer (50%), breast cancer (10% to 20%), and melanoma (10%).

Signs and symptoms depend on the size and location of the metastases, which can develop in the brain, leptomeninges, and spinal cord. Symptoms may be subtle, so a high level of suspicion is justified in patients with known underlying primary tumors. MRI with contrast is the diagnostic study of choice and typically shows rounded, contrast-enhancing lesions at the gray-white junction with surrounding edema (**Figure 21**). Brain metastases may sometimes be the first manifestation of cancer elsewhere in the body, necessitating workup for the underlying primary malignancy. Tissue diagnosis is required and is generally best obtained from the primary lesion. When the primary lesion cannot be identified or is inaccessible, stereotactic brain biopsy can be considered.

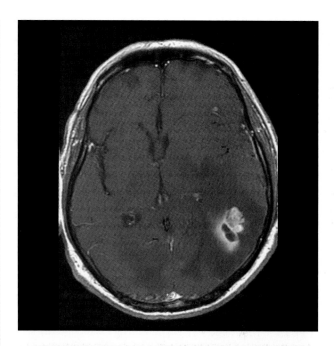

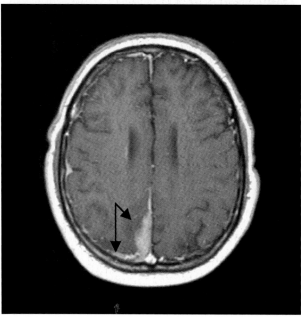

FIGURE 21.
Central nervous system metastases.
Top, axial postcontrast T1-weighted MRI showing a strongly enhancing nodular lesion in the left parietal lobe with marked surrounding edema and mass effect causing a left-to-right shift. *Bottom,* axial postcontrast T1-weighted MRI showing leptomeningeal enhancement from metastasis (*arrows*) that is seen most prominently over the right hemisphere and posteriorly along the falx cerebri.

The prognosis for patients with brain metastases is poor. Treatment focuses on improving quality of life. For patients with a single metastatic lesion and otherwise limited systemic disease, standard treatment is surgical resection followed by whole-brain radiation therapy. Median survival is 10 to 16 months. For patients with multiple metastases, radiation therapy can be administered for palliation. Median survival is 3 to 6 months.

Paraneoplastic Syndromes of the Nervous System

Paraneoplastic syndromes involve signs and symptoms of organ dysfunction in a patient with cancer that are unexplained by the direct effect of the tumor, metastatic disease, or treatment side effects. Although any organ system can be involved, deficits of the central and peripheral nervous systems are most commonly encountered. Paraneoplastic syndromes are rare and affect less than 1% of all cancer patients. Early recognition is important because the neurologic disorder often causes significant, irreversible morbidity. In addition, paraneoplastic symptoms are often the first sign of an underlying malignant tumor, which may still be focal and potentially curable. The most frequently identified primary tumors associated with paraneoplastic syndromes are small cell lung cancer; breast, ovarian, and testicular cancer; Hodgkin lymphoma; and thymoma. Although paraneoplastic syndromes occur at any age, they most often develop in older adults (median age, 65 years).

A paraneoplastic syndrome should be suspected in any patient with an otherwise unexplained, subacute, progressive neurologic disorder. Any part of the neuraxis may be affected, and involvement is often multifocal. Signs and symptoms include sensory or motor neuropathy, muscle weakness, cranial nerve palsies, ataxia, memory loss, psychiatric changes, and seizures. The cause is most likely autoimmune, and the diagnosis is made by detecting antibodies in either serum or cerebrospinal fluid (**Table 29**). Although individual antibodies were once believed to correlate with specific clinical patterns, syndrome overlap is increasingly recognized. Therefore, diagnostic testing should evaluate a broad panel of known antibodies. Once detected, however, an individual antibody may guide further evaluation toward a specific underlying tumor.

Diagnostic studies to identify the underlying tumor include CT or MRI of the chest, abdomen, and pelvis, as well

TABLE 29 Selected Neuronal Paraneoplastic Antibodies

Antibody	Tumor	Associated Syndromes
ANNA-1 (anti-Hu)	SCLC	Encephalomyelitis Cerebellar degeneration Sensory neuropathy Autonomic neuropathy
ANNA-2 (anti-Ri)	SCLC Breast cancer	Ataxia Neuropathy Opsoclonus-myoclonus
MA	SCLC Breast cancer Testicular cancer	Encephalomyelitis Cerebellar degeneration
PCA-1 (anti-Yo)	Breast cancer Ovarian cancer	Cerebellar degeneration
PCA-2	SCLC	Encephalomyelitis Cerebellar degeneration
CRMP-5	SCLC Thymoma	Encephalomyelitis Cerebellar degeneration Neuropathy Chorea
Amphiphysin	SCLC Breast cancer	Encephalomyelitis Neuropathy Stiff-man syndrome
VGCC	SCLC	Lambert-Eaton myasthenic syndrome Encephalomyelitis Cerebellar degeneration Neuropathy
VGKC	SCLC Thymoma	Limbic encephalitis

ANNA = antineuronal nuclear antibody; CRMP = collapsin response mediator protein; MA = monoclonal antibody; PCA = Purkinje cell antibody; SCLC = small cell lung cancer; VGCC = voltage-gated calcium channel; VGKC = voltage-gated potassium channel.

as testicular ultrasonography or mammography when appropriate. If these studies are unrevealing, whole-body [^{18}F] fluorodeoxyglucose positron emission tomography may improve detection of small tumors.

Primary treatment is aimed at the underlying tumor. If the neoplastic process can be cured, the paraneoplastic syndrome will remit. Neurologic deficits may not be reversible, but further progression can possibly be avoided. If the cancer is incurable, immune-modifying therapies (such as plasma exchange or intravenous immune globulin) and immunosuppressive agents (such as corticosteroids) are used. However, these treatments have had only variable success in alleviating neurologic symptoms. (For specific treatment options for Lambert-Eaton myasthenic syndrome, see Neuromuscular Disorders.)

KEY POINTS

- A paraneoplastic syndrome should be suspected in any patient with an otherwise unexplained subacute progressive neurologic disorder.

- The cause of paraneoplastic syndromes is most likely autoimmune, and the diagnosis is made by detecting antibodies in either serum or cerebrospinal fluid.

Bibliography

Buckner JC, Brown PD, O'Neill BP, Meyer FB, Wetmore CJ, Uhm JH. Central nervous system tumors. Mayo Clin Proc. 2007;82(10):1271-1286. [PMID: 17908533]

Darnell RB, Posner JB. Paraneoplastic syndromes involving the nervous system. N Engl J Med. 2003;349(16):1543-1554. [PMID: 14561798]

Ferreri AJ, Reni M. Primary central nervous system lymphoma. Crit Rev Oncol Hematol. 2007;63(3):257-268. [PMID: 17590348]

Hoffman S, Propp JM, McCarthy BJ. Temporal trends in incidence of primary brain tumors in the United States, 1985-1999. Neuro Oncol. 2006;8(1):27-37. [PMID: 16443945]

Epilepsy

Approach to the Patient with a Suspected Seizure

Patients may experience many types of spells, faints, and other episodic attacks that resemble epileptic seizures. The first step in evaluating a patient with a suspected seizure is to rule out other conditions, such as syncope or transient ischemic attack, by taking a careful history, performing a physical examination, and obtaining appropriate diagnostic testing. If the event is in fact determined to have been a seizure, the next step is to distinguish between an acute symptomatic seizure and one that was unprovoked. Acute symptomatic seizures are directly attributable to an acute insult to the central nervous system or to a systemic metabolic derangement (**Table 30**). Appropriate treatment of acute symptomatic seizures involves correcting the underlying cause, rather than initiating an antiepileptic medication. Epilepsy, on the other hand, is a condition of repeated unprovoked seizures and is diagnosed only when two or more such seizures have occurred.

KEY POINT

- Appropriate treatment of acute symptomatic seizures is correction of the underlying cause, rather than initiation of antiepileptic medication.

Epidemiology, Pathophysiology, and Classification of Seizures

Approximately 10% of the population worldwide will experience a single seizure in their lifetime. Epilepsy affects 3 million people in the United States, with a lifetime cumulative incidence of 3%. Although seizures can occur in patients of any age, the most common times are during childhood and after age 60 years, with the greatest incidence in the latter group. In 60% to 70% of patients with epilepsy, no cause of the seizures is identified. Elderly patients are more likely to have an identified remote symptomatic etiology, with one third of epilepsy cases in this age group attributed to cerebrovascular disease.

Seizures represent abnormal bursts of synchronous electrical activity arising from cortical neurons. These abnormal bursts can result from excess excitatory neuronal activity, failure of inhibitory pathways, or changes in ion channels that control neuronal membrane potential. The clinical manifestations vary depending on the cortical area involved and can include motor, sensory, psychic, and autonomic phenomena and changes in the level of consciousness. Seizures are divided

TABLE 30 Common Causes of Acute Symptomatic Seizures

Head trauma (immediate—seizure occurs at impact)
Intoxication
Prescription drugs
Alcohol
Illicit drugs (cocaine, amphetamines)
Drug withdrawal
Alcohol
Benzodiazepines, barbiturates
Metabolic
Hypo- or hyperglycemia
Hyponatremia
Hypocalcemia
Cardiovascular
Acute stroke
Acute intracerebral hemorrhage
Infectious

into two types—partial and generalized—on the basis of the region of the cortex involved in seizure initiation.

Generalized seizures involve both hemispheres diffusely from the onset. The most familiar form of generalized seizure is the generalized tonic-clonic or grand-mal seizure. The initial tonic phase manifests as a sustained muscular contraction that results in stiffening of the jaw, trunk, and limbs. Tonic contraction of the diaphragm may result in a characteristic vocal cry and in cyanosis. The clonic phase follows, with symmetric rhythmic jerking of the extremities. There can be urinary and occasionally bowel incontinence. The seizure typically stops spontaneously in 1 to 2 minutes and may be followed by a period of lethargy, confusion, or agitation lasting minutes to hours. Prolonged postictal confusion must be differentiated from ongoing subtle seizure activity. Other types of generalized seizures include absence, myoclonic, and atonic seizures. Absence seizures are typified by staring and unresponsiveness lasting several seconds. Myoclonic seizures are sudden, brief, shock-like muscle contractions, which may be focal, multifocal, or generalized in distribution. Atonic seizures consist of a sudden loss of muscle tone that causes a drop to the ground and carries a high risk of injury. With the exception of myoclonus, generalized seizures are all characterized by loss of consciousness.

In contrast, partial seizures arise in a focal area of the cortex. The manifestation of a partial seizure depends on the area of cortical involvement. The larger the area involved, the greater the likelihood of impaired consciousness. Partial seizures with fully maintained consciousness are subclassified as simple partial, and those with altered awareness are called complex partial. Partial seizures may spread to involve the cortex diffusely, a state referred to as secondary generalization.

The temporal lobe is the most common site of origin for partial seizures. Simple partial seizures in this area may manifest as an "indescribable feeling," a rising epigastric sensation, an unpleasant olfactory or gustatory sensation, a psychic phenomenon (such as déjà vu), or autonomic disturbances (such as flushing, diaphoresis, or lightheadedness). Some patients may report auditory distortion or vertigo. These symptoms typically last less than 1 minute and are often referred to as an aura. Complex partial seizures arising in the temporal lobe classically manifest with behavioral and speech arrest lasting less than 2 minutes. Automatisms (nonpurposeful stereotyped motor behaviors) are often exhibited and may include repetitive lip smacking, chewing, swallowing, or fumbling or picking behaviors with the ipsilateral hand. A period of postictal confusion lasting minutes to hours is common.

In contrast, frontal lobe seizures tend to be brief, nocturnal events that are less likely to be followed by postictal confusion. Seizures arising in frontal lobe structures outside the motor cortex can present with bizarre motor phenomena, including violent thrashing, bicycling movements, or clapping. Patients may experience intense fear or other emotions

and significant autonomic changes. Such unusual motor activity and emotional features commonly lead to frontal lobe seizures being misdiagnosed as psychogenic events. Frontal lobe seizures may tend to cluster or to generalize secondarily. Simple partial seizures arising in the primary motor cortex will present as localized tonic or clonic activity in the contralateral body. Seizure activity can spread to adjacent regions of the motor strip, a phenomenon called jacksonian march. The most common clinical manifestation of a jacksonian seizure is twitching of the thumb, which then spreads up the arm and into the ipsilateral face. Transient weakness of the involved limbs after the seizure has ended is common and is referred to as Todd paralysis, which usually lasts minutes but can persist for hours. When weakness is prolonged, it is important to rule out continued subtle seizure activity or, if it occurs after a first seizure, an underlying structural lesion or stroke.

Parietal and occipital lobe seizures are rare. Parietal seizures usually involve sensory phenomena, such as electric sensations, pain, or a feeling of pins and needles. Like seizures arising in the motor strip, jacksonian spread can be described by patients who experience it. Poorly formed visual hallucinations consisting of vague shapes and shadows may also be reported. Occipital lobe seizures usually manifest as unformed visual phenomena, such as flashes of light or loss of vision.

KEY POINTS

- The incidence of epilepsy is greatest in patients older than 60 years.
- Generalized seizures are those that involve both hemispheres diffusely from the onset, whereas partial seizures arise in a focal area of the cortex.
- Partial seizures with maintained consciousness are subclassified as simple partial, whereas those with altered awareness are called complex partial.

Epilepsy Syndromes and Their Diagnosis

Epilepsy is defined as a predilection for recurrent, unprovoked seizures and is typically diagnosed when two such seizures have occurred. Epilepsy is not a single disease but, rather, a group of disorders that share seizures as one manifestation. Epilepsy syndromes are defined by type of seizure, associated neurologic or systemic symptoms, age of onset, findings on an electroencephalogram (EEG), and family/genetic history. Appropriate identification of the epilepsy syndrome can be helpful in determining prognosis and appropriate treatment.

Classification of Epilepsy Syndromes

In the International League Against Epilepsy (ILAE) system, epilepsy syndromes are divided according to cause. Epilepsy attributable to a known brain abnormality is called symptomatic, whereas the term cryptogenic is used when an underlying brain disorder is suspected but unidentified. Epilepsies unrelated to a structural lesion or disorder are classified as idiopathic and are generally presumed to have a genetic cause. Like single seizures, epilepsy syndromes are also classified as generalized and partial. Generalized epilepsies typically manifest in childhood or adolescence, whereas new-onset epilepsy in adults (of all ages) is almost always partial.

Commonly Encountered Epilepsy Syndromes

Juvenile Myoclonic Epilepsy

Juvenile myoclonic epilepsy is an idiopathic generalized epilepsy syndrome characterized by both myoclonic seizures on awakening and generalized tonic-clonic seizures. These seizure types occur independently, but a flurry of myoclonic seizures may presage a generalized tonic-clonic seizure. Onset is usually in adolescence. Seizures may be provoked by sleep deprivation, alcohol, or flickering lights. The EEG demonstrates generalized spike and wave discharges of 4 to 6 Hz. Most patients with juvenile myoclonic epilepsy have an excellent response to medication, with lamotrigine and valproic acid considered first-line treatments. Although juvenile myoclonic epilepsy can usually be successfully controlled with treatment, the susceptibility to seizure persists over the patient's lifetime, and 75% to 100% of patients will relapse if medication is withdrawn. Juvenile myoclonic epilepsy is thought to be a multigene disorder, with familial studies demonstrating a strong but complex inheritance pattern.

Lennox-Gastaut Syndrome

Lennox-Gastaut syndrome is characterized by mental retardation and intractable seizures. Onset is usually by age 5, and the disorder is lifelong. A unique finding is the presence of multiple seizure types in the same patient, including atonic, atypical absence, myoclonic, and generalized tonic-clonic seizures. Status epilepticus (discussed later) is common. The EEG shows a characteristic pattern of generalized slow spike and wave discharges superimposed on a slow background. In about 60% of patients with the disorder, Lennox-Gastaut syndrome is attributable to a known symptomatic cause, such as tuberous sclerosis, meningoencephalitis, or hypoxic-ischemic injury.

Intractable Epilepsy

Medically refractory, or intractable, epilepsy is a clinically useful categorization, although not formally part of the ILAE classification system. Approximately 30% to 40% of patients with epilepsy do not respond to treatment with currently available anticonvulsant drugs. There is no single accepted criterion by which refractory epilepsy is defined. However, failure to attain seizure control despite adequate trials of two appropriate antiepileptic drugs is a commonly used indicator of intractability. Patients whose seizures persist despite such treatment have a less than 10% likelihood of achieving seizure freedom with subsequent medication trials. The consequences of uncontrolled seizures include increased mortality, greater adverse medication effects, cognitive decline, and impairment

of psychosocial functioning, including mood, interpersonal relationships, and employment. It is important, therefore, to recognize patients with intractable epilepsy early in their disease course. Referral to a comprehensive epilepsy care center to explore nonmedical management is appropriate.

KEY POINTS

- Patients with juvenile myoclonic epilepsy require life-long antiepileptic drug therapy.
- Approximately 30% to 40% of patients with epilepsy do not respond to treatment with currently available anticonvulsant drugs.
- Failure to attain seizure control in patients despite adequate trials of two appropriate antiepileptic drugs has been shown to correlate with a less than 10% likelihood of achieving seizure freedom with subsequent medication trials in those patients.

Risk Factors

Risk factors for the development of epilepsy include meningoencephalitis, childhood febrile convulsions, a history of head trauma, and a family history of epilepsy. Among diagnosed cases of epilepsy, 70% have no identifiable cause. For the 30% with a known etiology, leading causes are cerebrovascular disease, developmental brain disorders, remote head trauma, brain tumor, and neurodegenerative conditions. For patients with epilepsy, commonly cited seizure triggers include sleep deprivation, alcohol, flickering lights, and menstruation. Many prescription medications, including quinolone antibiotics, antipsychotic agents, and antidepressants, may also lower seizure threshold. When these medications are necessary, adjustment in antiepileptic therapy may be needed to maintain seizure control.

KEY POINTS

- Risk factors for the development of epilepsy include meningoencephalitis, childhood febrile convulsions, a history of head trauma, and a family history of epilepsy.
- Among diagnosed cases of epilepsy, 70% have no identifiable cause.

Differential Diagnosis and Diagnostic Evaluation

Diagnosis of seizures and epilepsy requires obtaining a detailed and accurate history. Because patients who have experienced a seizure are often unaware of what occurred, obtaining an eyewitness account is invaluable.

Many physiologic events can mimic seizures and should be part of the differential diagnosis. In adults, cardiac syncope, arrhythmia, transient ischemic attack, migraine, metabolic derangements, intoxication, and vertigo are among the common conditions that can present similarly to seizures (**Table 31**). Psychiatric conditions must also be considered. Psychogenic nonepileptic spells are seizure-like events that occur in patients with a conversion or somatoform disorder. Such spells occur with an estimated prevalence of 1.5 per 100,000 persons and are commonly misdiagnosed as epilepsy. Because psychogenic spells can also occur in 10% to 20% of patients with epilepsy, care must be taken in patients with suspected psychogenic spells to definitively exclude the diagnosis of epilepsy. Panic attacks should also be considered in the differential diagnosis of seizure. Carefully detailed questions about the episodes and about risk factors for epilepsy, including minor or major head trauma and concomitant medications, must be asked.

Further diagnostic testing is often needed to confirm or clarify the cause of a seizure-like episode. Depending on the history, evaluation of metabolic derangements, cardiac disease, cerebrovascular disorders, or vestibular dysfunction may be appropriate. A general laboratory survey should include a complete blood count, measurement of serum electrolyte and plasma glucose levels, and a toxicology screen, if appropriate. A lumbar puncture is generally only indicated if there are signs or symptoms suggesting an underlying infection of the central nervous system or if the patient is immunocompromised. Electroencephalography and neuroimaging should be standard components of the diagnostic work-up of patients suspected to have epilepsy.

Electroencephalography

EEGs are useful both to diagnose seizure and to classify the seizure type (partial or generalized). A routine EEG is a scalp recording of electric potentials from the brain for a period of 20 to 60 minutes. Although seizures are rarely recorded in this fashion, a routine EEG may show interictal epileptiform discharges, a finding highly correlated with a tendency for clinical seizures. In general, such discharges are found in the first EEG in only 25% to 50% of patients with epilepsy. Moreover, the sensitivity of EEGs for showing interictal epileptiform discharges may vary considerably, depending on seizure frequency, epilepsy syndrome, and site of seizure onset; sensitivity can be increased by obtaining the EEG during sleep, hyperventilation, or photic stimulation and by obtaining serial studies. When present on an EEG, interictal epileptiform discharges are highly specific and suggest a seizure diagnosis; however, it is important to interpret the EEG findings relative to the overall clinical scenario. Detection of interictal epileptiform discharges from frontal lobe structures is relatively low. Moreover, normal findings on an EEG do not rule out a diagnosis of seizure. When a routine EEG is unrevealing and seizures remain a diagnostic concern, prolonged recording with an ambulatory EEG recording device or with inpatient continuous video and EEG monitoring can be considered. These longer studies have a greater chance of detecting interictal epileptiform discharges and of allowing the recording of a seizure, which is the gold standard for diagnosis.

KEY POINT

- Normal findings on an electroencephalogram do not rule out a diagnosis of epilepsy, especially because interictal epileptiform discharges are found on the first electroencephalogram in only 25% to 50% of patients with epilepsy.

TABLE 31 Characteristics That Distinguish Between Common Mimics of Seizure in Adults

Characteristic	Seizure	Syncope	TIA	Migraine	Vertigo
Warning/aura	Variable (<1 minute)	Faint feeling	None	Variable (15-60 minutes)	None
Duration	1-2 minutes	Seconds to minutes	Minutes to hours	Hours	Minutes to days
Effect of posture	None	Variable	None	None	Variable
Symptoms during episode	Tonic-clonic movement, paresthesias, aphasia	Loss of tone, brief clonic jerks	Hemiparesis, hemisensory loss, visual loss, aphasia	Simple visual disturbance, vertigo, paresthesias	Nausea, ataxia, tinnitus
Altered consciousness	Common	Yes	Rare	Rare	No
Incontinence	Variable	Variable	No	No	No
Heart rate	Increased	Irregular/ decreased	Variable	No effect	Variable
Symptoms after episode	Confusion, fatigue	Alert	Alert	Fatigue	Alert
EEG during event	Epileptiform pattern	Diffuse slowing	Focal slowing	Rare slowing	No effect

EEG = electroencephalogram; TIA = transient ischemic attack.

Imaging Studies

For patients presenting with acute seizure, head imaging is important to rule out an underlying symptomatic cause, such as stroke, intracerebral hemorrhage, or malignancy, which may itself require emergency intervention. MRI is superior to CT for detection of epileptogenic lesions with the exception of acute blood products, such as those associated with subarachnoid hemorrhage or hemorrhagic stroke. All patients with a seizure should have a brain MRI, unless there is convincing evidence from the history and EEG of a primary generalized seizure disorder or if there is an unrelated contraindication to MRI (such as a pacemaker or aneurysm clip). Commonly identified structural lesions on MRIs that can cause epilepsy include mesial temporal sclerosis (**Figure 22**), vascular malformations (**Figure 23**), tumors, and malformations of cortical development (**Figure 24**), most of which are poorly visualized or not detectable with a CT scan. Studies suggest that, depending on the lesion type, these lesions will be missed 20% to 100% of the time on a CT scan. Functional imaging tests, such as single photon emission CT, positron emission tomography, and functional MRI, are used during evaluation of patients for epilepsy surgery.

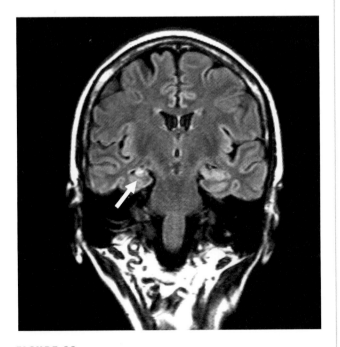

FIGURE 22.
Mesial temporal sclerosis.
Coronal flair MRI shows increased signal intensity and atrophy of the right mesial temporal lobe (*arrow*).

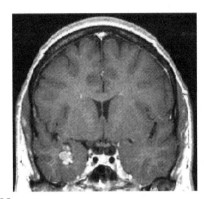

FIGURE 23.
Cavernous malformation.
Coronal T1-weighted MRI shows an intra-axial mass (cavernous hemangioma) in the right temporal lobe with a surrounding hemosiderin ring.

Treatment of Epilepsy

The decision to initiate antiepileptic drug therapy is based on a careful consideration of the risk of seizure recurrence and the risk-benefit ratio of the available treatment options. In addition to the potential morbidity or mortality that might result from future seizures, the adverse psychosocial consequences, such a loss of driving privileges, must also be considered. The goals of seizure treatment are to prevent future seizures and related injury and to maintain quality of life. In most patients, treatment involves long-term therapy with medication. Patients should be counseled to avoid potential seizure triggers, such as sleep deprivation and excess alcohol intake. Physicians should recall that epilepsy is a highly stigmatized condition, which often affects patients' willingness to accept the diagnosis and colors decisions regarding management. Maintaining quality of life means not only keeping patients free of seizures and adverse medication side effects, but also maintaining employment and driving. Driver's license privileges are restricted in every state in the United States for persons who have experienced a seizure. Specific restrictions vary by state, with typical requirements of a seizure-free period of 3 to 12 months in order to operate a private motor vehicle. Driving restrictions generally do not distinguish between persons with a single seizure and those with epilepsy or between the presence and absence of treatment with an anticonvulsant medication.

It is important to address and treat associated psychiatric comorbidity. Depression affects a disproportionate number of patients with epilepsy. Antidepressants are generally well tolerated, although the potential for lowered seizure threshold with these medications may necessitate closer seizure monitoring or adjustment of anticonvulsant therapy. Unless other options are not available, buproprion should be avoided in patients with epilepsy due to adverse effects on seizure control.

Antiepileptic Pharmacotherapy

Epilepsy is controlled with the first or second medication in 60% of patients with the disorder. Older, first-generation

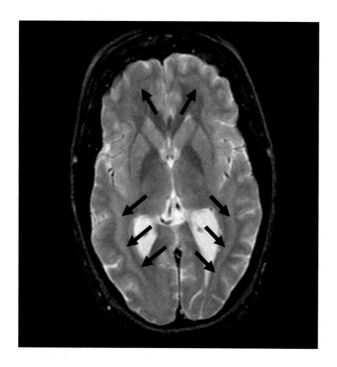

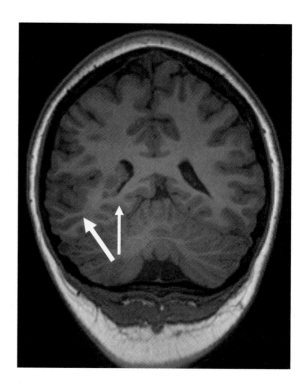

FIGURE 24.
Cortical dysplasia.
Left, subcortical band heterotopia. Axial MRI shows a widespread cortical malformation with simplification of the normal pattern of folding of the cortex and an underlying band of neuronal tissue (*arrows*), sometimes referred to as a double cortex. *Right,* focal cortical dysplasia with periventricular nodular heterotopia. Coronal MRI showing a focal area of thickened cortex in the right temporal region (*thick arrow*) and nodules of abnormal neuronal tissue along the ventricular surface (*thin arrow*).

antiepileptic drugs include phenobarbital, phenytoin, carbamazepine, valproic acid, and ethosuximide. (Ethosuximide is generally used only for treatment of childhood absence epilepsy and is rarely prescribed for adults.) Many newer drugs have become available in the last 15 years, which has expanded the therapeutic options. Second-generation agents include felbamate, gabapentin, lamotrigine, tiagabine, topiramate, levetiracetam, zonisamide, oxcarbazepine, and pregabalin.

When To Initiate Pharmacotherapy

The decision to initiate treatment of epilepsy after a single unprovoked seizure is based on an assessment of recurrence risk. In general, a greater risk of recurrence is predicted by a partial seizure, Todd paralysis, family history of epilepsy, age greater than 65 years, and abnormal findings on neurologic examination. Patients with abnormal results on EEG or head MRI are also at high risk for recurrent seizure and should be placed on an antiepileptic drug. In patients whose EEGs and MRIs are normal, the 2-year recurrence risk after a first seizure has been shown to be approximately 40%; unless special circumstances exist, medication is generally not started for these patients. For patients who have had two or more seizures, the risk of future recurrence is 60% or greater; antiepileptic medication should be started in these patients, unless the seizures were widely spaced in time (years apart) or were nondisabling, simple sensory events.

Discontinuation of Pharmacotherapy

As a general rule, patients who have been free of seizures for 2 years should be considered for medication withdrawal. For adult patients, the reported rate of relapse after stopping medication is 25% to 60% over 2 years. It is therefore necessary to consider the risks and benefits of medication discontinuation for each individual patient. Stopping medication can alleviate both acute and long-term drug side effects and the inconvenience and financial burden of chronic medication. In addition, most patients report improved quality of life when antiepileptic drugs are stopped. Potential risks associated with drug withdrawal include the negative effects of recurrent seizure on quality of life (working, driving) and the small potential risk of a seizure-related injury or status epilepticus.

Relapse risk is higher in the presence of an underlying structural abnormality, mental retardation, or abnormal neurologic examination findings. Seizure recurrence is also greater in those with a poor initial response to treatment. Knowledge of the epilepsy syndrome can be useful in guiding decisions about stopping medication. For example, patients with juvenile myoclonic epilepsy require lifelong medication, but those with certain benign epilepsy syndromes, such as benign rolandic epilepsy, should almost never be treated long term. If a decision is reached to discontinue seizure therapy, the medications should be slowly tapered, as rapid withdrawal has been linked to a greater likelihood of seizure recurrence.

Single-Agent Pharmacotherapy

Newly diagnosed epilepsy should be treated with single-agent pharmacotherapy. Monotherapy is better tolerated, is less expensive, and results in improved patient compliance compared with polytherapy. Furthermore, there is no compelling evidence that polytherapy results in improved seizure control. The chosen drug should be titrated upward until the patient is free of seizures or until limiting side effects develop. If seizures persist, a second drug should be tried as a monotherapy regimen. When the medication is changed, it is generally safer to slowly titrate up the new agent and slowly withdraw the first as the second reaches therapeutic levels rather than attempting an abrupt changeover. If seizures continue on the second agent, a third drug can be tried as a single agent or added for a two-drug regimen.

Dosing and Monitoring of Serum Levels of Antiepileptic Medications

Antiepileptic drugs are better tolerated when started at a low dose and slowly titrated upward. Monitoring of serum drug levels can be helpful when initiating treatment to confirm a therapeutic level or if symptoms suggesting medication toxicity are reported. In some cases, measuring serum concentrations may be helpful to establish an effective therapeutic baseline for an individual patient. Serum testing can also be used to confirm medication adherence. Additionally, when a new medication that may interact with an established antiepileptic drug is added to a patient's regimen, measurement of the serum level of the antiepileptic drug can guide any necessary dose adjustment. For highly protein-bound drugs, such as phenytoin, measurement of both total and free plasma concentrations is recommended if there is concern about low serum protein levels or if the patient is taking another highly protein-bound medication. Although most of the first-generation antiepileptic drugs have well-established therapeutic serum ranges, these ranges should not be interpreted as a strict dosing guideline. Rather, dose adjustments should be based on clinical seizure control and drug side effects. Regarding second-generation drugs, although their serum levels can also be measured, most are not highly protein bound and so do not have well-defined therapeutic serum concentrations. Thus, checking serum drug levels for the newer agents is often less helpful in guiding clinical management.

Common Side Effects

Commonly reported side effects for individual antiepileptic drugs are summarized in **Table 32**. The potential to cause sedation, unsteadiness, and imbalance is common to all antiepileptic drugs. These symptoms often develop with initiation of a new drug or with increased dosages and have the potential to improve with time.

Severe idiosyncratic reactions are relatively rare but can be potentially life-threatening. Drug rash, including Stevens-Johnson syndrome, has been linked with phenytoin, phenobarbital, carbamazepine, oxcarbazepine, tiagabine, zonisamide, and lamotrigine. Valproic acid has been associated with rare cases of acute hepatic failure and pancreatitis, particularly in children. Felbamate carries a 1 in 5000 risk of aplastic anemia and a 1 in 30,000 risk of hepatic failure. Because of this risk of a life-threatening idiosyncratic reaction, use of felbamate is limited to patients with seizures that are refractory to other treatments and that are of sufficient severity to justify the risk of a serious side effect. Liver chemistry test results and complete blood counts must be closely monitored.

Chronic use of first-generation antiepileptic drugs has been associated with increased risk of osteoporosis and vitamin D deficiency. The risk of bone disease with long-term use of newer antiepileptic drugs has not been established. Periodic bone density analysis should be considered for patients on chronic seizure therapy. Prophylactic calcium (1500 mg/d) and vitamin D supplementation (800 U/d) are

Drug	Side Effects
TABLE 32 Common Side Effects of Current Antiepileptic Drugs	
Carbamazepine	Rash, hepatic dysfunction, hyponatremia, bone disease
Felbamate	Hepatic failure, aplastic anemia, weight loss, nausea, headache
Gabapentin	Somnolence, lower extremity edema, weight gain
Lamotrigine	Rash
Levetiracetam	Irritability, depression
Oxcarbazepine	Rash, nausea, hyponatremia
Phenobarbital	Sedation, cognitive/mood disturbance, bone disease, hepatic dysfunction
Phenytoin	Rash, ataxia, hepatic dysfunction, bone disease, gingival hyperplasia, anemia
Pregabalin	Weight gain, lower extremity edema
Topiramate	Cognitive effects, nephrolithiasis, acute angle closure glaucoma, anorexia, metabolic acidosis
Tiagabine	Cognitive effects, tremor, nausea
Valproic acid	Weight gain, tremor, hair loss, hepatic dysfunction, thrombocytopenia, hyperammonemia, menstrual irregularity, bone disease
Zonisamide	Sedation, anorexia, nephrolithiasis, rash, visual field defect

also often recommended, although they are not of proven benefit in this population.

The potential for drug interaction should be considered both when choosing a new antiepileptic drug and when starting any new medication in patients requiring chronic seizure therapy. Drug interactions can lead to increased toxicity or to decreased antiepileptic drug efficacy with breakthrough seizures. One of the most common sources of pharmacodynamic drug interaction is alteration of hepatic metabolism. Phenobarbital, phenytoin, carbamazepine, and oxcarbamazepine all induce hepatic cytochrome P450 enzymes, and valproic acid inhibits them. When avoidance of altered hepatic metabolism, whether due to drug interaction or underlying liver disease, is desired, gabapentin, pregabalin, and levetiracetam should be considered.

Treatment During Pregnancy

The rate of major congenital malformations in newborns exposed to antiepileptic drugs during the first trimester of pregnancy is 4% to 6%, which is twice the rate reported for the general population. The greatest risk from antiepileptic drug exposure is likely during the first several weeks of gestation when major organogenesis occurs, typically before a woman even realizes she is pregnant. Current evidence suggests that valproic acid carries the highest risk of malformation and that polytherapy is worse than monotherapy. Current outcome data from pregnancy registries, however, are only available in sufficiently high numbers for older antiepileptic drugs and lamotrigine. There is insufficient evidence to establish the risks related to other second-generation antiepileptic drugs at this time. Potential harm related to antiepileptic drug use during pregnancy must be weighed against the risk posed by a seizure to both the mother and the fetus.

Ideally, pregnancy in women with epilepsy will be planned so there is time for medication adjustment before conception. Withdrawal of antiepileptic drugs should be attempted, when possible, according to the same general guideline for discontinuation of medication already discussed. Most women with epilepsy, however, will require antiepileptic drug treatment throughout pregnancy. For these patients, the aim is to use the smallest number of medications and the lowest dose that will maintain seizure control. Monotherapy is ideal. Reduction of medications after conception is unlikely to be effective in lowering malformation risk and can place the mother at increased risk for seizure.

Because many pregnancies are unplanned, all women on antiepileptic drug therapy should receive counseling about the risk of birth defects and be advised to take a daily folic acid supplement; dosage recommendations range from 0.4 to 5.0 mg per day. When pregnancy is not desired, it is essential to ensure that women taking antiepileptic drugs have an adequate birth control plan. Antiepileptic drugs that induce cytochrome P450 enzymes (phenobarbital, phenytoin, carbamazepine, oxcarbazepine, and high-dose topiramate) can interfere with the effectiveness of hormonal contraceptive agents.

KEY POINTS

- After a single unprovoked seizure, a greater risk of recurrence is predicted by a partial seizure, Todd paralysis, a family history of epilepsy, age greater than 65 years, and abnormal findings on neurologic examination.
- For adult patients, the reported rate of relapse after stopping antiepileptic medication is 25% to 60% over 2 years.
- Monotherapy antiepileptic drug regimens are preferred over polytherapy regimens.
- Chronic use of older antiepileptic drugs has been associated with an increased risk of osteoporosis.
- Exposure to antiepileptic drugs during pregnancy results in a 4% to 6% risk of major congenital malformation in newborns, which is twice the rate seen in the general population.

Selection of an Antiepileptic Medication

Knowledge of the type of seizure (partial or generalized) and seizure syndrome a patient has experienced will inform not only the decision to begin treatment, but also the choice of an appropriate drug (**Table 33**). Valproic acid and lamotrigine are often used as first-line drugs for generalized epilepsy, whereas carbamazepine and lamotrigine are good initial choices for partial epilepsy. For some patients, the side effect profile of a particular drug may be the major reason for choosing it, besides its likely effectiveness. Additional considerations include the timing of titration to an effective dose, ease of the dosing regimen, and cost. Because no single perfect drug exists, antiepileptic drug selection must rely on careful consideration of what is best for the individual patient.

Efficacy

Individual drugs vary in efficacy for given seizure types (see Table 33). In general, there is no evidence of greater efficacy for newer versus older antiepileptic drugs. Nevertheless, 30% of patients with epilepsy are refractory to current medical therapies. Before deciding that a patient will not respond to epilepsy medications, however, one should determine that the diagnosis of epilepsy is correct, that the medication(s) given was (were) appropriate for the seizure type, that the medication dosage was correct, and that the patient was adherent with taking the medication.

Tolerability

Epilepsy drugs are just as likely to be ineffective in particular patients because of adverse effects as from lack of efficacy. Approximately 5% of patients will discontinue the first antiepileptic drug prescribed because of a serious idiosyncratic reaction. Another 15% will discontinue because of non–life-threatening adverse effects, such as sedation, mood disorder, or weight gain.

TABLE 33 Spectrum of Action of Current Antiepileptic Drugs

| Drug | Type of Seizure | | | |
	Partial	Tonic-Clonic (First Generation)	Myoclonic	Absence
Carbamazepine	X	X	—	—
Ethosuximide	—	—	—	X
Felbamate	X	X	?	?
Gabapentin	X	—	—	—
Lamotrigine	X	X	X	X
Levetiracetam	X	X	X	—
Oxcarbazepine	X	?	—	—
Phenobarbital	X	X	?	—
Phenytoin	X	X	—	—
Pregabalin	X	—	—	—
Topiramate	X	X	X	X
Tiagabine	X	—	—	—
Valproic acid	X	X	X	X
Zonisamide	X	?	?	?

X = proved efficacy; — = no proved efficacy; ? = probable efficacy.

Nonpharmacologic Therapy

Epilepsy Surgery

Epilepsy surgery is a therapeutic option for patients with partial epilepsy who continue to have disabling, medically refractory seizures. Seizures must be severe and frequent enough to adversely affect quality of life before surgery is considered. Major medical comorbidity and progressive degenerative neurologic conditions are generally contraindications to surgical intervention. Patients who have undergone two medication trials without success are appropriately referred to a specialized epilepsy center for surgical evaluation.

The goal of epilepsy surgery is to remove the area of cortex from which seizures are generated. Potentially curative procedures include lesionectomy, focal cortical resection, and lobectomy. When resective surgery is not a reasonable option because of the involvement of the eloquent cortex (the primary language, motor, sensory, or visual cortex), the extent of involved tissues, or the underlying epilepsy syndrome, palliative surgical procedures, such as multiple subpial transection, hemispherectomy, corpus callosotomy, or placement of a vagus nerve stimulator, may be options.

Vagus Nerve Stimulator

Vagus nerve stimulation is a reasonable treatment option for medically refractory seizures in patients who are not candidates for traditional epilepsy surgery. The stimulator is an electronic signal generator implanted in the upper chest, just as a cardiac pacemaker is, that provides programmed pulsed electrical stimulation to the vagus nerve in the neck. Although the mechanism by which vagus nerve stimulation alters seizure activity is unclear, approximately half of the patients who receive this treatment report a 50% reduction in seizure frequency within 1 year of implantation. In addition to the programmed stimulation, patients are given a magnet that can be used to trigger on-demand stimulation, which may have some effect in aborting or limiting a seizure if used at onset. A benefit of vagus nerve stimulation over adding another antiepileptic drug is the avoidance of sedation or cognitive side effects. The device is generally well tolerated but can result in hoarseness, throat pain, cough, and shortness of breath. The implantation procedure is typically performed under general anesthesia and has a low complication rate. The presence of a vagus nerve stimulator is a contraindication to subsequent MRI, with the exception of head MRI under special circumstances. Therefore, such a device should not be used without careful consideration in patients with underlying malignancy or other conditions that may require serial MRI scans.

KEY POINTS

- Patients with disabling partial seizures that have not responded to treatment with two anticonvulsant drugs should be considered for epilepsy surgery.

- Vagus nerve stimulation is a reasonable treatment option for medically refractory seizures in patients who are not candidates for traditional epilepsy surgery.

Status Epilepticus

Status epilepticus is a neurologic emergency that has significant associated morbidity and mortality. Status epilepticus has been defined as occurring when a seizure persists or recurs without recovery for 30 minutes. Operationally, however, treatment efforts should begin when a seizure continues after 5 minutes. Although any seizure type can potentially exist as status epilepticus, generalized convulsive status epilepticus is the most common and potentially dangerous form. The incidence of generalized convulsive status epilepticus in the United States is 20 to 40 per 100,000 persons per year. More than half of patients who present with status epilepticus have no seizure history. In adults, the most common underlying causes are subtherapeutic levels of antiepileptic drugs, cerebrovascular disease, hypoxic injury, alcohol or drug intoxication, and metabolic derangements. The overall mortality rate is approximately 20%. Potential long-term complications include future seizures, cognitive impairment, aphasia, and motor deficits.

Early recognition and treatment of status epilepticus are key to the best possible outcome. Therefore, internists should be familiar with the presentation and management of the disorder. Persistent seizure activity results in acute systemic complications, including fever, hemodynamic instability, acidosis, rhabdomyolysis, and pulmonary edema, all of which must be carefully managed. Airway, breathing, and circulatory status should be assessed at presentation and monitored continuously. Many patients will require intubation and ventilatory support. Initial laboratory studies should include a complete blood count, measurement of serum electrolyte (including sodium) and plasma glucose levels, toxicology screen, and measurement of serum antiepileptic drug levels, when appropriate. Thiamine and glucose can be administered if alcohol abuse is suspected or the cause of the status epilepticus is unknown. Emergent head imaging can also be useful in the absence of a known underlying cause but should not delay treatment. Convulsive motor activity will become increasingly subtle over time and might, for example, only involve twitching of the eyes or face, which makes it challenging to distinguish between ongoing nonconvulsive status epilepticus and a postictal state. For this reason, continuous EEG monitoring is strongly advocated.

Medications for status epilepticus are outlined in **Table 34**. Benzodiazepines are generally considered first-line agents, to be followed by phenytoin or phenobarbital.

Approximately 30% of patients with status epilepticus do not respond to these interventions, a condition defined as refractory status epilepticus. These patients are generally placed in a medication-induced coma and must be monitored with EEG to guide dosing and assess response to therapy.

KEY POINTS

- Treatment of status epilepticus should commence after 5 minutes of continuous seizure activity because of an overall mortality rate of approximately 20% and neurologic sequelae, including future seizures, cognitive impairment, aphasia, and motor deficits.

- Benzodiazepines are the first-line treatment for status epilepticus.

- In patients who are unresponsive or somnolent after status epilepticus, continuous EEG monitoring is strongly advocated to distinguish between ongoing nonconvulsive status epilepticus and postictal states.

Bibliography

Annegers JF, Shirts SB, Hauser WA, Kurland LT. Risk of recurrence after an initial unprovoked seizure. Epilepsia. 1986;27(1):43-50. [PMID: 3081336]

Callaghan N, Garret A, Goggin T. Withdrawal of anticonvulsant drugs in patients free of seizures for two years. N Engl J Med. 1988;318(15):942-946. [PMID: 3127710]

Cunnington M, Tennis P; International Lamotrigine Pregnancy Registry Scientific Advisory Committee. Lamotrigine and the risk of malformations in pregnancy. Neurology. 2005;64(6):955-960. [PMID: 15781807]

Kim LG, Johnson TL, Marson AG, Chadwick DW; MRC MESS Study Group. Prediction of risk of seizure recurrence after a single seizure and early epilepsy: further results from the MESS trial. Lancet Neurol. 2006;5(4):317-322. [PMID: 16545748]

Kwan P, Brodie MJ. Early identification of refractory epilepsy. N Engl J Med. 2000;342(5):314-319. [PMID: 10660394]

Marson AG, Al-Kharusi AM, Alwaidh M, et al; SANAD Study Group. The SANAD study of effectiveness of carbamazepine, gabapentin, lamotrigine, oxcarbazepine, or topiramate for treatment of partial epilepsy: an unblended, randomised controlled trial. Lancet. 2007;369(9566):1000-1015. [PMID: 17382827]

Marson AG, Al-Kharusi AM, Alwaidh M, et al; SANAD Study Group. The SANAD study of effectiveness of valproate, lamotrigine, or topiramate for generalised and unclassifiable epilepsy: an unblended randomized controlled trial. Lancet. 2007;369(9566):1016-1026. [PMID: 17382828]

TABLE 34 Treatment of Status Epilepticus in Adults		
Setting	**Drug (Dose)[a]**	**Time Course[b]**
Prehospital or ED	Lorazepam (2-4 mg) *or* diazepam (5-10 mg)	0-20 minutes
ED or ICU	Phenytoin (20 mg/kg) *or* fosphenytoin (20 mg/kg)	20-60 minutes
ED or ICU	Phenobarbital (20 mg/kg)	60-90 minutes
ICU	Pentobarbital *or* midazolam *or* propofol *or* thiopental (as a continuous infusion)	90+ minutes

ED = emergency department; ICU = intensive care unit.

[a]All drugs are administered intravenously.

[b]Time from onset of treatment of status epilepticus.

Morrow J, Russell A, Guthrie E, et al. Malformation risks of antiepileptic drugs in pregnancy: a prospective study from the UK Epilepsy and Pregnancy Register. J Neurol Neurosurg Psychiatry. 2006;77(2):193-198. [PMID: 16157661]

Sillanpää M, Schmidt D. Prognosis of seizure recurrence after stopping antiepileptic drugs in seizure-free patients: a long-term population-based study of childhood-onset epilepsy. Epilepsy Behav. 2005;8(4):713-719. [PMID:16616648]

Wiebe S, Blume WT, Girvin JP, Eliasziw M; Effectiveness and Efficiency of Surgery for Temporal Lobe Epilepsy Study Group. A randomized controlled trial of surgery for temporal lobe epilepsy. N Engl J Med. 2001;345(5):11-18. [PMID: 11484687]

Disorders of the Spinal Cord

Presenting Symptoms and Signs of Myelopathies

Spinal cord disorders, or myelopathies, have a myriad of causes. The diagnostic process involves recognizing a myelopathic syndrome, using neuroimaging to detect compressive lesions and provide clues about noncompressive causes, and ordering focused laboratory testing to identify systemic medical disorders.

Spinal cord disease presents as motor or sensory dysfunction of the limbs and trunk. Typical patterns include symmetric or asymmetric spastic paraparesis (associated with a cervical or thoracic lesion) or quadriparesis (associated with a cervical lesion). Some patients note a sensory level below which they perceive numbness or neuropathic discomfort (burning, prickling, or a tight band-like sensation around the limb or trunk). Lhermitte sign, an electrical shock–like sensation that travels down the spine or extremities and is elicited by neck flexion, suggests a cervical spinal cord lesion. Neck or back pain may accompany a structural or inflammatory lesion, and the presence of pain at a truncal dermatomal level may identify the segment of spinal cord involved. Bowel dysfunction, impotence, and urinary urgency, frequency, and incontinence may also occur. Cauda equina lesions cause radicular pain, bladder dysfunction, and lower extremity sensorimotor symptoms without upper motoneuron signs (because the cauda is comprised of spinal roots); these can be difficult to differentiate from myelopathy.

Examination findings include paraparesis or quadriparesis accompanied by spasticity, hyperreflexia, and extensor plantar responses; a truncal sensory level detected with pinprick examination; impaired vibratory and proprioceptive sensation; and abnormal gait.

Clinical Presentation, Diagnosis, and Management of Compressive Myelopathies

Spinal cord compression is a neurologic emergency because delayed diagnosis and therapy result in irreversible neurologic disability. Back pain is typically the sentinel symptom. Paraparesis or quadriparesis occurs over days; motor deficit severity at diagnosis is the strongest predictor of posttherapeutic ambulatory ability. Disorders that mimic metastatic compression include epidural hematomas (usually in the setting of anticoagulation) and epidural abscess (associated with fever and elevated erythrocyte sedimentation rate).

In patients with suspected cord compression, an MRI of the entire spinal cord should be obtained immediately both to establish the diagnosis and because of the high incidence of multiple compressive sites. Cervical and thoracic spine imaging detects lesions that compress the spinal cord, whereas lumbar spine imaging reveals lesions affecting the conus medullaris or the cauda equina. CT myelography reliably detects compressive lesions but is more time-consuming than MRI and does not detect intrinsic cord lesions.

Epidural metastasis requires treatment with corticosteroids (typically, intravenous dexamethasone, 96 mg immediately and then 24 mg every 6 hours) followed by radiation therapy, decompressive surgery, or both. Indications for surgery include spinal instability and the presence of a known tumor type that is radiotherapy resistant, such as lung or renal clear-cell carcinoma. A randomized trial demonstrated that the combination of decompressive surgery and radiotherapy resulted in superior ambulatory outcomes to that achieved by radiotherapy alone. Patients with radiosensitive tumors, such as leukemia, lymphoma, myeloma, and germ-cell tumors, were excluded from this protocol.

In contrast to the acute spinal cord compression syndromes, spinal degenerative changes usually cause a subacute to chronic compressive myelopathy. Cervical spondylotic myelopathy is common and is associated with hypertrophic changes of the vertebral bodies, facet joints, and ligaments, with or without superimposed disk herniations, that result in cervical canal stenosis (**Figure 25**). Onset is usually insidious, with imbalance, numbness in the upper and lower extremities, and spastic gait. Upper motoneuron findings (hyperreflexia, extensor plantar responses, spasticity) are present in the lower extremities, and lower motoneuron findings (muscle atrophy, reduced or absent reflexes) may be present in the upper extremities. Neck pain is often present, but cervical radicular pain is typically absent. Cervical spine MRI reveals canal narrowing and compression of the spinal cord. Abnormal signal within the cord may represent compression-related myelomalacia (scarring), but coexisting disorders, such as vitamin B_{12} deficiency or multiple sclerosis, must be considered. Surgical decompression for cervical spondylotic myelopathy has been anecdotally reported to halt clinical progression of neurologic deficits but may not improve existing deficits.

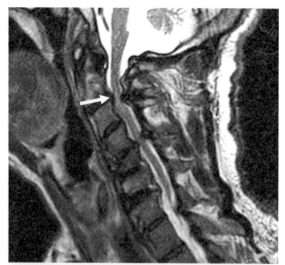

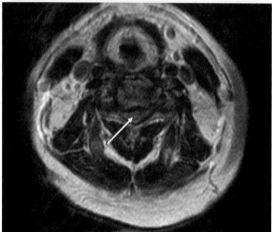

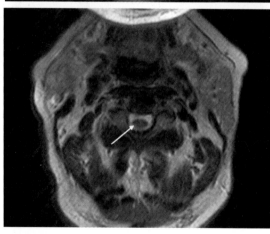

FIGURE 25.
Spinal cord compression.
Top, MRI of the cervical spine of a patient with spinal cord compression due to cervical spondylosis. There is stenosis at several levels, worst at C2 to C3 (*arrow*). *Middle*, axial MRI view of a cervical spinal cord showing effacement of the subarachnoid space, cord compression, and bright signal within the cord indicating myelomalacia (*arrow*). *Bottom*, axial MRI view of a normal cervical spinal cord and spinal canal for comparison with middle panel. The white margin surrounding the spinal cord is the subarachnoid space containing cerebrospinal fluid, and the cord is of normal caliber and shape (*arrow*).

Clinical Presentation, Diagnosis, and Management of Noncompressive Myelopathies

Noncompressive myelopathy can be categorized by cause, that is, demyelinating, inflammatory, infectious, nutritional, toxic/metabolic, vascular, and genetic/hereditary causes.

Demyelinating diseases are a leading cause of myelitis and are discussed in Demyelinating Diseases. Inflammatory myelopathies may occur with disorders such as sarcoidosis, Sjögren syndrome, and systemic lupus erythematosus. Diagnosis requires establishing the presence of active systemic disease or, in the case of sarcoidosis, obtaining a tissue biopsy. Treatment includes corticosteroids and long-term immunosuppressive therapy dictated by the specific diagnosis.

Inflammatory myelopathies may also be associated with infectious agents or postinfectious syndromes. Herpesviruses, enteroviruses, West Nile virus, human T-lymphotropic virus type 1, and HIV, among others, may directly infect the cord. Numerous other viruses and bacteria, such as *Mycoplasma pneumoniae*, have been implicated as triggers of a postinfectious, presumably autoimmune inflammatory myelopathy. *Mycobacterium tuberculosis* may be a triggering antigen for sarcoidosis.

Subacute combined degeneration of the cord is caused by vitamin B_{12} deficiency. The selective degeneration of the corticospinal tracts and dorsal columns results in sensory ataxia (because of dysfunctional proprioception), lower extremity weakness, and paresthesias. Vitamin B_{12} deficiency may be caused by autoimmune pernicious anemia, but malabsorption syndromes resulting from gastric surgery, especially gastric bypass procedures, are increasingly common causes. Nitrous oxide exposure, either acutely (from anesthesia induction in a patient with a borderline serum vitamin B_{12} level) or chronically (from recreational abuse) can interfere with vitamin B_{12} metabolic pathways and trigger a deficiency syndrome. Vitamin B_{12} deficiency is confirmed by demonstrating a low blood level, but some patients with borderline low levels can be diagnosed by detecting elevated levels of serum methylmalonic acid and homocysteine (see MKSAP 15 Hematology and Oncology). Replacement therapy usually halts progression, and some patients improve over time.

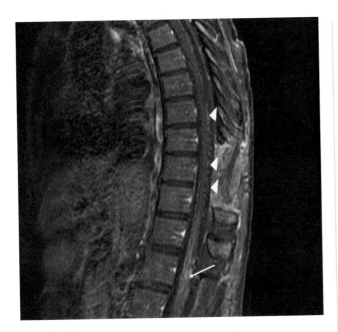

FIGURE 26.
Dural arteriovenous fistula of the spinal cord.
Sagittal T1-weighted MRI of the thoracolumbar spine with gadolinium shows enhancement of the spinal cord caused by venous congestion (*arrow*) and prominent tortuous veins along the dorsal cord surface (*arrowheads*).

Copper deficiency causes a progressive myelopathy similar to subacute combined degeneration. It may occur as a malabsorption syndrome after gastric bypass or in the setting of zinc overingestion from purposeful or accidental oversupplementation or overuse of zinc-containing drugs. Measurement of serum copper and zinc levels can lead to the diagnosis; controlled supplementation may arrest progression or mildly improve symptoms.

Vascular myelopathies include arterial cord infarctions and dura-based arteriovenous fistulas. Ischemic cord infarcts usually involve the anterior spinal artery and result in sudden weakness with spared sensation. Although some patients have vascular risk factors, most cases are idiopathic. Dural arteriovenous fistulas cause venous congestion due to abnormal connections between high-pressure arterial and low-pressure venous systems supplying the cord. Myelopathy typically evolves subacutely or chronically, with periods of stepwise deterioration that may indicate venous infarction. A spinal cord MRI often shows characteristic findings (**Figure 26**). Spinal angiography establishes the vascular anatomy and guides therapeutic options, such as endovascular embolization or surgical ligation.

Hereditary spastic paraplegia presents as a slowly progressive myelopathy with prominent spasticity and relatively mild weakness. There are autosomal dominant and recessive forms, some of which are detectable by genetic testing.

KEY POINTS

- Noncompressive myelopathy can result from demyelinating, inflammatory, infectious, nutritional, toxic/metabolic, vascular, and genetic/hereditary causes.

- Subacute combined degeneration of the spinal cord may be caused by vitamin B_{12} deficiency, nitrous oxide exposure, or copper deficiency.

- Dural arteriovenous fistula should be suspected in any patient with progressive myelopathy and superimposed episodes of rapid, stepwise clinical deterioration.

Bibliography

de Seze J, Stojkovic T, Breteau G, et al. Acute myelopathies: clinical, laboratory and outcome profiles in 79 cases. Brain. 2001;124(Pt 8):1509-1521. [PMID: 11459743]

Jellema K, Tijssen CC, van Gijn J. Spinal dural arteriovenous fistulas: a congestive myelopathy that initially mimics a peripheral nerve disorder. Brain. 2006;129(Pt 12):3150-3164. [PMID: 16921175]

Juhasz-Pocsine K, Rudnicki SA, Archer RL, Harik SI. Neurologic complications of gastric bypass surgery for morbid obesity. Neurology. 2007;68:1843-1850. [PMID: 17515548]

Masson C, Pruvo JP, Meder JF, et al. Spinal cord infarction: clinical and magnetic resonance imaging findings and short term outcome. J Neurol Neurosurg Psychiatry. 2004;75(10):1431-1435. [PMID: 15377691]

Patchell RA, Tibbs PA, Regine WF, et al. Direct decompressive surgical resection in the treatment of spinal cord compression caused by metastatic cancer: a randomised trial. Lancet. 2005;366(9486):643-648. [PMID: 16112300]

Self-Assessment Test

This self-assessment test contains one-best-answer multiple-choice questions. Please read these directions carefully before answering the questions. Answers, critiques, and bibliographies immediately follow these multiple-choice questions. The American College of Physicians is accredited by the Accreditation Council for Continuing Medical Education (ACCME) to provide continuing medical education for physicians.

The American College of Physicians designates MKSAP 15 Neurology for a maximum of 11 *AMA PRA Category 1 Credits*™. Physicians should only claim credit commensurate with the extent of their participation in the activity. Separate answer sheets are provided for each book of the MKSAP program. Please use one of these answer sheets to complete the Neurology self-assessment test. Indicate in Section H on the answer sheet the actual number of credits you earned, up to the maximum of 11, in ¼-credit increments. (One credit equals one hour of time spent on this educational activity.)

Use the self-addressed envelope provided with your program to mail your completed answer sheet(s) to the MKSAP Processing Center for scoring. Remember to provide your MKSAP 15 order and ACP ID numbers in the appropriate spaces on the answer sheet. The order and ACP ID numbers are printed on your mailing label. If you have *not* received these numbers with your MKSAP 15 purchase, you will need to acquire them to earn CME credits. E-mail ACP's customer service center at custserv@acponline.org. In the subject line, write "MKSAP 15 order/ACP ID numbers." In the body of the e-mail, make sure you include your e-mail address as well as your full name, address, city, state, ZIP code, country, and telephone number. Also identify where you have made your MKSAP 15 purchase. You will receive your MKSAP 15 order and ACP ID numbers by e-mail within 72 business hours.

CME credit is available from the publication date of July 31, 2009, until July 31, 2012. You may submit your answer sheets at any time during this period.

Self-Scoring Instructions: Neurology

Compute your percent correct score as follows:

Step 1: Give yourself 1 point for each correct response to a question.

Step 2: Divide your total points by the total number of questions: 90.

The result, expressed as a percentage, is your percent correct score.

	Example	Your Calculations
Step 1	77	
Step 2	77 ÷ 90	÷ 90
% Correct	86%	%

Directions

Each of the numbered items is followed by lettered answers. Select the **ONE** lettered answer that is **BEST** in each case.

Item 1

An 84-year-old man is evaluated for a 5-year history of a gradually worsening gait and a 2-year history of cognitive impairment and urinary incontinence. Twelve years ago, he sustained a closed head injury that caused a mild traumatic subarachnoid hemorrhage and a 5-hour loss of consciousness. Medications include zolpidem (when needed as a sleep aid) and a daily multivitamin.

On physical examination, temperature is 36.2 °C (97.2 °F), blood pressure is 128/78 mm Hg, pulse rate is 76/min, respiration rate is 14/min, and BMI is 27. The patient's gait is slow and unsteady and is marked by small, shuffling steps. His level of alertness, speech, posture, arm swing, and muscle tone are all normal, and he has no tremor. He scores 24/30 on the Folstein Mini–Mental State Examination, losing one point in the orientation portion for incorrectly stating today's date, three points in the serial calculation portion, and two points in the recall portion.

Results of a complete blood count, a basic metabolic panel, serum vitamin B$_{12}$ measurement, thyroid function tests, and a urinalysis are normal.

An MRI of the brain is shown.

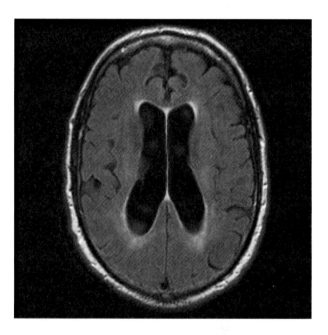

Which of the following is the most likely diagnosis?

(A) Alzheimer dementia
(B) Normal pressure hydrocephalus
(C) Parkinson disease
(D) Vascular dementia

Item 2

An 18-year-old male college student is evaluated for a single generalized tonic-clonic seizure that began when he was asleep in his dormitory and resolved uneventfully. He has no history of head trauma, meningitis, or prior seizure and no family history of epilepsy. He takes no medications.

Results of physical examination, including a neurologic examination, are normal.

Results of laboratory studies, including a complete blood count, a serum electrolyte panel, and a urine toxicology screen, are also normal.

An MRI of the brain and an electroencephalogram show no abnormalities.

Which of the following is the most appropriate management of this patient's seizure?

(A) Initiate no drug therapy at this time
(B) Initiate therapy with carbamazepine
(C) Initiate therapy with lamotrigine
(D) Initiate therapy with valproic acid
(E) Refer for epilepsy surgery evaluation

Item 3

A 36-year-old woman is evaluated in the office for a history of migraine, with and without aura, since age 16 years. She has an average of three attacks each month and consistently experiences an attack 2 days prior to menstruation; this headache is more difficult to treat than those not associated with menstruation. Although she typically obtains pain relief within 2 hours of taking sumatriptan, the headache recurs within 24 hours after each dose during the period of menstrual flow. Sumatriptan, orally as needed, is her only medication.

Results of physical examination are unremarkable.

Which of the following is the most appropriate perimenstrual treatment for this patient's headaches?

(A) Estrogen-progestin contraceptive pill
(B) Mefenamic acid
(C) Sumatriptan plus naproxen, orally
(D) Sumatriptan, subcutaneously
(E) Topiramate

Item 4

A 52-year-old woman is evaluated for a 2-year history of burning feet. Symptoms are constant and are worse at night. The patient is overweight and has a history of hypertension treated with lisinopril. There is no known family history of peripheral neuropathy.

On physical examination, the patient is afebrile; blood pressure is 134/88 mm Hg, pulse rate is 66/min, respiration rate is 12/min, and BMI is 28. Neurologic examination shows diminished pinprick and temperature sensation on the dorsal and plantar surfaces of both feet. Cranial nerve examination and testing of manual muscle strength, deep tendon reflexes, proprioception, and coordination reveal no abnormalities.

Laboratory studies show a fasting plasma glucose level of 102 mg/dL (5.7 mmol/L). Results of a complete blood count, vitamin B_{12} measurement, and serum protein electrophoresis are all normal.

Electromyographic testing shows a mild reduction in the sensory nerve action potential in the legs, compatible with a mild peripheral neuropathy. An MRI of the lumbar spine is normal.

Which of the following is the most appropriate next diagnostic test?

(A) Cerebrospinal fluid examination
(B) Genetic testing for Charcot-Marie-Tooth disease
(C) Glucose tolerance test
(D) Skin biopsy

Item 5

A 41-year-old man is evaluated in the emergency department for a 3-day history of confusion and visual loss and a 10-day history of gradually increasing headache. Two weeks ago, he had a 3-day history of severe gastroenteritis with diarrhea, nausea, and vomiting. A review of medical records shows that he is a factor V Leiden heterozygote.

On physical examination, vital signs are normal. The patient has papilledema, a very mild right pronator drift, right homonymous hemianopsia, and fluent aphasia.

Results of laboratory studies and a CT scan of the head are normal.

Which of the following is the most appropriate next diagnostic test in this patient?

(A) Carotid ultrasonography
(B) Electroencephalography
(C) Lumbar puncture
(D) Magnetic resonance venography

Item 6

A 45-year-old woman is evaluated in the emergency department for a 2-day history of increased leg weakness, ataxia, fatigue, and urinary incontinence. She has no other systemic symptoms. The patient has a 20-year history of multiple sclerosis, which has followed a progressive course over the past 5 years. Her baseline neurologic status, recorded 1 month ago, includes moderate bilateral spastic leg weakness, bilateral extensor plantar responses, mild sensory loss, and ambulation with a cane. Her only medication is interferon beta-1a; her dosage has been stable for the past 3 years.

On physical examination, temperature is 38.1 °C (100.6 °F), blood pressure is 110/70 mm Hg, pulse rate is 90/min, and respiration rate is 16/min. The patient is unable to ambulate because of severe leg weakness. There is no costovertebral angle tenderness. Results of general physical and neurologic examinations are otherwise normal, including tests of mental status, cranial nerve function, and upper extremity neurologic status.

Results of a complete blood count show a leukocyte count of 11,000/µL (11×10^9/L). Her urine is cloudy and is positive for nitrites and leukocyte esterase on urinalysis.

Results of serum electrolyte measurement, liver chemistry studies, and renal function tests are all normal.

A radiograph of the chest reveals no abnormalities.

Which of the following is the best drug therapy for this patient?

(A) Baclofen
(B) Ciprofloxacin
(C) Methylprednisolone
(D) Prednisone

Item 7

A 50-year-old woman is evaluated in the emergency department after having a witnessed generalized tonic-clonic seizure. Her husband reports hearing her fall and finding her on the kitchen floor convulsing. The event lasted 2 minutes and stopped spontaneously. The patient has never experienced a similar episode, has no personal history of head trauma or meningitis, and has no family history of a seizure disorder. She has a history of hypertension treated with hydrochlorothiazide.

On examination, the patient is lethargic but cooperative. She is afebrile, with a blood pressure of 146/80 mm Hg and a pulse rate of 70/min. She has mild weakness of the left face and arm that resolves over the next 3 hours.

Results of laboratory studies, including measurement of plasma glucose level, are normal.

An MRI of the brain shows chronic small-vessel ischemic disease but no acute abnormalities.

Which of the following findings predicts a greater risk of a future seizure in this patient?

(A) Age
(B) Hypertension
(C) Presence of secondary generalization
(D) Small-vessel ischemic changes on an MRI of the brain
(E) Todd paralysis

Item 8

A 70-year-old woman is evaluated in the emergency department for a 6-week history of back pain that has become increasingly severe over the past 6 days and a 2-day history of progressive bilateral leg weakness. Two years ago, the patient was treated for breast cancer with lumpectomy and local radiation therapy. She has no other pertinent personal or family medical history and takes no medications.

On examination, temperature is 37.1 °C (98.8 °F), blood pressure is 140/85 mm Hg, and pulse rate is 88/min. She had moderate spastic paraparesis and bilateral extensor plantar responses. A T8 sensory level, impaired bilateral lower extremity proprioception, and moderate gait ataxia are also noted.

Results of a complete blood count, erythrocyte sedimentation rate determination, and coagulation studies are all normal.

An MRI of the spinal cord reveals an epidural mass causing destruction of the T6 vertebral body with spinal instability and moderately severe compression of the adjacent spinal cord.

Which of the following is the most appropriate immediate treatment of this patient's spinal cord compression?

(A) Decompressive surgery

(B) Intravenous dexamethasone followed by decompressive surgery and chemotherapy

(C) Intravenous dexamethasone followed by decompressive surgery and radiation therapy

(D) Intravenous dexamethasone followed by radiation therapy and chemotherapy

Item 9

An 88-year-old woman is evaluated in the emergency department 1 hour after the acute onset of language disturbance and right-sided weakness. The family members who witnessed the onset say that the symptoms progressed over a few minutes and that there were accompanying symptoms of nausea and vomiting; they describe the patient holding her head as if in pain. She has a 20-year history of hypertension but no other medical problems; her only medication is lisinopril.

During the examination, the patient becomes increasingly difficult to arouse and vomits repeatedly. She is afebrile, blood pressure is 220/110 mm Hg, pulse rate is 110/min, and respiration rate is 20/min. There is no nuchal rigidity. Carotid upstrokes are normal; there are no bruits and no jugular venous distention. Other than tachycardia, the cardiopulmonary examination is unremarkable. Global aphasia and right hemiplegia are noted.

On the basis of her preliminary clinical evaluation, which of the following is the most likely diagnosis?

(A) Intracerebral hemorrhage

(B) Ischemic stroke

(C) Meningitis

(D) Transient ischemic attack

Item 10

A 61-year-old man is evaluated in the office for a 6-month history of progressive weakness of the lower extremities. He says he has difficulty rising from a seated position and walking up stairs and also has episodes of dry eyes, dry mouth, and erectile dysfunction. The patient reports no ptosis, diplopia, dysphagia, or dyspnea. He has a 15-year history of hypertension and a 42-pack year smoking history. Family history is unremarkable. His only medication is hydrochlorothiazide.

On physical examination, vital signs are normal. Manual muscle strength testing shows weakness in the proximal upper and lower limb muscles. Deep tendon reflexes are absent diffusely. Plantar responses are flexor. A sensory examination shows no abnormalities, and cranial nerve function is normal.

Laboratory studies show normal serum levels of sodium, potassium, calcium, creatinine, glucose, and creatine kinase. Results of liver chemistry studies are also normal.

Which of the following is the best diagnostic test for this patient?

(A) Measurement of acetylcholine receptor antibody level

(B) Measurement of parathyroid hormone level

(C) Measurement of voltage-gated P/Q-type calcium channel antibody level

(D) Muscle biopsy

Item 11

An 84-year-old man is evaluated for the gradual onset of progressive memory loss over the past 2 years. In the past 4 months, he has twice been unable to find his way home after going to the local supermarket; his wife now goes with him whenever he leaves the house. His wife also has assumed responsibility for the household finances after the patient overdrew their checking account for the third time because of subtraction errors in their checkbook. He has hypertension treated with hydrochlorothiazide and hypothyroidism treated with levothyroxine. His mother had onset of Alzheimer dementia at age 79 years and died at age 86 years. His only other medication is a daily multivitamin.

On physical examination, temperature is 36.9 °C (98.4 °F), blood pressure is 130/80 mm Hg, pulse rate is 72/min, respiration rate is 14/min, and BMI is 25. His level of alertness, speech, and gait are normal. His score on the Folstein Mini–Mental State Examination is 24/30, including 0/3 on the recall portion.

Results of laboratory studies, including a complete blood count, serum vitamin B_{12} measurement, thyroid function tests, and a basic metabolic panel, are normal.

An unenhanced MRI of the brain shows no abnormalities.

Which of the following is the most appropriate treatment at this time?

(A) Donepezil

(B) Memantine

(C) Quetiapine

(D) Sertraline

(E) Discontinuation of all current medications

Item 12

A 30-year-old woman is evaluated in the office for a 6-week history of severe left facial pain. She says the pain occurs multiple times each day, is confined to the left cheek and jaw, and is stabbing in quality. Each pain episode lasts only 2 seconds, but she may experience multiple consecutive episodes. The pain can be triggered by drinking cold fluid, chewing on the left side of the mouth, or touching the left cheek. Three years ago, she had intermittent paresthesias of the hands and feet, which led to a diagnosis of anxiety. She has been taking ibuprofen for pain control since her current symptoms began, but it has been ineffective.

On physical examination, vital signs are normal. Pain is triggered during the examination by touching the left cheek. She has no long-tract pyramidal signs or pathologic reflexes. Facial sensation and strength are normal, as are findings of funduscopic examination.

Which of the following is the most appropriate next step in management?

(A) Administration of baclofen
(B) CT of the head
(C) Lumbar puncture
(D) MRI of the brain
(E) Nerve conduction studies of the extremities

Item 13

A 62-year-old woman is evaluated in the emergency department for a 2-week history of progressive shortness of breath, which has culminated over the past 3 days in a change in the sound of her speech and occasional swallowing difficulties. She says that approximately 8 weeks ago, she began to have blurred vision late in the day, particularly when driving home from work, and occasional weakness in the upper and lower limbs. Three weeks ago, she had a urinary tract infection treated with ciprofloxacin. The patient takes no other medications

On physical examination, blood pressure is 118/56 mm Hg, pulse rate is 68/min, respiration rate is 22/min, and arterial oxygen saturation on ambient air is 98%. Her lungs are clear to auscultation. She has moderate bilateral proximal weakness in the upper and lower limbs, with mild weakness distally. Deep tendon reflexes are normal, and there is no appendicular or truncal ataxia. She has fluctuating ptosis and diminished facial strength. Speech is nasal and slurred; her language is normal.

Which of the following is the best treatment option for this patient?

(A) Plasma exchange
(B) Prednisone
(C) Pyridostigmine
(D) Repeat ciprofloxacin therapy

Item 14

A 33-year-old man is evaluated for a 3-year history of progressive gait dysfunction accumulating in a stepwise manner, with periods of rapid worsening followed by a plateau in symptoms until the next relapse. He has no personal history of other medical problems.

On physical examination, vital signs are normal. Severe spastic paraparesis, moderate loss of all sensory modalities in the lower extremities, and a T10 sensory level are noted.

An MRI of the thoracic spinal cord is shown to the right. An MRI of the brain shows no abnormalities. Cerebrospinal fluid analysis detects no oligoclonal bands.

Which of the following is the most appropriate next diagnostic test?

(A) Repeat lumbar puncture
(B) Repeat MRI of the brain
(C) Spinal angiography
(D) Spinal cord biopsy

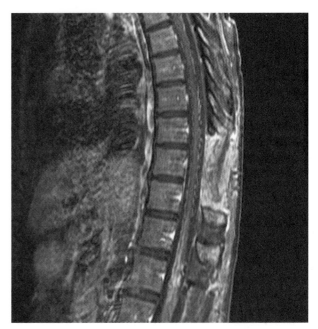

ITEM 14.

Item 15

A previously healthy 50-year-old woman is admitted to the hospital after three recent, transient episodes of nonfluent aphasia and right-hand numbness and weakness. One week before onset of these focal neurologic symptoms, she developed aching left jaw pain, which has persisted. She has no other medical problems and takes no medications.

On physical examination, vital signs are normal. A left carotid bruit is heard on auscultation. Left miosis and left ptosis are noted.

Results of laboratory studies and a CT scan of the head are normal.

Which of the following is the most likely diagnosis?

(A) Cluster headache
(B) Giant cell arteritis
(C) Spontaneous left internal carotid artery dissection
(D) Spontaneous left vertebral artery occlusion

Item 16

A 75-year-old woman is seen for a follow-up evaluation. Two weeks ago, she was brought to the emergency department after slipping in the bathroom and hitting her head on the tub. A CT scan of the head obtained at that time showed a small calcified lesion over the right sphenoid wing. A subsequent outpatient contrast-enhanced MRI of the brain showed a 2-cm dura-based lesion with homogeneous enhancement, consistent with a meningioma; no mass effect or edema was detected. She is otherwise healthy, has no general or neurologic symptoms, and takes no medications.

Vital signs and physical examination findings are normal.

Which of the following is the best management option for this patient?

(A) Chemotherapy

(B) Serial MRIs of the brain

(C) Stereotactic radiosurgery

(D) Surgical resection

Item 17

A 36-year-old woman is evaluated in the office for a 6-year history of headache. The patient says her headaches occur approximately three times each month, are associated with occasional nausea and pain that can be moderately severe and disabling, have a squeezing quality, and begin in the neck, radiating forward to involve the frontal head region bilaterally. Her headaches are preceded by yawning and irritability, last up to 24 hours, and can be triggered by stress or changes in barometric pressure. She has a history of mild depression treated with fluoxetine. Her mother and sister have a history of sinus headaches.

On physical examination, blood pressure is 124/86 mm Hg, pulse rate is 78/min, and BMI is 21. Results of general physical and neurologic examinations are normal. The patient's mood appears euthymic.

Which of the following is the most likely diagnosis?

(A) Chronic migraine

(B) Medication overuse headache

(C) Migraine without aura

(D) Sinus headache

(E) Tension-type headache

Item 18

A 70-year-old woman is evaluated for recent loss of consciousness. She says she had a "strange feeling" before losing consciousness. Her husband, who accompanied her on this visit and witnessed the event, reports that she fell to the ground and exhibited generalized stiffening and then shaking. He further states that her eyes rolled back in her head and that she was unresponsive for 1 minute, had urinary incontinence, and was profoundly confused, speaking garbled, nonsensical sentences, for 2 to 3 minutes after regaining consciousness. She had a similar episode 2 months ago; evaluation at that time, which included electrocardiography, stress electrocardiography, and a continuous-loop event electrocardiographic recorder, revealed no abnormal findings. The patient takes no medications.

Results of a physical examination, including a neurologic examination, are normal.

Results of MRI of the brain and electroencephalography during waking and sleeping are also normal.

Which of the following is the most likely diagnosis?

(A) Cardiac arrhythmia

(B) Partial seizure with secondary generalization

(C) Transient ischemic attack

(D) Vasovagal syncope

Item 19

A 53-year-old woman is evaluated in the office for a 1-week history of paresthesias that began symmetrically in the feet and progressed to involve the distal legs and, more recently, the hands. She says she is unsteady when walking, has lower limb weakness, and has difficulty going upstairs. The patient has no history of pain or bowel or bladder impairment. Personal and family medical history is noncontributory, and she takes no medications.

On physical examination, vital signs are normal. Weakness of distal lower extremity muscles is noted, with stocking-glove sensory loss and areflexia. Deep tendon reflexes are absent. Plantar responses are flexor, and gait is unsteady. No sensory level is present across the thorax. Mental status, language, and cranial nerve function are normal.

Complete blood count results, erythrocyte sedimentation rate, serum creatinine and creatine kinase levels, and liver chemistry test results are normal.

A chest radiograph shows no abnormalities.

Which of the following is the most appropriate next diagnostic test?

(A) Electromyography

(B) MRI of the spinal cord

(C) Serologic testing for West Nile virus

(D) Sural nerve biopsy

Item 20

A previously healthy 42-year-old woman is evaluated in the emergency department for the sudden onset of a severe occipital headache during defecation 8 hours ago, followed by two episodes of vomiting. She reports no neck stiffness or neurologic symptoms. Her mother and two sisters have a history of migraine.

On physical examination, temperature is 36.8 °C (98.2 °F), blood pressure is 148/88 mm Hg, pulse rate is 90/min, and respiration rate is 20/min. The patient is in obvious distress as a result of the pain. No evidence of meningismus, papilledema, or focal neurologic signs is found.

Cerebrospinal fluid examination reveals a normal level of protein and glucose and no leukocytes or erythrocytes.

A noncontrast CT scan of the head shows no abnormalities.

Which of the following is the most appropriate next step in management?

(A) Admission to the hospital for overnight observation

(B) Administration of sumatriptan, subcutaneously

(C) CT angiography of the head and neck

(D) Repeat lumbar puncture

Item 21

A 74-year-old man is brought to the emergency department by ambulance 1 hour after he had an acute witnessed onset of aphasia and right hemiparesis. He has a history of hypertension and atrial fibrillation. His current medications are hydrochlorothiazide, metoprolol, and warfarin.

On physical examination, blood pressure is 178/94 mm Hg and pulse rate is 80/min and irregular. Neurologic examination confirms nonfluent aphasia, a right pronator drift, a right leg drift, and an extensor plantar response on the right.

Results of laboratory studies performed within 1 hour of his arrival at the emergency department show an INR of 1.5.

An electrocardiogram obtained on the patient's arrival at the emergency department confirms atrial fibrillation. A CT scan of head obtained within 1 hour of his arrival reveals no early ischemic changes.

Which of the following is the best treatment?

(A) Aspirin

(B) Continuous intravenous heparin

(C) Intra-arterial recombinant tissue plasminogen activator (rtPA)

(D) Intravenous labetalol

(E) Intravenous rtPA

Item 22

A 65-year-old man is evaluated for worsening gait unsteadiness and falls. He first noticed the unsteadiness 1 year ago while walking and has started to fall recently, falling four times in the past 2 weeks. Approximately 3 years ago, he developed erectile dysfunction and has had increasing constipation ever since that time.

On physical examination, vital signs are normal except for the supine blood pressure, which is 190/105 mm Hg; blood pressure decreases to 76/50 mm Hg when he stands without a compensatory increase in the pulse rate. Results of mental status testing are normal. He has mildly slurred speech. Testing of cranial nerve function, including testing of extraocular movements, reveals no abnormalities. Manual muscle strength in the upper and lower extremities is normal, but he has mild rigidity of the extremities and mild appendicular ataxia. His gait is slow with a reduced stride length and arm swing, and he has marked postural instability.

Which of the following is the most likely diagnosis?

(A) Dementia with Lewy bodies

(B) Multiple system atrophy

(C) Parkinson disease

(D) Progressive supranuclear palsy

Item 23

A 60-year-old man is admitted to the hospital for generalized tonic-clonic seizures that began 30 minutes ago. Clinical seizure activity continues for another 60 minutes, during which time the patient is intubated, placed on a ventilator, and given lorazepam and fosphenytoin, both intravenously. After his seizures stop, he is transferred to the intensive care unit, where he remains comatose. The patient has been receiving chemotherapy and whole-brain radiation

therapy for recently diagnosed small cell lung cancer. He indicated at the time of his diagnosis that he wants everything possible done to prolong his life ("full code").

On examination, the patient is comatose, with no response to deep pain stimulation. Cranial nerve examination is significant for reactive pupils.

Results of laboratory studies are noncontributory.

Other than sinus tachycardia, the electrocardiogram is unremarkable.

Which of the following is the most appropriate next step in management?

(A) Continuous electroencephalographic monitoring

(B) Discussion of withdrawal of care with the family

(C) Intravenous phenobarbital

(D) MRI of the brain

Item 24

A 71-year-old woman is admitted to the hospital after having a witnessed morning seizure. She has a 3-week history of increasing gait unsteadiness and daytime somnolence and a 3-month history of progressive confusion and headaches; she typically naps 3 hours daily. Six month ago, the patient had fungal pneumonia caused by *Coccidioides immitis* infection. She has a 20-year history of type 2 diabetes mellitus and no relevant family history. Current medications are insulin glargine, metformin, and intravenous fosphenytoin (started on hospital admission).

On physical examination, temperature is 38.2 °C (100.8 °F), blood pressure is 116/70 mm Hg, pulse rate is 96/min, respiration rate is 18/min, and BMI is 32. The patient is somnolent but arouses to voice. She is disoriented to time and place and scores only 12/30 on the Folstein Mini–Mental State Examination. There is mild diffuse symmetric hyperreflexia, and plantar responses are extensor bilaterally; the patient moves all four limbs equally. There is no papilledema.

Leukocyte count is 14,000/μL (14×10^9/L), and erythrocyte sedimentation rate is 64 mm/h. All other results of laboratory studies, including measurement of serum vitamin B_{12} level, a basic metabolic panel, thyroid function tests, and urinalysis, are normal.

A noncontrast CT scan of the head shows mildly dilated ventricles. An electroencephalogram shows moderately severe diffuse slowing but no epileptiform activity.

Which of the following is the most appropriate next diagnostic test for this patient?

(A) Apolipoprotein E genotyping

(B) Cerebral CT angiography

(C) Cisternography

(D) Lumbar puncture and cerebrospinal fluid analysis

(E) Repeat electroencephalography

Item 25

A 30-year-old man has a recent diagnosis of multiple sclerosis (MS). He experienced two transient neurologic episodes in the past 6 months, one involving optic neuritis and the other minor partial myelitis; he recovered completely from both events and is currently asymptomatic. MS was diagnosed after an MRI of the brain showed white matter lesions typical of the disease. He has no other pertinent personal or family medical history.

Which of the following MS subtypes best describes the course of his disease?

(A) Benign
(B) Primary progressive
(C) Relapsing-remitting
(D) Secondary progressive

Item 26

A 22-year-old man is evaluated in the emergency department for a 12-hour history of mild headache, nausea, and vomiting. His roommate had similar symptoms the previous day. He is given intravenous fluids and prochlorperazine and begins to feel better until his head suddenly becomes stiff and turns to the right; he cannot move it to the midline or to the left, and he reports cramping and aching in the right neck muscles.

Neurologic examination shows the head to be turned to the right with sustained contraction of the left sternocleidomastoid muscle but is otherwise unremarkable.

Which of the following is the best treatment for this patient?

(A) Benztropine
(B) Botulinum toxin
(C) Phenytoin
(D) Recombinant tissue plasminogen activator
(E) Tetanus immune globulin

Item 27

A 41-year-old man is evaluated in the emergency department for a 3-hour history of a severe headache. The headache began abruptly while he was at work and involved the left frontal temporal region and the left ear and jaw. The pain is pulsatile and severe. There are no associated symptoms. He has a history of migraine without aura.

On physical examination, temperature is 36.2 °C (97.2 °F), blood pressure is 146/88 mm Hg, pulse rate is 68/min, respiration rate is 18/min, and BMI is 26. The patient has mild left ptosis and mild anisocoria (3 mm pupil on the left and 4 mm on the right). There is no meningismus. The remainder of the neurologic examination and funduscopic examination findings are normal. An electrocardiogram shows normal findings.

Laboratory studies show a normal complete blood count, erythrocyte sedimentation rate, and serum chemistry levels. Results of a cerebrospinal fluid analysis are normal.

An unenhanced CT scan of the head and neck shows no abnormalities. A magnetic resonance angiogram of the neck (*left*) and an MRI of the brain (*right*) are shown below.

Which of the following is the most appropriate next step in treatment?

(A) Intra-arterial nimodipine
(B) Intravenous dihydroergotamine
(C) Intravenous heparin
(D) Intravenous nitroglycerin
(E) Stent-assisted aneurysm coiling

Item 28

A 73-year-old retired woman is evaluated in the emergency department 6 hours after experiencing the sudden, explosive onset of a severe headache. The patient has hypertension controlled by diet and exercise. There is no relevant

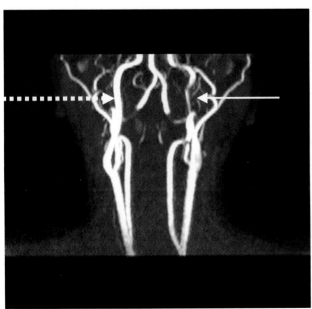

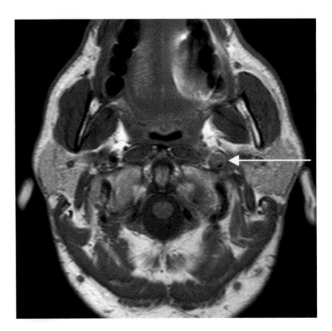

ITEM 27.

family history. She has no allergies and takes no over-the-counter medications.

On physical examination, she is in obvious distress from the headache. Temperature is normal, blood pressure is 179/108 mm Hg, pulse rate is 119/min, and respiration rate is 14/min. There is no meningismus. No subhyaloid retinal hemorrhages are noted. Neurologic examination shows a normal level of consciousness and no focal abnormalities.

Results of laboratory studies and a CT scan of the head without contrast are normal.

Which of the following is the most appropriate next diagnostic test?

(A) CT angiogram of the head
(B) Lumbar puncture
(C) Magnetic resonance angiogram of the brain
(D) Magnetic resonance venogram of the brain
(E) MRI of the brain

Item 29

A 25-year-old woman comes to the office to ask about discontinuing her epilepsy medication because she is concerned about its potential long-term adverse effects. She has a 9-year history of generalized tonic-clonic seizures and rapid, shock-like body jerks consistent with myoclonic seizures on awakening. After her first seizure, she had an MRI with normal findings and an electroencephalogram showing generalized polyspike and wave abnormalities. She was started on lamotrigine and has done relatively well, having only rare seizures when she does not get adequate sleep or indulges in binge alcohol drinking. Her last generalized tonic-clonic seizure occurred 1 year ago.

Results of physical examination, including neurologic examination, are normal.

Which of the following is the best advice regarding discontinuation of the lamotrigine?

(A) Begin a slow taper over the next 3 months
(B) Continue life-long treatment
(C) Discontinue after she is seizure free for 2 years
(D) Discontinue now

Item 30

An 81-year-old man is evaluated for the gradual onset and progression of memory loss over the past year. He says he has difficulty recalling the names of familiar people, has misplaced his wallet on numerous occasions, and is slower to find his car in large, crowded parking lots. He continues to manage his finances, travel with his wife, and perform the activities of daily living without difficulty. He has borderline hyperlipidemia that is managed by diet alone. A paternal uncle developed Alzheimer dementia at age 74 years. His only medications are aspirin and a daily multivitamin.

On physical examination, temperature is 36.7 °C (98.1 °F), blood pressure is 126/82 mm Hg, pulse rate is 68/min, respiration rate is 14/min, and BMI is 26. His level of alertness, speech, and gait are normal. He

scores 26/30 on the Folstein Mini–Mental State Examination, losing all three points on the recall portion and one point on the orientation section for incorrectly stating today's date.

Results of a complete blood count, serum vitamin B_{12} measurement, thyroid function tests, and a basic metabolic panel are normal.

An MRI of the brain without contrast shows no abnormalities.

Which of the following is the most likely diagnosis at this time?

(A) Alzheimer dementia
(B) Dementia with Lewy bodies
(C) Frontotemporal dementia
(D) Mild cognitive impairment
(E) Vascular dementia

Item 31

A 31-year-old woman is evaluated for an 8-month history of diurnal fatigue. She has a 3-year history of relapsing-remitting multiple sclerosis (MS) treated with interferon. The fatigue, which is worse in the early afternoon, has been present since her last MS attack, from which she has otherwise recovered completely. The patient, who has two young children, reports no current problems with sleep or mood and no interferon-related side effects. She exercises regularly. She has a history of depression and hypothyroidism. Current medications are interferon beta-1a and levothyroxine.

On physical examination, temperature is 36.9 °C (98.4 °F), blood pressure is 95/70 mm Hg, pulse rate is 76/min, and BMI is 23. Results of general physical and neurologic examinations are normal.

Results of laboratory studies are also normal, including a complete blood count, erythrocyte sedimentation rate, liver chemistry studies, and serum folate, thyroid-stimulating hormone, and vitamin B_{12} levels.

Which of the following is the most appropriate next step in treatment?

(A) Amantadine administration
(B) Corticosteroid therapy
(C) Discontinuation of the interferon beta-1a
(D) Vitamin B_{12} injections

Item 32

A 35-year-old woman is evaluated in the office for a 5-month history of right-hand numbness and tingling. She says that these symptoms involve the entire hand, seem to be worse when she drives or holds a book or newspaper, and have been awakening her at night. She reports no history of neck pain or hand weakness. Personal and family medical history is noncontributory, and she takes no medication.

General physical examination reveals no abnormalities. Neurologic examination shows normal strength but sensory loss in the distribution of the median nerve in the right hand. Percussion elicits paresthesias at the wrist (Tinel sign).

An electromyogram shows a mild right median neuropathy at the wrist, with no evidence of cervical radiculopathy.

Which of the following is the most appropriate initial step in treatment?

(A) Corticosteroid injection into the carpal tunnel
(B) Gabapentin
(C) Surgical referral for carpal tunnel release
(D) Wrist splints

Item 33

A 28-year-old woman in her first trimester of pregnancy is evaluated in the office for severe and frequent migraine attacks occurring up to four times per week. These attacks are associated with severe pain, nausea, and emesis and last up to 24 hours; acetaminophen and NSAIDs do not relieve her symptoms. The patient has a 10-year history of migraine.

Results of physical examination, including a neurologic examination, are normal.

Which of the following is the most appropriate treatment for this patient?

(A) Amitriptyline at bedtime
(B) Ergotamine tartrate as needed
(C) Metoclopramide as needed
(D) Valproic acid (extended release) twice daily
(E) Verapamil three times daily

Item 34

A 65-year-old man is evaluated for possible epilepsy. He reports three similar "spells" over the past month of which he recalls a feeling of déjà vu followed by a loss of awareness. He says that family members who witnessed these episodes have described him as being unresponsive during them, recounting that he stares and repetitively smacks his lips for 1 minute, followed by a few minutes of confusion and garbled speech before he returns to normal awareness. He has no significant personal or family medical history and takes no medications.

Physical examination, including neurologic examination, reveals no abnormalities.

Which of the following is the most likely diagnosis?

(A) Absence seizure
(B) Generalized tonic-clonic seizure
(C) Myoclonic seizure
(D) Partial complex seizure
(E) Simple partial seizure

Item 35

A 53-year-old woman is evaluated in the office for a 4-month history of tremor. The tremor affects both upper extremities and is present "most of the time." She has a 15-year history of type 2 diabetes mellitus; she also has a history of hypertension, gastroparesis, and chronic kidney

disease. Medications are insulin glargine, insulin lispro, lisinopril, hydrochlorothiazide, and metoclopramide.

On examination, she has diminished pedal pulses. Speech, language, and mental status are normal. Cranial nerve function is normal, although a paucity of facial expression is noted. Movements are slow, and there is mild bilateral upper and lower extremity rigidity. Deep tendon reflexes are normal, as are results of manual muscle strength testing. Sensory examination reveals distal sensory loss. She had a mildly stooped posture but no postural instability. A 4-Hz resting tremor in both upper extremities is noted, as is a prominent postural tremor.

Which of the following is the most likely diagnosis?

(A) Dementia with Lewy bodies
(B) Drug-induced parkinsonism
(C) Multiple system atrophy
(D) Parkinson disease

Item 36

An 81-year-old woman is evaluated in the office for increasing difficulty with activities of daily living, including dressing and feeding herself, over the past 6 months. She has had gradually progressive cognitive decline for the past 5 years and now needs 24-hour help from a caregiver; Alzheimer dementia was previously diagnosed. The patient also has hypertension and hypothyroidism. Her mother had onset of Alzheimer dementia at age 80 years and died at age 87 years. Current medications are donepezil, 10 mg/d; lisinopril, 5 mg/d; levothyroxine, 0.1 mg/d; and a daily multivitamin.

On physical examination, temperature is 36.4 °C (97.5 °F), blood pressure is 120/78 mm Hg, pulse rate is 68/min, respiration rate is 14/min, and BMI is 24. Her level of alertness, speech, and gait are normal. The patient scores only 12/30 on the Folstein Mini–Mental State Examination.

Results of a complete blood count, a basic metabolic panel, a serum vitamin B_{12} measurement, and thyroid function tests are normal.

A CT scan of the head without contrast shows no evidence of tumor, hemorrhage, or infarction.

Which of the following is the most appropriate next step in treatment?

(A) Add memantine
(B) Add quetiapine
(C) Add sertraline
(D) Increase the dosage of donepezil
(E) Stop all medications

Item 37

A 75-year-old man is evaluated in the emergency department for a 2-day history of impaired balance, left-leg weakness, and urinary urgency and a 3-day history of constant midthoracic pain with occasional shooting pain in the left thorax at approximately the T7 dermatome. There is no history of trauma. The patient has degenerative arthritis of the lumbosacral spine. He is a current smoker with a 50-pack-year smoking history. The patient takes occasional ibuprofen or acetaminophen for back pain.

On physical examination, temperature is normal, blood pressure is 140/85 mm Hg, pulse rate is 80/min, and respiration rate is 14/min. Neurologic examination shows left lower extremity weakness, hyperreflexia, an extensor plantar response, bilateral sensory impairment below the T7 dermatome, and gait ataxia. Findings from mental status, cranial nerve, and upper extremity motor and sensory examinations are normal.

Results of a complete blood count, coagulation panel, and erythrocyte sedimentation rate measurement are also normal.

A radiograph of the chest shows a parenchymal lesion in the right lung apex.

Which of the following is the most likely diagnosis?

(A) Acute L5 disk herniation
(B) Epidural abscess
(C) Epidural hematoma
(D) Epidural metastases

Item 38

A 68-year-old man is admitted to the intensive care unit because of an exacerbation of chronic obstructive pulmonary disease (COPD). His course becomes complicated over the next 2 days by pneumonia and acute kidney injury, and he requires noninvasive positive-pressure ventilation with bilevel positive airway pressure. After 10 days, his medical condition stabilizes, but profound weakness of the extremities is noted. Besides COPD, the patient has a history of hypertension, hypothyroidism, and hyperlipidemia. One week before admission, he was started as an outpatient on prednisone, 60 mg/d, for his COPD; other medications include piperacillin-tazobactam, metoprolol, levothyroxine, and simvastatin.

On physical examination, blood pressure is 134/90 mm Hg, pulse rate is 90/min, and arterial oxygen saturation is 96% on nasal oxygen, 2 L/min. Neurologic examination shows profound symmetric weakness of bilateral upper and lower extremity muscles. Deep tendon reflexes and cranial nerve function are normal.

Laboratory studies show an elevated serum creatinine level at 1.5 mg/dL (114.5 µmol/L). Serum levels of creatine kinase and electrolytes are normal, as are results of liver chemistry studies.

Which of the following is the most appropriate therapy for this patient?

(A) Increased dosage of prednisone
(B) Intravenous administration of immune globulin
(C) Physical and occupational therapy
(D) Plasma exchange

Item 39

A 40-year-old woman is evaluated in the emergency department 30 minutes after having a 1-minute episode of involuntary jerking of the right hand that spread up the right arm and a subsequent 2-minute episode of loss of consciousness and witnessed generalized tonic-clonic seizure activity. She has a 1-month history of increasing confusion and low-grade headache. Two years ago, she was treated for cutaneous melanoma.

On physical examination, the patient is awake and alert. Vital signs are normal. There are no signs of meningismus and no papilledema. She has mild right-sided facial droop and only antigravity strength in the right arm; strength is normal elsewhere.

Laboratory studies, including a complete blood count, measurement of serum electrolyte and plasma glucose levels, and a urine toxicology screen, show no abnormalities.

Which of the following is the most appropriate next diagnostic test for this patient?

(A) CT of the head
(B) Electroencephalography
(C) Gadolinium-enhanced MRI of the brain
(D) Lumbar puncture
(E) Positron emission tomography

Item 40

A 48-year-old woman is evaluated in the office for memory loss of gradual onset and progression over the past year. She says she has difficulty recalling names of familiar people, has misplaced her glasses on numerous occasions, and is slower to find her car in large or crowded parking lots. The patient now requires help from her daughter to manage her finances and prepare large meals. She has no other problems or personal medical history, but several members of her family developed dementia between age 46 and 54 years, including her mother, maternal uncle, and maternal grandfather. Her only medication is a daily multivitamin.

On physical examination, temperature is 36.7 °C (98.1 °F), blood pressure is 116/74 mm Hg, pulse rate is 72/min, respiration rate is 14/min, and BMI is 24. Her level of alertness, speech, and gait are normal. She scores 24/30 on the Folstein Mini–Mental State Examination, losing two points on the orientation section for misstating the date and year, one point in the serial calculation portion, and all three points on the recall portion.

Results of a complete blood count, basic metabolic panel, serum vitamin B_{12} measurement, and thyroid function tests are normal. Genetic testing is positive for the presenilin-1 mutation.

An MRI of the brain without contrast shows no abnormalities.

Which of the following is the most likely diagnosis?

(A) Autosomal recessive Parkinson disease with dementia
(B) Creutzfeldt-Jakob disease
(C) Early-onset familial Alzheimer dementia
(D) Frontotemporal dementia
(E) Vascular dementia

Item 41

A 79-year-old woman is to be transferred from the emergency department to a hospital ward for ongoing care. She awoke at home 5 hours ago with slurred speech, difficulty swallowing food and drink, and left hemiparesis. A right hemispheric ischemic stroke was diagnosed in the emergency department after a CT scan of the head confirmed a right hemispheric infarction. Because the time of stroke onset could not be determined, no recombinant tissue plasminogen activator was administered. The patient has no other medical problems and takes no medications.

On physical examination, blood pressure is 168/86 mm Hg, pulse rate is 80/min, and respiration rate is 18/min. Neurologic assessment reveals dysarthria, dysphagia, left facial droop, and left hemiparesis.

Laboratory studies show a plasma LDL cholesterol level of 158 mg/dL (4.09 mmol/L) but no other abnormalities.

Which of the following is the most appropriate first step in management after transfer is completed?

(A) Bedside screening for dysphagia
(B) Oral administration of an angiotensin-converting enzyme inhibitor
(C) Oral administration of a statin
(D) Physical therapy and rehabilitation consultation

Item 42

A 50-year-old man is evaluated for a 12-year history of slowly progressive left leg weakness and trouble ambulating. There is no history of transient neurologic symptoms. He has a history of hypertension, coronary artery disease, and chronic low back pain. Current medications are sublingual nitroglycerin, atenolol, aspirin, and occasional NSAIDs.

On physical examination, vital signs are normal. The patient has moderately severe spastic paraparesis that is worse on the left, with prominent circumduction of the left leg during ambulation. He requires a cane to ambulate 100 meters.

Cerebrospinal fluid analysis reveals the presence of oligoclonal bands.

MRIs of the brain and spine show lesions consistent with chronic multiple sclerosis.

Which of the following is the most appropriate treatment for this patient?

(A) Glatiramer acetate
(B) Interferon beta-1a
(C) Natalizumab
(D) Physical therapy

Item 43

A 30-year-old man is evaluated in the office for an 8-month history of intensely painful headaches, which occur up to 10 times per day and last approximately 15 minutes each. The pain is most severe around the left eye, and he has no pain between attacks. Each attack is associated with rhinorrhea, lacrimation, and conjunctival injection. The patient has a 12-pack-year smoking history. He takes a combination of acetaminophen, caffeine, and aspirin, usually taking a total of five tablets daily.

Results of a physical examination, including a neurologic examination, are normal.

Which of the following is the most likely diagnosis?

(A) Cluster headache
(B) Medication overuse headache
(C) Paroxysmal hemicrania
(D) SUNCT syndrome (Short-lasting Unilateral Neuralgiform headache attacks with Conjunctival injection and Tearing)

Item 44

A 62-year-old woman is evaluated for a 1-year history of tremor that affects both upper extremities. She says that her handwriting has become sloppier since she first noticed the tremor and that she occasionally spills her morning coffee because of it. Although she feels otherwise healthy, she is concerned that she may have Parkinson disease. The patient has a history of hyperlipidemia controlled by diet and exercise but is otherwise healthy. Her mother, who died at age 79 years, had a similar tremor. Her only medication is a daily multivitamin.

On examination, she has a mild tremor in the upper extremities that is present with the arms extended and during finger-to-nose testing. No resting tremor is apparent. Muscle tone and gait and limb coordination are normal.

Administration of which of the following drugs is the most appropriate treatment of this patient?

(A) Carbidopa-levodopa
(B) Clonazepam
(C) Propranolol
(D) Ropinirole

Item 45

A 50-year-old man is admitted to the hospital after having two generalized tonic-clonic seizures in a 24-hour period. He has had seizures in the past, which were always attributed to alcohol withdrawal. Ten years ago, he was in a major motor vehicle collision that was related to alcohol intoxication. He has end-stage liver disease secondary to alcoholic cirrhosis but has been sober for 2 years and is awaiting a liver transplant. His kidney function is normal. His current medications include nadolol, spironolactone, and furosemide.

On physical examination, the patient is awake and alert, is afebrile, and has a normal blood pressure and pulse rate. Neurologic examination findings are normal. The general physical examination reveals changes consistent with chronic liver disease, including jaundice and ascites.

Laboratory studies show a serum creatinine level of 0.6 mg/dL (45.8 μmol/L) and no blood ethanol. Serum electrolyte levels are normal.

An MRI of the brain shows an area of chronic encephalomalacia in the left frontotemporal head region, consistent with old trauma. An electroencephalogram shows left temporal sharp waves.

Which of the following is the best treatment for this patient?

(A) Levetiracetam
(B) Oxcarbazepine
(C) Phenytoin
(D) Valproic acid

Item 46

A 74-year-old woman is admitted to the hospital after sustaining a severe left hemispheric ischemic stroke while alone at home. Her son found her collapsed in the living room when he went to visit her. The patient has hypertension for which she takes enalapril but no history of ischemic heart disease or heart failure.

On physical examination, blood pressure is 190/105 mm Hg, pulse rate is 80/min, and respiration rate is 16/min. The patient has right hemiparesis, right facial droop, aphasia, and dysarthria. The remainder of the physical examination, including the cardiovascular examination, is normal.

Results of laboratory studies, including serum creatinine level, are normal.

A CT scan shows frank ischemic changes that occupy most of the left middle cerebral artery territory. An electrocardiogram and chest radiograph show normal findings.

Which of the following is the most appropriate treatment of her hypertension at this time?

(A) Intravenous labetalol
(B) Intravenous nicardipine
(C) Oral nifedipine
(D) Withholding of all antihypertensive medications

Item 47

A 44-year-old woman is evaluated for a 4-month history of worsening gait and bilateral leg numbness. She underwent gastric bypass surgery 8 years ago but has no other relevant personal or family medical history. Her only medications are a daily multivitamin and vitamin B_{12}.

On physical examination, temperature is normal, blood pressure is 130/80 mm Hg, pulse rate is 90/min, respiration rate is 14/min, and BMI is 29. The patient has moderate gait ataxia, lower extremity spasticity, hyperreflexia, and bilateral extensor plantar responses. Strength is normal, but vibration and proprioceptive sensation is impaired in both feet.

Results of laboratory studies show a mild normocytic anemia. Serum vitamin B_{12}, vitamin E, methylmalonic acid, and homocysteine levels are all normal.

Nerve conduction studies and an electromyogram reveal a moderate axonal peripheral neuropathy. MRIs of the cervical spinal cord and the thoracic spinal cord show no abnormalities.

Which of the following is the most appropriate next diagnostic study?

(A) Antinuclear antibody testing
(B) Measurement of serum copper and zinc levels
(C) MRI of the brain
(D) Serum neuromyelitis optica (NMO)-IgG autoantibody test

Item 48

A 68-year-old man is evaluated for fatigue. He says that for the past 2 weeks, he has been awakening at approximately 2 AM with a left-sided tremor and left-sided stiffness. Parkinson disease was diagnosed 3 years ago after he noted a left-hand tremor and a change in his handwriting; examination at that time showed mild parkinsonian signs, and he was started on carbidopa-levodopa. He currently takes immediate-release carbidopa-levodopa, which results in near-resolution of his parkinsonian symptoms; he notes, however, that the medication wears off if too much time passes between doses. During this recent period of early-morning awakening, he has occasionally taken extra carbidopa-levodopa, which has allowed him to fall asleep again.

Results of a general medical examination are normal. Neurologic examination reveals slurred speech and a paucity of facial expression. Deep tendon reflexes are normal, as are results of manual muscle strength testing and sensory examination. He has mild upper extremity rigidity that is greatest in the left arm and a very mild resting tremor of the left upper limb. No appendicular or truncal ataxia is noted.

Which of the following should be added to this patient's drug regimen to treat his fatigue?

(A) Clonazepam, before bedtime
(B) Donepezil
(C) Extended-release carbidopa-levodopa, before bedtime
(D) Fluoxetine

Item 49

A 38-year-old woman is evaluated in the office for a 10-month history of increasingly frequent headache. The headache is often worse in the morning on awakening. She has recently started keeping a headache diary, which reveals episodes on approximately 25 days of each month. The headache varies from a near-daily bilateral frontal dull throbbing to a severe left hemicranial throbbing associated with nausea, photophobia, and phonophobia. The patient has a 20-year history of migraine without aura and a history of depression. Her mother also has a history of migraine and depression, and her sister has a history of migraine. The patient has been taking propranolol for 3 months; a mixed analgesic containing butalbital, caffeine, and acetaminophen for mild or moderate headache at least 3 days per week for 9 months; rizatriptan for severe headache at least 2 days per week for 4 months; and citalopram for 1 year. Rizatriptan has become increasingly ineffective over the past month.

Physical examination findings, including neurologic examination findings, are normal.

Which of the following is the most likely diagnosis for her current symptoms?

(A) Chronic migraine
(B) Chronic tension-type headache
(C) Idiopathic intracranial hypertension
(D) Medication overuse headache

Item 50

A 68-year-old man is admitted to the hospital for evaluation of a transient 15-minute episode of left facial droop, slurred speech, and left arm weakness. Three years ago, the patient had a radical neck dissection as treatment of head and neck cancer and subsequently had radiation therapy. He also has hypertension and hyperlipidemia and has a 40-pack-year smoking history. Family history is noncontributory. Current medications are lisinopril, atorvastatin, and aspirin.

On physical examination, temperature is normal, blood pressure is 156/88 mm Hg, pulse rate is 88/min, and respiration rate is 14/min. A right carotid bruit is heard on auscultation. No abnormal findings are noted on neurologic examination.

Results of laboratory studies are normal.

An MRI of the brain reveals a small wedge-shaped, cortical diffusion–weighted positive region of signal change occupying the right hemisphere. A magnetic resonance angiogram of the neck shows 80% stenosis of the right internal carotid artery.

In addition to aspirin therapy, which of the following is the most appropriate next step in treatment?

(A) Carotid angioplasty and stenting
(B) Carotid endarterectomy
(C) External carotid to internal carotid artery bypass surgery
(D) Intravenous administration of heparin

Item 51

A 69-year-old woman is evaluated in the office for visual hallucinations that have occurred several times over the past 3 months. During the past year, she and others have noticed that she is walking more slowly, has a mildly stooped posture, and occasionally has saliva accumulating at the corner of her mouth. Over the past 3 years, she has had increasing difficulty organizing financial records, has forgotten appointments, and twice became lost in crowded but familiar parts of her town. According to her husband, who accompanied her to this appointment, her sleep over the past 10 years has been marked by semipurposeful and flailing limb movements and occasional clear speech, once taking the form of a speech to employees. Her mother had onset of Alzheimer dementia at age 77 years and died at age 82 years. Her only medication is a daily multivitamin.

On physical examination, temperature is 36.6 °C (97.9 °F), blood pressure is 142/76 mm Hg supine and 110/68 mm Hg standing, pulse rate is 80/min supine and does not change with standing, respiration rate is 14/min, and BMI is 22. There is trace cogwheeling of the right upper limb. When the patient walks, her posture is slightly stooped, right arm swing is slightly diminished, and gait is slow without frank shuffling. Rapid alternating movements are mildly reduced in speed and amplitude in the right hand. She has mildly reduced facial expression and mildly reduced inflection of speech. She scores 27/30 on the Folstein Mini–Mental State Examination, losing one point for misstating the date and two points on the memory portion of the test. Her level of alertness is normal, and she has no tremor.

Results of a complete blood count, basic metabolic panel, serum vitamin B_{12} measurement, and thyroid function tests are normal.

An MRI of the brain without contrast shows no abnormalities.

Which of the following is the most likely diagnosis?

(A) Alzheimer dementia
(B) Creutzfeldt-Jakob disease
(C) Dementia with Lewy bodies
(D) Frontotemporal dementia
(E) Vascular dementia

Item 52

A 32-year-old woman is seen for a follow-up evaluation. She had a witnessed generalized tonic-clonic seizure 1 week ago and was evaluated in the emergency department, where results of physical examination, complete blood count, measurement of serum electrolyte levels, and urine toxicology screen were all normal. She is otherwise healthy, has no significant personal or family medical history, and takes no medications.

Results of a repeat physical examination are also normal.

In addition to electroencephalography, which of the following diagnostic tests should be performed next?

(A) CT of the head
(B) Lumbar puncture
(C) MRI of the brain
(D) Positron emission tomography

Item 53

A 50-year-old man is evaluated because of abnormal findings on a brain MRI. Two weeks ago, he was involved in a motor vehicle accident in which he sustained shoulder, upper back, and neck injuries and head trauma without loss of consciousness. Results of an MRI of the cervical spine were normal, but an MRI of the brain revealed the white matter abnormalities shown on the next page.

The patient has a 15-year history of hypertension but no personal or family history of neurologic disease. His only medication is quinapril.

On physical examination, blood pressure is 155/90 mm Hg; all other vital signs are normal. Results of neurologic examination are also normal.

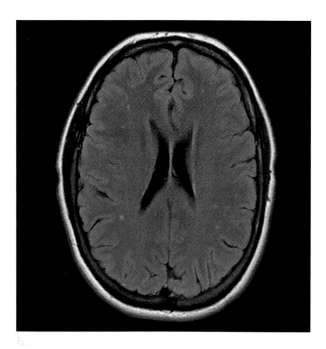

Which of the following is the most appropriate next step in diagnosis?

(A) Lumbar puncture
(B) Repeat MRI in 3 months
(C) Visual evoked potential studies
(D) No further testing

Item 54

A 56-year-old man is evaluated in the office for a 1-month history of intermittent weakness of the left foot, a 6-month history of progressive right arm weakness, and 1-year history of muscle cramps. He says he feels lately as if he is "catching" his foot on things when ambulating. He has noticed no shortness of breath, dysphagia, or other bulbar symptoms and reports no other pain, sensory loss, or bowel or bladder impairment. The patient is otherwise healthy, has no history of disease, and is unaware of any family history of neurologic disorders. He takes no medications.

Results of a general medical examination are normal. Neurologic examination reveals normal speech, language, and mental status. His tongue appears atrophic with fasciculations. He has diffuse weakness and atrophy of the proximal muscles in the right arm; fasciculations are noted. Left arm strength and muscle bulk are normal. Moderate weakness of the distal muscles in the left leg is noted, with fasciculations present in both lower extremities. Deep tendon reflexes are brisk in the upper and lower limbs, and the plantar response is extensor bilaterally. Sensory examination reveals no abnormalities, and there is no appendicular ataxia.

Laboratory studies show a serum creatine kinase level of 602 U/L. Results of a complete blood count; measurement of serum creatinine, electrolyte, and vitamin B_{12} levels; and liver chemistry studies are normal.

A radiograph of the chest shows no abnormalities.

Which of the following is the most likely diagnosis?

(A) Amyotrophic lateral sclerosis
(B) Cervical myelopathy
(C) Chronic inflammatory demyelinating polyradiculoneuropathy
(D) Primary lateral sclerosis

Item 55

A 32-year-old man is evaluated in the office for a 6-month history of excruciating headaches, which occur up to 12 times per day and last approximately 10 minutes each. He is pain free between attacks. The pain is centered around and behind the left eye, and each attack is associated with conjunctival injection, lacrimation, and rhinorrhea. The patient has an 8-pack-year smoking history. He takes a combination of acetaminophen, caffeine, and aspirin, usually taking a total of four to six tablets daily.

Results of a physical examination, including a neurologic examination, are normal.

Which of the following is the most appropriate treatment for this patient's condition?

(A) Indomethacin
(B) Lamotrigine
(C) Prednisone
(D) Verapamil

Item 56

A 72-year-old man with a 3-year history of progressive dementia is evaluated in the emergency department for increased weakness, difficulty arising from a seated position, gross unsteadiness and slowness of pace while walking, and a 1-week history of urinary incontinence. His wife reports that after a fall 3 weeks ago in which he sustained no head trauma, he started to become weaker and more confused and now cannot ambulate without holding onto someone or using a walker. Although the patient has exhibited progressive mild gait change with shuffling and reduced left-sided arm swing over the past 2 years, he has not previously required a gait aid. At an evaluation 2 months ago, he scored 19/30 on the Folstein Mini–Mental State Examination. The patient also has chronic atrial fibrillation. There is no relevant family medical history. Current medications are donepezil, memantine, atenolol, and warfarin.

On physical examination, temperature is 36.5 °C (97.8 °F), blood pressure is 96/60 mm Hg, pulse rate is 84/min and irregular, respiration rate is 16/min, and BMI is 23. The patient attends to the examiner but cannot rise from a seated position without assistance. His posture is stooped and he walks slowly with a shuffling gait, is very unsteady, and requires the assistance of the examiner to walk without falling. The patient fatigues rapidly after walking a few feet. There are no cranial bruises or other signs of trauma. He now scores 5/30 on the Folstein Mini–Mental State Examination.

Laboratory studies show an INR of 2.3. Results of a complete blood count, a basic metabolic panel, measurement of serum vitamin B_{12} and thyroid-stimulating hormone levels, and a urinalysis are normal.

A chest radiograph shows clear lung fields. An electrocardiogram shows atrial fibrillation, with a heart rate of 84/min.

Which of the following is the most appropriate next diagnostic test?

(A) Awake and asleep electroencephalography
(B) Cerebrospinal fluid analysis
(C) CT of the head
(D) Echocardiography

Item 57

A 45-year-old woman is admitted to the hospital with mild left hemiplegia, left hemineglect, and dysarthria. A CT scan of the head reveals a large right hemispheric infarction due to an occluded right middle cerebral artery. She has a history of anti–phospholipid antibody syndrome diagnosed 3 years ago after an episode of iliofemoral venous thrombosis. She was treated for 18 months with warfarin but elected to discontinue treatment. There is no relevant family history. Her only medication is aspirin.

Forty-eight hours later, a progressive deterioration of her mental status is noted. The patient had previously stated that she wants everything possible done to prolong her life ("full code").

Examination now shows that she has severe left hemiplegia and that her head and eyes are deviated to the right.

A repeat CT scan of the head reveals a large hypodense region occupying the entire right middle cerebral artery territory, a local mass effect, and a 7-mm midline shift from right to left.

Which of the following is the most appropriate therapy at this time?

(A) Decompressive hemicraniectomy
(B) Intra-arterial thrombolysis
(C) Intravenous heparin
(D) Use of an endovascular mechanical clot-retrieval device

Item 58

A 58-year-old man is evaluated for a 5-month history of gait impairment and falls and a 1-week history of difficulty swallowing. His wife, who accompanied him, says that she has noticed a change in his speech over the past few weeks. He has no significant medical history, and there is no known family history of neurologic problems.

General physical examination findings are normal; no orthostatic decrease in blood pressure is noted. Neurologic examination shows normal orientation and memory. Speech is slow and mildly dysarthric, and he appears to have decreased facial expression. Cranial nerve examination shows an impairment in vertical gaze. There is evidence of moderate axial and mild bilateral appendicular rigidity. No tremor is noted. Muscle strength and deep tendon reflexes are normal, as are sensory examination findings. There is no

appendicular ataxia. Gait is slow, and there is significant postural instability.

Which of the following is the most likely diagnosis?

(A) Amyotrophic lateral sclerosis
(B) Corticobasal degeneration
(C) Parkinson disease
(D) Progressive supranuclear palsy

Item 59

A 58-year-old man is evaluated in the emergency department after having a generalized tonic-clonic seizure 1 hour ago while sleeping; the seizure was witnessed by his wife. The patient has postictal lethargy and confusion. Stage IV non–small cell lung cancer characterized by a large, surgically nonresectable lesion in the right lung and by liver and pancreatic metastases was diagnosed 6 months earlier. He has been receiving chemotherapy for the past 5 months.

On examination, the patient is afebrile; other vital signs are also normal. He is lethargic but arousable and is oriented to self but not to time or place. Mild weakness and incoordination of the right upper extremity are noted.

Results of laboratory studies are normal.

An MRI of the brain with contrast shows nine ring-enhancing lesions at the gray-white junction that involve both cerebral hemispheres and are consistent with metastases. The largest of these is in the left precentral gyrus and is associated with edema in the surrounding white matter.

Which of the following is the best management option?

(A) Brain biopsy
(B) Palliative whole-brain radiation therapy and corticosteroid administration
(C) Stereotactic radiosurgery of the left precentral gyrus
(D) Surgical resection of accessible cerebral metastases

Item 60

A 33-year-old man is evaluated for a 3-day history of worsening weakness and numbness of the right arm and leg. He has a 5-year history of multiple sclerosis. His only current medication is glatiramer acetate.

On physical examination, temperature is 36.5 °C (97.7 °F), blood pressure is 105/75 mm Hg, pulse rate is 68/min, and respiration rate is 14/min. Moderate right arm and leg weakness, hyperreflexia, an extensor plantar response, and vibratory sense impairment are noted.

Which of the following should this patient receive to treat his acute relapse?

(A) Empiric antibiotic therapy
(B) Immune globulin, intravenously
(C) Methylprednisolone, intravenously
(D) Plasmapheresis
(E) Prednisone, orally

Item 61

A 17-year-old male high school student is evaluated in the emergency department 1 hour after having a generalized tonic-clonic seizure while eating breakfast with his family. He says he was out late the night before with classmates and drank six cans of beer over the course of the evening. He reports having sudden, involuntary jerks of his arms this morning before the convulsion and having had similar jerks on awakening over the past 2 months when sleep deprived. He reports no history of regular alcohol or illicit substance abuse. He takes no medications.

Physical examination and neurologic examination findings are normal.

Results of laboratory studies (including a complete blood count; measurements of serum electrolyte, plasma glucose, and serum ethanol levels; and a urine toxicology screen) are normal.

A CT scan of the head shows no abnormalities.

Which of the following is the most likely diagnosis?

(A) Alcohol withdrawal seizure
(B) Benign rolandic epilepsy
(C) Juvenile myoclonic epilepsy
(D) Temporal lobe epilepsy

Item 62

A 78-year-old man is re-evaluated after a 5-mm left middle cerebral artery aneurysm is discovered incidentally on an MRI of the brain obtained because of a previous symptom of extreme dizziness, which has since resolved. The patient has no other relevant personal or family medical history and takes no medications.

On physical examination, blood pressure is 138/82 mm Hg, pulse rate is 80/min, and respiration rate is 18/min. Results of physical examination, including neurologic examination, are normal.

A magnetic resonance angiogram (MRA) shows a solitary unruptured aneurysm but no additional intracranial aneurysms. No hemorrhage, infarction, mass, or mass effect is evident.

Which of the following is the most appropriate next step in the management of this patient's aneurysm?

(A) Annual MRA
(B) Endovascular coiling of the aneurysm
(C) Nimodipine administration
(D) Surgical clipping of the aneurysm

Item 63

A 64-year-old woman is evaluated for a 1-year history of increasing difficulty finding the right word in conversation and completing sentences; she sometimes says the wrong word accidentally. Her family now has difficulty understanding her, and she no longer has any interest in speaking on the telephone. Her ability to drive, shop, pay bills, and cook seems unimpaired. She has no other relevant personal or family medical history. Her only medication is aspirin, 81 mg/d.

On physical examination, temperature is 36.6 °C (97.9 °F), blood pressure is 122/78 mm Hg, pulse rate is 80/min, respiration rate is 14/min, and BMI is 23. The patient is right-handed. Her level of alertness is normal, and her comprehension appears to be intact, with her correctly executing the commands to show the right thumb and two fingers on the left hand. Spontaneous speech is effortful, and she talks in short, telegraphic sentences filled with many mispronunciations (such as "posital" for "hospital"). She makes similar errors when trying to write words rather than speak them, can repeat no more than two words or four numbers at a time, and can repeat essentially no sentences.

Results of a complete blood count, a basic metabolic panel, a serum vitamin B$_{12}$ measurement, and thyroid function tests are normal.

An MRI of the brain without contrast shows mild atrophy but is otherwise unremarkable.

This patient's impairment in speech and writing is most likely due to which of the following disorders?

(A) Alzheimer dementia
(B) Creutzfeldt-Jakob disease
(C) Dementia with Lewy bodies
(D) Frontotemporal lobar degeneration
(E) Vascular dementia

Item 64

A 28-year-old man is evaluated in the office for a 3-day history of blurred vision in the left eye and pain with eye movement. He has a history of rare migraine headaches but no other disorders. There is no pertinent family history. The patient takes no medications.

On physical examination, temperature is 36.8 °C (98.2 °F), blood pressure is 105/65 mm Hg, pulse rate is 78/min, respiration rate is 12/min, and BMI is 22. A left central scotoma is noted on visual field testing. Corrected visual acuity is 20/50 in the right eye and 20/20 in the left; red desaturation and a relative afferent pupillary defect are noted in the left eye. Other findings of physical and neurologic examinations, including funduscopy, are normal.

Results of laboratory studies are normal.

An orbital MRI reveals enhancement of the left optic nerve with intravenous administration of gadolinium. An MRI of the brain shows six periventricular white matter lesions, each measuring 3 to 5 mm in diameter and one enhancing with gadolinium administration. Ophthalmologic consultation confirms that the clinical features are compatible with optic neuritis.

Which of the following best describes this patient's approximate risk of developing multiple sclerosis over the next 10 to 15 years?

(A) 10%
(B) 20%
(C) 50%
(D) 90%

Item 65

A 40-year-old man is evaluated in the emergency department for ongoing seizure activity. His wife says that he was having a generalized tonic-clonic seizure when she awoke 45 minutes ago and that she called the paramedics when the seizure continued for more than 5 minutes; she also reports that he had three seizures yesterday, each consisting of staring and unresponsiveness with repetitive lip smacking and each lasting 2 minutes. The patient has a known history of partial epilepsy secondary to a cavernous malformation in the left temporal lobe and has an average of four seizures each year. He is on phenytoin therapy.

On examination, he is comatose with continuous rhythmic twitching of the right face and arm. Blood pressure is 120/70 mm Hg, pulse rate is 80/min, and arterial oxygen saturation rate by pulse oximetry is 85% (on ambient air). The patient is intubated.

Which of the following is the most appropriate next step in management?

(A) CT of the head
(B) Electroencephalography
(C) Intravenous administration of lorazepam
(D) Measurement of serum phenytoin level

Item 66

A 55-year-old man is evaluated in the postanesthesia care unit for an inability to move his right arm and leg and a marked delay in his ability to obey commands and instructions. Two hours ago, he underwent femoropopliteal bypass surgery because of severe lower extremity peripheral artery disease. The neurologic deficits were first noticed 15 minutes ago, immediately after extubation. In addition to peripheral artery disease, the patient has a history of hypertension, hyperlipidemia, coronary artery disease, and type 2 diabetes mellitus. Medications include aspirin, metoprolol, lisinopril, simvastatin, and metformin.

On physical examination, blood pressure is 162/88 mm Hg, pulse rate is 80/min, respiration rate is 18/min, and BMI is 31. Pupils are 3 mm in diameter, symmetric, and reactive to light. He is aphasic, has right hemiparesis, and has a right extensor plantar response.

An immediately obtained CT scan of the head shows a subtle hyperdensity of the left middle cerebral artery in the sylvian fissure but no other obvious abnormalities.

Which of the following is the most appropriate next step in management?

(A) Administration of naloxone
(B) Intra-arterial clot extraction
(C) Intravenous administration of recombinant tissue plasminogen activator
(D) MRI of the brain

Item 67

A 65-year-old man is hospitalized because of a 6-week history of progressive weakness and incoordination of the left arm and leg. He is otherwise healthy, with no relevant personal or family medical history. He takes no medications.

Vital signs and other general physical examination findings are normal. Neurologic examination confirms mild weakness of the left arm and leg with decreased rapid alternating movements.

A complete blood count and peripheral blood smear are normal.

A contrast-enhanced MRI of the brain is shown.

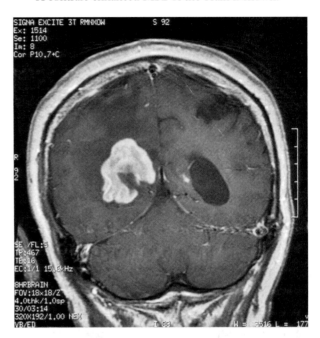

Lumbar puncture is ordered, and no abnormalities are found on subsequent analysis of the cerebrospinal fluid, including cytologic examination and flow cytometry.

Which of the following is the most appropriate next step in management?

(A) Chemotherapy with intrathecal methotrexate
(B) Corticosteroid administration
(C) Hospice referral
(D) Stereotactic brain biopsy
(E) Whole-brain radiation therapy

Item 68

A 24-year-old woman is evaluated in the office for an 8-week history of severe daily headache. The headache is generalized and throbbing in quality and is associated with intermittent nausea and vomiting, episodes of visual blurring provoked by coughing and laughing, and the perception that she can hear her heartbeat. The headache has been unresponsive to oral administration of two different triptans and to a 1-month course of amitriptyline. The patient has a history of migraine without aura since age 13 years. Her only current medication is ibuprofen, as needed.

On physical examination, her temperature is 36.4 °C (97.5 °F), blood pressure is 128/80 mm Hg, pulse rate is 88/min, respiration rate is 20/min, and BMI is 34. She has impaired lateral gaze with the left eye, indistinct disc margins, and no retinal venous pulsations. There is no impairment of visual acuity or visual fields to confrontation.

Results of a complete blood count, liver chemistry studies, and measurements of serum creatinine, electrolyte, and thyroid-stimulating hormone levels are normal.

An MRI of the brain and magnetic resonance venography of the brain show no abnormalities.

Lumbar puncture reveals an opening pressure of 380 mm H_2O. Results of cerebrospinal fluid analysis are normal.

Which of the following is the most appropriate treatment at this time?

(A) Acetazolamide
(B) Nortriptyline
(C) Propranolol
(D) Sumatriptan, subcutaneously
(E) Valproic acid

Item 69

A 54-year-old man with a 1-year history of Parkinson disease is brought to the office by his wife, who is concerned about her husband's recent excessive gambling. She says that in the past 6 months, he has been spending increasing amounts of time at a casino, where he rarely enjoyed going before the diagnosis of Parkinson disease. His behavior is otherwise unchanged. The patient has been taking ropinirole since the diagnosis and has had a marked diminution in tremor as a result; he has had no difficulties with or change in mood, cognition, or sleep.

General physical examination findings are normal. Neurologic examination shows normal speech, language, mood, and mental status. There is mild left upper limb rigidity and a minimal resting tremor, but no other abnormalities are detected.

Which of the following is the most likely cause of this patient's gambling problem?

(A) Bipolar disorder
(B) Frontotemporal dementia
(C) Medication-related compulsive behavior
(D) Parkinson-related dementia

Item 70

A 33-year-old woman is evaluated in the emergency department for paresthesia that began in the left face and spread over 30 minutes to the left arm and leg, clumsiness of the left hand that began 30 minutes ago, and an emerging right-sided throbbing headache. She is otherwise healthy but has a family history of migraine. Her only medication is a daily oral contraceptive pill.

On physical examination, temperature is normal, blood pressure is 140/82 mm Hg, pulse rate is 110/min, and respiration rate is 20/min. All other examination findings are normal.

Results of laboratory studies and a CT scan of the head are also normal.

Which of the following is the most likely diagnosis?

(A) Migraine with aura
(B) Multiple sclerosis
(C) Sensory seizure
(D) Transient ischemic attack

Item 71

A 25-year-old woman with epilepsy comes to the office seeking advice about pregnancy. She first developed seizures after sustaining a head injury in a motor vehicle collision at age 16 years. MRIs obtained since then have shown an area of encephalomalacia in the right temporal lobe. Her seizures were initially refractory to carbamazepine and valproic acid monotherapy. Carbamazepine was stopped, and lamotrigine was added to the valproic acid 1 year ago. She has not had any seizures since that time.

Which of the following is the most appropriate management?

(A) Advise the patient not to become pregnant
(B) Continue the valproic acid and lamotrigine
(C) Discontinue the valproic acid and continue the lamotrigine
(D) Discontinue the valproic acid and lamotrigine
(E) Substitute phenobarbital for her current medications

Item 72

A 79-year-old woman was hospitalized 4 days ago after sustaining a right hip fracture in a fall. She underwent surgical repair with right hip replacement 3 days ago and did not awaken from general anesthesia until 12 hours after extubation. As her alertness has increased, she has become increasingly agitated, yelling at the nurses and flailing her arms; mechanical four-limb restraints were placed 2 days ago. The patient has a 4-year history of progressive cognitive decline diagnosed as Alzheimer dementia. She also has chronic atrial fibrillation treated with chronic warfarin therapy. She has no other pertinent personal or family medical history. Current medications are donepezil, memantine, atenolol, warfarin, and low-molecular-weight heparin.

On physical examination today, temperature is 37.2 °C (99.0 °F), blood pressure is 100/68 mm Hg, pulse rate is 100/min and irregular, respiration rate is 18/min, and BMI is 21. The patient can move all four limbs with guarding of the right lower limb. She is inattentive and disoriented to time and place and exhibits combativeness alternating with hypersomnolence. The remainder of the neurologic examination is unremarkable, without evidence of focal findings or meningismus.

Which of the following is the most likely diagnosis?

(A) Acute cerebral infarction
(B) Acute worsening of Alzheimer dementia
(C) Meningitis
(D) Postoperative delirium

Item 73

A 36-year-old woman is evaluated in the emergency department for a 3-day history of confusion and falls. Her husband, who accompanied her, says that her symptoms seem to be getting worse. She has a 20-year history of Crohn disease that necessitated a partial small bowel resection because of stricture formation 5 years ago; she had a partial colectomy for fistulae 2 years ago and has had recent weight loss due to diarrhea. Current medications include prednisone and azathioprine.

On physical examination, temperature is 35.6 °C (96.0 °F), blood pressure is 142/76 mm Hg, pulse rate is 90/min, respiration rate is 14/min, and BMI is 17. Temporal muscle wasting, sunken supraclavicular fossae, and absent adipose stores are noted. Abdominal examination reveals surgical scars and a few low-pitched bowel sounds, but results are otherwise normal. On neurologic examination, the patient is confused; she is unable to state the date and does not know the name of the hospital. Marked nystagmus is noted. There is no nuchal rigidity or obvious motor weakness. Deep tendon reflexes are reduced, and plantar responses are flexor. The patient has a markedly ataxic gait.

Which of the following is the best initial management?

(A) Electroencephalography
(B) Haloperidol
(C) Thiamine
(D) Vancomycin, ampicillin, and ceftriaxone

Item 74

A 65-year-old woman comes to the office for her annual examination. She reports that she had a tonic-clonic seizure at age 24 years after the birth of her daughter but has been seizure free on phenytoin since that time. The patient also has osteoporosis, diagnosed after a screening bone density scan. Current medications include phenytoin, alendronate, calcium, and vitamin D.

Physical examination findings are normal.

Which of the following is the most appropriate next step in management?

(A) Check the serum phenytoin level
(B) Continue the current dosage of phenytoin
(C) Discontinue the phenytoin in a tapered fashion
(D) Substitute lamotrigine for the phenytoin

Item 75

A 25-year-old woman is evaluated in the office for a 1-week history of numbness of the left leg. She also had a 2-week history of diplopia and vertigo 1 year ago; an MRI obtained at that time is shown to the right. There is no family history of neurologic problems. She takes no medications.

On physical examination, vital signs are normal. Plantar response is extensor on the left. There is mild loss of

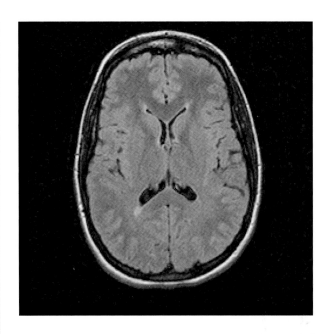

vibratory sense in both feet with a patchy, reduced pain sensation throughout the left lower extremity.

Laboratory studies are noncontributory.

A repeat MRI of the brain shows only the same periventricular white matter lesion. MRIs of the cervical spine and thoracic spine show no abnormalities.

Which of the following is the most appropriate next step in diagnosis?

(A) Electronystagmography
(B) Lumbar puncture
(C) Magnetic resonance angiography
(D) Magnetic resonance spectroscopy

Item 76

An 88-year-old man is brought to the emergency department within 45 minutes of the witnessed onset of dysarthria and right face, arm, and leg weakness. Recombinant tissue plasminogen activator is administered intravenously 105 minutes after symptom onset. The patient is then admitted to the intensive care unit, and 4 hours after thrombolysis, his neurologic symptoms and signs are rapidly improving.

On physical examination, vital signs are normal, except for a blood pressure of 190/105 mm Hg. There is right pronator drift, right facial droop, and mild residual dysarthria.

Which of the following is the most appropriate treatment of this patient's elevated blood pressure?

(A) Intravenous labetalol
(B) Intravenous nitroprusside
(C) Oral nifedipine
(D) Withholding of antihypertensive medications

Item 77

A 34-year-old woman is evaluated in the office for right-sided facial paralysis that she noticed on awakening 1 hour ago. She has a 10-pack-year smoking history. Personal and family medical history is noncontributory. Her only medication is a daily oral contraceptive.

On physical examination, temperature is 36.5 °C (97.7 °F), blood pressure is 110/70 mm Hg, pulse rate is 82/min, respiration rate is 14/min, and BMI is 26. Limb strength, reflexes, and tone are normal bilaterally. Findings from a sensory examination, which included her face, are also normal. When asked to raise her eyebrows, the patient does not elevate the right side. When asked to shut her eyes, she cannot close the right one, but the globe rotates upward, partially covering the iris. When asked to smile, the patient does not move the right side of her face.

Which of the following is the most likely diagnosis?

(A) Graves ophthalmopathy
(B) Left cerebral infarction
(C) Right facial nerve (Bell) palsy
(D) Right trigeminal neuralgia

Item 78

A 46-year-old man is evaluated in the office for a 6-month history of a resting right-arm tremor. He says that his writing has gotten smaller during this time and that he has had difficulty buttoning his dress shirts. The patient reports no prior medical problems and is not aware of any neurologic problems in his family. He takes no medications.

Results of a general medical examination are normal. Neurologic examination shows a paucity of facial expression (hypomimia). Cranial nerve function is normal. Motor examination shows normal strength but mild left upper limb rigidity and a 5-Hz resting tremor of the right upper limb. Deep tendon reflexes are normal, as are results of sensory examination. There is no truncal or appendicular ataxia. Diminished arm swing is noted bilaterally, but it is worse on the right. A tremor in the right upper limb is noted during ambulation. Left upper limb alternating motion rates are diminished.

Which of the following is the best treatment for this patient?

(A) Amantadine
(B) Pramipexole
(C) Primidone
(D) Propranolol

Item 79

A 70-year-old man is seen in the office for routine follow-up of partial seizures that began 2 years ago after a stroke. At that time, he was started on phenytoin, 300 mg/d, and has had no subsequent seizures; he tolerates the medication well, with no reported adverse effects. His current medications are phenytoin, an angiotensin-converting enzyme inhibitor, a statin, and aspirin.

Results of physical examination, including a neurologic examination, are normal.

Laboratory studies show a total serum phenytoin level of 9 mg/L (35.6 μmol/L) (therapeutic range, 10-20 mg/L

[39.6-79.2 μmol/L]). Results of a complete blood count and liver chemistry tests are normal.

Which of the following is the most appropriate next step in management?

(A) Continue the phenytoin at the current dosage
(B) Increase the phenytoin dosage
(C) Measure the free serum phenytoin level
(D) Substitute gabapentin for the phenytoin

Item 80

A 26-year-old woman is evaluated in the office for a change in migraine symptoms. She began having migraine attacks shortly after menarche at age 13 years, experiencing an attack approximately every 2 months. For the past 8 weeks, these attacks have been associated with visual aura. The neurologic symptoms evolve over a period of 10 minutes, last less than 60 minutes, and are followed within 30 minutes by a severe, unilateral throbbing headache associated with nausea. Sumatriptan relieves the headache within 30 minutes. The patient also has asthma. Her mother and sister have a history of migraine. Current medications are an oral contraceptive pill started 9 weeks ago, sumatriptan as needed, a daily inhaled corticosteroid, and an inhaled β-agonist as needed.

Results of physical examination, including neurologic examination, are normal.

Complete blood count results, erythrocyte sedimentation rate, serum chemistry study results, thyroid-stimulating hormone level, and anticardiolipin and antinuclear antibody levels are normal.

An MRI of the brain shows no abnormalities.

Which of the following is the most appropriate next step in management?

(A) Add propranolol
(B) Add verapamil
(C) Discontinue the oral contraceptive pill
(D) Discontinue the sumatriptan
(E) Measure serum lactate and pyruvate levels

Item 81

An 82-year-old man is evaluated in the office for an episode of hesitancy in speech, word-finding difficulty, right facial droop, and weakness and awkwardness of the right hand and arm. The episode occurred early yesterday, lasted 20 minutes, and was witnessed by his wife. The patient has a history of coronary artery disease, hypertension, and hyperlipidemia. Current medications are metoprolol, aspirin, hydrochlorothiazide, and lovastatin.

On physical examination, temperature is normal, blood pressure is 148/88 mm Hg, pulse rate is 70/min, and respiration rate is 12/min. Neurologic examination reveals no abnormalities.

Which of the following is the most appropriate next step in management?

(A) Add clopidogrel
(B) Admit to the hospital
(C) Order outpatient diagnostic studies
(D) Schedule a follow-up visit in 1 week

Item 82

A 33-year-old woman is admitted to the hospital for evaluation and treatment of new-onset transverse myelitis that has resulted in severe paraparesis. The patient also has had two recent episodes of optic neuritis. She reports no systemic symptoms, such as fever, rash, arthralgias, or pulmonary problems. She has a history of hypothyroidism but no family history of any neurologic disorders. Her only medication is levothyroxine.

Vital signs are normal on physical examination. Visual acuity is 20/200 in the right eye and 20/30 in the left. Bilateral optic disc pallor and severe spastic paraparesis with loss of all sensory modalities below T10 are noted. The patient requires bilateral assistance to ambulate 5 meters.

Results of laboratory studies are normal, including a complete blood count, liver chemistry and renal function tests, and measurement of erythrocyte sedimentation rate and C-reactive protein level. The antinuclear antibody is positive, but anti–double-stranded DNA and anti–SSA/SSB antibodies are negative. Analysis of the cerebrospinal fluid shows a normal IgG index and no abnormalities in oligoclonal banding.

An MRI of the spinal cord reveals an increased signal extending over five vertebral segments with patchy gadolinium enhancement. An MRI of the brain shows no abnormalities.

Which of the following is the most appropriate next diagnostic test?

(A) Electromyography
(B) Serum antineutrophil cytoplasmic antibody test
(C) Serum neuromyelitis optica (NMO)-IgG autoantibody test
(D) Testing of visual evoked potentials

Item 83

A 30-year-old man with epilepsy is evaluated for disabling seizures that occur once a month despite adherence to his drug therapy. He also reports excess sedation and cognitive slowing related to his medication. The patient has had partial complex seizures since age 16 years and has been previously treated with appropriate dosages of phenytoin, carbamazepine, and valproic acid; he currently takes lamotrigine, 200 mg twice daily (dose range, 100-600 mg/d). He is otherwise in excellent health and has no other medical problems.

Physical examination, including neurologic examination, reveals no abnormal findings.

An MRI of the brain shows an increased T2 signal and atrophy of the right hippocampus, both consistent with

mesial temporal sclerosis. An electroencephalogram shows right temporal sharp waves.

Which of the following is the most appropriate next step in management?

(A) Add another anticonvulsant to his drug regimen
(B) Increase the dosage of lamotrigine
(C) Refer him for epilepsy surgery evaluation
(D) Refer him for implantation of a vagus nerve stimulator

Item 84

A 73-year-old woman is evaluated in the emergency department for the onset of a severe, "explosive" headache 8 hours ago. She initially rested in a dark bedroom after headache onset, but when the pain did not abate, her husband drove her to the hospital. The patient has hypertension controlled with lisinopril. Family medical history is noncontributory.

As assessment in the emergency department begins, she becomes nauseated, vomits, and then becomes rapidly and progressively more obtunded. Intubation and mechanical ventilation are required.

On physical examination, temperature is normal, blood pressure is 188/102 mm Hg, pulse rate is 120/min, and respiration rate is 20/min. The patient exhibits a flaccid quadriplegia, and meningismus is present. Both pupils are 4 mm in diameter and nonreactive; the oculocephalic reflex is absent, and the corneal reflex is absent bilaterally. She has a depressed level of consciousness, with a Glasgow Coma Scale score of 3. Subhyaloid hemorrhages are noted on funduscopy.

Results of a complete blood count (with differential) are normal, as are blood urea nitrogen, serum creatinine, and serum electrolyte levels.

A CT scan of the head shows an extensive acute subarachnoid hemorrhage and mild prominence of the temporal tips of the lateral ventricles.

Which of the following neurologic complications is most likely to have caused this patient's rapid deterioration?

(A) Hydrocephalus
(B) Rebleeding
(C) Syndrome of inappropriate antidiuretic hormone secretion
(D) Vasospasm

Item 85

A 32-year-old woman is evaluated for a gradual increase in migraine frequency and severity over the past 6 months. Migraine attacks, which formerly occurred two or three times each month, are now occurring approximately three times each week, with each attack lasting at least 12 hours. She has a 15-year history of asthma, a 10-year history of migraine without aura, and a 4-year history of type 2 diabetes mellitus controlled by diet. Her mother and sister also have a history of migraine. Current medications are almotriptan as needed for acute migraine, an inhaled corticosteroid, and an albuterol inhaler as needed for wheezing.

On physical examination, blood pressure is 130/80 mm Hg, pulse rate is 88/min, and BMI is 34. Results of a physical examination, including a neurologic examination, are normal.

An MRI of the brain shows no abnormalities.

Which of the following is the most appropriate treatment for this patient?

(A) Gabapentin
(B) Nortriptyline
(C) Propranolol
(D) Topiramate
(E) Valproic acid

Item 86

A 24-year-old woman is evaluated for a 2-month history of abnormal movements affecting both arms. She describes these movements as intermittent and irregular writhing movements and says she cannot suppress them. The patient had an unprovoked deep venous thrombosis in her right leg 2 years ago and a miscarriage 8 months ago but has had no other medical problems. She has no known family history of neurologic disease or thrombophilia and takes no medications.

General physical examination findings are normal. Neurologic examination reveals random, irregular movements of the hands and arms but is otherwise unremarkable.

Which of the following is the most likely diagnosis?

(A) Anti–phospholipid antibody syndrome
(B) Huntington disease
(C) Parkinson disease
(D) Wilson disease

Item 87

A 31-year-old woman with a history of migraine is evaluated in the office for several severe migraine attacks that are not well controlled with over-the-counter analgesics. The headaches are severe, are associated with severe nausea and vomiting, and began 2 weeks ago after she delivered a healthy baby boy. She is currently breast feeding.

Results of physical examination, including neurologic examination, are normal.

Which of the following is the most appropriate treatment for this patient?

(A) Butalbital
(B) Extra-strength acetaminophen
(C) Frovatriptan
(D) Metoclopramide
(E) Prochlorperazine

Item 88

A 30-year-old man is reevaluated for management of partial epilepsy. He first developed seizures 1 year ago after surgical treatment of a ruptured aneurysm of the right middle cerebral artery. He was started on phenytoin (400 mg/d) at that time but continues to have monthly episodes in which he experiences a rising epigastric sensation followed by loss of awareness lasting 1 to 2 minutes and then several hours of confusion and significant fatigue. He also reports gait imbalance and excessive fatigue related to the phenytoin. He takes no other medications.

Physical and neurologic examination findings are noncontributory.

Laboratory studies show a current serum phenytoin level of 18 mg/L (71.3 µmol/L) (therapeutic level, 10-20 mg/L [39.6-79.2 µmol/L]).

Which of the following is the most appropriate next step in management?

(A) Add another antiepileptic drug to his current regimen
(B) Gradually transition from phenytoin to a new antiepileptic drug
(C) Increase the dosage of phenytoin
(D) Refer for epilepsy surgery evaluation
(E) Refer for vagus nerve stimulation

Item 89

A 68-year-old man is evaluated in the office for a 4-week history of continuous left leg pain and weakness. The pain is severe, burning, and in the distribution of the anterior thigh. He has had a 4.5-kg (10-lb) weight loss in the last 3 weeks. The patient had prostate cancer 1 year ago and underwent radiation therapy to the pelvis. He also has hypertension treated with lisinopril.

General physical examination findings are normal, except for a BMI of 31. Neurologic examination shows normal speech, language, and cranial nerve function. Strength and deep tendon reflexes are normal in the upper extremities and in the right leg. There is diffuse weakness, greatest in the quadriceps, hip adductor, and iliopsoas muscles, and absent knee and ankle jerks in the left leg; plantar response is flexor. Sensory loss is evident in the distribution of the saphenous sensory nerve on the left.

Laboratory studies show an elevated fasting plasma glucose level of 132 mg/dL (7.3 mmol/L). All other laboratory results, including erythrocyte sedimentation rate; serum electrolyte, creatinine, and thyroid-stimulating hormone levels; and liver chemistries, are normal.

Which of the following is the most likely diagnosis?

(A) Cauda equina syndrome
(B) Diabetic lumbosacral radiculoplexus neuropathy
(C) Myelopathy
(D) Radiation-induced lumbosacral plexopathy

Item 90

A 69-year-old woman is evaluated in the emergency department for the sudden onset of headache, nausea, vomiting, and imbalance. The patient has hypertension for which she takes lisinopril. She has no other relevant personal or family medical history.

On physical examination, blood pressure is 160/90 mm Hg, pulse rate is 80/min, and respiration rate is 18/min. Her Glasgow Coma Scale score is 12 (of a possible 15), which indicates moderate brain injury. Right finger-to-nose and heel-to-shin testing reveals dysmetria.

Results of laboratory studies, including a complete blood count, a metabolic profile, and coagulation tests, are normal.

A CT scan of the head shows an acute right cerebellar hemorrhage (>4 cm in diameter), perihematoma edema, compression of the right pons, and effacement but no compression of the fourth ventricle.

Which of the following is the most appropriate next step in management?

(A) Hematoma evacuation
(B) Labetalol, intravenously
(C) Recombinant factor VII, intravenously
(D) Ventriculostomy

Answers and Critiques

Item 1   Answer: B
Educational Objective: Diagnose normal pressure hydrocephalus.

This patient exhibits the classic triad of gait impairment (specifically, gait apraxia), dementia, and urinary incontinence that typifies the potentially reversible syndrome of normal pressure hydrocephalus (NPH). This triad of symptoms eventually occurs in most patients with dementia, and the diagnosis of NPH is often considered but much less often proved to be the correct diagnosis. In this patient, however, strong evidence supports a diagnosis of NPH, including the MRI evidence of ventriculomegaly. Although Alzheimer dementia (AD) is also associated with cognitive impairment and impaired gait, gait does not improve after removal of cerebrospinal fluid in AD as it does in NPH. AD is so common in elderly patients with cognitive impairment that excluding it as a cause can delay the diagnosis of NPH; this delay may help explain some of the eventual shunt failures that occur even in patients with well-diagnosed NPH. Therefore, recognizing reversible dementia syndromes as soon as possible is imperative because of the therapeutic opportunity these syndromes represent.

The only symptom this patient has that is shared by patients with Parkinson disease is a shuffling gait. Otherwise, his presentation—normal posture, arm swing, and muscle tone and the absence of a tremor—is quite different.

Likewise, this patient has no history of or symptoms suggesting stroke or vascular disease, such as sudden onset of neurologic signs or symptoms, which makes vascular dementia unlikely. Although coincident vascular, Alzheimer-type, and Parkinson-type pathology is a common finding in autopsy studies, even in neurologically unimpaired healthy elderly adults, this fact should not constitute the basis for a diagnosis in the setting of a classic reversible dementia syndrome.

> **KEY POINT**
> - The triad of gait apraxia, dementia, and urinary incontinence, especially when accompanied by enlarged ventricles, is suggestive of normal pressure hydrocephalus.

Bibliography
Graff-Radford NR. Normal pressure hydrocephalus. Neurol Clin. 2007;25(3):809-832, vii-viii. [PMID: 17659191]

Item 2   Answer: A
Educational Objective: Manage a single unprovoked seizure.

Drug therapy should not be initiated in this patient at this time. After a single unprovoked seizure, the risk of recurrence in the subsequent 2 years has been reported to be 30% to 40%. The risk of recurrence is greatest in patients with status epilepticus on presentation, with an identifiable underlying neurologic cause, or with abnormal results on an electroencephalogram (EEG). Patients with a partial seizure who are age 65 years or older or who have a family history of epilepsy may also be in a higher-risk category. The appropriate recommendation for this young patient, who has experienced a single idiopathic seizure but has no personal or family history of epilepsy, no identified neurologic cause of his seizure, and normal results on an EEG, is that no medication be started. As with all medical treatment recommendations, patient preference must be taken into account, and some patients in the low-risk group may elect to start therapy after a single seizure, particularly if they have a high-risk occupation. If a second seizure occurs in the future, the recurrence risk is greater than 60%, and antiepileptic medical therapy should be recommended at that time.

Of note, driver's license privileges are restricted in every state in the United States for persons who have experienced a seizure. Specific restrictions vary by state, with typical requirements of a seizure-free period of 3 to 12 months in order to again operate a motor vehicle; a few states make exceptions for a single seizure. Reinstatement of driving privileges depends on demonstrating freedom from seizures for the specified period and there being a reasonable expectation of future seizure control. Initiation of antiepileptic medication is not required by law.

Epilepsy surgery is reserved for patients who have disabling seizures that cannot be controlled with medication. Such surgery is not indicated for this patient, who had a single seizure that resolved uneventfully.

> **KEY POINT**
> - Unless special circumstances exist, drug therapy is generally not started in patients with a single unprovoked seizure.

Bibliography
Kim LG, Johnson TL, Marson AG, Chadwick DW; MRC MESS Study Group. Prediction of risk of seizure recurrence after a single seizure and early epilepsy: further results from the MESS trial [erratum in Lancet Neurol. 2006;5(5):383]. Lancet Neurol. 2006;5(4):317-322. [PMID: 16545748]

Item 3   Answer: B

Educational Objective: Treat a menstrually related migraine with an evidence-based modality.

This patient should be treated with mefenamic acid. She has migraine with aura, migraine without aura, and menstrually related migraine. Her menstrually related headaches are less responsive to acute therapy than are the non–menstrually related attacks, and headache recurs daily throughout menses. The best management for this patient is, therefore, the perimenstrual use of a prophylactic agent. There is evidence that supports the use of mefenamic acid for perimenstrual prophylaxis, with treatment starting 2 days prior to the onset of flow or 1 day prior to the expected onset of the headache and continuing for the duration of menstruation. In this patient, that would mean beginning 3 days before the onset of menstrual flow and continuing throughout menstruation.

The use of combined oral contraceptive therapy (estrogen plus progestin) is contraindicated in this woman because of her history of migraine with aura. Women with migraine with aura are at a two-fold increased risk of ischemic stroke, ischemic myocardial infarction, and venous thromboembolism. The risk of stroke is increased further, up to eight-fold, in women with migraine with aura who use combined oral contraceptive pills.

No evidence supports the oral use of either sumatriptan plus naproxen sodium or topiramate for the perimenstrual prophylaxis of menstrually related migraine. Similarly, there is no evidence supporting the subcutaneous use of sumatriptan in this setting. In fact, the higher recurrence rate with the subcutaneous formulation may prove counterproductive.

KEY POINT

- Evidence supports the use of mefenamic acid for perimenstrual prophylaxis of menstrually related migraines, with treatment starting 2 days prior to the onset of flow or 1 day prior to the expected onset of the headache and continuing for the duration of menstruation.

Bibliography

Pringsheim T, Davenport WJ, Dodick D. Acute treatment and prevention of menstrually related migraine headache: evidence-based review. Neurology. 2008;70(17):1555-1563. [PMID: 18427072]

Item 4   Answer: C

Educational Objective: Test for diabetes mellitus and impaired glucose tolerance in a patient with suspected small-fiber peripheral neuropathy.

A 2-hour glucose tolerance test to detect diabetes mellitus or impaired glucose tolerance is the most appropriate next diagnostic study for this patient. The patient's history of burning feet, in conjunction with neurologic examination findings showing only distal sensory loss (with normal reflexes and muscle strength), suggests a small-fiber peripheral neuropathy. The most common identifiable cause of small-fiber peripheral neuropathy is diabetes or impaired glucose tolerance. This patient's fasting plasma glucose level, which is just over the upper limit of normal, should prompt a 2-hour glucose tolerance test. This test is more sensitive and can detect patients with diabetes and a normal fasting plasma glucose level. Approximately 30% of patients with normal fasting plasma glucose levels will have an oral glucose tolerance test diagnostic for diabetes. A result of 140 mg/dL to 199 mg/dL (7.8 mmol/L to 11.0 mmol/L) from this test establishes a diagnosis of impaired glucose tolerance, and a result of 200 mg/dL (11.1 mg/dL) or greater is diagnostic of diabetes.

An examination of cerebrospinal fluid (CSF) obtained on lumbar puncture is not indicated in this patient. CSF studies should be considered in patients with acute or rapidly progressive neuropathy or polyradiculoneuropathy and in patients with severe weakness, sensory loss, or absent deep tendon reflexes. In patients with Guillain-Barré syndrome or chronic inflammatory polyradiculoneuropathy, CSF examination typically shows a normal cell count with elevated CSF protein level (albuminocytologic dissociation). CSF testing in such patients also helps to exclude infectious disorders, such as West Nile virus, HIV, and polyradiculoneuropathy caused by cytomegalovirus, which can present similarly.

Given the symptom of burning feet and the absence of high arches, hammertoes, or abnormalities on strength and reflex testing, Charcot-Marie-Tooth disease is not likely. Although Charcot-Marie-Tooth disease is a common cause of peripheral neuropathy, patients with this disorder typically do not have neuropathic pain, and many patients also do not have sensory symptoms, despite having sensory loss on examination. Many patients in whom Charcot-Marie-Tooth disease is ultimately diagnosed are unaware of a family history of peripheral neuropathy, so the lack of family history in this patient does not necessarily exclude the diagnosis. Genetic testing is commercially available for many of the different forms of this disease, but genetic testing should be considered only in those patients with a known family history or in those with long-standing neuropathic symptoms and high arches and hammertoes on examination. Other inherited causes of small-fiber peripheral neuropathy include the hereditary burning feet syndrome, hereditary amyloidosis, and the hereditary sensory autonomic neuropathies.

A skin biopsy is not indicated in this patient, given that the electromyographic (EMG) study was abnormal and showed objective evidence of peripheral neuropathy. Abnormalities on EMG testing in patients with suspected small-fiber peripheral neuropathy are seen in only 25% to 30% of patients. When EMG studies are normal, skin biopsy or autonomic nervous system testing should be considered to establish the diagnosis of a small-fiber peripheral neuropathy. Skin testing for small-fiber peripheral neuropathy is commercially available and can show reduced numbers of nerve fibers in the epidermis. Because small-fiber nerves also make up the autonomic nervous system, autonomic nervous system testing can also establish the presence of a small-fiber peripheral neuropathy.

> **KEY POINT**
> * A history of burning or lancinating distal extremity pain and examination findings showing only sensory loss suggest a small-fiber peripheral neuropathy, which is most frequently associated with diabetes mellitus and impaired glucose tolerance.

Bibliography

Singleton AR, Smith AG. Therapy insight: neurological complications of prediabetes. Nat Clin Pract Neurol. 2006;2(5):276-282. [PMID: 16932564]

Item 5   Answer: D

Educational Objective: Evaluate suspected cerebral venous sinus thrombosis.

This patient should undergo magnetic resonance venography. The most likely diagnosis, given his known hypercoagulability, likely dehydration, symptoms of mounting intracranial pressure, and eventual focal deficits, is cerebral venous sinus thrombosis with possible venous ischemia. Cerebral venous sinus thrombosis may present with signs and symptoms of intracranial hypertension, such as headache, papilledema, and visual problems; focal neurologic findings or seizures; and mental status changes, stupor, and coma. Major risk factors for cerebral venous sinus thrombosis in adults include conditions that predispose to spontaneous thromboses, such as inherited or acquired thrombophilia, pregnancy, oral contraceptive use, malignancy, sepsis, and head trauma.

Magnetic resonance venography can readily detect obstruction of the venous sinuses by a thrombus and the damage to the brain caused by the resultant increased pressure and so is the most appropriate next diagnostic test. Of all the possible imaging modalities, magnetic resonance venography is the most sensitive test for detecting the thrombus and the occluded dural sinus or vein.

Carotid ultrasonography assesses the extracranial vasculature but does not assist in the assessment of the intracranial vasculature. The patient's clinical presentation suggests elevated intracranial pressure from venous stasis. The intracranial venous sinuses need assessment, not the extracranial carotid arteries.

Seizures are a recognized complication of cerebral venous sinus thrombosis. However, electroencephalography does not assist with the establishment of a preliminary diagnosis and should not be performed next.

A lumbar puncture is contraindicated in this patient with evidence of elevated intracranial pressure.

> **KEY POINT**
> * Cerebral venous sinus thrombosis should be considered in the differential diagnosis of any patient with headache, features of elevated intracranial pressure, progressive reduction in the level of consciousness, and seizures, especially if there is a known risk of hypercoagulability.

Bibliography

Paciaroni M, Palmerini F, Bogousslavsky J. Clinical presentations of cerebral vein and sinus thrombosis. Front Neurol Neurosci. 2008;23:77-88. [PMID: 18004054]

Item 6   Answer: B

Educational Objective: Differentiate pseudorelapses from true relapses in multiple sclerosis.

Ciprofloxacin is the best drug therapy for this patient. In light of her new urinary incontinence, fever, and abnormal results on urinalysis, she most likely has a urinary tract infection, which is manifesting clinically as a worsening of her baseline neurologic deficits (leg weakness and ambulatory impairment). She is experiencing a pseudorelapse of her multiple sclerosis (MS)—a neurologic deterioration caused by a change in general health status or by factors in the external environment (such as heat). Pseudorelapses are usually caused by systemic infections or medications. Treatment of the underlying cause (in this patient, with the antibiotic agent ciprofloxacin), obtaining a urine culture to ensure the appropriate antibiotic choice, and supportive care with an antipyretic agent constitute the appropriate treatment. Pseudorelapses need to be differentiated from true MS relapses, which are not associated with systemic symptoms, such as fever. Patients with chronic, progressive forms of MS and moderate or severe baseline neurologic impairment are at high risk for pseudorelapses. Occult urinary tract infection is a common culprit.

Symptomatic therapy with antipyretic and antispasticity drugs only is not appropriate for this patient because her primary infection would be left untreated. Additionally, antispasticity drugs, such as baclofen, are likely to worsen her leg weakness.

Pseudorelapses are typically self-limited, and spontaneous neurologic improvement usually occurs during or shortly after successful treatment of the underlying infection. Therefore, inclusion of a corticosteroid at treatment onset is unnecessary and could interfere with the treatment of the infection. Because corticosteroids do not treat and may aggravate the primary infection, high-dose methylprednisolone or prednisone should never be given as the only therapy to patients with MS and a suspected urinary tract infection. Occasionally, a systemic infection triggers a new MS relapse; in patients with such a relapse, corticosteroids could be used to treat the neurologic impairment after cure of the infection and exclusion of other causes of deterioration have been documented.

KEY POINT

- Pseudorelapses in multiple sclerosis are the worsening of neurologic symptoms because of another cause, such as a systemic infection requiring antibiotic treatment or supportive care, and should be differentiated from true relapses, which may require corticosteroid treatment.

Bibliography

Noseworthy JH, Lucchinetti C, Rodriguez M, Weinshenker BG. Multiple sclerosis. N Engl J Med. 2000;343(13):938-952. [PMID: 11006371]

Item 7   Answer: E

Educational Objective: Evaluate the risk of seizure recurrence after a generalized tonic-clonic seizure.

The presence of Todd paralysis predicts a greater risk of future seizures in this patient. After a single unprovoked seizure, recurrence risk in the subsequent 2 years has been reported to be 30% to 40%. Many historical or examination findings predict a higher risk of recurrence, including presentation in status epilepticus, age greater than 65 years, known underlying neurologic disorder(s) or structural lesion(s), and Todd paralysis. Partial-onset seizures are also more likely to recur, perhaps because of the increased likelihood of there being an underlying causative structural lesion. Todd paralysis is a transient unilateral or focal weakness often seen after partial seizures, with or without secondary generalization. Todd paralysis or other focal abnormalities on the neurologic examination predict a greater risk of a future seizure. Patients with an electroencephalogram or head imaging scan showing a potentially epileptogenic lesion are also in the higher-risk category.

Elderly patients have been shown to have a higher risk of recurrence after a first seizure compared with younger adults. This 50-year-old woman would not be in a higher risk category on the basis of age alone.

Cerebrovascular disease, including prior stroke and intracranial hemorrhage, is a commonly identified cause of epilepsy in older adults. However, the presence of hypertension and other cerebrovascular risk factors does not predict a greater risk of future seizures.

The presence or absence of secondary generalization does not affect the rate of future events and so is not relevant for determining this patient's risk.

The relatively nonspecific finding of small-vessel ischemic disease on an MRI of the brain is not significantly correlated with seizure risk. More concerning vascular lesions include acute or chronic stroke or hemorrhagic lesions involving cortical structures.

KEY POINT

- After a single unprovoked seizure, a greater risk of recurrence is predicted if the event was a partial seizure or if the patient has Todd paralysis, status epilepticus on presentation, an age greater than 65 years, or abnormal findings on neurologic examination.

Bibliography

Berg AT. Risk of recurrence after a first unprovoked seizure. Epilepsia. 2008;49 Suppl 1:13-18. [PMID: 18184149]

Item 8   Answer: C

Educational Objective: Treat metastatic epidural spinal cord compression.

This patient has a typical presentation of epidural spinal cord compression, most likely from recurrence of the patient's previously treated breast cancer. The best treatment is intravenous dexamethasone followed by decompressive surgery and radiation therapy. The corticosteroid infusion likely reduces the tumor-related mass effect and edema, surgery provides immediate physical decompression of the spinal cord and the opportunity to stabilize the spine (if necessary), and radiotherapy targets the residual macroscopic and microscopic tumor burden.

Observational studies support the use of intravenous corticosteroids in all patients with epidural spinal cord compression. Surgery is also warranted because of the concern about spinal instability. Furthermore, a randomized, multicenter, controlled clinical trial of therapy for epidural spinal cord compression, which included patients with metastatic breast cancer, showed that the combination of decompressive surgery and radiotherapy was associated with better ambulatory outcome than either treatment alone. In some scenarios, such as early spinal cord compression by a very radiosensitive tumor (including lymphoma and myeloma), intravenous dexamethasone plus radiotherapy may be appropriate. However, patients with such tumors were not included in the previously mentioned trial.

There is no role for chemotherapy in the immediate treatment of epidural spinal cord compression. Chemotherapy may be indicated as part of a comprehensive program to control metastatic disease but will not provide the urgent relief needed for this cancer emergency.

KEY POINT

- Epidural spinal cord compression usually requires immediate therapy with intravenous corticosteroids followed by decompressive surgery and radiation therapy.

Bibliography

Patchell RA, Tibbs PA, Regine WF, et al. Direct decompressive surgical resection in the treatment of spinal cord compression caused by metastatic cancer: a randomised trial. Lancet. 2005;366(9486): 643-648. [PMID: 16112300]

Item 9   Answer: A

Educational Objective: Diagnose intracerebral hemorrhage in a patient with hypertension.

This patient most likely has had an intracerebral hemorrhage. The classic presentation of an intracerebral hemorrhage is the sudden onset of a focal neurologic deficit with subsequent symptomatic progression over minutes to hours. Headache, vomiting, hypertension, and an impaired level of consciousness are its most common clinical accompaniments and help distinguish an intracerebral hemorrhage from an ischemic stroke. Intracranial hemorrhage, which accounts for 11% of stroke deaths, has symptoms similar to those of ischemic stroke at presentation; therefore, it cannot always be reliably distinguished from ischemic stroke by clinical criteria alone. The definitive diagnostic study is CT of the head or MRI of the brain. Imaging provides diagnostic and prognostic information. The volume of intracranial hemorrhage and level of consciousness are the two most powerful predictors of outcome in this setting.

A severe hemispheric ischemic stroke can cause severe focal neurologic dysfunction but generally does not progress or worsen as rapidly as occurred with this patient.

Meningitis, although sometimes fulminant, is rarely this acute in presentation. As with subarachnoid hemorrhage, it may be associated with nuchal rigidity. Encephalitis, but not meningitis, can cause cerebral dysfunction, such as aphasia.

A transient ischemic attack is a brief episode of focal neurologic dysfunction, without progressive worsening, that usually lasts less than 30 minutes and so is unlikely to be the correct diagnosis in this patient.

KEY POINT

- **The classic presentation of intracerebral hemorrhage is the sudden onset of a focal neurologic deficit with subsequent symptomatic progression over minutes to hours.**

Bibliography

Demaerschalk B, Aguilar MI. Treatment of acute intracerebral hemorrhage. Curr Treat Options Neurol. 2008;10(6):453-465. [PMID: 18990314]

Item 10   Answer: C

Educational Objective: Evaluate suspected Lambert-Eaton myasthenic syndrome.

This patient most likely has Lambert-Eaton myasthenic syndrome, as suggested by his history of proximal upper and lower limb weakness, the presence of autonomic symptoms (dry eyes/mouth, erectile dysfunction), and the finding of absent deep tendon reflexes on examination. These are characteristic signs and symptoms of the syndrome. Lambert-Eaton myasthenic syndrome is a neuromuscular junction disorder caused by disordered calcium channel function on the presynaptic nerve terminal. In most patients with this disorder, antibodies to voltage-gated P/Q-type calcium channel receptors exist. Lambert-Eaton myasthenic syndrome is typically a paraneoplastic syndrome, caused by or associated with an underlying malignancy, particularly small cell lung cancer. The diagnosis of Lambert-Eaton myasthenic syndrome precedes the clinical diagnosis of cancer in up to 50% of affected patients; therefore, in patients with newly diagnosed Lambert-Eaton myasthenic syndrome, a thorough search for an underlying cancer should be performed. If no evidence of malignancy is found, these patients should be evaluated serially for occult malignancy. In addition to elevated levels of voltage-gated P/Q-type calcium channel antibodies, the diagnosis can be confirmed through electrodiagnostic studies, particularly repetitive nerve stimulation studies, which show an increase in the muscle action potential (increment) after brief exercise.

Elevated levels of antibodies against acetylcholine receptors are present in 90% of patients with generalized myasthenia gravis. Myasthenia gravis is an autoimmune disorder that results in neuromuscular transmission failure, causing weakness of limb and cranial muscles. The diagnosis is confirmed through electrodiagnostic testing, including repetitive nerve stimulation studies and, in some patients, single-fiber electromyography. The presence of an elevated acetylcholine receptor antibody level may provide additional confirmatory evidence supporting the diagnosis of myasthenia gravis. In this patient, the absence of any bulbar signs or symptoms, such as ptosis, visual symptoms (blurred vision or diplopia), or dysphagia, in conjunction with absent deep tendon reflexes, would argue against myasthenia gravis.

Hyperparathyroidism, either primary or secondary, can result in proximal limb weakness. The normal calcium level in this patient would argue against a significant parathyroid disorder. Additionally, absent deep tendon reflexes would not be expected in a patient with hyperparathyroidism. Measurement of the parathyroid hormone level is therefore not indicated.

Muscle biopsy is not likely to offer any additional diagnostic information in this patient with normal serum creatine kinase levels. Muscle biopsy is indicated primarily in patients with suspected inflammatory myopathies, such as polymyositis, dermatomyositis, or inclusion body myositis, and in certain hereditary myopathic disorders. Symptom onset in the seventh decade argues against a hereditary myopathy, as does the normal creatine kinase level. Although serum creatine kinase levels can be normal in patients with inclusion body myositis, deep tendon reflexes are typically normal, and weakness is most prominent in quadriceps and deep finger flexor muscles.

- The diagnosis of Lambert-Eaton myasthenic syndrome, a neuromuscular junction disorder that causes progressive proximal muscle weakness and areflexia, precedes the clinical recognition of cancer in up to 50% of patients.

Bibliography

Mareska M, Gutmann L. Lambert-Eaton myasthenic syndrome. Semin Neurol. 2004;24(2):149-153. [PMID: 15257511]

Item 11   Answer: A

Educational Objective: Treat memory loss in a patient with Alzheimer dementia.

This patient should receive donepezil. The Folstein Mini–Mental State Examination (MMSE) discriminates well between the major stages of dementia used for prognosis and management purposes. The MMSE score range of 21 to 25 corresponds to mild dementia, 11 to 20 to moderate dementia, and 0 to 10 to severe dementia. This patient has Alzheimer dementia and is at a mild to moderate stage of impairment. The most appropriate medication with which to begin treatment is an acetylcholinesterase inhibitor of which there are currently three: donepezil, rivastigmine, and galantamine. Multiple large, prospective, randomized, double-blind, placebo-controlled studies have shown in patients with mild, moderate, or severe Alzheimer dementia the efficacy of donepezil (and its superiority to placebo) in the preservation of instrumental and functional activities of daily living and in the reduction of caregiver stress. Other studies have found that patients treated with donepezil have improved cognitive function compared with those treated with placebo. Donepezil was safe and well tolerated in this patient group.

Memantine is also used to treat Alzheimer dementia, but only in patients with moderate to severe impairment. There is no evidence that memantine has any effect in earlier stages of Alzheimer dementia or that it alters the course of the disease. With a score of 24/30 on the MMSE, this patient has mild dementia, which makes memantine an inappropriate treatment. In patients with severe dementia, memantine can be used alone or added to an acetylcholinesterase inhibitor.

Quetiapine is an antipsychotic drug, and sertraline is an antidepressant agent. Although both can be used in patients with Alzheimer dementia, their use is limited to treatment of behavioral symptoms of psychosis and depression, respectively, neither of which this patient has exhibited. However, if these medications are to be used in such patients, the risks must first be carefully weighed against the benefits. The U.S. Food and Drug Administration has reported that the use of second-generation antipsychotic medications (aripiprazole, olanzapine, quetiapine, and risperidone) in elderly patients with dementia is associated with increased mortality.

Although it is important to consider the potential cognitive side effects of prescription (and nonprescription) medications, those taken by this patient are not associated with such effects. Therefore, there is no need to risk potential harm to this patient by discontinuing his blood pressure and thyroid medications.

- First-line pharmacotherapy for mild Alzheimer dementia is an acetylcholinesterase inhibitor.

Bibliography

Blass DM, Rabins PV. In the clinic. Dementia. Ann Intern Med. 2008;148(7):ITC4-1-ITC4-16. [PMID: 18378944]

Item 12   Answer: D

Educational Objective: Evaluate trigeminal neuralgia.

This patient, whose history is most compatible with a diagnosis of trigeminal neuralgia, should have an MRI of the brain. In 90% of patients with trigeminal neuralgia, idiopathic disease presents after age 40 years. Trigeminal neuralgia in a patient this young should prompt evaluation for secondary causes, such as multiple sclerosis, posterior fossa tumors, and vascular or aneurysmal compression of the trigeminal nerve. In light of her history of transient paresthesias 3 years ago, multiple sclerosis is high among the diagnostic possibilities for this patient. An MRI can show the demyelination typical of multiple sclerosis.

Baclofen, although sometimes used in this scenario, is not a first-line drug for treatment of trigeminal neuralgia and should not be initiated at this stage because there is insufficient evidence from randomized, controlled trials to show significant benefit from non–antiepileptic drugs in trigeminal neuralgia.

CT of the head is not the imaging procedure of choice for this patient. The resultant scan will not show demyelinating lesions and may not detect posterior fossa or skull-based lesions involving the trigeminal nerve.

Although the detection of abnormalities on cerebrospinal fluid examination can be useful in supporting a diagnosis of multiple sclerosis, brain-imaging procedures should precede lumbar puncture, especially as long as other structural intracranial lesions are still part of the differential diagnosis. Once such lesions are excluded by the results of imaging studies, lumbar puncture may be appropriate to perform.

Nerve conduction studies of the extremities are inappropriate for this patient because the paresthesias have been transient, the neurologic examination discloses no evidence of a peripheral neuropathy, and the structural and demyelinating causes of trigeminal neuralgia are best excluded with an MRI of the brain.

- **Because trigeminal neuralgia usually presents after age 40 years, its diagnosis in a younger patient should prompt an evaluation for secondary causes, such as multiple sclerosis, posterior fossa tumors, and vascular or aneurysmal compression of the trigeminal nerve.**

Bibliography

Cheshire WP. Trigeminal neuralgia: for one nerve a multitude of treatments. Expert Rev Neurother. 2007;7(11):1565-1579. [PMID: 17997704]

Item 13   Answer: A

Educational Objective: Treat myasthenic crisis.

This patient has a rapidly progressive neurologic disorder with weakness of limb, bulbar, and respiratory muscles and should undergo plasma exchange. Given the absence of sensory loss and normal deep tendon reflexes, myasthenia gravis is the most likely diagnosis. Because of the rapid progression of the disease and the involvement of respiratory and bulbar muscles, the patient should be admitted to the hospital for management of a myasthenic crisis. Myasthenic crisis is a potentially life-threatening neurologic emergency characterized by weakness that is severe enough to necessitate intubation. Electromyographic studies, including repetitive stimulation of motor nerves, are indicated to establish a diagnosis of myasthenia gravis.

Plasma exchange is the treatment of choice in patients with myasthenic crisis. Myasthenia gravis is an autoimmune disorder that results from antibody-mediated attacks on the postsynaptic neuromuscular junction. This process may impair neuromuscular transmission by functional blockade of the acetylcholine receptor, by accelerating the degradation of acetylcholine receptors, and by causing damage to the postsynaptic membrane of the neuromuscular junction. Plasma exchange presumably removes these circulating antibodies.

Prednisone is an effective therapy in the treatment of patients with myasthenia gravis. However, it is not appropriate as the initial, sole therapy in patients in the midst of a myasthenic crisis. A worsening of muscular weakness is seen in some patients within the first 3 weeks of the initiation of this medication. Even if this complication does not occur, the beneficial effects from prednisone typically do not occur for 3 to 4 weeks after drug initiation. In a patient with myasthenic crisis, prednisone is often initiated after the patient has been stabilized and is improving with plasma exchange. Used in this fashion, prednisone should reach maximum efficacy by the time the beneficial effects of plasma exchange have waned (6-8 weeks).

Pyridostigmine is an inhibitor of acetylcholinesterase, which increases the amount of acetylcholine in the neuromuscular junction. This medication can be given orally or intravenously and may offer symptomatic benefit in patients with myasthenia gravis. Patients with mild symptoms due to myasthenia gravis can occasionally be treated with pyridostigmine alone. Although this medication may be of some benefit in patients with myasthenic crisis and should be considered, definitive immune-modulating therapy is indicated as the most appropriate treatment.

Ciprofloxacin and other fluoroquinolone medications are contraindicated in patients with myasthenia gravis; the ciprofloxacin the patient received 3 weeks ago to treat a urinary tract infection may have precipitated her current myasthenic crisis. Other medications that should be avoided in patients with myasthenia gravis include lithium, aminoglycosides, magnesium, and macrolide antibiotics.

- **Myasthenic crisis, a potentially life-threatening neurologic emergency characterized by muscle weakness severe enough to necessitate intubation, typically requires plasma exchange therapy.**

Bibliography

Bershad EM, Feen ES, Suarez JI. Myasthenia gravis crisis. South Med J. 2008;101(1):63-69. [PMID: 18176295]

Item 14   Answer: C

Educational Objective: Evaluate a suspected spinal dural arteriovenous fistula.

The most appropriate next diagnostic test for this patient is spinal angiography for the specific purpose of confirming the presence of a spinal dura-based arteriovenous fistula. Dural arteriovenous fistula should be suspected in any patient with a chronic or subacute progressive myelopathy with episodes of more rapid, stepwise clinical deterioration.

In this patient, the diagnosis is suggested by the clinical history of stepwise spinal cord dysfunction without significant recovery and the MRI finding of a swollen spinal cord with dorsal flow voids, which is indicative of tortuous blood vessels. The spinal cord lesion represents cord congestion due to an abnormal connection between the high-pressure arterial and low-pressure venous drainage systems serving the spinal cord circulation. Patients with such spinal fistulas are often mistakenly diagnosed as having multiple sclerosis (MS), which is the most common nontraumatic disabling disease of young adults.

Although repeating the cerebrospinal fluid analysis and the MRI of the brain would be a reasonable way to reevaluate the validity of an MS diagnosis, the spinal cord MRI findings in this patient are not typical of MS and make these repeated studies unnecessary.

Spinal cord biopsy would be useful if there were a strong clinical suspicion of an unusual inflammatory myelopathy or a cord tumor. Nothing in the patient's examination or laboratory and imaging findings suggests either possibility.

KEY POINT

- Spinal dural arteriovenous fistula should be suspected in any patient with a chronic or subacute progressive myelopathy with episodes of more rapid, stepwise clinical deterioration.

Bibliography

Jellema K, Tijssen CC, van Gijn J. Spinal dural arteriovenous fistulas: a congestive myelopathy that initially mimics a peripheral nerve disorder. Brain. 2006;129(Pt 12):3150-3164. [PMID: 16921175]

Item 15   Answer: C

Educational Objective: Diagnose carotid artery dissection.

The most likely clinical diagnosis to explain this patient's focal neurologic symptoms is a left internal carotid artery dissection with resultant transient ischemic attacks (TIAs). Carotid dissection characteristically develops after head or neck trauma but may occur spontaneously. Manifestations of this condition include ipsilateral throbbing neck, head, or orbital pain with possible Horner syndrome. The pain from carotid dissection may occur suddenly or develop gradually. Such a dissection can cause a TIA or ischemic stroke by one of two mechanisms: either the mural hematoma expands to the point of occluding the lumen, or a thrombus forms and embolizes to cause distal arterial branch occlusion. Dissection of the cervical arteries, although an infrequent occurrence, is a leading cause of stroke in young and otherwise healthy persons. Magnetic resonance angiography of the carotid arteries and carotid duplex ultrasonography are indicated in the clinical evaluation of possible carotid dissection.

A cluster headache is an excruciating unilateral headache of extreme intensity, with a typical duration of 15 minutes to 3 hours. Its pain is lancinating or boring in quality and is located behind the eye (periorbital) or in the temple, sometimes radiating to the neck or shoulder. The cardinal symptoms of a cluster headache attack are ptosis (drooping eyelid), conjunctival injection (redness of the conjunctiva), lacrimation (tearing), rhinorrhea (a runny nose), and, less commonly, facial blushing, swelling, or sweating. These features are known as the autonomic symptoms. The neck is often stiff or tender in the aftermath of a headache, with jaw or tooth pain sometimes present. Although this patient had ptosis and jaw pain, there were no other features to support a diagnosis of cluster headache. Additionally, one would not expect a patient with a cluster headache to have focal cortical dysfunction (such as aphasia).

Giant cell arteritis (or temporal arteritis) is a granulomatous vasculitis that predominantly affects the extracranial branches of the carotid artery. This condition occurs almost exclusively in patients older than 50 years of age and has a female predominance. Clinical manifestations of giant cell arteritis include headache, jaw or tongue claudication, scalp tenderness, systemic symptoms, and fever. Involvement of the primary branches of the aorta also may cause limb claudication. Giant cell arteritis is not associated with pain along the carotid artery or cerebral hemispheric symptoms and would be an unusual diagnosis in this relatively young patient.

The patient's clinical symptoms are aphasia, right hemiparesis, and right hemisensory loss; all are referable to the middle cerebral artery territory of the dominant left hemisphere and thus are consistent with an anterior circulation stroke event. There are no posterior circulation symptoms (in the vertebrobasilar artery territory) to suggest that a vertebral artery occlusion has occurred. Although an ipsilateral Horner syndrome can accompany a lateral medullary infarction secondary to a vertebral artery occlusion, a patient with this condition would also be expected to have dysphagia, hoarseness, a reduced gag reflex, vertigo, nystagmus, vomiting, ipsilateral cerebellar findings, ipsilateral loss of pain and temperature sensations in the face, and contralateral loss of pain and temperature sensations in the body, none of which this patient has.

KEY POINT

- Dissection of the cervical arteries, although an infrequent occurrence, is a leading cause of stroke in young and otherwise healthy persons.

Bibliography

Jensen MB, Chacon MR, Aleu A. Cervicocerebral arterial dissection. Neurologist. 2008;14(1):5-6. [PMID: 18195650]

Item 16   Answer: B

Educational Objective: Manage asymptomatic meningioma.

This patient should have serial MRIs of the brain. Meningiomas are benign, slow-growing tumors that are often discovered as an incidental finding when head imaging is obtained for evaluation of unrelated symptoms. Their appearance on CT scans and MRIs is diagnostic. Appropriate management depends on the age of the patient and the size and location of the tumor. For this patient, who is elderly and has a small, asymptomatic meningioma, the most appropriate management strategy is to follow up with serial MRIs of the brain. In patients with incidentally diagnosed meningiomas, most clinicians perform imaging studies every 3 to 6 months during the first year. If the tumor remains stable, yearly imaging may be performed for the next 5 to 10 years. Densely calcified meningiomas are particularly indolent.

Chemotherapy is not warranted in this patient because meningiomas are usually benign in histology and behavior. In patients with large or symptomatic meningiomas, surgical resection is the treatment of choice, whereas observation usually is appropriate for small, asymptomatic meningiomas until evidence of progressive enlargement or symptoms develop.

Stereotactic radiosurgery, which selectively irradiates a sharply defined target, is used for symptomatic meningiomas that are not amenable to surgical resection. Surgical resection is generally recommended only for patients who are symptomatic or for young patients in whom it is likely that symptoms will develop over time with a slow-growing tumor.

KEY POINT

- Small, asymptomatic meningiomas in older adults should be monitored with serial imaging.

Bibliography

Yano S, Kuratsu J; Kumamoto Brain Tumor Research Group. Indications for surgery in patients with asymptomatic meningiomas based on an extensive experience. J Neurosurg. 2006;105(4):538-543. [PMID: 17044555]

Item 17   Answer: C

Educational Objective: Distinguish migraine from sinus and tension-type headaches.

This patient most likely has migraine without aura. Approximately 90% of patients in an ambulatory care setting with a chief symptom of recurrent, moderately severe headache have a form of migraine. Her 6-year history of episodic headache meets the International Classification of Headache Disorders criteria for migraine. There is no single criterion that is necessary or sufficient to make the diagnosis of migraine. In this particular example, this patient does not have unilateral or throbbing pain, and there is no associated photophobia, phonophobia, or vomiting, features that are often considered necessary for the diagnosis. Her headache is preceded by premonitory symptoms (yawning and irritability), which occur in approximately 75% of patients with migraine. In addition, her attacks are triggered by stress and changes in barometric pressure, both of which are frequent triggers for migraine. Depression is a comorbid disorder that often leads to a misdiagnosis of tension-type headache.

Chronic migraine (previously referred to as "transformed" migraine) is a very common cause of chronic daily headaches and is defined as headaches occurring on more than 15 days per month that meet the diagnosis of migraine without aura or respond to ergots or triptans (migraine-specific drugs) on at least 8 of those days. This patient does not meet the diagnostic criteria for this type of headache.

Another chronic daily headache often confused with chronic migraine is medication overuse headache. This type of headache, which typically occurs when (or soon after) a patient awakens, is defined as more than 15 headache days per month and more than 10 days of use of acute headache medication per month. Analgesic therapy may decrease headache intensity, but the headache usually will not completely remit. Although the symptoms of this condition may be identical to those of migraine or tension-type headache, the efficacy of migraine-specific therapy in patients with medication overuse headache is intermittent or poor. Patients with this condition respond only when the medication overuse is addressed. Again, the patient described in the vignette does not meet the diagnostic criteria for this type of headache.

Headache triggered by changes in barometric pressure is often mistakenly diagnosed as sinus headache. Patients with acute rhinosinusitis and sinus headache have symptoms consisting of nasal congestion, purulent nasal secretions, sinus tenderness, and facial pain. These findings are not present in this patient.

Tension-type headache is a dull, bilateral, or diffuse headache that is often described as a pressure or squeezing sensation of mild to moderate intensity. This type of headache has no accompanying migraine features (such as nausea), and its pain does not prohibit activity, characteristics that do not match this patient's symptoms. Headache triggered by stress is often mistaken as tension-type headache, even though stress is one of the most commonly reported migraine triggers. Up to 75% of patients with migraine report neck pain that precedes or occurs during the attack, and this scenario is frequently mistaken for tension-type headache.

KEY POINT

- Approximately 90% of patients who present in an ambulatory care setting with a chief symptom of recurrent, moderately severe headache have a form of migraine.

Bibliography

Headache Classification Subcommittee of the International Headache Society. The international classification of headache disorders: 2nd edition. Cephalalgia. 2004;24 Suppl 1:9-160. [PMID: 14979299]

Item 18   Answer: B

Educational Objective: Diagnose a partial seizure with secondary generalization.

The history and provided eyewitness account are most consistent with the diagnosis of a partial seizure with secondary generalization. This type of seizure is characterized by sensory, motor, autonomic, or psychic (déjà vu, depersonalization) phenomena with or without altered awareness at onset followed by generalized tonic-clonic activity. Accurate classification of a seizure relies predominantly on the clinical history, with diagnostic testing used to confirm or clarify the suspected cause. When a patient has loss of consciousness with urinary incontinence and stiffening and shaking lasting 1 to 2 minutes, seizure should always be very strongly considered as the cause. When there is a high clinical suspicion of epilepsy, as in this patient, normal findings on an MRI of the brain and electroencephalogram

(EEG) do not rule out that diagnosis. An MRI shows an epileptogenic lesion in only 10% to 20% of patients with epilepsy, and a routine EEG shows abnormalities in only 25% to 50% of patients with confirmed epilepsy.

Approximately one third of syncopal episodes are reflex mediated or neurocardiogenic. Cardiac arrhythmias are responsible for approximately 15% of syncopal episodes and are most common in patients with cardiac risk factors or evidence of structural heart disease. Onset is usually sudden, may or may not be associated with palpitations, and can occur in any position. However, this patient's previous normal cardiac evaluation decreases the likelihood of an arrhythmia, and incontinence rarely results from causes of transient loss of consciousness other than seizure. The extended postictal period of confusion and speech impairment seen in this patient is also atypical of cardiac arrhythmia. Patients recovering from loss of consciousness due to arrhythmia are more typically alert or at most mildly confused after the loss of consciousness. Although the premonitory aura this patient experienced is most suggestive of seizure, such an aura has also been reported in cases of cerebral hyperperfusion from cardiac arrhythmia or neurocardiogenic syncope.

A transient ischemic attack is not associated with this patient's findings and is not associated with loss of consciousness.

Vasovagal syncope occurs as the result of sudden vasodilatation and bradycardia resulting in hypotension and cerebral hypoperfusion and is the most common cause of neurocardiogenic syncope. Syncope with pain, emotional stress, cough, micturition, or defecation supports a vasovagal cause, which is often preceded by warning symptoms of lightheadedness, nausea, and diaphoresis. Generalized stiffening and shaking lasting seconds can occur with vasovagal syncope due to reduced cerebral blood flow, but this type of syncope does not explain the aura, prolonged loss of consciousness, postictal confusion, and incontinence experienced by the patient. Thus, this diagnosis is unlikely.

KEY POINT

- **Normal findings on an electroencephalogram and MRI do not rule out a diagnosis of seizure.**

Bibliography

Pillai J, Sperling MR. Interictal EEG and the diagnosis of epilepsy. Epilepsia. 2006;47 Suppl 1:14-22. [PMID: 17044820]

Item 19   Answer: A

Educational Objective: Evaluate suspected Guillain-Barré syndrome.

This patient should undergo electromyography (EMG). She has a rapidly progressive disorder affecting the peripheral nervous system, most compatible with a clinical diagnosis of Guillain-Barré syndrome. Patients with Guillain-Barré syndrome typically develop paresthesias distally in the lower extremities that are followed by limb weakness and gait unsteadiness. In addition to sensory loss and limb weakness, deep tendon reflexes are characteristically absent or markedly reduced. The diagnosis is confirmed by EMG, which usually shows a demyelinating polyradiculoneuropathy. Cerebrospinal fluid (CSF) analysis characteristically shows albuminocytologic dissociation, whereby the spinal fluid cell count is normal but the spinal fluid protein level is elevated. CSF analysis may also yield normal results early in the course of the disease. However, a normal CSF cell count is useful in excluding other infectious conditions, such as polyradiculoneuropathies associated with HIV and cytomegalovirus infection, infection due to West Nile virus, and carcinomatous or lymphomatous nerve root infiltration. By definition, symptoms in patients with Guillain-Barré syndrome peak within 4 weeks of onset. Poor prognostic features include rapid symptom progression, respiratory failure, EMG evidence of axonal degeneration, and advanced age. Intravenous immune globulin and plasma exchange are equally efficacious in the treatment of Guillain-Barré syndrome.

MRI of the spinal cord would be inappropriate as the next diagnostic test. The patient's presentation of distal extremity sensory loss with areflexia suggests a disorder of the peripheral nervous system. A spinal cord lesion (myelopathy) would be an unlikely cause of the symptoms noted on clinical examination. The absence of bowel or bladder impairment, the lack of a sensory level across the thorax, and the upper and lower limb areflexia argue against a central nervous system disorder affecting the spinal cord.

West Nile virus infection should be considered in every patient with symptoms of extremity weakness that begin acutely and progress over days to weeks. However, the presence of paresthesias and sensory loss on examination are not typical of West Nile virus infection. This enteroviral illness affects the anterior horn cells, causing limb weakness in the absence of sensory loss. Most cases of West Nile virus infection cause only minor symptoms that are indistinguishable from those of other viral illnesses.

Biopsy of the sural nerve is considered in the diagnostic evaluation of patients with a marked peripheral neuropathy of unknown cause. The sural nerve is a sensory nerve that supplies sensation to the lateral distal leg and lateral aspect of the foot. Sural nerve biopsy is appropriate in patients with suspected vasculitis or amyloidosis and occasionally in patients with chronic inflammatory demyelinating polyradiculoneuropathy; it is also used to exclude neuropathic conditions resulting from neoplastic infiltration or other inflammatory conditions, such as sarcoidosis. Symmetric signs and symptoms and diffuse areflexia are not typical of vasculitis. The acute onset and rapid symptom progression would argue against amyloidosis, chronic inflammatory demyelinating polyradiculoneuropathy, or other infiltrating peripheral nerve disorders. Sural nerve biopsy is not necessary in patients with suspected Guillain-Barré syndrome.

Bibliography

Winer JB. Guillain-Barré syndrome. BMJ. 2008;337:a671. doi: 10.1136/bmj.a671. [PMID: 18640954]

Item 20   Answer: C

Educational Objective: Manage a thunderclap headache.

This patient should undergo CT angiography of the head and neck. She has experienced a thunderclap headache, which is a severe and explosive headache that is maximal in intensity at or within 60 seconds of onset. Every thunderclap headache must be immediately evaluated to detect potentially catastrophic conditions, especially subarachnoid hemorrhage. Most of the other causes of thunderclap headache, such as an unruptured cerebral aneurysm, a carotid or vertebral artery dissection, cerebral venous sinus thrombosis, and reversible cerebral vasoconstriction syndrome, can be excluded by noninvasive angiography. Therefore, CT angiography of the head and neck is the most appropriate next step in management. CT angiography can detect unruptured aneurysms as small as 3 mm in diameter and thus is adequate to exclude this diagnosis. Magnetic resonance angiography (MRA) would also be appropriate in this setting. Both CT angiography and MRA can be performed with a venous phase to exclude cerebral venous sinus thrombosis. Given that most causes of thunderclap headache can be excluded by such noninvasive angiography and that prior cerebrospinal fluid analysis has shown no evidence of a subarachnoid hemorrhage in this patient, conventional cerebral angiography, in which a catheter is inserted into a large artery and advanced through the carotid artery, is unnecessary.

Because of the potential for neurologic morbidity associated with several of the causes of thunderclap headache, admission for observation without evaluation of the cerebral vasculature would not be the best management option.

Similarly, treatment with a vasoconstrictive drug, such as sumatriptan, would not be appropriate until the other causes of thunderclap headache have been excluded. Drugs with the potential to constrict extracranial and intracranial cerebral vessels can precipitate or exacerbate the cerebral ischemia that may be associated with arterial dissection and reversible cerebral vasoconstriction syndromes.

Although it may take up to 6 hours for subarachnoid blood to sediment into the lumbar thecal sac, this patient's first lumbar puncture occurred more than 8 hours after the onset of symptoms. Repeating the lumbar puncture would, therefore, be unnecessary.

Bibliography

Schwedt TJ, Matharu MS, Dodick DW. Thunderclap headache. Lancet Neurol. 2006;5(7):621-631. [PMID: 16781992]

Item 21   Answer: E

Educational Objective: Treat an acute hemispheric stroke.

This patient should receive intravenous recombinant tissue plasminogen activator (rtPA). He has clinical symptoms and signs and radiologic evidence of an acute left hemispheric stroke. The probable mechanism of stroke is a cardioembolism, given his history of atrial fibrillation and his subtherapeutic INR. He was brought to the emergency department within 1 hour of the witnessed onset of stroke symptoms, and his evaluation is completed 1 hour later. He does not appear to have any clinical, radiologic, or laboratory contraindication to receiving the preferred treatment of intravenous rtPA, and he can receive it within the recommended window of 3 hours from stroke onset. The standard dose is 0.9 mg/kg. Although he is on warfarin, rtPA is not contraindicated because his INR is 1.5; an INR less than or equal to 1.7 is required for rtPA administration in a patient on anticoagulation.

Aspirin is indicated for acute ischemic stroke in patients who are not eligible for rtPA, as this patient is. For patients with acute stroke who are eligible for thrombolysis, aspirin should be withheld in the emergency department and for 24 hours after rtPA administration.

Although long-term anticoagulation is an effective treatment for prevention of cardioembolic stroke in patients with atrial fibrillation, acute anticoagulation with heparin has not been shown to be beneficial in patients with acute ischemic stroke.

Intra-arterial administration of rtPA is indicated for selected patients with acute stroke who have major intracranial artery occlusion within 6 hours of symptom onset and who are not otherwise candidates for intravenous administration of rtPA. This patient was eligible for intravenous administration of rtPA within 3 hours of stroke onset. The latter treatment takes precedence.

Elevated blood pressure is common at the time of initial stroke presentation, even among patients without chronic hypertension. Rapid lowering of blood pressure may further impair cerebral blood flow and worsen the ischemic injury. Elevated blood pressure often will resolve spontaneously or improve gradually during the first few days after a stroke. The threshold for acute blood pressure lowering in patients with acute stroke who are eligible for thrombolysis is 185/110 mm Hg. In such a setting, preferred agents include intravenous infusions of labetalol or nicardipine. Because this patient's blood pressure is already below that threshold, there is no indication for intravenous use of labetalol at this time.

KEY POINT

- **A patient with acute ischemic stroke who is taking warfarin but who has a subtherapeutic INR (≤1.7) is still eligible to receive thrombolysis with intravenous recombinant tissue plasminogen activator within the recommended window of 3 hours from stroke onset.**

Bibliography

Adams HP Jr, del Zoppo G, Alberts MJ, et al. Guidelines for the early management of adults with ischemic stroke: a guideline from the American Heart Association/American Stroke Association Stroke Council, Clinical Cardiology Council, Cardiovascular Radiology and Intervention Council, and the Atherosclerotic Peripheral Vascular Disease and Quality of Care Outcomes in Research Interdisciplinary Working Groups: the American Academy of Neurology affirms the value of this guideline as an educational tool for neurologists [errata in Stroke. 2007;38(6):e138 and Stroke. 2007;38(9):e96]. Stroke. 2007;38(5):1655-1711. [PMID: 17431204]

Item 22   Answer: B

Educational Objective: Diagnose multiple system atrophy.

Multiple system atrophy is the most likely diagnosis in this patient. He has a progressive neurologic disorder characterized by signs and symptoms that suggest impairment of multiple neurologic systems; these include the autonomic nervous system (orthostatic hypotension, erectile dysfunction, constipation), the extrapyramidal system (rigidity, impaired gait), and the cerebellum (limb ataxia). Multiple system atrophy is a progressive, ultimately fatal neurodegenerative disorder that typically causes dysautonomia, parkinsonism, and ataxia, in some combination, in affected patients. Multiple system atrophy is a clinical diagnosis that is suggested by the presence of these various features in the same patient.

Dementia with Lewy bodies is also typically associated with parkinsonian features and should be considered in the differential diagnosis of this patient. Dementia with Lewy bodies is associated with cognitive impairment, parkinsonian signs and symptoms, and possible evidence of dysautonomia. However, gait or limb ataxia is not expected, and the degree of dysautonomia typically is not as severe as that seen in multiple system atrophy.

The prominent dysautonomia, early falls, absence of a resting tremor, and presence of appendicular ataxia in this patient argue against Parkinson disease as the diagnosis.

Early multiple system atrophy can, however, be difficult to distinguish from Parkinson disease, especially because some affected patients may respond initially to carbidopa-levodopa, a medication used to treat parkinsonian symptoms in Parkinson disease.

Progressive supranuclear palsy should also be part of the differential diagnosis in this patient. A rare neurodegenerative disorder, progressive supranuclear palsy is associated with parkinsonian signs and early falls due to marked postural instability. However, significant dysautonomia and ataxia are not expected. Marked impairment in vertical gaze is a hallmark of progressive supranuclear palsy.

KEY POINT

- **Multiple system atrophy is a sporadic, heterogeneous, neurodegenerative disorder that causes impairment of multiple neurologic systems, including the autonomic nervous system, the extrapyramidal system, and the cerebellum.**

Bibliography

O'Sullivan SS, Massey LA, Williams DR, et al. Clinical outcomes of progressive supranuclear palsy and multiple system atrophy. Brain. 2008;131(Pt 5):1362-1372. [PMID: 18385183]

Item 23   Answer: A

Educational Objective: Manage nonconvulsive status epilepticus.

This patient should undergo continuous electroencephalographic monitoring. Generalized convulsive status epilepticus, which this patient initially exhibited, is a neurologic emergency with significant morbidity and mortality. Complications include hemodynamic instability, acidosis, rhabdomyolysis, pulmonary edema, respiratory failure, and irreversible brain injury. His early treatment with lorazepam was appropriate as first-line therapy. Over time, the clinical manifestations of status epilepticus can become increasingly subtle, but the electrical seizures can continue unabated, a state referred to as subtle or nonconvulsive status epilepticus. Motor manifestations may be limited to rhythmic muscle twitching in the face or eyes or to low-amplitude multifocal myoclonus in an obtunded or comatose patient. The unwary or inexperienced observer may mistake subtle generalized convulsive status epilepticus for postictal obtundation. Failure to diagnose and treat ongoing status epilepticus increases the risk of an adverse outcome, even with ventilatory and critical care support. Ongoing electrical seizure activity will lead to increasing physiologic derangement and neuronal injury. In this patient and others who remain unresponsive or have persistent altered mentation after treatment for clinical status epilepticus, it may be impossible to distinguish on clinical grounds alone the effect of ongoing electrical seizure activity from postictal lethargy or the side effects of medication. For this reason, continuous electroencephalographic monitoring is strongly advocated for optimal management. If ongoing status epilepticus is demonstrated, additional intravenous antiepileptic drugs should be administered at doses sufficient to terminate the electroencephalographic seizures.

Withdrawal of care at this point is premature because the patient has not yet had an adequate evaluation.

Adding phenobarbital or other medications to this patient's drug regimen carries the risk of complications, such as hypotension, and thus would not be the best choice, unless the patient were still experiencing seizures.

Obtaining an MRI of the brain should never delay other necessary diagnostic tests or therapies required to treat the status epilepticus. MRI is also unlikely to provide useful additional information in this patient whose cerebral metastasis constitutes a known underlying cause of his seizure activity.

KEY POINT

- Continuous electroencephalographic monitoring is indicated for patients who remain unresponsive after resolution of clinical status epilepticus to distinguish nonconvulsive status epilepticus from a postictal state.

Bibliography

Manno EM. New management strategies in the treatment of status epilepticus. Mayo Clin Proc. 2003;78(4):508-518. [PMID: 12683704]

Item 24   Answer: D

Educational Objective: Evaluate chronic meningitis masquerading as dementia.

This patient has fungal meningitis due to *Coccidioides immitis* infection and thus should undergo lumbar puncture and subsequent cerebrospinal fluid analysis to detect the potentially reversible cause of her cognitive and other impairments. A 71-year-old woman with declining cognition may seem an obvious candidate for Alzheimer dementia, but any pathologic process affecting the brain can impair cognition. The symptoms described—subacute onset, headache, fluctuating level of alertness, fever, peripheral blood markers of inflammation, and mildly dilated ventricles on the CT scan—should all provoke suspicion of an infectious, inflammatory, or otherwise reversible cause rather than a degenerative one. The scenario described is of a patient with encephalopathy whose clinical, laboratory, and radiologic findings suggest some type of meningitic process. Because of the time course, an atypical infectious agent, such as fungal meningitis, should be considered, especially in light of her history of fungal pneumonia in the past. Other causes of chronic or subacute meningoencephalitis, such as autoimmune encephalopathy and carcinomatous meningitis, need also be considered.

Apolipoprotein E (APOE) genotyping will not provide useful information in this patient. Specifically, discovering if this patient carries the APOE e4 allele and thus has an elevated risk for Alzheimer dementia would not help explain or treat her current symptoms and signs but could delay finding the probable infectious, inflammatory, or related cause of her symptoms.

Although cerebral vasculitis can produce a clinical picture similar to this one, cerebral CT angiography is not sufficiently sensitive to diagnose vasculitis of the central nervous system. Making that diagnosis usually requires either invasive intra-arterial angiography or brain and leptomeningeal biopsy. The more usual application of cerebral CT angiography is in the assessment of acute stroke, of which there is no evidence in this patient.

The finding of mildly dilated ventricles on this patient's CT scan is not relevant to her signs and symptoms, so further confirmatory testing by cisternography is unlikely to reveal the underlying cause of her findings.

It is highly unlikely that a repeat electroencephalogram (EEG) will give much further insight into this patient's condition, given that the EEG obtained during the patient's symptomatic period showed no epileptiform activity. Seizures are a potential complicating feature of any meningitic or encephalitic process, but the occurrence of a seizure or EEG finding of occasional interictal epileptiform activity will not provide any additional information about the underlying cause of this patient's symptoms.

KEY POINT

- Cerebrospinal fluid analysis should be considered in any patient with potentially reversible causes of impaired cognition, particularly if meningoencephalitis is suspected.

Bibliography

Johnson RH, Einstein HE. Coccidioidal meningitis. Clin Infect Dis. 2006;42(1):103-107. [PMID: 16323099]

Item 25   Answer: C

Educational Objective: Diagnose relapsing-remitting multiple sclerosis.

This patient experienced an episode of transient neurologic dysfunction (an attack) at disease onset and thus has relapsing-remitting multiple sclerosis (MS). Eighty-five percent of patients with MS have this type of disease onset. In relapsing-remitting MS, relapse frequency declines over time, and relapses do not become more severe with increasing disease duration; however, recovery from individual events may be slower and less complete.

Primary progressive MS, which the other 15% of patients with MS have at disease onset, is defined as gradually worsening neurologic function over more than 1 year without recovery. This patient has recovered completely from two neurologic episodes and is currently asymptomatic. Therefore, he cannot be classified as having primary progressive MS.

Secondary progressive MS is characterized by gradual, unremitting development of new symptoms over months to years in a patient who previously had a relapsing-remitting course. The lifetime risk of conversion from relapsing-remitting to secondary progressive disease is greater than 50%, but the onset and rate of the progressive phase are highly variable and not predictable for individual patients. The median time from MS onset until conversion to the secondary progressive phase typically ranges from 10 to 15 years. The establishment of a secondary progressive course is a risk factor for substantial disability, such as loss of independent ambulatory function; the median time from MS onset to the point at which unilateral gait assistance (such as a cane) is required is 15 to 25 years. This patient first had transient symptoms only 6 months ago and thus cannot be characterized as having secondary progressive disease.

Benign MS is defined loosely as no or minimal neurologic impairment 15 or more years after MS onset. This category may encompass as many as 20% of all patients with MS. The definition of benign MS is controversial because continued follow-up of such patients often uncovers late progressive disease and disability accrual. However, a small minority of patients with MS live a long and essentially unrestricted life. The factors that predict a benign course early in the disease have not yet been identified. This patient's MS diagnosis is too recent to be categorized as benign at this point.

KEY POINT

- Multiple sclerosis begins as a relapsing-remitting disorder in 85% of patients and a primary progressive disorder in 15% of patients; those with the relapsing-remitting type have a greater than 50% risk of developing a secondary progressive disease course.

Bibliography
Vukusic S, Confavreux C. Natural history of multiple sclerosis: risk factors and prognostic indicators. Curr Opin Neurol. 2007;20(3):269-274. [PMID: 17495619]

Item 26   Answer: A
Educational Objective: Treat an acute dystonic reaction.

This patient is experiencing a prochlorperazine-induced dystonic reaction, which is best treated with benztropine. Acute dystonic reactions are characterized as torticollic (twisted or a turned head, neck, or face), oculogyric (deviated or rolling gaze), buccolingual (pulling sensation of the tongue), or opisthotonic (trunk or entire-body spasm). Medications, such as prochlorperazine, that block dopaminergic receptors in the extrapyramidal system can result in acute dystonic reactions. Intravenous anticholinergic agents, such as benztropine or diphenhydramine, are the treatment of choice in the acute treatment of dystonic reactions. Benzodiazepine medications can also be helpful in the acute setting. Oral anticholinergic medications are continued for 48 to 72 hours to prevent relapse.

Cervical dystonia, or spasmodic torticollis, is a chronic condition associated with abnormal head posturing and tremor. Botulinum toxin is often beneficial for this condition.

Acute dystonic reactions can be misdiagnosed as seizures, tetanus, stroke, and other conditions. Phenytoin is an antiseizure medication, tissue plasminogen activator is appropriate treatment for strokes under certain conditions, and tetanus immune globulin is administered for tetanus prophylaxis. None of these drugs is indicated for acute dystonic reactions.

KEY POINT

- Medications that block dopamine receptors can cause acute dystonic reactions, which can be readily treated with benztropine.

Bibliography
Dressler D, Benecke R. Diagnosis and management of acute movement disorders. J Neurol. 2005;252(11):1299-1306. [PMID: 16208529]

Item 27   Answer: C
Educational Objective: Treat an acute carotid dissection in a patient with headache.

This patient has a carotid dissection, for which he should receive heparin. Acute headache with oculosympathetic paresis (Horner syndrome) is a common presentation of carotid dissection and must be assumed to be carotid dissection until proved otherwise. Such a headache may precede the onset of cerebral ischemia (transient ischemic attack or stroke) by days to weeks. Additional manifestations of this condition may include ipsilateral throbbing neck or orbital pain. The pain from carotid dissection may occur suddenly or develop gradually. Neurologic abnormalities due to ischemia in the ipsilateral hemisphere (causing contralateral numbness or weakness) or retina (causing ipsilateral monocular visual symptoms) also may occur. Magnetic resonance angiography of the carotid arteries and carotid duplex ultrasonography are indicated in the clinical evaluation of possible carotid dissection. Although the management of carotid dissection is controversial, most experts agree on the intravenous use of heparin in the acute setting to prevent distal embolism and stroke.

Acute severe headache always requires imaging of the neck and cerebral blood vessels to rule out a vascular cause. This patient's magnetic resonance angiogram of the neck shows a long, tapered stenosis of the left internal carotid artery in the neck, which indicates dissection. Although this patient's CT scan of the head and neck had normal results and MRI of the brain reveals no abnormalities of the brain parenchyma, the MRI does show dissection of the internal carotid artery.

There is no evidence to support the use of intra-arterial nimodipine or intravenous nitroglycerin in this setting. The carotid stenosis in this patient is due to the mural hematoma in the wall of a blood vessel, not to an arterial spasm. In addition, these drugs may decrease systemic arterial pressure and cerebral perfusion pressure distal to the severe carotid stenosis.

Despite his migraine history and his severe unilateral and pulsatile headache, this patient's current headache does not fulfill the diagnostic criteria for migraine; there are no associated features of nausea, vomiting, photophobia, or phonophobia. Because of its potent α-adrenergic stimulation, dihydroergotamine, a migraine therapy, is contraindicated in patients with conditions that predispose them to vasospastic reactions. This medication is thus not appropriate in the presence of a carotid dissection.

Stent-assisted aneurysm coiling is not indicated in this patient because he does not have an intracerebral aneurysm, according to the results of his imaging studies.

KEY POINT

- **Acute unilateral headache with associated Horner syndrome represents acute carotid dissection until proved otherwise.**

Bibliography

Schievink WI. Spontaneous dissection of the carotid and vertebral arteries. N Engl J Med. 2001;344(12):898-906. [PMID: 11259724]

Item 28   Answer: B

Educational Objective: Evaluate a subarachnoid hemorrhage.

This patient should have a lumbar puncture. A thunderclap headache is a severe and explosive headache that is maximal in intensity at or within 60 seconds of onset. CT scanning is the first test to be conducted in a patient with thunderclap headache in whom a subarachnoid hemorrhage is suspected; a ruptured intracranial aneurysm is the most serious cause of such headaches. The ability to detect subarachnoid hemorrhage is dependent on the amount of subarachnoid blood, the interval after symptom onset, the resolution of the scanner, and the skills of the radiologist. On the day of the hemorrhage, extravasated blood will be present in more than 95% of patients, but in the following days, this proportion falls sharply. If an initial CT scan of the head reveals nothing, a lumbar puncture should be performed next in patients with this presentation. In an important minority (<5%) of patients with thunderclap headache who have no abnormalities on a CT scan and no blood in the cerebrospinal fluid (CSF), the CSF contains metabolites of hemoglobin that may be detected by spectrophotometry. This finding is diagnostic for subarachnoid hemorrhage. Subsequent angiography can confirm the presence of a ruptured aneurysm. It should be noted that spectrophotometry is not universally available in all hospitals.

CT angiography and magnetic resonance angiography have similar test characteristics. Their sensitivity for detecting a ruptured aneurysm, with the more invasive conventional angiography as the gold standard, is currently 95%. CT angiography can be performed faster than can magnetic resonance angiography, but the latter uses no radiation and no contrast injection. Both modalities can play a role in the work-up of a patient with undiagnosed thunderclap headache when lumbar puncture and standard CT are nondiagnostic. Conditions other than aneurysm in the differential diagnosis of thunderclap headache can also be detected by CT angiography or magnetic resonance angiography, including arterial dissection and reversible cerebral vasoconstriction syndrome.

Magnetic resonance venography may be necessary in a patient with thunderclap headache, but only when cerebral venous sinus thrombosis is part of the differential diagnosis. Cerebral venous sinus thrombosis is more common in young adults. Major risk factors for such thrombosis in adults include conditions that predispose to spontaneous thromboses, including inherited or acquired thrombophilia, pregnancy, oral contraceptive use, malignancy, sepsis, and head trauma.

An MRI is as sensitive as a CT scan in the acute phase of subarachnoid hemorrhage but is not superior. Any subarachnoid blood not evident on a CT scan is unlikely to be seen on an MRI. A few days after the hemorrhage, an MRI is better for detecting blood, with fluid-attenuated inversion recovery (FLAIR) and T2-star images being the most sensitive. An MRI can also help in the detection of other conditions in the differential diagnosis, such as an acute ischemic stroke, pituitary apoplexy, a third-ventricle colloid cyst, and an acute hypertensive crisis.

KEY POINT

- **A lumbar puncture with subsequent cerebrospinal fluid analysis is necessary in any patient with thunderclap headache and normal findings on a CT scan to fully evaluate a possible subarachnoid hemorrhage.**

Bibliography

van Gijn J, Kerr RS, Rinkel GJ. Subarachnoid haemorrhage. Lancet. 2007;369(9558):306-318. [PMID: 17258671]

Item 29   Answer: B

Educational Objective: Manage juvenile myoclonic epilepsy in a young adult.

This patient requires life-long treatment of her epilepsy. Appropriate recognition of specific epilepsy syndromes is essential because it will guide the clinician in selecting the appropriate therapy, making the correct prognosis, and, in some instances, providing genetic counseling. A history of myoclonic and generalized tonic-clonic seizures on awakening with onset in adolescence is highly suggestive of the syndrome of juvenile myoclonic epilepsy, which is one of the most commonly encountered forms of epilepsy, possibly affecting 5% to 10% of all patients with epilepsy.

Seizures in juvenile myoclonic epilepsy are generally well controlled with medication, but relapses can be provoked by sleep deprivation, alcohol, or exposure to flickering lights. If medication is withdrawn, seizures will recur in 75% to 100% of patients. Therefore, in this patient with a history of juvenile myoclonic epilepsy, medication withdrawal is not recommended either now, 3 months from now, or in 2 years; juvenile myoclonic epilepsy requires lifelong therapy.

KEY POINT

- **Juvenile myoclonic epilepsy requires lifelong antiepileptic drug therapy.**

Bibliography

Sokic D, Ristic AJ, Vojvodic N, Jankovic S, Sindjelic AR. Frequency, causes and phenomenology of late seizure recurrence in patients with juvenile myoclonic epilepsy after a long period of remission. Seizure. 2007;16(6):533-537. [PMID: 17574449]

Item 30   Answer: D

Educational Objective: Diagnose mild cognitive impairment.

This patient has mild cognitive impairment (MCI), which denotes abnormal cognitive decline that is not severe enough to produce disability. His self-reported memory loss, which is confirmed by his performance on the Folstein Mini–Mental State Examination, is his only symptom; there are no other signs of dementia. Memory loss is nonspecific and is part of many dementia syndromes. However, the lack of any functional impairment in this patient makes MCI the most likely diagnosis at this time. Although there are no universally accepted criteria for MCI, the disorder has been defined as a memory abnormality corroborated by objective memory impairment on standardized tests, without general cognitive impairment or an effect on functional independence. The rate of progression to dementia is approximately 10% to 15% per year.

Alzheimer dementia is the most common cause of MCI involving memory loss. Because this patient has no functional disabilities and thus does not meet the criteria for frank dementia, Alzheimer dementia is an incorrect diagnosis at this point. He may eventually develop the disease, given that the conversion rate of MCI to dementia is roughly 10% to 15% per year and that, at autopsy, approximately 80% of patients originally diagnosed with MCI have Alzheimer dementia.

Early-stage symptoms that are characteristic of frontotemporal dementia include changes in behavior and personality, such as increasing apathy, disinhibition, or perseverative (repetitive to an exceptional degree) fixations. This patient has exhibited no such changes.

The onset of dementia with Lewy bodies could also be characterized by memory loss. Besides clearly not having dementia of any sort at this stage of his illness, this patient lacks any of the other symptoms of dementia with Lewy bodies, such as parkinsonism, visual hallucinations, psychomotor slowing, and dream enactment behavior.

Typical manifestations of vascular dementia include psychomotor slowing, a stepwise progression, and a history of stroke, none of which pertains to this patient.

KEY POINT

- **Mild cognitive impairment denotes abnormal cognitive decline that is not severe enough to produce disability.**

Bibliography

Petersen RC, Stevens JC, Ganguli M, Tangalos EG, Cummings JL, DeKosky ST. Practice parameter: early detection of dementia: mild cognitive impairment (an evidence-based review). Report of the Quality Standards Subcommittee of the American Academy of Neurology. Neurology. 2001;56(9):1133-1142. [PMID: 11342677]

Item 31   Answer: A

Educational Objective: Treat fatigue related to multiple sclerosis.

This patient should receive a course of amantadine. Fatigue is the most common symptom of multiple sclerosis (MS) but is also highly prevalent in the general population. The fact that the patient's fatigue began with a relapse strengthens its association with her MS, but evaluation for other causes is still required. Her review of systems, physical examination, and laboratory studies do not reveal another likely cause, and she is already sleeping and exercising regularly. Therefore, pharmacologic therapy can reasonably be offered. Amantadine has been shown in several small placebo-controlled studies to reduce MS-related fatigue. The mechanism is not clearly understood but is likely related to the drug's stimulant properties.

Although a brief course of corticosteroids may provide a temporary boost of energy, this strategy is not a practical solution because the beneficial effects will by definition be brief. Longer-term use of corticosteroids is also not advised because of the high risk of adverse effects.

Discontinuation of interferon beta-1a is unnecessary because the patient does not perceive any adverse effects from the drug. Flu-like symptoms and fatigue related to interferon beta-1a are usually temporally related to individual injections.

Although fatigue can also be related to vitamin B_{12} deficiency, injection of the vitamin is not indicated for this patient because the patient's physical examination and normal laboratory values show that she is not vitamin B_{12} deficient.

KEY POINT

- **Adequate rest and regular physical exercise can reduce multiple sclerosis–related fatigue, but many patients require treatment with stimulants, such as amantadine.**

Bibliography

Lapierre Y, Hum S. Treating fatigue. Int MS J. 2007;14(2):64-71. [PMID: 17686346]

Item 32   Answer: D

Educational Objective: Manage mild carpal tunnel syndrome.

This patient should be treated with wrist splints. She reports symptoms typical of carpal tunnel syndrome. The electromyogram (EMG) confirms the presence of a mild median neuropathy at the wrist. Given the mild symptoms and the presence of only mild changes on the EMG, a trial of conservative therapy is most appropriate. Conservative treatment approaches offer advantages over surgical treatment in terms of decreased short-term morbidity and surgical risk; also, the adverse effects of drug therapy may be avoided if nondrug modalities are used and prove to be beneficial. Conservative therapies include wrist splints, physical therapy, ergonomic adjustments, and corticosteroid injections. The role of occupational and recreational activities using the hands is highly variable, but ergonomic education and modification can be considered if thought to be relevant for individual patients.

For this patient with mild signs and symptoms of carpal tunnel syndrome, a trial of conservative therapy using wrist splints is indicated. A recently reported randomized controlled trial, which identified workers through a carpal tunnel syndrome surveillance protocol, assigned them to either the control group, who received ergonomic education, or the treatment group, who participated in a 6-week nocturnal splinting trial. Participants in the splinting group showed greater improvement than the control group, and this benefit was still present at 1 year.

The initial response rate to corticosteroid injections at or near the wrist is 70%. The duration of response is quite variable, however, and patients often require repeat injections or, ultimately, carpal tunnel surgery. Patients with mild to moderate symptoms who do not respond to wrist splinting should be considered for corticosteroid injection.

Gabapentin and other medications used to treat neuropathic pain are typically not indicated in carpal tunnel syndrome.

Carpal tunnel surgery should be considered in patients who have not responded to conservative therapy and in patients with moderate to severe signs or symptoms, unless there is a contraindication to surgery. A recent systematic review of the different surgical treatment options for carpal tunnel syndrome failed to reveal improved outcomes in open versus endoscopic carpal tunnel release.

KEY POINT

- **Wrist splinting is an effective, conservative treatment of carpal tunnel syndrome in patients with mild symptoms.**

Bibliography

Werner RA, Franzblau A, Gell N. Randomized controlled trial of nocturnal splinting for active workers with symptoms of carpal tunnel syndrome [erratum in Arch Phys Med Rehabil. 2007;88(4):544]. Arch Phys Med Rehabil. 2005;86(1):1-7. [PMID: 15640980]

Item 33   Answer: C

Educational Objective: Treat migraine during pregnancy.

Metoclopramide has been shown to have efficacy for both the pain and nausea associated with migraine. This drug has a U.S. Food and Drug Administration (FDA) rating of pregnancy category B. Acute medications with an FDA rating of pregnancy category A or B carry the lowest risk of harm to the fetus and should be used preferentially for the treatment of migraine during pregnancy.

Amitriptyline and verapamil are used for migraine prophylaxis. Both have an FDA rating of pregnancy category C (risk to the fetus cannot be ruled out) and are not contraindicated for pregnant women. However, prophylactic migraine therapy should be avoided whenever possibly during pregnancy, especially in the first trimester. Often, migraine improves during the second and third trimesters of pregnancy, so acute therapy during the first trimester is preferred. If migraine continues to be disabling and occurs frequently during the second and third trimesters, prophylactic therapy could be considered, especially if the health of the mother and/or the fetus is compromised.

Ergotamine tartrate and valproic acid have an FDA rating of pregnancy category X (studies have shown fetal abnormalities) and are contraindicated during pregnancy.

KEY POINT

- **Migraines during pregnancy that do not respond to simple analgesia can be safely and effectively treated with metoclopramide.**

Bibliography

Loder E. Migraine in pregnancy. Semin Neurol. 2007;27(5):425-433. [PMID: 17940921]

Item 34   Answer: D

Educational Objective: Diagnose partial complex seizure arising in the temporal lobe.

This patient's "spells" were most likely partial complex epileptic seizures. The incidence of epilepsy is greatest in infants and older adults, with half of new-onset seizures presenting in persons older than 65 years. In large part, the latter fact reflects the increased prevalence of underlying brain diseases—particularly cerebrovascular disease, neurodegenerative conditions (such as Alzheimer disease), and brain tumors— that increase seizure risk in this segment of the population.

Epilepsy is classified as partial or generalized on the basis of the areas of the brain involved at onset. Seizures that present in adulthood are usually partial in onset; partial seizures in which the patient maintains full awareness are classified as simple partial, whereas those involving an alteration of consciousness, as in this patient, are classified as partial complex. The most common site of onset for partial seizures is the temporal lobe. As described by this patient, temporal lobe events often begin with an aura of déjà vu, a rising epigastric sensation, or autonomic disturbances. Although automatisms, such as lip smacking, are occasionally reported in absence seizures, these features are atypical for that type of seizure and are more suggestive of partial complex ones. In this patient, the age of onset, duration (several minutes) of the event, presence of oral automatisms, and reported postictal confusion and speech impairment all suggest a partial complex seizure.

Absence, generalized tonic-clonic, and myoclonic seizures are all manifestations of generalized epilepsy and are correlated with generalized epileptiform discharges on an electroencephalogram. Absence seizures are characterized by brief periods of staring and unresponsiveness, typically lasting seconds, with an immediate return to normal awareness. Absence seizures usually present in childhood. The length of this patient's episodes, his confusion before returning to normal awareness, and his age argue against absence seizure being the diagnosis.

Generalized tonic-clonic (grand mal) seizures are characterized by stiffening of the trunk and extremities followed by generalized symmetric jerking. Such features were not reported in this patient.

Myoclonic seizures consist of brief, shock-like muscle jerks without loss of awareness. These features are not consistent with the history this patient provides.

KEY POINT

- Epilepsy that presents in adulthood is usually partial in onset; partial seizures that involve altered awareness are classified as complex partial seizures.

Bibliography

Trost LF III, Wender RC, Suter CC, et al; National Epilepsy Management Panel. Management of epilepsy in adults. Diagnosis guidelines. Postgrad Med. 2005;118(6):22-26 [PMID: 16382762]

Item 35   Answer: B

Educational Objective: Diagnose drug-induced parkinsonism.

Drug-induced parkinsonism is the most likely diagnosis in this patient. This disorder has classically been associated with neuroleptic medications but can occur with any dopamine-blocking medications, including metoclopramide. Although metoclopramide causes drug-induced parkinsonism in one third of all patients using it, the disorder is particularly underdiagnosed in such patients. Establishing a diagnosis of

drug-induced parkinsonism is critical because stopping dopamine-blocking medications can reverse or improve parkinsonian features in these patients.

Cognitive impairment in conjunction with parkinsonism occurs in patients with dementia with Lewy bodies, but the latter diagnosis is unlikely in this patient, given her apparently normal cognition.

Multiple system atrophy is a heterogeneous, progressive, and ultimately fatal neurodegenerative disorder associated with parkinsonian features and with cerebellar and autonomic signs and symptoms of variable severity. Early multiple system atrophy would be a consideration in this patient if she were not on a medication known to induce signs and symptoms of parkinsonism. The parkinsonism in some patients with early multiple system atrophy cannot be distinguished from Parkinson disease and may even be responsive initially to levodopa. Most patients with multiple system atrophy, however, have bilateral parkinsonian signs and lack significant tremor, findings that are atypical of Parkinson disease.

Parkinson disease should be part of the differential diagnosis but is an unlikely cause of the symptoms in this patient. Although there are parkinsonian signs and symptoms, there are several atypical features that should prompt consideration of an alternative diagnosis. The presence of symmetric signs and symptoms (tremor and rigidity) and the postural tremor in this patient suggest a condition other than Parkinson disease. Other features that suggest an alternative condition in patients with parkinsonian signs and symptoms include early falls, rapid progression, poor or waning levodopa response, dementia, early autonomic failure, and ataxia. Moreover, this patient is taking metoclopramide, a medication known to cause parkinsonism.

KEY POINT

- Drug-induced parkinsonism is a potential complication of dopamine-blocking medications, including metoclopramide.

Bibliography

Esper CD, Factor SA. Failure of recognition of drug-induced parkinsonism in the elderly. Mov Disord. 2008;23(3):401-404. [PMID: 18067180]

Item 36   Answer: A

Educational Objective: Treat functional decline in a patient with advanced Alzheimer dementia.

This patient has Alzheimer dementia that is moderately advanced and now has difficulties with basic activities of daily living. The N-methyl-D-aspartate receptor antagonist memantine is the only drug approved by the U.S. Food and Drug Administration as first-line treatment of moderate to advanced Alzheimer dementia. Although evidence is limited, there is some suggestion that the stepped approach of adding memantine to a regimen that includes a cholinesterase inhibitor (such as donepezil) results in a modest additional benefit over substituting memantine for the cholinesterase inhibitor.

Quetiapine is an antipsychotic medication and sertraline is an antidepressant agent. Although both drugs can be used in patients with Alzheimer dementia, their use is limited to the treatment of the behavioral symptoms of psychosis and depression, respectively, neither of which this patient has at this time.

There is no approved indication for using donepezil beyond its recommended maximum dosage of 10 mg/d. In fact, data suggest that doing so is associated with increased adverse effects and not with increased efficacy.

Discontinuing the donepezil taken by this patient without substituting another drug to manage her functional decline would not help slow or otherwise improve the course of her disease. Although the potential cognitive side effects of the other prescription (and nonprescription) medications taken by this patient must also be considered, lisinopril, levothyroxine, and daily multivitamins have no association with such effects.

KEY POINT

- **Memantine is a first-line agent for treatment of moderate to advanced Alzheimer dementia.**

Bibliography

Areosa SA, Sherriff F, McShane R. Memantine for dementia. Cochrane Database Syst Rev. 2005;(2):CD003154. [PMID: 15846650]

Item 37   Answer: D

Educational Objective: Diagnose epidural spinal cord compression.

The most likely diagnosis is epidural spinal cord compression from metastatic cancer of the spine. The clinical feature of weakness accompanied by upper motoneuron signs (such as hyperreflexia and an extensor plantar response) and the detection of a sensory level localize the process to the thoracic spinal cord. The shooting thoracic pain is a localizing symptom that indicates involvement of the left T7 spinal nerve root. The patient is a long-standing smoker and has a lung mass suspicious for malignancy. Lung cancer is among the most common primary malignancies that metastasize to the spine. New and progressive symptoms referable to the spinal cord represent a neurologic emergency that should prompt evaluation for a compressive lesion. Clinical outcome, including ambulatory ability and mortality, depends on neurologic status at diagnosis.

A lumbar disk herniation at the L5 level would typically cause low back pain and radicular pain (sciatica) in one lower extremity because most herniations are unilateral or asymmetric. The thoracic location of the pain and sensory level and the presence of upper motoneuron signs in this patient exclude that diagnosis.

Other compressive lesions, such as an abscess or a hematoma, could result in the clinical symptoms and signs

exhibited by this patient. However, epidural abscesses are usually accompanied by fever and an elevated erythrocyte sedimentation rate, both of which were absent in this patient. Likewise, epidural hematoma development is strongly associated with anticoagulant use; this patient was not taking any such medications, and he had normal results on a coagulation panel.

KEY POINT

- **New and progressive symptoms referable to the spinal cord represent a neurologic emergency that should prompt evaluation for a compressive lesion.**

Bibliography

Loblaw DA, Perry J, Chambers A, Laperriere NJ. Systematic review of the diagnosis and management of malignant extradural spinal cord compression: the Cancer Care Ontario Practice Guidelines Initiative's Neuro-Oncology Disease Site Group. J Clin Oncol. 2005;23(9):2028-2037. [PMID: 15774794]

Item 38   Answer: C

Educational Objective: Treat critical illness myopathy.

This patient should have physical and occupational therapy. His history is quite typical of critical illness myopathy. Critical illness refers to the syndrome of sepsis and multiple organ failure. Critical illness myopathy or neuropathy is usually recognized in the intensive care unit, either in patients who have difficulty weaning from mechanical ventilation (up to 30% of patients) or in patients who have developed severe limb weakness during or after recovery from critical illness. Electrodiagnostic testing with electromyography should be considered in patients who develop generalized weakness or fail to wean from ventilation in this setting. Such testing can help exclude other conditions, such as neuromuscular junction disorders or polyradiculoneuropathy (Guillain-Barré syndrome), and confirm the diagnosis of critical illness myopathy or neuropathy.

Physical and occupational therapy is ideally initiated immediately on recognition of this syndrome. Respiratory therapy is important to minimize the risk of superimposed pulmonary infection. Stretching and passive range-of-motion exercises help maintain joint mobility and prevent contractures. Later, as the patient improves, strengthening of upper and lower extremity muscle groups and training in activities of daily living can be performed. Most patients will transition into the inpatient rehabilitation unit once medically stable.

Corticosteroids, such as prednisone, should be avoided, if possible, in patients with critical illness who develop peripheral neuropathy or myopathy during the course of their illness. Corticosteroids may play a role in the pathogenesis of critical illness myopathy, but myopathy can develop in patients who are critically ill even with no history of corticosteroid exposure.

Treatment of critical illness polyneuropathy with intravenous immune globulin has been attempted, but this therapy has not been shown to be of benefit in this disease or in critical illness myopathy. Some attempts to target and interrupt the cascade of humoral factors associated with sepsis have been promising, but treatment of critical illness myopathy is supportive at this time. The primary, initial approach is directed toward the prevention and management of sepsis, the systemic inflammatory response syndrome, and multiple organ dysfunction. Aggressive treatment of infection, hypoxemia, and hypotension is critical.

There is no evidence of a role for plasma exchange in the treatment of critical illness myopathy or neuropathy at this time.

KEY POINT

- **Therapy for critical illness myopathy, a frequent complication in sepsis or multiorgan failure that can cause failure to wean from mechanical ventilation and limb weakness, involves physical and occupational rehabilitative therapies and avoidance of corticosteroids.**

Bibliography

Bolton CF. Neuromuscular manifestations of critical illness. Muscle Nerve. 2005;32(2):140-163. [PMID: 15825186]

Item 39   Answer: C

Educational Objective: Evaluate suspected brain metastases in a patient with known primary cancer.

This patient should have a gadolinium-enhanced MRI. Her melanoma has most likely metastasized to her brain. Brain metastases are 10 times more common than primary brain tumors, and metastatic disease of the central nervous system (CNS) is estimated to occur in 20% to 40% of adults with cancer. The tumors most likely to metastasize to the CNS in adults are lung and breast carcinoma and melanoma. Presenting signs and symptoms vary according to the size and location of the metastatic lesion(s) and occur as a result of local mass effect or increased intracranial pressure; common symptoms include seizure, headache, behavioral changes, and subacute progressive focal neurologic deficits. A high level of clinical suspicion for CNS metastasis is therefore justified when new neurologic deficits develop in patients such as this one with a known primary tumor.

Contrast-enhanced MRI is the diagnostic modality of choice when brain metastasis is suspected. MRI has a higher sensitivity and specificity than CT scanning and is also safer because MRI contrast does not cause nephrotoxicity, and allergies are extremely rare. Furthermore, normal findings on a CT scan do not exclude the presence of a brain tumor, so a follow-up MRI would be required.

Despite her witnessed tonic-clonic seizure, electroencephalography is not appropriate as the next diagnostic step because brain imaging is more likely to reveal a potential underlying cause for the seizure. MRI is the study of choice to detect tumors, gliosis associated with encephalitis, head trauma, and stroke that may be causing seizures.

Lumbar puncture is also inappropriate in this patient because seizures are almost never present as the sole manifestation of a CNS infection or subarachnoid hemorrhage; lumbar puncture is indicated only if there are other indicators of these conditions. CNS infection is indicated by the presence of fever or altered mental status. Patients with subarachnoid hemorrhage may also have seizures, but this type of hemorrhage is associated with severe headache, altered mental status, syncope, and neurologic deficits and usually will be identified by CT or MRI imaging.

Positron emission tomography (PET) can be used to identify malignant tumors with high metabolic rates and may be helpful in planning the next diagnostic step (which lesion to biopsy) and in prognosis. However, the use of PET before the establishment of a brain tumor with MRI is premature and not indicated.

KEY POINT

- **Contrast-enhanced MRI is the diagnostic modality of choice when brain metastasis is suspected.**

Bibliography

Soffietti R, Cornu P, Delattre JY, et al. EFNS guidelines on diagnosis and treatment of brain metastases: report of an EFNS task force. Eur J Neurol. 2006;13(7):674-681. [PMID: 16834697]

Item 40   Answer: C

Educational Objective: Diagnose early-onset familial Alzheimer dementia.

This patient's personal and family medical history is striking for dementia at an unusually young age. Her maternal family history in particular is strongly suggestive of early-onset familial Alzheimer dementia, which typically has symptomatic onset in a person's forties or fifties. Although genetic testing is not routine in the evaluation of dementia, all known causes of early-onset familial Alzheimer dementia involve an autosomal dominant mutation. Therefore, genetic testing was appropriate for this patient and should be considered in all patients with early-onset dementia that seems to follow an autosomal dominant pattern of inheritance. The presenilin-1 mutation is specific for early-onset familial Alzheimer dementia. Although mutations of the amyloid precursor protein and presenilin-2 gene are other known autosomal dominant mutations that can cause the disease, the presenilin-1 mutation is by far the most common cause, and testing for this mutation is commercially available. Because the mutation has been identified in this patient, it is appropriate to offer genetic counseling to her daughter.

Because the presenilin-1 mutation is specific for early-onset familial Alzheimer dementia and because no evidence of parkinsonism was found on examination, it is unlikely that this patient has autosomal recessive Parkinson disease with dementia. In addition to evidence of parkinsonism, mutations in the parkin, α-synuclein, LRRK2, and other genes are associated with this disorder. The autosomal dominant mutations seen in early-onset familial Alzheimer dementia are not.

Besides the specificity of presenilin-1 for Alzheimer dementia, this patient is also unlikely to have Creutzfeldt-Jakob disease or vascular dementia because characteristic MRI findings in those disorders are absent. Specifically, there is no "cortical ribbon" sign typical of Creutzfeldt-Jakob disease and no sign of previous cerebral infarction, which is seen in most patients with vascular dementia.

No details are provided that suggest a frontotemporal pattern of dementia, although patients with Alzheimer dementia may occasionally exhibit such a pattern. Frontotemporal dementia and Alzheimer dementia are thus sometimes difficult to distinguish on clinical grounds alone. Even in the presence of a frontotemporal pattern of cognitive deficits, however, a presenilin-1 mutation is specific for early-onset familial Alzheimer dementia.

KEY POINT

- **The presenilin-1 mutation is specific for early-onset familial Alzheimer dementia.**

Bibliography

The structure of the presenilin 1 (S182) gene and identification of six novel mutations in early onset AD families. Alzheimer's Disease Collaborative Group. Nat Genet. 1995;11(2):219-222. [PMID: 7550356]

Item 41   Answer: A

Educational Objective: Manage in-hospital stroke care.

On admission to a hospital ward, a patient with stroke should be given nothing by mouth (kept NPO) until a swallowing assessment is conducted. Dysphagia screening is especially appropriate for this patient, who had difficulty swallowing when she first awoke with stroke symptoms. Dysphagia occurs in 45% of all hospitalized patients with stroke and can lead to poor outcomes, including aspiration pneumonia and death. Bedside screening of swallowing ability should thus be completed before oral intake of any medication or food; if the screening results are abnormal, a complete examination of swallowing ability is recommended. The American Heart Association/American Stroke Association recommends a water swallow test performed at the bedside by a trained observer as the best bedside predictor of aspiration. A prospective study of the water swallow test demonstrated a significantly decreased risk of aspiration pneumonia of 2.4% versus 5.4% in patients who were not screened.

Angiotensin-converting enzyme inhibitors, statins, and aspirin are appropriate treatments for secondary stroke prevention in some patients, but they should not be orally administered before ruling out the risk of aspiration.

Like most patients with stroke, this patient will undoubtedly require physical therapy and rehabilitation during her recovery. However, consulting with the department(s) responsible for such care is not an immediate concern and should not be the first step taken when the patient arrives in the hospital ward.

KEY POINT

- **In a patient with stroke, dysphagia screening should be performed before food, oral medication, or liquids are administered.**

Bibliography

Hinchey JA, Shephard T, Furie K, Smith D, Wang D, Tonn S; Stroke Practice Improvement Network Investigators. Formal dysphagia screening protocols prevent pneumonia. Stroke. 2005;36(9):1972-1976. [PMID: 16109909]

Item 42   Answer: D

Educational Objective: Treat a patient with primary progressive multiple sclerosis.

This patient has primary progressive multiple sclerosis (MS); no treatments have been shown to affect the disease course. Therefore, physiatry consultation for evaluation and treatment of his spasticity and back pain are most appropriate at this time. His gradually worsening neurologic function is very likely due to a degenerative loss of axons in the central nervous system; active inflammation, the hallmark of clinical relapses, plays a much less significant role in primary progressive MS than in the relapsing-remitting type. This patient's function and pain could likely be improved substantially with a focus on symptomatic therapies, beginning with physiatry consultation for evaluation and treatment of his spasticity, impaired mobility, and musculoskeletal pain. Symptomatic therapy in patients with multiple sclerosis can have a marked beneficial effect on patient comfort, function, and quality of life, even when further disease progression cannot be effectively stopped.

Beta interferons, glatiramer acetate, and natalizumab, the currently approved MS therapies, are all most effective in altering the immunologic mechanisms that underlie relapses and thus are only appropriate for relapsing-remitting disease.

KEY POINT

- **No therapies have convincing effects on the neurodegenerative processes that underlie progressive forms of multiple sclerosis.**

Bibliography

Miller DH, Leary SM. Primary-progressive multiple sclerosis. Lancet Neurol. 2007;6(10):903-912. [PMID: 17884680]

Item 43   Answer: C

Educational Objective: Diagnose paroxysmal hemicrania.

This patient has paroxysmal hemicrania, one of the trigeminal autonomic cephalalgias. These cephalalgias are characterized by pain referred to the first division of the trigeminal nerve and cranial autonomic symptoms, including lacrimation and rhinorrhea. They differ from one another in the duration and frequency of attacks. A paroxysmal hemicrania attack has an intermediate duration (mean, 15 minutes) and an intermediate episode frequency (mean, 11 per day).

Cluster headache, another trigeminal autonomic cephalalgia, closely resembles paroxysmal hemicrania except in the duration and frequency of attacks. Cluster headache is associated with one to eight attacks per day, and each attack has a mean duration of 60 minutes. Because this patient's headaches only last approximately 15 minutes each, cluster headache is unlikely.

Although this patient overuses over-the-counter analgesics, he does not have a background of diffuse low-grade headache associated with medication overuse headache.

The syndrome of Short-lasting Unilateral Neuralgiform headache attacks with Conjunctival injection and Tearing, or SUNCT syndrome, is another trigeminal autonomic cephalalgia with a very similar phenotype to paroxysmal hemicrania. However, SUNCT syndrome is usually associated with more than 30 attacks per day and a duration of 30 to 120 seconds for each attack. These parameters do not match this patient's symptoms.

It is important to distinguish between the trigeminal autonomic cephalalgias because they are treated differently. Verapamil, indomethacin, and lamotrigine are, respectively, the treatments of first choice for cluster headache, paroxysmal hemicrania, and SUNCT syndrome.

KEY POINT

- **The various trigeminal autonomic cephalalgias, characterized by pain referred to the first division of the trigeminal nerve and accompanying cranial autonomic symptoms, can be distinguished by the duration and frequency of each attack.**

Bibliography

Boes CJ, Swanson JW. Paroxysmal hemicrania, SUNCT, and hemicrania continua. Semin Neurol. 2006;26(2):260-270. [PMID: 16628536]

Item 44   Answer: C

Educational Objective: Treat essential tremor.

This patient should be treated with propranolol. She has a history and examination findings consistent with the presence of essential tremor. Essential tremor primarily occurs when a patient maintains a posture, such as when the hands are outstretched. Essential tremor also may be present during movement, particularly postural adjustments. Autosomal dominant transmission occurs in approximately half of patients with this condition. Essential tremor most commonly affects the upper extremities; however, the legs, head, trunk, face, and vocal cords may be involved. Up to 15% of patients with essential tremor have major disability associated with this condition. Progression of essential tremor is typically slow, with intermittent lengthy periods of stable symptoms. Features that may be predictive of a more severe essential tremor include a positive family history of tremor, longer tremor duration, voice tremor, and unilateral tremor onset. Alcoholic beverage consumption suppresses symptoms in most patients with this condition.

Treatment options for essential tremor are often limited and frequently only partially effective. It has been estimated that 50% of patients with essential tremor have no response to medical treatment. First-line medications used to treat essential tremor include propranolol, primidone, gabapentin, and topiramate. Propranolol is typically the drug of choice in most patients with essential tremor because of its effectiveness, which has been established in multiple well-designed randomized clinical trials.

Essential tremor is distinguished from Parkinson disease by its lack of parkinsonian features, such as rigidity, bradykinesia, postural instability, and resting tremor. Carbidopa-levodopa can be an appropriate choice to treat Parkinson disease but is not useful in the treatment of essential tremor. This tremor is typically postural and kinetic, with a frequency of 6 to 12 Hz.

Clonazepam is considered a second-line medication in patients with refractory essential tremor and thus should not be used as the initial pharmacotherapy, given its questionable effectiveness in two randomized clinical studies and its frequent association with drowsiness.

Ropinirole is a dopamine agonist medication used to treat Parkinson disease. Given the absence of any other signs of Parkinson disease, this medication would not be indicated in this patient.

KEY POINT

- **First-line medications used to treat essential tremor include propranolol, primidone, gabapentin, and topiramate.**

Bibliography

Lorenz D, Deuschl G. Update on pathogenesis and treatment of essential tremor. Curr Opin Neurol. 2007;20(4):447-452. [PMID: 17620881]

Item 45   Answer: A

Educational Objective: Treat epilepsy in a patient with liver disease.

Given his clinical history, MRI findings, and electroencephalographic findings, this patient is likely to have epilepsy. Treatment of epilepsy in a patient with an underlying hepatic disease requires careful selection and management of the antiepileptic medication. Levetiracetam, gabapentin, and pregabalin are the preferred choices in patients with significant liver disease because they do not undergo significant hepatic metabolism and have low protein binding. Therefore, levetiracetam is most appropriate for this patient.

For antiepileptic drugs that are hepatically metabolized or highly protein bound, alterations of hepatic enzymatic pathways and hypoalbuminemia can result in unexpected drug toxicity. For these reasons, oxcarbazepine, phenytoin, and valproic acid would be less favored options for this patient. Additionally, some antiepileptic drugs should be avoided because of their potential hepatoxicity, particularly valproic acid and felbamate.

In patients who have undergone or are expected to undergo organ transplantation, it is particularly important to consider potential drug interactions that might alter the effectiveness of their immunosuppression regimen. Cytochrome P450 enzyme inducers, including phenytoin and oxcarbazepine, and inhibitors, including valproic acid, can be problematic in this population. Highly protein-bound drugs, such as phenytoin, are also best avoided when possible. Levetiracetam, gabapentin, and pregabalin are preferred for these patients because of the lack of significant drug interactions. Because these three medications are renally excreted, the dosage may need to be lowered in the presence of renal insufficiency. Dosing should be based on clinical response rather than the serum drug level because the therapeutic range for these agents is quite broad.

KEY POINT

- **For patients who should avoid hepatically metabolized antiepileptic drugs, either because of drug interaction or underlying liver disease, levetiracetam, gabapentin, and pregabalin can be used.**

Bibliography

Lacerda G, Krummel T, Sabourdy C, Ryvlin P, Hirsch E. Optimizing therapy of seizures in patients with renal or hepatic dysfunction. Neurology. 2006;67(12 Suppl 4):S28-33. [PMID: 17190918]

Item 46   Answer: D

Educational Objective: Manage hypertension in a patient with an acute ischemic stroke.

For uncomplicated ischemic strokes in patients without concurrent acute coronary artery disease or heart failure, consensus exists that antihypertensive medications, such as intravenous labetalol or nicardipine, should be withheld if the systolic blood pressure is less than 220 mm Hg or the diastolic blood pressure is less than 120 mm Hg, unless there are other manifestations of end-organ damage. This patient's systolic and diastolic blood pressure levels are below these limits. Many such patients have spontaneous declines in blood pressure during the first 24 hours after stroke onset.

Oral nifedipine is an inappropriate treatment for this patient not only because of its antihypertensive qualities, but also because of its route of administration. Given the severity of her stroke deficits, in particular the dysarthria, she should receive nothing by mouth until a swallowing evaluation is carried out because of the high risk of aspiration.

Notably, the patient is not eligible for recombinant tissue plasminogen activator therapy because the time interval between now and her previous symptom-free state is unknown. Aspirin (160 to 325 mg/d) administered within 48 hours of stroke onset results in a small but significant reduction in the risk for recurrent stroke during the first 2 weeks after the stroke and improves outcome at 6 months. Therefore, aspirin is recommended as initial therapy for most patients with acute stroke. However, aspirin should not be administered for at least 24 hours after administration of thrombolytics.

KEY POINT

- **For uncomplicated ischemic strokes in patients without concurrent acute coronary artery disease or heart failure, antihypertensive medications should be withheld if the systolic blood pressure is less than 220 mm Hg or the diastolic blood pressure is less than 120 mm Hg, unless there are other manifestations of end-organ damage.**

Bibliography

Adams HP Jr, del Zoppo G, Alberts MJ, et al. Guidelines for the early management of adults with ischemic stroke: a guideline from the American Heart Association/American Stroke Association Stroke Council, Clinical Cardiology Council, Cardiovascular Radiology and Intervention Council, and the Atherosclerotic Peripheral Vascular Disease and Quality of Care Outcomes in Research Interdisciplinary Working Groups: the American Academy of Neurology affirms the value of this guideline as an educational tool for neurologists [errata in Stroke. 2007;38(6):e38 and Stroke. 2007;38(9):e96]. Stroke. 2007;38(5):1655-1711. [PMID: 17431204]

Item 47   Answer: B

Educational Objective: Evaluate copper deficiency myeloneuropathy.

Serum copper and zinc levels should be measured in this patient. She has a progressive myeloneuropathy syndrome and mild anemia, both caused by copper deficiency. Gastric bypass surgery is a risk factor for this clinical syndrome, which can be caused by vitamin B_{12} deficiency, copper deficiency, or both. Given that her serum vitamin B_{12} level is normal, copper deficiency is the most likely cause. Overingestion of zinc can also impair copper absorption. Therefore, both serum copper and zinc levels should be evaluated. In patients with copper deficiency, the spinal cord MRI can be normal or demonstrate signal changes involving the dorsal columns.

Antinuclear antibody testing is useful for detection of an inflammatory or a rheumatologic abnormality, but such a disorder is unlikely in the absence of any clinical symptoms or signs suggesting a systemic inflammatory disease.

An MRI of the brain may be appropriate in some patients with myelopathy to investigate for multifocal diseases, such as multiple sclerosis (MS). This patient, however, has no cerebral symptoms or signs, and the clinical syndrome exhibited and electromyography results suggest a myeloneuropathy.

Neuromyelitis optica (NMO) can be distinguished from MS by the NMO-IgG autoantibody test. Long considered an MS variant, NMO is now recognized as a distinct demyelinating disease with a predilection for the optic nerves and spinal cord. An MRI of the spinal cord typically shows extensive lesions in patients with NMO. This patient's normal results on spine MRI make the diagnosis of NMO unlikely and the NMO-IgG autoantibody test unnecessary.

KEY POINT

- **Vitamin B$_{12}$ and copper deficiencies are associated with malabsorption syndromes related to gastric bypass surgical procedures and can cause anemia and a syndrome of progressive myeloneuropathy.**

Bibliography

Juhasz-Pocsine K, Rudnicki SA, Archer RL, Harik SI. Neurologic complications of gastric bypass surgery for morbid obesity. Neurology. 2007;68(21):1843-1850. [PMID: 17515548]

Item 48   Answer: C

Educational Objective: Treat a sleep disorder in a patient with Parkinson disease.

This patient should take extended-release carbidopa-levodopa before bedtime. Patients with Parkinson disease develop both motor and nonmotor complications. One of the major nonmotor complications is fatigue, which occurs in roughly half of patients with Parkinson disease. The first step in evaluating fatigue in these patients is to ensure that their dosage of levodopa or a dopamine agonist is high enough to adequately treat their parkinsonian symptoms. Standing blood pressures should also be obtained in these patients, when symptomatic, to exclude orthostatic hypotension as the cause of fatigue. Sleep disorders are common in patients with Parkinson disease, and poor sleep is the likely cause of fatigue in this patient. The patient reports increasing stiffness and tremor at night, symptoms that reflect a "wearing-off" effect of levodopa. Taking extended-release carbidopa-levodopa immediately before bedtime should allow a more restful night's sleep and lessen his fatigue. The extended-release version of this medication has a longer duration of efficacy than the immediate-release version.

Sleep disorders are also common in patients with Parkinson disease. Its motor manifestations (such as tremor, rigidity, and dystonia), as exhibited by this patient, can disrupt sleep. Restless legs syndrome, periodic limb movement disorder, rapid eye movement (REM) sleep behavior disorder, and obstructive sleep apnea are other sleep disorders that can all occur in patients with Parkinson disease and disrupt sleep. REM sleep behavior disorder is characterized by the lack of normal muscle atonia during REM sleep and may result in patients physically acting out their dreams, such that they may yell, punch, grab, shout, or even jump out of bed. REM sleep behavior disorder may precede other clinical signs of Parkinson disease. Although this disorder and periodic limb movements of sleep may respond to clonazepam, this drug is not indicated in this patient, who lacks a history of such movements.

Donepezil is indicated in the treatment of patients with dementia and is therefore not appropriate for this patient who has no evidence of dementia.

Psychiatric disorders can develop in up to 60% of patients with Parkinson disease. After dopaminergic therapy is optimized, most clinicians use selective serotonin reuptake inhibitors, such as fluoxetine, to treat depression in patients with Parkinson disease. These drugs and serotonin-norepinephrine reuptake inhibitors are first-line agents for those requiring drug treatment. Given the absence of any other symptoms of depression, fluoxetine is not indicated in this patient. Moreover, although depression is often associated with fatigue, this patient's fatigue is more likely the result of an inadequate dosage of medication.

KEY POINT

- **Motor symptoms of Parkinson disease, such as tremor, rigidity and dystonia, can develop nocturnally and cause sleep disturbances; such symptoms may respond to extended-release carbidopa-levodopa therapy.**

Bibliography

Ferreri F, Agbokou C, Gauthier S. Recognition and management of neuropsychiatric complications in Parkinson's disease. CMAJ. 2006;175(12):1545-1552. [PMID: 17146092]

Item 49   Answer: D

Educational Objective: Diagnose medication overuse headache.

This patient has medication overuse headache. She has a 20-year history of migraine but a 10-month history of chronic daily headache on more than 15 days per month. She has been using an acute headache medication (butalbital, caffeine, and acetaminophen) more than 10 days per month and a combination of this medication and rizatriptan on some of these days. These features define a medication overuse headache.

Although the patient does have chronic migraine, her current symptoms most likely result from her overuse of acute medications and not from her long history of migraine. Medication overuse headache typically presents when or soon after a patient awakens, and the efficacy of migraine-specific therapy in patients with medication overuse headache is intermittent or poor. Furthermore, some of this patient's headaches lack the classic features of migraine, including a pounding, unilateral headache of approximately 1-day's duration associated with nausea and disability (taking to bed).

Despite the patient's depression, her headaches are not fully characteristic of chronic tension-type headache, which is typically mild to moderate in severity, lasts from 30 minutes to 7 days, and is often described as a "band-like" constriction around the head. Tension-type headaches are not associated with nausea and vomiting, photophobia, or phonophobia.

Idiopathic intracranial hypertension is a disturbance of increased intracranial pressure without evidence of intracranial disease, such as mass lesion, hydrocephalus, or venous sinus thrombosis. This disorder occurs most commonly in obese women of childbearing age but also may be associated with tetracycline therapy, oral contraceptive use, and hypervitaminosis A. Affected patients typically develop new onset of daily nonthrobbing headaches that may worsen with coughing and sneezing or in the supine position. Other clinical symptoms may include diplopia, transient episodes of monocular or binocular visual loss, and pulsatile tinnitus. Characteristic findings in patients with this condition are papilledema, an enlarged blind spot or visual field abnormalities, and possible sixth cranial nerve palsy. This patient's findings are not consistent with idiopathic intracranial hypertension.

KEY POINT

- Medication overuse headache is generally defined as a headache for more than 15 days per month and the use of acute headache medication on more than 10 days per month.

Bibliography

Dodick DW. Clinical practice. Chronic daily headache [erratum in N Engl J Med. 2006;354(8):884]. N Engl J Med. 2006;354(2):158-165. [PMID: 16407511]

Item 50   Answer: A

Educational Objective: Treat symptomatic severe extracranial carotid artery stenosis.

This patient, who has had an ischemic stroke and has symptomatic severe internal carotid artery stenosis (>70% stenosis), should undergo carotid angioplasty and stenting. Although carotid endarterectomy is still considered the gold standard of surgical therapies for patients with such stenosis, it cannot be performed in those who have stenosis that is difficult to access surgically (above the C2 level), medical conditions that greatly increase the risk of surgery,

or other specific conditions, such as radiation-induced stenosis or restenosis after carotid endarterectomy. For such patients, the less invasive combination of carotid angioplasty and stenting is preferable. The U.S. Food and Drug Administration has approved carotid angioplasty and stenting for patients with symptomatic severe carotid artery stenosis who are classified as high surgical risk or who have unfavorable anatomy that precludes a surgical approach. Other candidates for nonsurgical treatment of severe stenosis include patients with a history of radical neck surgery, spinal immobility, dissection, an ostial lesion below the clavicle, the presence of a tracheostomy stoma, and contralateral laryngeal nerve paralysis.

External carotid to internal carotid artery bypass surgery was shown not to be effective for the surgical treatment of carotid artery stenosis, but this surgery may be considered for symptomatic carotid artery occlusion (that is, 100% occlusion).

Studies of unfractionated and low-molecular-weight heparin have not shown any benefit for the vast majority of patients with acute ischemic stroke. Overall, the small reduction in recurrent ischemic stroke associated with anticoagulants is counterbalanced by an increase in hemorrhagic strokes. The American Heart Association and the American Academy of Neurology recommend that patients with ischemic stroke should not be treated with anticoagulation. Therefore, heparin administration is not appropriate for this patient.

KEY POINT

- Carotid angioplasty and stenting should be used in patients with symptomatic severe (>70%) internal carotid artery stenosis who are not eligible for surgical treatment with carotid endarterectomy.

Bibliography

Sacco RL, Adams R, Albers G, et al. Guidelines for prevention of stroke in patients with ischemic stroke or transient ischemic attack: a statement for healthcare professionals from the American Heart Association/American Stroke Association Council on Stroke: cosponsored by the Council on Cardiovascular Radiology and Intervention and the American Academy of Neurology: the American Academy of Neurology affirms the value of this guideline. Stroke. 2006;37(2):577-617. [PMID: 16432246]

Item 51   Answer: C

Educational Objective: Diagnose dementia with Lewy bodies.

This patient has symptoms of dream-enactment behavior, cognitive decline, parkinsonism, and visual hallucinations, which together are the hallmark features of dementia with Lewy bodies. Also characteristic of this type of dementia are the physical findings of orthostatic hypotension and features of mild parkinsonism, such as a reduced degree of facial expression (hypomimia), reduced arm swing, stooped posture, and mild cogwheeling.

Alzheimer dementia is a common comorbidity in patients with dementia with Lewy bodies. However, this diagnosis clearly does not in itself sufficiently account for the additional features of parkinsonism, dream enactment behavior, visual hallucinations, and dysautonomia.

Creutzfeldt-Jakob disease is a rapidly progressive dementia that is associated with early age at onset and prominent myoclonus and typically results in death within a year of onset. This patient's 10-year history of symptoms and absence of myoclonus rule out that diagnosis.

Because the hallmark features of frontotemporal dementia, such as apathy, perseveration, hoarding, disinhibition, and other personality changes, are lacking in this patient, that diagnosis is unlikely.

This patient has no cerebrovascular risk factors for or history of stroke. Additionally, her MRI has no features to suggest a vascular etiology of her symptoms. Therefore, vascular dementia is very unlikely.

KEY POINT

- **Dementia with Lewy bodies is characterized by dream-enactment behavior, cognitive decline, parkinsonism, and visual hallucinations.**

Bibliography

Weisman D, McKeith I. Dementia with Lewy bodies. Semin Neurol. 2007;27(1):42-47. [PMID: 17226740]

Item 52   Answer: C

Educational Objective: Evaluate a new-onset seizure with electroencephalography and MRI.

For patients whose clinical history includes new onset of a seizure for which no obvious provocative cause is identified, the standard evaluation consists of electroencephalography and MRI of the brain. These tests will help not only to confirm the diagnosis, but also to predict the risk of future recurrence and rule out any underlying condition (such as a brain tumor) that might require treatment in itself. MRI has been shown to be clearly superior to CT in detecting potentially epileptogenic lesions. For example, in one retrospective case series of 117 patients with refractory epilepsy, MRI detected 95% of histologically identifiable lesions, whereas CT only detected 32%.

CT is the imaging modality of choice for new-onset seizures only when there is a suspicion of an acute cerebral hemorrhage or when a contraindication to MRI is present. Neither condition pertains to this patient.

For adults with new-onset seizures, lumbar puncture is generally only indicated when the patient's history or physical examination findings lead to a significant clinical suspicion of an underlying infection or inflammatory cause. Infection of the central nervous system is indicated by the presence of fever or altered mental status. Patients with a subarachnoid hemorrhage, for whom lumbar puncture is sometimes appropriate, may also have seizures, but such a hemorrhage is associated with severe headache, altered mental status, syncope, and neurologic deficits and usually will be identified on a CT scan or MRI. Given this patient's uneventful prior history and normal results on physical examination, lumbar puncture is inappropriate.

Positron emission tomography is sometimes used as part of a surgical evaluation for medically refractory epilepsy. It does not presently have any role in the evaluation of new-onset seizures.

KEY POINT

- **MRI is superior to CT for detection of epileptogenic lesions.**

Bibliography

So EL. Role of neuroimaging in the management of seizure disorders. Mayo Clin Proc. 2002;77(11):1251-1264. [PMID: 12440562]

Item 53   Answer: D

Educational Objective: Interpret nonspecific white matter abnormalities incidentally discovered on an MRI of the brain.

This patient requires no further testing. He has MRI evidence of white matter lesions but no history or examination findings that suggest a diagnosis of multiple sclerosis (MS). Misinterpretation of white matter abnormalities incidentally discovered on the MRIs of patients with nonspecific symptoms is a leading cause of MS misdiagnosis. The lesions noted on this patient's MRI are not typical of those seen in MS; given his age and long-standing and incompletely controlled hypertension, they are most likely related to small-vessel cerebrovascular disease. MS lesions are typically larger, ovoid, and periventricular in location, as in the MRI shown.

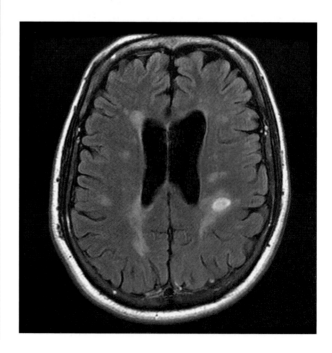

They sometimes enhance with gadolinium. The patient can be reassured that MS is extremely unlikely and counseled that he needs to improve his blood pressure control and be aware of other modifiable vascular risk factors.

Lumbar puncture and visual evoked potential studies might be useful if MS were a serious clinical consideration but are unnecessary for this patient. There is currently no indication to repeat the MRI in 3 months for diagnostic purposes; additionally, findings will not influence management of his hypertension or other modifiable risk factors.

KEY POINT

- **Misinterpretation of nonspecific white matter lesions discovered on brain MRIs of patients without specific symptoms is a leading cause of the misdiagnosis of multiple sclerosis.**

Bibliography

Frohman EM, Goodin DS, Calabresi PA, et al. The utility of MRI in suspected MS: report of the Therapeutics and Technology Assessment Subcommittee of the American Academy of Neurology. Neurology. 2003;61(5):602-611. [PMID: 12963748]

Item 54   Answer: A

Educational Objective: Diagnose amyotrophic lateral sclerosis.

Amyotrophic lateral sclerosis (ALS) is the most likely diagnosis in this patient. Patients with ALS typically have progressive, asymmetric, painless extremity or bulbar weakness on presentation. The absence of sensory loss and the lack of bowel or bladder impairment are also suggestive of ALS. The combination of upper motoneuron findings (hyperreflexia, extensor plantar response) and lower motoneuron signs (atrophy, fasciculations) seen on neurologic examination strongly suggests ALS, which is a fatal, neurodegenerative motoneuron disease that affects both the upper and lower motoneurons. The term motoneuron disease is used to describe the heterogeneous group of disorders affecting the upper motoneuron, the lower motoneuron, or both; for example, progressive muscular atrophy is a motoneuron disease that affects the lower motoneuron, and primary lateral sclerosis is a motoneuron disease that affects the upper motoneuron. It is unclear whether different motoneuron disorders are distinct disorders or reflect different manifestations of a single disease. What is established, however, is that ALS has the worst prognosis of them all, with a mean survival of 3 to 5 years.

Cervical myelopathy should be considered in patients presenting with arm and leg weakness but is an unlikely cause of this patient's symptoms. The presence of tongue atrophy and fasciculations, absence of sensory loss, and lack of bowel or bladder impairment would not be typical of a cervical myelopathy. Nonetheless, MRI studies are indicated in patients with suspected ALS to exclude myelopathy.

Chronic inflammatory demyelinating polyradiculoneuropathy is a treatable neurologic condition that causes weakness, sensory loss, and depressed deep tendon reflexes. The absence of sensory loss and the hyperreflexia seen in this patient are not typical of this disorder. Chronic inflammatory demyelinating polyradiculoneuropathy is an immune-mediated, inflammatory disorder that causes demyelination of peripheral nerves and nerve roots. An elevated cerebrospinal fluid protein level, characteristic findings on an electromyogram showing demyelination and conduction block, or a sural nerve biopsy can establish the diagnosis. Chronic inflammatory demyelinating polyradiculoneuropathy is a neurologic disorder that is expected to respond to immune-modulating therapy. Corticosteroids, intravenous immune globulin, plasma exchange, mycophenolate mofetil, and azathioprine have been the primary therapies used in its treatment.

Primary lateral sclerosis is not the diagnosis in this patient, given the lower motoneuron findings of atrophy and fasciculations on examination. A motoneuron disorder affecting the upper motoneuron, primary lateral sclerosis causes slowly progressive weakness and spasticity. In affected patients, spasticity predominates over weakness and is typically symmetric and lower limb predominant. Later in the disease course, most patients develop pseudobulbar features, with dysarthria and emotional lability. Primary lateral sclerosis is a clinical diagnosis that can be established only by excluding other diseases. Spinal cord MRIs are particularly useful in this regard. Primary lateral sclerosis is a slowly progressive neurodegenerative disorder with a much better prognosis than ALS; long-term survival is expected. There are no medications approved by the U.S. Food and Drug Administration for the treatment of primary lateral sclerosis.

KEY POINT

- **Both upper and lower motoneuron findings are typically present in amyotrophic lateral sclerosis, which helps distinguish this disorder from its mimickers, such as multifocal motor neuropathy, chronic inflammatory demyelinating polyradiculoneuropathy, and primary lateral sclerosis.**

Bibliography

Tartaglia MC, Rowe A, Findlater K, Orange JB, Grace G, Strong MJ. Differentiation between primary lateral sclerosis and amyotrophic lateral sclerosis: examination of symptoms and signs at disease onset and during follow-up. Arch Neurol. 2007;64(2):232-236. [PMID: 17296839]

Item 55   Answer: A

Educational Objective: Treat paroxysmal hemicrania.

This patient should receive indomethacin. He most likely has paroxysmal hemicrania, one of the trigeminal autonomic cephalalgias, which are characterized by pain referred to the first division of the trigeminal nerve and by accompanying cranial autonomic symptoms, including lacrimation and rhinorrhea. An attack of paroxysmal hemicrania has an intermediate duration (mean, 15 minutes) and an intermediate episodic frequency (mean, 11 per day). Treatment with indomethacin can immediately and completely resolve the headache. Usually, the response occurs within the first 48 hours after treatment is initiated. Indomethacin is not effective for treating any of the other trigeminal autonomic cephalalgias. Therefore, a positive response to the drug helps distinguish between paroxysmal hemicrania and the other trigeminal autonomic cephalalgias.

Lamotrigine is the most effective drug for the treatment of the syndrome of Short-lasting Unilateral Neuralgiform headache attacks with Conjunctival injection and Tearing (SUNCT syndrome), another trigeminal autonomic cephalalgia. There is no evidence supporting its usefulness in the treatment of paroxysmal hemicrania.

Prednisone and verapamil are commonly used treatments for cluster headache, yet another trigeminal autonomic cephalalgia. As with lamotrigine, there is no evidence supporting their usefulness in the treatment of paroxysmal hemicrania.

KEY POINT

- **Indomethacin is the treatment of choice for paroxysmal hemicrania.**

Bibliography

Boes CJ, Swanson JW. Paroxysmal hemicrania, SUNCT, and hemicrania continua. Semin Neurol. 2006;26(2):260-270. [PMID: 16628536]

Item 56   Answer: C

Educational Objective: Evaluate a suspected subdural hematoma in a patient with chronic dementia.

This patient should undergo CT of the head. His chronic course seems most compatible with a degeneratively based etiology, such as dementia with Lewy bodies. Although impaired cognition and gait are expected in this setting, the disease course tends to be slow and steady. The subacute deterioration affecting both cognitive and motor skills that this patient has exhibited most likely resulted from his fall. Although there was no witnessed direct head trauma, minor, even indirect head trauma is possible because he takes warfarin and thus is at increased risk for bleeding. The manner in which the patient has declined is itself nonspecific, and common medical causes of such decline, such as urinary tract infection, pneumonia, and some common metabolic disturbances, are unlikely. The possibility of greatest concern is some form of intracranial disturbance, specifically, a subdural hematoma. A CT scan of the head is thus the most reasonable test to perform because other tests have not revealed a more obvious cause for the patient's decline.

The patient's course does not suggest a seizure, and so electroencephalography (EEG) is not appropriate as the next diagnostic test. If a subdural hematoma is diagnosed, the patient and family should be counseled that seizures may complicate his future clinical course and that EEG is now reasonable to evaluate any epileptiform symptoms that may arise.

In the absence of concern about meningitis, cerebrospinal fluid analysis should not be considered until it is known whether there is increased intracranial pressure related to a subdural hematoma or other trauma-induced intracranial hemorrhage. There is an increased risk of brainstem herniation with lumbar puncture and of cardioembolic cerebral infarction from the reversal of anticoagulation needed before performing a lumbar puncture.

Echocardiography would be reasonable if brain imaging disclosed a recent cerebral infarction as the cause of the decline. In the absence of such evidence, this test is inappropriate.

KEY POINT

- **In elderly patients with chronic dementia who take warfarin, minor, even indirect head trauma can lead to bleeding and cause abrupt worsening of confusion.**

Bibliography

Manjunath BR. Computed tomography or not? A case report of an acute subdural hematoma without any external head injury in an elderly patient of advanced dementia. J Am Geriatr Soc. 2008; 56(2):378-379. [PMID: 18251834]

Item 57   Answer: A

Educational Objective: Treat malignant brain edema in a patient with ischemic stroke.

This patient has malignant brain edema as a result of her ischemic stroke and should be treated with decompressive hemicraniectomy. Young patients with major infarctions affecting the cerebral hemisphere or cerebellum have a heightened risk of brain edema and increased intracranial pressure. Reducing any edema and close monitoring for signs of neurologic worsening, particularly during the first 3 to 5 days after the stroke when the edema maximizes, are recommended. Meta-analyses of randomized, controlled trials have shown that decompressive hemicraniectomy for malignant stroke reduces morbidity and mortality.

Intra-arterial thrombolysis is an option for the treatment of selected patients who have had a major stroke within the past 6 hours due to occlusion of a major intracranial artery. Although this patient's stroke was caused by an occluded right middle cerebral artery, she is long past the time window for this acute stroke therapy. Delay is associated with an increased risk of hemorrhagic conversion and reduced symptomatic benefit.

Long-term anticoagulation may play a role in the prevention of recurrent ischemic stroke in a patient with anti–phospholipid antibody syndrome. However, acute intravenous administration of heparin in this patient who has a large acute cerebral infarction is more likely to accelerate the possibility of hemorrhagic conversion of the infarction and thus to worsen her current clinical state.

The endovascular mechanical clot-retrieval device has been used to extract thrombi from occluded intracranial arteries. However, guidelines recommend that such a device must be used within 8 hours of a stroke. This patient is now beyond that 8-hour time window.

KEY POINT

- Decompressive surgery can be a life-saving intervention in a patient who develops malignant brain edema after a hemispheric stroke.

Bibliography

Adams HP Jr, del Zoppo G, Alberts MJ, et al. Guidelines for the early management of adults with ischemic stroke: a guideline from the American Heart Association/American Stroke Association Stroke Council, Clinical Cardiology Council, Cardiovascular Radiology and Intervention Council, and the Atherosclerotic Peripheral Vascular Disease and Quality of Care Outcomes in Research Interdisciplinary Working Groups: the American Academy of Neurology affirms the value of this guideline as an educational tool for neurologists [errata in Stroke. 2007;38(6):e38 and Stroke. 2007;38(9):e96]. Stroke. 2007;38(5):1655-1711. [PMID: 17431204]

Item 58   Answer: D

Educational Objective: Diagnose progressive supranuclear palsy.

This patient's history and examination findings are most consistent with a diagnosis of progressive supranuclear palsy. A sporadic, neurodegenerative disorder, progressive supranuclear palsy typically manifests as gait impairment and falls, slurred speech, and impaired swallowing. The presence of reduced facial expression, axial rigidity, and impairment of vertical eye movements on examination further suggests the diagnosis.

Amyotrophic lateral sclerosis is not associated with parkinsonian signs such as rigidity and postural instability. Patients with bulbar-onset amyotrophic lateral sclerosis present with slurred speech (dysarthria) and swallowing dysfunction, later followed by the development of diffuse extremity weakness, atrophy, and fasciculations.

Corticobasal degeneration is also a rare, sporadic, neurodegenerative disorder that can manifest as gait impairment, slurred speech, dystonia, or myoclonus. Parkinsonian signs are evident on examination and are characteristically asymmetric. Alien limb phenomena can occur, whereby an extremity will move independently of voluntary, conscious control.

The lack of a resting tremor, the symmetric bradykinesia and rigidity, and the early falls distinguish this patient's condition from Parkinson disease. Patients with progressive supranuclear palsy do not respond favorably to levodopa therapy, a mainstay of Parkinson disease management.

KEY POINT

- Early falls, symmetric bradykinesia and rigidity, and lack of a resting tremor or levodopa responsiveness characterize progressive supranuclear palsy and help distinguish it from Parkinson disease.

Bibliography

Lubarsky M, Juncos JL. Progressive supranuclear palsy: a current review. Neurologist. 2008;14(2):79-88. [PMID: 18332837]

Item 59   Answer: B

Educational Objective: Manage multiple brain metastases.

The recommended treatment for this patient who has multiple cerebral metastases is palliative whole-brain radiation therapy and corticosteroid administration. Brain metastases are a common complication of systemic cancer and are associated with a poor prognosis. Treatment decisions are based on the location and number of cerebral lesions, the severity of neurologic symptoms, and the extent and prognosis of the systemic cancer. The main goal of therapy is to improve neurologic deficits by reducing the volume of the space-occupying metastases and the surrounding edema and to prevent symptom progression. Treatment response is directly related to the time from diagnosis to radiation therapy.

In the presence of a known primary tumor with a likelihood of metastasizing to the central nervous system, such as lung cancer, brain biopsy to confirm the metastatic nature of the lesions is not needed.

Stereotactic radiosurgery and surgical resection are generally restricted to patients with a single metastatic lesion and with reasonably controlled systemic disease. Neurosurgery will occasionally be considered for palliation in patients with multiple metastases, but only if there is a single lesion causing immediately life-threatening or severely disabling symptoms. In this patient, the presenting symptoms of seizure and mild weakness would not justify such aggressive intervention; these symptoms would be better treated with whole-brain radiation therapy and corticosteroids.

KEY POINT

- Patients with multiple cerebral metastases and/or advanced systemic disease are not candidates for neurosurgical resection and should instead receive palliative treatment.

Bibliography

Tsao MN, Lloyd N, Wong R, Chow E, Rakovitch E, Laperriere N. Whole brain radiotherapy for treatment of multiple brain metastases. Cochrane Database Syst Rev. 2006;3:CD003869 [PMID: 16856022]

Item 60   Answer: C

Educational Objective: Treat an acute relapse of multiple sclerosis.

Evidence from placebo-controlled trials involving multiple sclerosis (MS) and optic neuritis supports the intravenous use of methylprednisolone to speed recovery from acute MS relapses. The long-term outcome of an individual MS attack, however, is not affected by the therapy chosen. Therefore, in light of the potential adverse effects of such drugs, intravenous administration of corticosteroids should be offered only for relapses that result in substantial discomfort or reduced function. This patient's 3-day history of worsening weakness and numbness of the right arm and leg qualifies him for corticosteroid therapy.

It is necessary to rule out infection as a cause of neurologic worsening in patients with MS because infections can cause a "pseudoexacerbation"; this patient, however, is asymptomatic except for his neurologic symptoms and is afebrile. Patients with moderate or severe MS-related disability are more susceptible to the effects of mild infections, especially urinary tract infections, and investigation for such infections is warranted, even in the absence of systemic symptoms. However, empiric antibiotic therapy to treat a possible occult infection is not warranted in the absence of evidence or a high clinical suspicion of infection.

Intravenously administered immune globulin is an effective treatment for a number of immune system–mediated diseases, but evidence of its efficacy for MS is lacking. Clinical trials have found no benefit from immune globulin, either as add-on treatment to methylprednisolone for acute MS attacks or as monotherapy for acute optic neuritis.

Plasma exchange therapy may be beneficial in the treatment of fulminant attacks of multiple sclerosis that are unresponsive to corticosteroids. Such therapy appears to be particularly useful in patients with severe attacks of neuromyelitis optica that do not improve with corticosteroids. However, plasmapheresis is not indicated for this patient at this time before a trial of methylprednisolone.

Oral administration of prednisone was not as effective as intravenous administration of methylprednisolone in the Optic Neuritis Treatment Trial and so should not be the first choice to treat acute MS relapses.

KEY POINT

- **Multiple sclerosis relapses may resolve more rapidly with intravenous methylprednisolone therapy.**

Bibliography

Noseworthy JH, Lucchinetti CF, Rodriguez M, Weinshenker BG. Multiple sclerosis. N Engl J Med. 2000;343(13):938-952. [PMID: 11006371]

Item 61   Answer: C

Educational Objective: Diagnose juvenile myoclonic epilepsy.

This patient most likely has juvenile myoclonic epilepsy. Recognizing the specific epilepsy syndrome affecting a patient is crucial in selecting the appropriate therapy, making the correct prognosis, and, in some cases, providing genetic counseling. A history of myoclonic (rapid, unprovoked jerks) and generalized tonic-clonic seizures on awakening with onset in adolescence strongly suggests a diagnosis of juvenile myoclonic epilepsy. One of the most commonly encountered forms of epilepsy, juvenile myoclonic epilepsy may affect 5% to 10% of all patients with epilepsy. Seizures are often provoked by sleep deprivation, alcohol, or exposure to flickering lights.

Alcohol withdrawal seizures develop in chronic users of alcohol and are generally seen in combination with other signs and symptoms of alcohol withdrawal, such as delirium, tremor, tachycardia, and diaphoresis. This patient's history does not suggest alcohol withdrawal as the likely cause of his recurrent seizures.

Benign rolandic epilepsy is a syndrome seen in younger children and adolescents who have seizures, usually during sleep, that begin with focal sensory and/or motor symptoms involving the face, mouth, and throat that can then secondarily generalize. This benign syndrome is not associated with myoclonic seizures and so is not the diagnosis in this patient.

Temporal lobe epilepsy is the most common of the localization-related epilepsies, a type of epilepsy resulting from a focal brain abnormality. Temporal lobe epilepsy can often be further categorized as the result of a focal abnormality of the mesial temporal lobe. The most common seizure classification associated with mesial temporal lobe epilepsy is complex partial seizure. Characteristically, patients with complex partial seizures are awake but exhibit altered awareness, such as unresponsiveness or staring. Patients also exhibit automatisms—such as lip smacking, swallowing, picking, or manipulating objects—or automatic (purposeless, repetitive) behaviors. Patients often describe a preceding aura and, most commonly, autonomic symptoms. About one third of complex partial seizures will generalize as tonic-clonic seizures. This patient's myoclonic jerking is not compatible with temporal lobe epilepsy.

KEY POINT

- **Juvenile myoclonic epilepsy is characterized by myoclonic and generalized tonic-clonic seizures on awakening that are often provoked by sleep deprivation or alcohol.**

Bibliography

Renganathan R, Delanty N. Juvenile myoclonic epilepsy: under-appreciated and under-diagnosed. Postgrad Med J. 2003;79(928):78-80. [PMID: 12612320]

Item 62   Answer: A

Educational Objective: Manage an unruptured intracranial aneurysm.

This patient should have an annual magnetic resonance angiogram (MRA) or CT angiogram to monitor aneurysmal growth. For patients without a prior subarachnoid hemorrhage, the lowest-risk aneurysms are those in the anterior circulation and less than 7 mm in diameter. The annual risk of rupture for an aneurysm of the size of this patient's is 0.05% annually. The risk of neurologic disability associated with intervention exceeds the potential benefit. After 3 successive years of annual monitoring, an MRA or CT angiogram obtained once every 3 years is sufficient.

The second report from the International Study of Unruptured Intracranial Aneurysms was a prospective observational study of patients who either underwent open or endovascular repair of asymptomatic intracranial aneurysms. Open surgery was associated with surgery-related death or poor neurologic outcome of nearly 13% at 1 year, compared with approximately 10% for endovascular repair. Complication rates increased with increasing age (30% at age 70 years or older), aneurysm size, and location of the aneurysm in the posterior circulation. Because the complication rate of intervention is likely to exceed the complication rate of observation alone, neither clipping nor coiling is indicated.

Nimodipine is administered routinely in patients with subarachnoid hemorrhage in order to prevent vasospasm. This drug is not appropriate for a patient with an unruptured intracranial aneurysm. It is generally recommended that patients should refrain from smoking, heavy alcohol consumption, amphetamines, cocaine, and excessive straining and the Valsalva maneuver when taking this drug.

> **KEY POINT**
> - **Annual magnetic resonance or CT angiography to monitor aneurysmal growth is appropriate as management of a low-risk unruptured intracranial aneurysm.**

Bibliography

Wiebers DO, Whisnant JP, Huston J III, et al; International Study of Unruptured Intracranial Aneurysms Investigators. Unruptured intracranial aneurysms: natural history, clinical outcome, and risks of surgical and endovascular treatment. Lancet. 2003;362(9378):103-110. [PMID: 12867109]

Item 63   Answer: D

Educational Objective: Diagnose frontotemporal lobar degeneration on the basis of progressive nonfluent aphasia.

This patient has progressive nonfluent aphasia that is most likely due to frontotemporal lobar degeneration. Progressive nonfluent aphasia, semantic dementia, and frontotemporal dementia comprise the three main syndromes of frontotemporal lobar degeneration. Symptom onset is insidious and progression is gradual over the course of several years. Her early decline in social interpersonal conduct is typical of this disorder, as is her aspontaneity and economy of speech. Approximately 10% of patients with frontotemporal lobar degeneration, especially frontotemporal dementia, have concurrent motoneuron disease.

The most prominent early symptom of Alzheimer dementia is memory impairment. Alzheimer dementia can also produce aphasia, although usually not a purely nonfluent form and not typically as an initial symptom. Other diagnoses should also be considered when the prominent early finding is a symptom other than recent memory impairment, such as impaired social behavior, gait difficulty, or hallucinations and delusions. Clinical suspicion for additional diagnoses also should be raised when the disease course is not insidious and chronically progressive. Finally, Alzheimer dementia typically begins at a later age than 64 years, an age that is more typical of frontotemporal lobar degeneration.

Creutzfeldt-Jakob disease is a rapidly progressive dementia producing death, typically within a year of onset. Although the specific symptoms of this disorder are highly variable, this patient's gradual disease course does not resemble the more rapid one of Creutzfeldt-Jakob disease.

This patient does not have two of the core clinical features (parkinsonism, fluctuations in cognition or level of alertness, and visual hallucinations) required for a diagnosis of dementia with Lewy bodies, and she is considerably younger than most patients with this disorder. As with Alzheimer dementia, aphasia can occur within the context of this dementia.

Progressive nonfluent aphasia is often mistaken for a stroke because of the obvious speech impairment produced. With stroke, however, the aphasia would be of sudden onset, and the patient would likely have MRI evidence of cerebral infarction, both of which are lacking in this instance. Additionally, the patient has exhibited no other signs or symptoms of stroke and has no history of vascular disease. Therefore, vascular dementia is unlikely.

> **KEY POINT**
> - **In frontotemporal lobar degeneration, which encompasses the syndromes of progressive nonfluent aphasia, semantic dementia, and frontotemporal dementia, symptom onset is insidious and progression gradual over the course of several years.**

Bibliography

Ogar JM, Dronkers NF, Brambati SM, Miller BL, Gorno-Tempini ML. Progressive nonfluent aphasia and its characteristic motor speech deficits. Alzheimer Dis Assoc Disord. 2007;21(4):S23-30. [PMID: 18090419]

Item 64   Answer: D

Educational Objective: Determine the risk for future conversion to multiple sclerosis of clinically isolated syndromes.

The results of a brain MRI in a patient with new-onset neurologic symptoms suggestive of demyelination provide the most powerful prognostic information about his or her risk of developing multiple sclerosis (MS). Symptomatic patients with as few as one MRI brain lesion compatible with demyelination on clinical presentation have a risk of up to 90% that they will experience a second clinical event over the next 10 to 15 years, thereby confirming MS. Conversely, if the brain MRI reveals no white matter lesions, their risk over the same time period is slightly less than 20%. The brain MRI typical of MS reveals ovoid lesions in the periventricular white matter that sometimes enhance with gadolinium.

This patient has also experienced left optic neuritis. When this occurs as a first-ever event of symptomatic central nervous system inflammatory demyelination, it is referred to as a clinically isolated syndrome, a term that implies some risk of developing MS in the future. Other such clinically isolated syndromes include brain stem or spinal cord events, such as myelitis.

Long-term follow-up studies of all patients presenting with optic neuritis show that only approximately 50% of them later develop MS. This risk, however, is increased over that of the general population. Coupled with the implications of the brain MRI in this patient, the finding of optic neuritis confirms his very high risk.

KEY POINT

- **If the brain MRI of a patient with a first-ever event of symptomatic central nervous system inflammatory demyelination shows lesions consistent with demyelination, the risk of developing multiple sclerosis approaches 90% over the next 10 to 15 years.**

Bibliography

Brex PA, Ciccarelli O, O'Riordan JI, Sailer M, Thompson AJ, Miller DH. A longitudinal study of abnormalities on MRI and disability from multiple sclerosis. N Engl J Med. 2002;346(3):158-164. [PMID: 11796849]

Item 65   Answer: C

Educational Objective: Manage status epilepticus.

This patient should receive lorazepam. He most likely has status epilepticus, a neurologic emergency defined as seizures that persist or recur without interval recovery for a period of 30 minutes or longer. Approximately 50% of patients with status epilepticus have an established diagnosis of epilepsy, and among these patients, nonadherence to medication is a common precipitating event. Convulsive status epilepticus has a mortality rate of approximately 20%. When generalized convulsive status epilepticus continues, clinical signs of ongoing electrical seizure activity will often become increasingly subtle and may only involve subtle twitching of the eyes, face, or limbs, as seen in this patient. However minimal, this continuing electrical seizure activity must be corrected to avoid potential morbidity and mortality. Persistent seizure activity results in acute systemic complications, including fever, hemodynamic instability, acidosis, rhabdomyolysis, and pulmonary edema, all of which must be carefully managed. Airway, breathing, and circulatory status should be assessed at presentation and monitored continuously. Early diagnosis and therapeutic intervention are critical because an increase in the duration of status epilepticus is directly correlated with increased mortality. Treatment should not be delayed for diagnostic testing. Intravenous administration of a benzodiazepine (lorazepam or diazepam) is accepted as first-line therapy and may be administered by emergency medical personnel in the field.

A CT of the head may ultimately be necessary to evaluate for bleeding of the cavernous malformation. Although emergent head imaging is often useful in the absence of a known underlying cause of status epilepticus, it should never delay treatment with a benzodiazepine.

Because this patient's symptoms are quite consistent with status epilepticus, confirming the diagnosis with an electroencephalogram (EEG) and thus delaying treatment is unnecessary. In patients who are unresponsive or somnolent after status epilepticus, continuous EEG monitoring is strongly advocated to distinguish between ongoing nonconvulsive status and postictal states.

Intravenous administration of phenytoin or phenobarbital is used as second-line therapy for status epilepticus not responsive to benzodiazepines. If administration of these agents is planned, it should not be delayed while awaiting results of serum drug levels.

KEY POINT

- **Benzodiazepines are the first-line treatment for status epilepticus.**

Bibliography

Manno EM. New management strategies in the treatment of status epilepticus. Mayo Clin Proc. 2003;78(4):508-518. [PMID: 12683704]

Item 66   Answer: B

Educational Objective: Manage a perioperative stroke.

This patient should undergo intra-arterial clot extraction. His presentation is not merely that of someone just emerging from anesthesia or still exhibiting the effects of narcotic analgesia. Rather, the patient is behaving clinically as if he sustained an intraoperative or postoperative stroke. A CT scan of the head obtained so soon after symptom onset will not yet reveal ischemic changes, although it will exclude hemorrhage as a cause of his neurologic symptoms. His

CT scan strongly supports the presence of an occluded left middle cerebral artery. The ideal acute treatment for a perioperative ischemic stroke in this patient, whose recent surgery makes him ineligible for recombinant tissue plasminogen activator (rtPA), is consultation with an endovascular neurosurgeon for intra-arterial clot extraction with a device approved by the U.S. Food and Drug Administration. As with the intra-arterial administration of thrombolytics, the use of these devices is limited to comprehensive stroke centers that have the expertise to perform these procedures safely. Although the clot extraction device is recognized by American Heart Association/American Stroke Association guidelines as a reasonable intervention for extraction of intra-arterial thrombi in carefully selected patients for the management of acute stroke, the expert panel also recognizes that the utility of the device in improving outcomes after stroke is unclear.

Although the narcotic analgesia he received during surgery may be contributing to this patient's small pupils, it is not the probable explanation for his hemiparesis. Therefore, administration of naloxone or any other opioid antagonist is not appropriate management.

The patient, who was last known to be neurologically intact 2 hours ago at the start of the operation, awoke from anesthesia with the neurologic deficit. Although he is within the traditional 3-hour time window for intravenous administration of recombinant tissue plasminogen activator, this therapy is contraindicated within 14 days of major surgery.

A diffusion-weighted MRI of the brain would be more sensitive than the CT scan was in detecting acute ischemia but is unnecessary in this patient. The diagnosis of acute ischemic stroke can satisfactorily be established clinically, and the MRI does not add anything of value to the patient's management.

KEY POINT

- **Recombinant tissue plasminogen activator as treatment of acute stroke is contraindicated in patients who have had major surgery in the past 14 days.**

Bibliography

Adams HP Jr, del Zoppo G, Alberts MJ, et al. Guidelines for the early management of adults with ischemic stroke: a guideline from the American Heart Association/American Stroke Association Stroke Council, Clinical Cardiology Council, Cardiovascular Radiology and Intervention Council, and the Atherosclerotic Peripheral Vascular Disease and Quality of Care Outcomes in Research Interdisciplinary Working Groups: the American Academy of Neurology affirms the value of this guideline as an educational tool for neurologists [errata in Stroke. 2007;38(6):e138 and Stroke. 2007;38(9):e96]. Stroke. 2007;38(5):1655-1711. [PMID: 17431204]

Item 67   Answer: D

Educational Objective: Manage primary central nervous system lymphoma.

This patient should undergo a stereotactic brain biopsy. He most likely has a primary central nervous system (CNS) lymphoma, given the distinctive radiographic signs. In immunocompetent patients, a primary CNS lymphoma is visualized most often as a solitary round mass with minimal surrounding edema that is situated in the deep white matter. Tumors are isointense to hypointense on T2-weighted MRI images and enhance homogeneously after contrast administration. Parenchymal brain metastases are rare in patients with systemic lymphoma. More commonly, parenchymal brain involvement occurs as an isolated site of disease (primary CNS lymphoma). Among patients presenting with a primary CNS lymphoma, occult systemic disease is present in less than 5%. The symptoms of CNS lymphoma are dependent on the site of tumor involvement. Primary CNS lymphoma is usually a B-cell non-Hodgkin lymphoma and is rare, accounting for less than 5% of intracranial tumors. It presents most commonly in the sixth and seventh decades of life in immunocompetent patients and in the fourth decade in HIV-infected patients.

Despite its characteristic appearance, a primary CNS lymphoma cannot be accurately diagnosed by clinical presentation or neuroimaging studies. Because other conditions, both malignant and nonmalignant, can mimic primary CNS lymphoma, a tissue diagnosis is required before treatment can be appropriately initiated. Diagnostic modalities include stereotactic brain biopsy or cerebrospinal fluid analysis to detect a clonal B-cell population.

Standard treatment of primary CNS lymphoma in immunocompetent patients consists of chemotherapy (usually high-dose methotrexate) followed by whole-brain radiation therapy if the patient's tumor is refractory to chemotherapeutic agents. However, neither of these treatments is appropriate before a biopsy establishes a tissue diagnosis.

When lymphoma is suspected but not confirmed, corticosteroids should be avoided unless mandated by high risk of immediate morbidity and mortality from mass effect because they may cause the lesion to dramatically shrink or even disappear. This corticosteroid response is temporary and can complicate diagnosis by reducing the yield of diagnostic biopsy and delay therapy.

The median survival of patients with CNS lymphoma is 3 years with combination chemotherapy and radiation therapy. Therefore, hospice referral is not indicated, particularly before the establishment of a tissue diagnosis.

KEY POINT

- **Primary central nervous system lymphoma is diagnosed by detection of a clonal B-cell population on cerebrospinal fluid analysis or by brain biopsy.**

Bibliography

Haldorsen IS, Krossnes BK, Aarseth JH, et al. Increasing incidence and continued dismal outcome of primary central nervous system lymphoma in Norway 1989-2003: time trends in a 15-year national survey. Cancer. 2007;110(8):1803-1814. [PMID: 17721992]

Item 68 Answer: A

Educational Objective: Treat idiopathic intracranial hypertension.

This patient should be treated with acetazolamide. She has idiopathic intracranial hypertension, a disease that primarily affects young obese women. She has a progressive daily headache associated with pulsatile tinnitus and transient visual obscurations, the most common symptoms of this disease. She also has papilledema and impaired lateral gaze to the left on presentation. These signs and symptoms suggest the possibility of a left sixth cranial nerve palsy. Abducens nerve palsies are sometimes seen in patients with idiopathic intracranial hypertension because of compression of the sixth cranial nerve as a result of elevated intracranial pressure. Definitive diagnosis is established by an elevated cerebrospinal fluid (CSF) pressure and normal results on CSF analysis. Because there is not yet evidence of visual field or visual acuity impairment, urgent surgical intervention is not necessary and medical therapy is appropriate. However, all patients with suspected idiopathic intracranial hypertension must undergo a thorough ophthalmologic evaluation, including formal visual perimetry testing, to detect enlargement of the blind spots or visual field defects that are not detected by confrontation visual field testing at the bedside.

Acetazolamide is the medical option of first choice for the treatment of idiopathic intracranial hypertension. Although its exact mechanism of action is unclear, acetazolamide is a carbonic anhydrase inhibitor that decreases the production of CSF and relieves intracranial hypertension.

No evidence suggests that nortriptyline, propranolol, and subcutaneously administered sumatriptan are appropriate treatments of idiopathic intracranial hypertension. Nortriptyline also has the potential adverse effect of weight gain, which could worsen the clinical course in this patient.

Valproic acid is approved by the U.S. Food and Drug Administration for the preventive treatment of migraine. Although this patient has a history of migraine and her current headache is associated with features often seen during acute migraine attacks (nausea, emesis, severe headache, throbbing quality), the headache does not otherwise resemble migraine because it is persistent, progressive, unresponsive to triptan medications, and associated with some abnormal findings on examination. Valproic acid is therefore not appropriate in this circumstance, especially with its potential for weight gain as an adverse effect.

KEY POINT

- Acetazolamide is the option of first choice for the medical treatment of idiopathic intracranial hypertension.

Bibliography
Friedman DI. Idiopathic intracranial hypertension. Curr Pain Headache Rep. 2007;11(1):62-68. [PMID: 17214924]

Item 69 Answer: C

Educational Objective: Diagnose potential adverse effects of dopamine agonist medications.

This patient has developed an excessive gambling behavior after receiving treatment with the dopamine agonist ropinirole for Parkinson disease. Patients who are initiated and maintained on dopamine agonist medications to control Parkinson disease should be warned about the potential for developing abnormal, compulsive behaviors, such as excessive gambling, excessive shopping, and hypersexuality. These adverse effects, which can also develop in patients taking such medications for restless legs syndrome, are likely due to effects on the dopaminergic reward centers in the brain. Factors that can increase the risk of these behaviors include a young age at diagnosis in men and a history of mood disorders, alcohol abuse, or obsessive-compulsive behaviors. Other potential adverse effects of dopamine agonist therapy include orthostatic hypotension, nausea, vomiting, hallucinations, and sleep attacks. These potential adverse effects of dopamine agonist medications should be discussed with patients. Sleep attacks, or the sudden irresistible urge to sleep, have garnered considerable medicolegal and social attention. There is controversy about whether such attacks are distinct from excessive daytime somnolence, an established potential side effect of dopamine agonist medications. However, there have been rare reports of sleep attacks occurring while driving and resulting in motor vehicle accidents. The current recommendation is to warn patients taking these medications about the risk of sleep attacks while driving.

Bipolar disorder is an illness characterized by periods of mood elevation and one or more episodes of depression. The period of mood elevation is characterized by a distinct period of abnormal and persistently elevated, expansive, or irritable mood that lasts at least 1 week. This patient's mood is described as normal and he lacks a history of depression, both of which make bipolar disorder unlikely.

Patients with frontotemporal dementia may develop compulsive behaviors but would be expected to also exhibit other signs of personality or behavioral change. This patient's only sign of such a change is his compulsive gambling.

The patient has no history or examination findings suggesting that Parkinson-related dementia has developed, which makes it an unlikely cause of his excessive gambling. Parkinson-related dementia is not associated with compulsive gambling behavior.

KEY POINT

- A potential adverse effect of dopamine agonist therapy is the development of compulsive behaviors, such as pathologic gambling, shopping, and hypersexuality.

Bibliography

Stamey W, Jankovic J. Impulse control disorders and pathological gambling in patients with Parkinson disease. Neurologist. 2008; 14(2):89-99. [PMID: 18332838]

Item 70   Answer: A

Educational Objective: Identify stroke mimickers.

This patient with stroke symptoms is most likely experiencing a migraine with aura and not a stroke. Migraine with aura is a stroke mimicker; stroke mimickers account for nearly one third of all stroke-alert calls in an emergency department. The clinical clues supporting a diagnosis of migraine are the patient's young age, the absence of vascular risk factors, the family history of migraine, and the presence and spread of the sensory symptoms. An MRI with diffusion-weighted imaging can rule out an acute ischemic stroke and thus help confirm the diagnosis of migraine with aura.

Although multiple sclerosis (MS) should be in the differential diagnosis, this patient is less likely to have MS than a migraine or stroke because her presentation was more acute than would be typical in MS. Finding evidence of central nervous system demyelination on an MRI is the usual way MS is diagnosed; when such evidence is lacking, demyelination can sometimes be suggested by abnormal findings in the cerebrospinal fluid.

Symptoms of stroke and transient ischemic attack (TIA) are described as negative or are said to involve loss of function. For example, there may be hemiparesis (a motor deficit affecting half the body) or bland sensory loss (numbness, loss of sensation, diminished sense of touch) in half the body. In contrast, partial seizures account for positive motor symptoms—such as involuntary unilateral muscle movement, twitching, and jerking—or positive sensory symptoms—such as paresthesia, tingling, or a feeling of "pins and needles." Sensory seizure symptoms generally reflect the anatomic organization of the sensory homunculus on the contralateral primary sensory cortex, whereas migraine symptoms may not. The sensory aura of a migraine generally spreads slowly over half the body. Rapidity of onset is another helpful clue in distinguishing migraine from TIA and seizure. A TIA comes on very rapidly (seconds), and seizures generally manifest in less than 1 minute. Migraine with aura, on the other hand, presents more slowly (over minutes, as with this patient), and symptoms spread slowly from region to region.

KEY POINT

- **When assessing a patient with the acute onset of focal neurologic deficits, the examiner should include stroke mimickers, such as migraine with aura, in the differential diagnosis.**

Bibliography

Adams HP Jr, del Zoppo G, Alberts MJ, et al. Guidelines for the early management of adults with ischemic stroke: a guideline from the American Heart Association/American Stroke Association Stroke Council, Clinical Cardiology Council, Cardiovascular Radiology and Intervention Council, and the Atherosclerotic Peripheral Vascular Disease and Quality of Care Outcomes in Research Interdisciplinary Working Groups: the American Academy of Neurology affirms the value of this guideline as an educational tool for neurologists [errata in Stroke. 2007;38(6):e138 and Stroke. 2007;38(9): e96]. Stroke. 2007;38(5):1655-1711. [PMID: 17431204]

Item 71   Answer: C

Educational Objective: Manage epilepsy in a woman who desires pregnancy.

This patient should discontinue taking the valproic acid but continue taking the lamotrigine. All current antiepileptic drugs are classified by the U.S. Food and Drug Administration (FDA) as pregnancy risk category C or D. Infants exposed to antiepileptic drugs during the first trimester of pregnancy have a risk of major congenital malformation that is twice that observed in the general population (4%-6% versus 2%-3%). This teratogenic risk is greatest in those whose mothers were on a polytherapy antiepileptic drug regimen or valproic acid monotherapy. Furthermore, there is early evidence indicating that maternal antiepileptic drug use during pregnancy can have an adverse effect on the long-term cognitive and behavioral development of the children born to these mothers. However, the potential for harm is not great enough to justify counseling every woman with epilepsy against becoming pregnant. In light of the potential risk to their offspring, women with epilepsy should discuss the risks and benefits of treatment with their care providers and modify any risk, if possible.

Because there is no antiepileptic drug in FDA pregnancy risk category A or B, the potential of safely discontinuing antiepileptic drugs should be assessed when a woman with epilepsy desires pregnancy. This patient has a known underlying structural lesion, has a history of seizures that were initially difficult to control, and has been seizure free for only 1 year. All these factors indicate it is unlikely that she could be safely taken off antiepileptic drugs at this time. Most women with epilepsy will require continued drug therapy during pregnancy, with the goal of reducing the medications to the greatest extent that can still reasonably be expected to maintain seizure control. Low-dose monotherapy is optimal; whenever possible, valproic acid should be discontinued or replaced because of its particularly high teratogenic potential. This patient has been seizure free since lamotrigine was added to her regimen. The most appropriate next step in management, therefore, is to discontinue the valproic acid and attempt to control her epilepsy with lamotrigine monotherapy.

There continues to be a common misconception that phenobarbital is safer than other antiepileptic drugs during pregnancy. However, current data from large pregnancy registry studies do not support this assumption but demonstrate instead a risk of major malformations and adverse effects on intelligence in children whose mothers took phenobarbital during pregnancy.

KEY POINT

- Infants exposed to antiepileptic medication during the first trimester of pregnancy have a 4% to 6% chance of having a major congenital malformation; malformation rates are greatest in infants exposed to valproic acid and polytherapy antiepileptic regimens.

Bibliography

Harden CL. Pregnancy and epilepsy. Semin Neurol. 2007;27(5):453-459. [PMID: 17940924]

Item 72   Answer: D

Educational Objective: Diagnose postoperative delirium in a patient with dementia.

Abrupt worsening of confusion in elderly patients with chronic dementia usually results from an acute medical problem. In addition, patients with chronic dementia from almost any cause are at greater risk for delirium after surgery with general anesthesia. This patient with a hip fracture who underwent right hip surgery with general anesthesia and did not recover from the anesthesia until 12 hours after extubation most likely has postoperative delirium. Such delirium is highly predictable and often easily managed by identification and correction of any underlying disorders and the removal or reduction of contributing factors.

In a patient with chronic atrial fibrillation who is confused postoperatively, the possibility of acute stroke must be considered. However, this patient has no clinical evidence of such an event, making this diagnosis extremely unlikely.

Surgery does not exacerbate the dementia of Alzheimer dementia (or of any other cause) but rather produces a superimposed delirium.

This patient has had dementia for 4 years that has abruptly gotten worse after surgery. Although not impossible, meningitis is highly unlikely in this setting, especially given the absence of any supporting physical examination findings, including meningeal irritation.

KEY POINT

- Patients with chronic dementia, such as Alzheimer dementia, are at greater risk for delirium after surgery with general anesthesia.

Bibliography

Rudolph JL, Jones RN, Rasmussen LS, Silverstein JH, Inouye SK, Marcantonio ER. Independent vascular and cognitive risk factors for postoperative delirium. Am J Med. 2007;120(9):807-813. [PMID: 17765051]

Item 73   Answer: C

Educational Objective: Manage Wernicke encephalopathy.

This patient should receive thiamine. She has Wernicke encephalopathy, a syndrome that results from deficiency of vitamin B_1, an important coenzyme in several biochemical pathways of the brain. Typical clinical manifestations of the disorder include mental status changes, nystagmus, ophthalmoplegia, and unsteady gait, all varying in intensity from minor to severe. The typical clinical triad of ataxia, areflexia, and ophthalmoplegia is seen in only 19% of affected patients. Conditions associated with Wernicke encephalopathy include AIDS, alcohol abuse, cancer, hyperemesis gravidarum, prolonged total parenteral nutrition, postsurgical status (particularly gastric bypass), and glucose loading (in a predisposed patient). The disorder develops in patients who are malnourished as a result of malabsorption, a poor diet, increased metabolic requirements during illness, or thiamine deficiency. Recognition of the disorder and treatment with intravenous administration of thiamine are essential.

Establishing a diagnosis of Wernicke encephalopathy can be difficult, but treatment with thiamine should not be withheld while considering other disorders. The diagnosis remains a clinical one and should be considered in any patient with poor nutrition or a disorder that can result in impaired absorption of food who exhibits one or more of the classic features of mental status change, gait impairment, and ocular signs. Measurements of serum thiamine level and erythrocyte transketolase activity lack specificity as diagnostic tests and may not be readily available. An MRI of the brain can help rule out other conditions and may show some characteristic changes of Wernicke encephalopathy, such as paraventricular signal changes in the thalamus, mamillary bodies, periaqueductal region, and cerebellum. Although these MRI changes seem to be quite specific for this disorder, their sensitivity is only 53%.

Because Wernicke encephalopathy remains a clinical diagnosis, other neurologic disorders should be considered in this patient after thiamine has been administered. Electroencephalography can help exclude a seizure disorder, such as nonconvulsive status epilepticus. Infections, including encephalitis and meningitis, for which intravenous administration of broad-spectrum antibiotic drugs (such as vancomycin, ampicillin, and ceftriaxone) may be appropriate also should be part of the differential diagnosis and can be excluded with cerebrospinal fluid analysis.

Haloperidol is not indicated in this patient, who is confused but has no apparent history of psychosis or agitation. Some patients with Wernicke encephalopathy do have agitation, hallucinations, and behavioral disturbances that can mimic an acute psychosis.

- Wernicke encephalopathy is due to thiamine deficiency; may result in mental status changes, ophthalmoplegia, nystagmus, and unsteady gait; and is best treated with thiamine.

Bibliography

Sechi G, Serra A. Wernicke's encephalopathy: new clinical settings and recent advances in diagnosis and management. Lancet Neurol. 2007;6(5):442-455. [PMID: 17434099]

Item 74   Answer: C

Educational Objective: Manage the withdrawal of antiepileptic drugs in a patient who has taken them for over 40 years.

Phenytoin therapy should be discontinued in this patient in a tapered fashion. Although lifelong antiepileptic drug therapy is required for some patients and for some types of epilepsy, this is by no means always the case. As a general rule, discontinuation of antiepileptic drugs should be considered for patients who have been seizure free for 2 or more years. Medications should not be withdrawn in patients with epilepsy syndromes known to be lifelong, with underlying structural brain lesions, with symptomatic neurologic disorders, or (in most cases) with a history of medically refractory seizures. The risk of recurrent seizure when the patient is no longer taking the medication must always be balanced against the risks associated with continued antiepileptic drug treatment. Unfortunately, too many patients are treated unnecessarily for years because of the common misconception that antiepileptic drug therapy can never be safely discontinued. This patient has been seizure free for more than 40 years; in fact, the decision to initiate therapy was questionable because she only had a single event. Now she has osteoporosis, a condition which can be worsened by continued exposure to phenytoin. Therefore, the most appropriate next step in management is to gradually withdraw the medication.

Because the phenytoin will be withdrawn, there is no need to determine a blood level prior to tapering the medication; the results will not affect when or how the medication will be tapered. This patient has been seizure free for more than 2 years and thus meets the criteria for careful withdrawal of the antiepileptic medication. There is no indication to substitute lamotrigine for the phenytoin or to continue the phenytoin.

- Patients on antiepileptic medication who have been seizure free for 2 years should be considered for medication withdrawal.

Bibliography

Callaghan N, Garrett A, Goggin T. Withdrawal of anticonvulsant drugs in patients free of seizures for two years. A prospective study

[erratum in N Engl J Med. 1988;319(3):188]. N Engl J Med. 1988;318(15):942-946. [PMID: 3127710]

Item 75   Answer: B

Educational Objective: Evaluate suspected multiple sclerosis.

This patient should next undergo lumbar puncture. There is already a high clinical suspicion of multiple sclerosis (MS) because of the patient's age, her prior transient neurologic symptoms, the abnormal findings on neurologic examination, and the periventricular white matter lesion seen on two MRIs of the brain. However, these imaging and examination results are insufficient to confirm that multiple regions of the central nervous system are affected at different times (dissemination in time and space), which is one of the diagnostic criteria of MS. Up to 85% of patients with MS have an abnormal finding on cerebrospinal fluid analysis, such as the presence of oligoclonal bands or elevation of the IgG index. Therefore, lumbar puncture is the most appropriate next step in diagnosis. Confirmation of the diagnosis of MS at this stage would allow intervention with immunomodulatory therapy and result in a lower risk of both future relapses and accumulation of neurologic impairment.

In the assessment of vestibular function, electronystagmography (ENG) uses electrodes to record eye movements to help discriminate between central and peripheral causes of vertigo. However, this patient's current leg numbness, history of diplopia and vertigo, and findings of an extensor plantar response, a loss of vibratory sense, and reduced pain sensation of the leg point to a process not confined to vestibular function but associated with manifestations that are separate in both time (two neurologic events over 2 years) and space (different parts of the central nervous system). This is most compatible with MS. Furthermore, in a patient without symptoms of vertigo, the ENG is likely to be normal.

For similar reasons, magnetic resonance angiography, a noninvasive imaging technique used to detect vascular lesions, is unlikely to be helpful in this patient with probable MS.

Magnetic resonance spectroscopy is at present a research technique that is not useful for MS diagnosis but may in the future play a role in monitoring disease progression and determining whether therapeutic interventions have neuroprotective effects.

- Cerebrospinal fluid analysis is useful when the clinical setting is suspicious for multiple sclerosis but neuroimaging is inconclusive.

Bibliography

Polman CH, Reingold SC, Edan G, et al. Diagnostic criteria for multiple sclerosis: 2005 revisions to the "McDonald Criteria". Ann Neurol. 2005;58(6):840-846. [PMID: 16283615]

Item 76   Answer: A

Educational Objective: Treat hypertension in a patient with ischemic stroke who has received recombinant tissue plasminogen activator, intravenously.

In patients who have received recombinant tissue plasminogen activator as treatment of stroke, systolic blood pressure should be maintained below 180 mm Hg and diastolic blood pressure below 105 mm Hg for at least the first 24 hours after thrombolysis treatment. According to current clinical guidelines, intravenous administration of labetalol or nicardipine can best achieve this goal (class II recommendation). Therefore, of the options listed, intravenous administration of labetalol is most appropriate for this patient whose systolic blood pressure is 190 mm Hg and whose diastolic blood pressure is 105 mm Hg.

Intravenous administration of nitroprusside should be instituted only if either labetalol or nicardipine proves unsuccessful in controlling this patient's blood pressure. Intravenous nitroprusside is considered second-line therapy because it may be associated with increased intracranial pressure.

Oral administration of nifedipine is inappropriate because of its rapid absorption, which can result in a secondary precipitous decline in blood pressure.

Withholding antihypertensive medications is inappropriate in this patient. Excessively high blood pressure is associated with an increased risk of symptomatic hemorrhagic transformation after thrombolytic therapy and may be prevented with careful adjustment of the blood pressure to target levels recommended by treatment guidelines.

KEY POINT

- **In a patient with ischemic stroke treated with recombinant tissue plasminogen activator (rtPA), systolic blood pressure should be kept below 180 mm Hg and diastolic below 105 mm Hg for 24 hours after rtPA treatment; intravenous labetalol or nicardipine can best achieve this goal.**

Bibliography

Adams HP Jr, del Zoppo G, Alberts MJ, et al. Guidelines for the early management of adults with ischemic stroke: a guideline from the American Heart Association/American Stroke Association Stroke Council, Clinical Cardiology Council, Cardiovascular Radiology and Intervention Council, and the Atherosclerotic Peripheral Vascular Disease and Quality of Care Outcomes in Research Interdisciplinary Working Groups: the American Academy of Neurology affirms the value of this guideline as an educational tool for neurologists [errata in Stroke. 2007;38(6):e138 and Stroke. 2007;38(9):e96]. Stroke. 2007;38(5):1655-1711. [PMID: 17431204]

Item 77   Answer: C

Educational Objective: Diagnose Bell palsy.

This patient's physical examination findings most strongly suggest right facial nerve (Bell) palsy. The precise cause of

Bell palsy is not known, and it is still considered an idiopathic disorder. Research strongly suggests it may be the result of herpes simplex virus infection of the facial nerve. Bell palsy is not considered contagious. The seventh cranial nerve innervates all muscles of facial expression (the mimetic muscles). Any cause of a complete facial neuropathy will therefore impair the entire hemiface, including the forehead corrugators typically spared by cerebral lesions. Bell phenomenon describes the reflexive rolling upwards of the globe during eye closure. When a patient is asked to close the eyes, forced eyelid opening will reveal this phenomenon, as will the selective paralysis of the orbicularis oculi due to a facial neuropathy. Facial neuropathies will otherwise spare the extraocular muscles that govern globe movement. Because Bell palsy is a diagnosis of exclusion, clinicians need to make every effort to exclude other identifiable causes of facial paralysis, such as Lyme disease, acute and chronic otitis media, cholesteatoma, and multiple sclerosis. Other common causes of acute peripheral facial paralysis will often have findings on history or physical examination that suggest the correct diagnosis.

Graves ophthalmopathy can cause proptosis or extraocular muscle edema with consequent eye movement abnormalities but is not associated with the facial hemiparalysis typical of facial nerve (Bell) palsy.

Cerebral infarction, brain hemorrhage, or any structural brain lesion can cause weakness of the lower face but not of the forehead because the bilateral cortical representation of the midline forehead spares the forehead corrugators. Some limb or sensory abnormality is also often, but not universally, observed in the setting of cerebral infarction; no such abnormality was observed in this patient. Therefore, despite her cerebrovascular risk factors of oral contraception and cigarette smoking, this patient is unlikely to have had a cerebral infarction.

The trigeminal nerve provides sensation, not movement, to the muscles of facial expression, so trigeminal neuralgia is not a likely diagnosis in this patient with normal sensation.

KEY POINT

- **Any cause of a complete facial neuropathy will impair the entire hemiface, including the forehead muscles.**

Bibliography

Tiemstra JD, Khatkhate N. Bell's palsy: diagnosis and management. Am Fam Physician. 2007;76(7):997-1002. [PMID: 17956069]

Item 78   Answer: B

Educational Objective: Treat Parkinson disease.

This patient should be treated with pramipexole. He has classic signs of Parkinson disease, including tremor, rigidity, and bradykinesia. There are no effective neuroprotective agents to treat this disorder. Dopamine agonist medications, either pramipexole or ropinirole, are indicated for the initial treatment of the parkinsonian symptoms in this young patient with apparent Parkinson disease. Motor complications, such as dyskinesias (abnormal involuntary movements), an end-of-dose "wearing-off" effect, and fluctuations, may be less frequent and less severe with dopamine agonist medications than with levodopa.

Levodopa, a precursor of dopamine, is the most efficacious medication used to treat the symptoms of Parkinson disease but is typically initiated only in patients older than 65 years. The associated development of motor fluctuations occurs at a rate of 10% annually in these patients but may develop more rapidly and be more severe in younger patients taking levodopa as an initial medication. Carbidopa is administered in conjunction with levodopa to prevent the peripheral conversion of levodopa to dopamine.

Amantadine has been used in the treatment of Parkinson disease since the 1970s but is not currently a medication of choice for initial therapy. Its mechanism of action in the treatment of Parkinson disease is unknown, but amantadine may increase dopamine release via antagonism at the *N*-methyl-D-aspartic acid receptor. The drug also has anticholinergic properties. Amantadine may reduce dyskinesias, one of the motor complications of Parkinson disease. However, any initial improvement in their parkinsonian symptoms that patients taking amantadine experience may be modest and not sustained.

Primidone is used in patients with essential tremor. Essential tremor is distinguished from Parkinson disease by its occurrence with limb movement and the lack of parkinsonian signs on examination. Likewise, propranolol would not be of any benefit in this patient with the typical resting tremor of Parkinson disease. Propranolol remains the drug of choice in the treatment of patients with essential tremor.

KEY POINT

- **Dopamine agonist medications are used as first-line treatment of Parkinson disease in patients younger than 65 years, whereas levodopa is used in patients age 65 years or older.**

Bibliography

Clarke CE. Parkinson's disease. BMJ. 2007;335(7617):441-445. [PMID: 17762036]

Item 79   Answer: A

Educational Objective: Treat a patient with an abnormal serum antiepileptic drug level.

The most important considerations that should guide decisions about adjusting epilepsy medication dosage or changing the type of drug used are the current clinical seizure control and the presence of adverse side effects. This patient reports a prolonged period of freedom from seizures and the absence of adverse effects while on a stable dosage of phenytoin. Although the patient's total serum phenytoin level is mildly subtherapeutic, this in itself is not a sufficient indication to make a change in the type or dosage of medication. Therefore, the patient should be kept on phenytoin at his present dosage of 300 mg/d as long as a seizure or adverse effect of medication does not occur.

Monitoring of serum antiepileptic drug levels can be useful when it is necessary to confirm that a level is therapeutic in a patient with uncontrolled seizures, when toxicity is suspected, or when medication adherence needs to be confirmed; none of these scenarios applies to this patient. Serum drug level monitoring can be particularly helpful with phenytoin because of its narrow therapeutic window and its nonlinear pharmacokinetics, which can result in unexpectedly large changes in serum concentration from small adjustments in oral dosage. For phenytoin and other highly protein-bound drugs, checking the free (as well as the total) serum drug levels may be necessary if there is concern about therapeutic effectiveness or toxicity in the presence of a low serum protein level or polypharmacy with other highly protein-bound drugs; again, these indications do not apply to this patient.

KEY POINT

- **Adjustments to the dosage or type of antiepileptic drug used by a patient with epilepsy should be based on clinical seizure control and drug side effects rather than strict serum drug levels.**

Bibliography

Jannuzzi G, Cian P, Fattore C, et al. A multicenter randomized controlled trial on the clinical impact of therapeutic drug monitoring in patients with newly diagnosed epilepsy. The Italian TDM Study Group in Epilepsy. Epilepsia. 2000;41(2):222-230. [PMID: 10691121]

Item 80   Answer: C

Educational Objective: Manage migraine with aura in a young woman taking oral contraceptives.

The American Academy of Obstetrics and Gynecology considers migraine with aura an absolute contraindication to the use of oral contraception. The International Headache Society strongly advises against the use of oral contraceptive pills in women who have migraine with aura that involves more than just the visual system and recommends stopping the pill in women who develop an aura after the pill is started. Patients who have migraine with aura have up to an eight-fold increased risk of ischemic stroke; this risk is tripled by smoking and quadrupled by the use of oral contraception. This patient, therefore, should discontinue using oral contraception.

There is little evidence to support the use of propranolol or verapamil for the prevention of migraine in this patient. In any case, the frequency of her migraines (approximately one every 2 months) does not justify the use of preventive medication.

Triptans are not contraindicated in patients with migraine with aura. Therefore, the sumatriptan can continue to be used for acute migraine relief in this patient.

Mitochondrial Encephalopathy with Lactic Acidosis and Stroke-like episodes (MELAS) is a maternally inherited mitochondrial disorder associated with lactic acidosis and a high prevalence of migraine with aura. The hallmark of MELAS is the occurrence of nonischemic stroke manifesting as hemiparesis, hemianopia, or cortical blindness. The course is progressive and leads to progressive neurologic impairment and dementia. Other features may include short stature, hearing loss, and muscle weakness. However, this patient has no clinical or imaging features of this disorder, and measuring her serum lactate and pyruvate levels would not be appropriate.

KEY POINT

- Oral contraceptive pills are contraindicated in women with migraine with aura, especially if the aura involves more than just simple visual aura, if there are additional stroke risk factors, or if the aura begins after the initiation of oral contraception.

Bibliography

Loder EW, Buse DC, Golub JR. Headache and combination estrogen-progestin oral contraceptives: integrating evidence, guidelines, and clinical practice. Headache. 2005;45(3):224-231. [PMID: 15836597]

Item 81   Answer: B

Educational Objective: Manage a transient ischemic attack.

This patient should be admitted to the hospital. Given his clinical history, he most likely has had a recent transient ischemic attack (TIA). His ABCD^2 score (based on Age, Blood pressure, Clinical features, the Duration of symptoms, and the presence of Diabetes) is 5: one point is for his age (>60 years), one point for his hypertension, one point for a symptom duration of greater than 10 minutes, and two points for the focal weakness he described. This score is moderately high and carries an estimated stroke risk of 5% over the next 2 days, 7% over the next week, 10% over the next 30 days, and 12% over the next 3 months. Therefore, the most appropriate response is for this patient to undergo urgent evaluation within the next 24 hours at an emergency department, at a hospital during a brief admission, or at an organized urgent TIA clinic.

It is reasonable to review the stroke prevention regimen of a patient with risk factors and make adjustments to any antiplatelet medications in the context of a new stroke or TIA. However, the priority is an expedited evaluation to determine the cause and mechanism of the stroke or TIA, such as symptomatic extracranial carotid artery stenosis

amenable to endarterectomy, intracranial stenosis amenable to angioplasty and stenting, or cardioembolism with requirements for long-term anticoagulation. Therefore, adding clopidogrel to this patient's drug regimen is not the most appropriate next step in management.

Outpatient diagnostic studies may play a role in the assessment of this patient, but only if they occur and results are back within 24 hours. Because this scenario is unlikely, such studies are clearly not the most appropriate next step in management.

Given the high probability of an acute ischemic stroke event and the high short-term risk of stroke in this patient, scheduling a follow-up appointment in 1 week in the absence of diagnostic testing or evaluation could be life threatening.

KEY POINT

- Patients with a diagnosis of a recent transient ischemic attack are at an appreciably high short-term risk of stroke and should be evaluated in a hospital in an expedited and emergent fashion.

Bibliography

Johnston SC, Nguyen-Huynh MN, Schwartz ME, et al. National Stroke Association guidelines for the management of transient ischemic attacks. Ann Neurol. 2006;60(3):301-313. [PMID: 16912978]

Item 82   Answer: C

Educational Objective: Evaluate suspected neuromyelitis optica in a patient with transverse myelitis and paraparesis.

This patient very likely has neuromyelitis optica (NMO), a severe demyelinating disease of the central nervous system that is distinct from multiple sclerosis (MS). She should be tested for the autoantibody marker NMO-IgG (anti–aquaporin-4). NMO occurs more commonly in nonwhite persons, is often associated with serum autoantibodies or other autoimmune diseases, and has a predilection for the optic nerves and spinal cord with relative sparing of the brain. This patient's spinal cord lesion is also characteristic of NMO because it extends over more than three vertebral segments; cord lesions in typical MS are usually less than two segments in length. The finding of the NMO-IgG autoantibody marker is approximately 75% sensitive and more than 90% specific for NMO. Differentiating between NMO and MS as early in the disease course as possible is important because the prognosis and treatment of the two diseases are different. NMO is a more severe disease treated with immunosuppressive drugs, whereas MS is initially treated with immunomodulatory therapies, such as β-interferon and glatiramer acetate.

There are no symptoms or signs of peripheral nerve or muscle involvement in this patient. Therefore, electromyography is not indicated.

Cytoplasmic and perinuclear-staining antinuclear cytoplasmic antibodies (ANCAs) may be detected in patients with systemic vasculitis. Although vasculitis is a rare cause of transverse myelitis, it is very unlikely to explain multiple episodes of optic neuritis and transverse myelitis in the absence of systemic symptoms.

Visual evoked potential testing will confirm the known involvement of the optic nerves in this patient but will not otherwise aid diagnosis and so is unnecessary.

KEY POINT

- Neuromyelitis optica (NMO) is a severe demyelinating disease of the central nervous system that is distinct from multiple sclerosis and associated with the autoantibody marker NMO-IgG (anti–aquaporin-4).

Bibliography

Wingerchuk DM, Lennon VA, Lucchinetti CF, Pittock SJ, Weinshenker BG. The spectrum of neuromyelitis optica. Lancet Neurol. 2007;6(9):805-815. [PMID: 17706564]

Item 83   Answer: C

Educational Objective: Manage medically refractory partial epilepsy.

For patients with medically refractory partial epilepsy whose seizures are adversely affecting their quality of life, referral for epilepsy surgery evaluation is the most appropriate next step in management. Seizures arising from mesial temporal sclerosis, as is suggested by this patient's MRI, are particularly amenable to surgical cure, with seizure-free rates reported to be as high as 80% after resection. The most common surgical procedure is surgical resection of mesial temporal lobe sclerotic lesions. Quality of life and social functioning improve after successful surgery, and surgical morbidity and mortality are low. In fact, surgery may improve long-term mortality.

Approximately 30% of patients with epilepsy have seizures that cannot be adequately controlled with currently available medical therapies. If seizures have not responded to two medications that are appropriate for the seizure disorder and are used at an adequate dosage, the likelihood of achieving complete control with subsequent medication trials is less than 10%. The patient described has continued disabling seizures despite trials of four medications, all appropriate for treating partial complex seizures and all given at adequate dosages. Therefore, adding another drug to his current regimen is unlikely to improve his condition.

His current dosage of lamotrigine, although not the theoretical maximal daily dosage, represents a reasonable trial of the drug. A further increase in the lamotrigine dosage is not the best choice for this patient who reports limiting adverse effects on the current regimen.

The vagus nerve stimulator is an approved therapy for medically refractory partial epilepsy that is best used as a palliative option for patients who are not candidates for resective surgery. This patient has no contraindications to such surgery.

KEY POINT

- Patients with disabling partial seizures that have not responded to treatment with two appropriate anticonvulsant drugs should be considered for epilepsy surgery.

Bibliography

Kwan P, Brodie MJ. Early identification of refractory epilepsy. N Engl J Med. 2000;342(5):314-319. [PMID: 10660394]

Item 84   Answer: B

Educational Objective: Differentiate between rebleeding, vasospasm, and hydrocephalus.

The most likely complication to have caused this patient's rapid deterioration is rebleeding. In the first few hours after an initial hemorrhage, up to 15% of affected patients have a sudden deterioration of consciousness, which strongly suggests rebleeding. In patients who survive the first day, the rebleeding risk is evenly distributed during the next 4 weeks, with a cumulative risk of 40% without surgical or endovascular interventions. Occlusion of the responsible aneurysm is thus the first aim in the management of a subarachnoid hemorrhage and is usually performed by coiling or clipping.

Typically, patients who develop hydrocephalus after having a subarachnoid hemorrhage are initially alert but then experience a gradual reduction in consciousness over the next 24 hours. Downward deviation of the eyes and small, unreactive pupils indicate dilatation of the proximal part of the cerebral aqueduct with dysfunction of the pretectal area. Although this patient may have secondarily developed hydrocephalus, her symptoms and examination findings suggest that the principal reason for her precipitous decline is early rebleeding. On average, one in five patients who sustain subarachnoid hemorrhages will have mildly enlarged ventricles on the initial CT scan but not frank hydrocephalus.

The syndrome of inappropriate antidiuretic hormone secretion is recognized as a potential complication in patients with subarachnoid hemorrhages and other critical care neurologic conditions. Its symptoms and signs are muscle cramps, weakness, altered sensorium, coma, and seizures. This syndrome causes the electrolyte disturbance of hyponatremia. This patient's serum electrolytes were determined to be in the normal range at the time of her evaluation in the emergency department.

Vasospasm-induced cerebral ischemia after a subarachnoid hemorrhage has a more gradual onset than occurred in this patient. It often involves more than the territory of a single cerebral artery. The clinical manifestations evolve gradually over several hours and consist of hemispheric focal deficits, a reduction of consciousness, or both. The peak frequency of vasospasm is from 5 to 14 days after the subarachnoid hemorrhage.

> **KEY POINT**
> - Rebleeding is the most imminent danger after a subarachnoid hemorrhage.

Bibliography

van Gijn J, Kerr RS, Rinkel GJ. Subarachnoid haemorrhage. Lancet. 2007;369(9558):306-318. [PMID: 17258671]

Item 85   Answer: D

Educational Objective: Treat a patient prophylactically for migraine.

Prophylactic treatment should generally be initiated in patients with two or more migraine attacks per week. There is level 1 evidence to support the use of topiramate for the prevention of migraine, and the U.S. Food and Drug Administration has approved the drug for this purpose. This patient is obese (BMI of 34) and has type 2 diabetes mellitus. Any medication with the potential for weight gain must, therefore, be used with caution, given the morbidity associated with obesity and the potential to worsen her underlying hyperglycemia. Topiramate is associated with weight loss.

Gabapentin is a second-tier drug because of the lower level of evidence supporting its use. It is also not approved by the FDA for the preventive treatment of migraine.

There is no evidence of nortriptyline's efficacy in the preventive treatment of migraine. Moreover, it is also associated with weight gain.

Propranolol, a nonselective β-blocker, is contraindicated in patients with persistent asthma and has a relative contraindication in patients with diabetes mellitus.

Valproic acid, although also supported by level 1 evidence and FDA approval for migraine prevention, is associated with weight gain and is not the best treatment for this patient. Additionally, in light of the potential teratogenicity associated with this drug, it is often avoided in women of childbearing potential.

> **KEY POINT**
> - Prophylactic medication should be initiated in patients with two or more migraine attacks per week.

Bibliography

Dodick DW, Silberstein SD. Migraine prevention. Pract Neurol. 2007;7(6):383-393. [PMID: 18024778]

Item 86   Answer: A

Educational Objective: Diagnose anti–phospholipid antibody syndrome in a patient with chorea.

This patient most likely has anti–phospholipid antibody syndrome. She has movements consistent with chorea, with no other identifiable neurologic signs or symptoms. Chorea is characterized by random, nonstereotyped movements that can affect virtually any body part. Anti–phospholipid antibody syndrome is characterized by a history of a thrombotic event (including recurrent fetal loss) in association with a persistent lupus anticoagulant or persistently elevated levels of anticardiolipin or B_2-glycoprotein I antibodies. Lupus anticoagulants or elevated levels of anti–phospholipid antibodies are often present in patients with systemic lupus erythematosus; they also occur in patients with cancer or infections and in association with the use of certain drugs (for example, hydralazine, procainamide, phenothiazines). A multitude of neurologic disorders can occur in patients with anti–phospholipid antibody syndrome, including chorea. Chorea has also been associated with systemic lupus erythematosus and may occur early in the course of either disorder, even before other signs develop. Levels of anticardiolipin antibodies, antinuclear antibodies, and anti–double-stranded DNA antibodies should be measured in the diagnostic evaluation of chorea.

Huntington disease is not likely in this patient. A progressive, autosomal dominant disorder, Huntington disease has a mean age of onset of approximately 40 years. A history of psychiatric disturbance may precede the motor manifestations of the disease, and cognitive abnormalities are present in nearly all affected patients, appearing early in the course of the disease. Chorea is also present in nearly all patients, and other extrapyramidal findings, such as dystonia and parkinsonian signs, are commonly seen.

Chorea commonly occurs in patients with Parkinson disease who are on dopamine therapy and is thought to reflect high levels of dopamine in the basal ganglia. Typically, these choreiform movements, also known as dyskinesias, occur at the peak of the dopamine medication effect and, if mild, may not be bothersome to the patient. Given that this patient has no symptoms of Parkinson disease, such as a resting tremor, and is not on medication, this diagnosis is very unlikely.

Wilson disease is an autosomal recessive disorder that most commonly results in psychiatric symptoms and parkinsonian signs, neither of which are present in this patient. Chorea occurs in approximately 15% of patients with Wilson disease.

> **KEY POINT**
> - Chorea can occur in patients with anti–phospholipid antibody syndrome or systemic lupus erythematosus.

Bibliography

Wild EJ, Tabrizi SJ. The differential diagnosis of chorea. Pract Neurol. 2007;7(6):360-373. [PMID: 18024776]

Item 87   Answer: C

Educational Objective: Treat migraine in a lactating mother.

This patient should be taking frovatriptan for her migraine attacks. Frovatriptan and sumatriptan are both considered compatible with breast feeding by the American Academy of Pediatrics. The patient has not responded to first-line therapy with simple analgesics and is reporting severe migraine attacks, for which a triptan is indicated.

The American Academy of Pediatrics has given butalbital and acetaminophen a rating of caution and metoclopramide and prochlorperazine a rating of concern for mothers who are breast feeding. Therefore, these drugs should be avoided in such mothers. In addition, the patient has already reported a lack of response to over-the-counter analgesics, so extra-strength acetaminophen is not likely to result in marked improvement.

KEY POINT

- **Using frovatriptan or sumatriptan for treatment of migraine is compatible with breast feeding, according to the American Academy of Pediatrics.**

Bibliography

Lay CL, Broner SW. Special considerations in the treatment of migraine in women. Semin Neurol. 2006;26(2):217-222. [PMID: 16628532]

Item 88   Answer: B

Educational Objective: Manage epilepsy that is not controlled with the first antiepileptic drug administered.

This patient should gradually transition to a new antiepileptic drug. He continues to have disabling seizures, despite taking phenytoin for 1 year and despite having a high therapeutic serum drug level. Only approximately half of the patients prescribed a first antiepileptic drug for seizure control will continue on that drug. For the others, initial therapy will be unsuccessful, either from lack of efficacy or from unacceptable side effects. When patients are unsuccessfully treated with a first antiepileptic drug, the recommendation is to try a second antiepileptic drug as monotherapy. It is generally recommended to gradually transition between drugs, titrating the new drug to therapeutic range before tapering off the initial agent.

There is no compelling evidence that polytherapy improves seizure control over monotherapy. However, the primary rationale for continued monotherapy in a patient unsuccessfully treated with a first antiepileptic drug is the increased rate of adverse effects and drug interactions when antiepileptic drugs are used in combination. Concerns about adherence and increased expense also play a role. Therefore, adding another antiepileptic drug to this patient's drug regimen is not appropriate as the next step in management.

Although an increase in phenytoin dosage might be considered in some cases, this patient has already reported clinically significant adverse effects from the drug. These would likely limit his ability to tolerate a higher dosage.

Epilepsy surgery and vagus nerve stimulation are reserved for patients with medically refractory seizure disorders and are generally not considered until at least two antiepileptic drugs have been shown to be ineffective in controlling seizures. This patient has thus far tried only phenytoin therapy. A referral for either of these treatments is premature at this point.

KEY POINT

- **Monotherapy is preferred over polytherapy drug regimens as treatment of epilepsy.**

Bibliography

Brodie MJ, Kwan P. Staged approach to epilepsy management. Neurology. 2002;58 (8 Suppl 5):S2-8. [PMID: 11971127]

Item 89   Answer: B

Educational Objective: Diagnose diabetic lumbosacral radiculoplexus neuropathy.

Diabetic lumbosacral radiculoplexus neuropathy, or diabetic amyotrophy, is the most likely diagnosis in this patient. This neuropathy is a subacute, progressive disorder that causes asymmetric leg pain, sensory loss, and weakness. Weight loss of 4.5 kg (10 lb) or more occurs in most affected patients. Many patients with this disorder are unaware that they have diabetes mellitus before the development of diabetic lumbosacral radiculoplexus neuropathy, and in most patients, glycemic control is not severely compromised. This disorder usually begins with unilateral leg pain followed by weakness and sensory loss, which spread to involve the contralateral leg nearly all the time. Weakness is often greatest proximally initially, but over time, diffuse weakness involving proximal and distal muscles ensues. Electromyographic studies characteristically show dysfunction at the level of multiple peripheral nerves, the lumbosacral plexus, and multiple nerve roots. MRI studies of the lumbosacral plexus are typically normal in this disorder but are most helpful in excluding an infiltrative neoplastic process, which can present similarly.

Cauda equina syndrome due to a compressive, infiltrating, or inflammatory process affecting multiple lumbosacral nerve roots should be considered in this patient. However, the absence of abnormal signs or symptoms in the right leg would be unusual in this syndrome. Patients with cauda equina syndrome typically have bilateral (but sometimes asymmetric) leg pain, weakness, and areflexia. Bowel and bladder impairment can occur, and saddle anesthesia is expected in affected patients.

Myelopathy due to demyelinating disease or other disorders should be considered in patients with lower limb weakness, sensory loss, and pain but is unlikely in this patient. Absent reflexes in the left leg suggest a lower motoneuron problem affecting either multiple nerve roots or the lumbosacral plexus in that limb. A myelopathy would be expected to cause hyperreflexia, spasticity, and an extensor plantar response in the lower limbs.

When there is a history of pelvic irradiation, radiation-induced lumbosacral plexopathy should be considered in patients with progressive leg weakness. However, the rapid progression of symptoms and the presence of pain in this patient are not typical of radiation-induced lumbosacral plexopathy. Moreover, the mean time to symptom onset after radiation exposure is 3 to 6 years, although it has been reported to range from 1 month to 18 years after radiation exposure. Radiation-induced damage can affect the brachial plexus (typically, in breast cancer) or lumbosacral plexus. The frequency of brachial plexus injury after radiation therapy has been reported to range from 1.8% to 9.0%. Typical symptoms include gradually progressive weakness and sensory loss.

KEY POINT

- **Diabetic lumbosacral radiculoplexus neuropathy (diabetic amyotrophy) is characterized by severe, initially unilateral lower limb pain and weakness.**

Bibliography

Dyck PJ, Windebank AJ. Diabetic and nondiabetic lumbosacral radiculoplexus neuropathies: new insights into pathophysiology and treatment. Muscle Nerve. 2002;25(4):477-491. [PMID: 11932965]

Item 90   Answer: A

Educational Objective: Treat intracerebral hemorrhage.

This patient has signs of neurologic deterioration, given her score on the Glasgow Coma Scale. She has an acute cerebellar hemispheric hemorrhage that is greater than 3 cm in diameter and thus should be considered for neurosurgical intervention. The priority in such cases is to decompress the posterior fossa by surgically evacuating the hematoma. Patients with posterior fossa hematomas are at risk for life-threatening complications, including herniation and hydrocephalus, without such intervention.

Blood pressure management in intracranial hemorrhage remains controversial. No trial has demonstrated that blood pressure control in this setting affects outcome, and there is concern about reducing cerebral perfusion pressure in patients with elevated intracranial pressure. The American Heart Association guidelines recommend that mean arterial blood pressure be kept between 70 mm Hg and 130 mm Hg. This patient's mean arterial blood pressure is 113 mm Hg, and thus intravenous administration of labetalol is not indicated. More importantly, urgent evacuation of the hematoma is likely to be life-saving and thus is the treatment of choice.

Recombinant factor VII was promising as an experimental therapy for acute intracerebral hemorrhages, but the definitive phase 3 trial did not yield efficacious results. It is not approved by the U.S. Food and Drug Administration for treatment of such hemorrhages.

A ventriculostomy may be indicated in a patient with a cerebellar hemorrhage who develops hydrocephalus. Because this patient's CT scan does not yet demonstrate that complication, ventriculostomy is inappropriate as the next step in management.

KEY POINT

- **Emergent surgical evacuation of the hematoma is indicated for patients with a cerebellar hemorrhage greater than 3 cm in diameter who are deteriorating neurologically or who have brain stem compression and/or hydrocephalus from ventricular obstruction.**

Bibliography

Kirollos RW, Tyagi AK, Ross SA, van Hille PT, Marks PV. Management of spontaneous cerebellar hematomas: a prospective treatment protocol. Neurosurgery. 2001;49(6):1378-1386. [PMID: 11846937]

Index